ALSO BY LYDIA DAVIS

NOVEL
The End of the Story

STORIES
The Thirteenth Woman and Other Stories
Story and Other Stories
Break It Down
Almost No Memory
Samuel Johnson Is Indignant
Varieties of Disturbance
The Collected Stories of Lydia Davis
Can't and Won't

POETRY
Two American Scenes (with Eliot Weinberger)

SELECTED TRANSLATIONS
Madame Bovary: Provincial Ways by Gustave Flaubert
Letters to His Neighbor by Marcel Proust
Swann's Way by Marcel Proust
Death Sentence by Maurice Blanchot
The Madness of the Day by Maurice Blanchot
The Spirit of Mediterranean Places by Michel Butor
Rules of the Game, I: Scratches by Michel Leiris
Rules of the Game, II: Scraps by Michel Leiris
Rules of the Game, III: Fibrils by Michel Leiris
Hélène by Pierre Jean Jouve
Grasses and Trees by A. L. Snijders

NONFICTION
Essays One

Essays Two

Essays Two

LYDIA DAVIS

ON PROUST,

TRANSLATION,

FOREIGN LANGUAGES,

AND THE CITY OF ARLES

Farrar, Straus and Giroux

New York

Farrar, Straus and Giroux
120 Broadway, New York 10271

Illustration credits can be found on pages 569–571.

Owing to limitations of space, all acknowledgments for permission to
reprint previously published material can be found on page 573.

Library of Congress Control Number: 2019020199
ISBN: 978-0-374-14886-7

www.fsgbooks.com
www.twitter.com/fsgbooks • www.facebook.com/fsgbooks

1   3   5   7   9   10   8   6   4   2

Contents

FABULAE FACILES

Preface

The present volume of essays, my second, is a little more single-minded in its themes and subject matter than my first, *Essays One*, which concentrated on writers and writing but also included essays on the visual arts, memory, the turn of the millennium, and the Bible. Here, in this volume, another large part of my life is represented, in which professional and recreational activities tend to overlap: my translations and my interest in how foreign languages may be learned.

As I mention in a couple of the essays that follow, an important experience behind my lifelong preoccupation with other languages must have been my exposure to German at the age of seven in a first-grade classroom in Graz, Austria, where I had no choice but to learn the language. I'm not sure that anyone talked much about the immersion method of language-learning in 1954, but it was effective: the other children were learning to read, and I, having been through first grade in the United States already, was learning to read again, this time in German. The language was all around me for most of a year, not only in the classroom, but as I played with friends, walked on the streets, rode the trolleys, went into stores, and passed through the corridors of the hotel

where, for the first weeks, my family and I lived. There, on
school mornings, I was expected to get up to the rattle of my
own alarm clock and dress on my own. If I arrived downstairs in the dining room on time, I could have *Schokolade
mit Schlag* (hot chocolate with whipped cream). If I was
late, I had *Schokolade ohne Schlag* (without). I had constant
practice in German, therefore, and even though I lost some
of the language when I returned to the United States, the
deeper sense of how a German sentence is constructed, as
well as much of the elementary (child's) vocabulary, never
went away.

This experience was also a child's thorough, lengthy
introduction to the concept that communication can take
other forms, with other sounds and orthographies. I theorize
now that I must have gone through a few weeks, at least,
of some frustration and bewilderment, as I listened to quite
alien sounds coming, though so naturally, from my classmates' mouths, accompanied by expressions on their faces
that were, by contrast, completely recognizable to me—of
concentration, pleasure, challenge, surprise, and good humor. Then, this frustration must have been followed by grad-
ual enlightenment as I became progressively more familiar
with the meaning of what I was hearing, and eventually it
must have implanted in me a hunger to repeat the experience, or at least a strong desire, at the sight of words that
mean nothing to me, to find out what they mean.

Lessons in other foreign languages followed. In school
back in the United States, I was introduced to French, then
to Latin; later, in college, to Italian. But before the end of
my time in high school, my parents went down to Argen-
tina for half a year, my father to teach in the university at La
Plata. I joined them after graduation and, living for a couple
of months of the summer in Buenos Aires, began to learn

Spanish—I would try to converse during the day and then study a little grammar in the evenings. (This still seems to me one good way to approach a language: practice using it, and then, later, look up the "rules" behind what you have been trying to do.)

There is much more to say about exposure to foreign languages, but, over the years, perhaps compelled by the mental conditioning of that first experience in Graz, I have spent countless hours of countless days studying other languages, either trying to reawaken my rudimentary German, Latin, Spanish, and Italian, or learning new languages on my own, chiefly through reading. Three of the essays in this volume are accounts of these experiences—returning to Spanish and learning Dutch and Norwegian. There is inevitably some overlap among the accounts, since I used more or less the same method for all three languages; I have trimmed back some of that overlap, but I have also deliberately left some.

What I have not yet written about is my struggle, one winter, to make my way sentence by sentence through Caesar's *The Gallic War*, trying each sentence in Latin and then looking at the facing-page English of the nice little Loeb Classical Library edition. By the end of the book I had still not managed, to my disappointment, to acquire any more feel for reading a Latin sentence than I had in the beginning, frustrated most obviously by the "unnatural" word order. I am not done trying to gain a more comfortable reading knowledge of Latin. I have a little old tan-covered book for children, a 1937 update of an 1880 publication of "easy" stories in Latin (*Fabulae Faciles*). This is an obvious place to start. Then I will try the sermons of St. Caesarius, the bishop whom I mention in the last essay. His style of Latin, I've been told, is deliberately "rustic," with short, simple sentences and basic vocabulary, in part so as to reach his listeners more effectively. And I doubt that I will be bored, since his sermons include stern warnings against some of the more colorful social behaviors of the people of sixth-century Arles.

One more note on language-learning: A friend once described to me his variation on my preferred learning-by-reading method. He said that in the morning, when his mind was fresh, he would read a portion of a given novel in the original language; then, at night, when he was tired, he would continue where he left off, but in the English translation. This seems like a more relaxing and entertaining method, and I am ready to try it.

Springing, of course, from my interest in foreign languages is my choice to work for most of my adult life as a translator, mainly from French but with later brief forays, for my own pleasure—the enjoyment of the challenge—into a list of other languages that has kept growing: German, Swedish, Norwegian, Spanish, Catalan, Dutch, Portuguese, Gascon . . . Some of these adventures were inspired by a resolution that I have not yet completely fulfilled: to attempt to translate at least one short work from each of the languages into which my own stories have been translated, so as to make a gesture, at least, toward a cultural exchange. Since my life is not yet over, I have left open the question of what I will do about a language (Japanese, Turkish, Farsi) that is completely unrelated to any language I know.

The translation of the Gascon fairy tale, which I write about in this volume, was not a result of this resolution. I was simply intrigued by the near incomprehensibility of its language even for someone who knows French, has some acquaintance with Spanish, and has attempted to learn Provençal, all of which do help. The tale itself I enjoyed, once I began figuring out how to decipher it. The tone and style of the essay is colored by the fact that in its first version it was a piece of fiction (made almost entirely of nonfictional material) told in the querulous voice of a determinedly pedantic scholar trying to read the difficult language on a noisy train.

I have also not yet written about the experience of translating German itself, my ur–foreign language (and the one that still seems to me, beyond the elementary level, and along with Latin, one of the most difficult I know). I have attempted a few stories by the early twentieth-century Viennese coffeehouse habitué Peter Altenberg—short-short autobiographical fiction—as well as a small selection from Walter Serner's whimsical, bizarre, tongue-in-cheek, and occasionally offensive 1920 Dada manifesto of rules by which to live. I have also translated a few short pieces by Robert Walser on visual art, and most recently and enthusiastically, some of the warmly human and insightful newspaper columns of the Swiss writer Peter Bichsel, a collection of whose work was handed to me a few years ago. He writes in somewhat the same form, with somewhat the same approach, as the Dutch A. L. Snijders, drawing on his own life experiences and offering thoughts on what he has learned or seen. Because he was held to a limited word count, the pieces share a certain pace and pattern of development. They are long enough to deliver something substantial, but occupy no more than a few pages.

For a translator of French, the project of translating Proust's *Du Côté de chez Swann* into English was obviously a high point, what looked at the time like the culmination of a career. The increased effort that I put into that project is reflected in this volume of essays by the number of pieces on the experience. One originated as a blog post, two as talks on the translation, the "Alphabet" as a project in itself—to plunder the "Proust diary" I kept as I went along, noting particular problems, linguistic discoveries, or curious choices made by the previous translators. In the "Alphabet," I will sometimes discuss a problem in more detail that I have touched upon elsewhere in the book. One more small note: In the course of discussing my Proust translation, I often mention his first translator, C. K. Scott Moncrieff. What may be confusing is that the full surname is a double one, Scott Moncrieff, unhyphenated, and I often refer to him that way.

For a much shorter, and yet, in the end, unexpectedly complicated Proust translation project—the rendering into English of his letters to an upstairs neighbor and her husband—I wrote quite a long essay as an afterword. What I felt the letters needed, as supplement, was a mental picture of Proust in situ, in the room where he wrote them. This also gave me the opportunity to describe my experience of visiting both that room and, separately, housed in a museum, its original contents.

One entire draft of my translation of *Fibrils*, volume 3 of *The Rules of the Game*, by Michel Leiris—an author belonging to a period very different from Flaubert's and from Proust's; he was still alive during most of the time I was working on the three volumes of his "autobiographical essay"— was done just before I started *Swann's Way*. I found that the Leiris translation had been a good exercise in handling complex syntax before I embarked on Proust's own variety of the hypotactic structure. In fact, I experienced what was really an ecstasy of literal translation doing the work, which unfortunately produced a less than fully readable version, so that I later—much later, years after the publication of the Proust—had to revise it extensively in order to bring it up to the level of competence the book deserved. I describe some of this in my essay on translating Leiris.

After the "culmination" of translating Proust, I thought I was done with book-length translation projects. But I was then invited to translate Flaubert's *Madame Bovary*. I hesitated but in the end could not resist this very different challenge. My essay on this project also includes thoughts and notes on translation generally, since it was written after so many years of that occupation.

The first essay in the book, on some of the pleasures of translating, also contains reflections on this consuming activity as I have experienced it since my early twenties. The essay began life as an enumeration of eleven pleasures—an ample number, I thought—and then grew over time as more pleasures were revealed. It paused at seventeen for a while, until I came to read it through for this collection, by which time I had discovered an eighteenth, which possibly subsumed a nineteenth. Now the pleasures number twenty-one, and the enumeration could go on, I'm sure. I have presented these pleasures not in any necessarily logical order, but in the order in which they occurred to me, which seemed the most natural and organic.

Another kind of translation, for me, was changing the original English of a text into another kind of English, or changing the form of a text without much altering its English, and in three of the essays I describe different varieties of this experience: "modernizing" a few pages of Laurence Sterne as an experiment; standardizing and simplifying the language of a classic children's dog story, *Bob, Son of Battle*, in order to make the book more accessible; and, lastly, converting parts of an ancestor's nineteenth-century memoir, which he called *Our Village*, into a narrative poem without changing the language more than necessary. The latter essay, as it evolved, came to focus largely on line breaks, which is not surprising, since the main problem in converting a piece of prose into poetry was, of course, where to break the lines; for me, this focus was a very helpful practice in isolating and studying on its own one particular aspect of writing verse, perhaps finally learning something about that elusive skill.

The concluding essay in the book, on the city of Arles, departs a little from the overall theme of foreign languages and translation, though not from an ongoing preoccupation with French history and culture. I include it partly to move away, finally, from the close concentration on language in the other essays and partly from a desire to convey at least some small part of what is so very interesting to me about this city, which I visited a couple of years ago—in what ways it is both so unusually rich in history and exceptional in its geography. What I include here is only a fraction of what I learned about it, during months of reading, and perhaps in time I will be able to make something more of this exploration.

ON TRANSLATION

Twenty-One Pleasures of Translating
(and a Silver Lining)

The translation problems that you have struggled with the hardest, perhaps never satisfied with your solutions, will stay with you for a long time—you can count on it. A few years ago, in June, on a trip to France, I was taken by French friends for a wine-tasting in the small Burgundian town of Beaune, south of Dijon. During the wine-tasting, we were at one point instructed to *mâchez le vin*—I can't remember now whether this was while we still held the wine in our mouths, or after we had swallowed or spat it out. Now, when this phrase was spoken, I became instantly alert, my translator-antennae going up: using the verb *mâcher*, "chew," for something that you can't actually chew was a problem I had spent several hours on during my translating of *Madame Bovary* some seven years before. The word occurs in a passage near the beginning of the novel, when Charles Bovary, at least, is still happy in his marriage, and Emma is not yet obviously restless or unhappy. This passage very well illustrates Flaubert's antiromanticism:

Et alors, sur la grande route qui étendait sans en finir son long ruban de poussière, par les chemins creux où les arbres se courbaient en berceaux, dans les sentiers dont les blés lui montaient jusqu'aux genoux, avec le soleil sur ses épaules et l'air du matin à ses narines, le coeur plein des félicités de la nuit, l'esprit tranquille, la chair contente, il s'en allait ruminant son bonheur, comme ceux qui mâchent encore, après dîner, le goût des truffes qu'ils digèrent.

This was how I translated it:

And then, on the road stretching out before him in an endless ribbon of dust, along sunken lanes over which the trees bent like an arbor, in paths where the wheat rose as high as his knees, with the sun on his shoulders and the morning air in his nostrils, his heart full of the joys of the night, his spirit at peace, his flesh content, he would ride along ruminating on his happiness, like a man continuing to chew, after dinner, the taste of the truffles he is digesting.

I like to reproduce the word order, and the order of ideas, of the original whenever possible. Flaubert ends this otherwise-lyrical paragraph with the words *truffes* and *digèrent*—in other words, his rhetorical buildup, in describing the sensuous, placid happiness of a man in love, ends with a reference to digestion and a black, smelly fungus. This is typical of Flaubert, who likes to create a traditional writerly effect, romantic or sentimental, and then, when we are well entranced, bring us back down to reality with a thud by offering us a mundane, preferably earthy image—truffles in this scene, potatoes in a later one.

The problem for me, however, was the word *mâchent*, which I translated as "chew." Of course I wanted to retain the idea of chewing, especially since it follows the lovely "ruminating," which is not only an apt word for Charles's idle thoughts, as his horse ambles along, but also yet another veiled reference to one of Flaubert's favorite metaphors—the bovine—which makes regular appearances in his work, even in character names such as Bovary and Bouvard.

But how do you chew a taste?

What I did not do, during the wine-tasting in Beaune— a cause for some lost sleep once I returned home—was ask the professional who was assisting us on our tour just how *he* translates *mâcher* into English, for English-speaking visitors, since there must be an accepted translation for this in the wine-tasting world, at least.

Still, the experience answered one question—the word *mâcher*, unlike "chew," can be used for something that, in my opinion, you don't chew.

In translating, you pose yourself a question—or it is posed to you by the text; you have no satisfactory answer, though you put something down on paper, and then years later the answer may turn up. Certainly you never forget the question.

I have had two literary occupations, and preoccupations, all my adult life, both evidently necessary to me, each probably enhancing the other—writing and translating. And this is one of the differences between them: in translation, you are writing, yes, but not only writing—you are also solving, or trying to solve, a set problem not of your own creation. The problem can't be evaded, as it can in your own writing, and it may haunt you later.

So, here we have the first two pleasures of translating: (1) the pleasure of writing; and (2) the pleasure of solving a puzzle.

———————

1) In translating, you are forming phrases and sentences that please you at least to some extent and most of the time. You have the pleasure of working with sound, rhythm, image, rhetoric, the shape of a paragraph, tone, voice. And—an important difference—you have this writing pleasure within the island of the given text, within its distinct perimeter. You are not beset by that very uncomfortable anxiety, the anxiety of invention, the commitment to invent a piece of work yourself, one that may succeed but may also fail, and whose success or failure is unpredictable.

I am writing, but not my own work. The words are my choices, but only within limits. I am working very hard at one aspect of writing, but I am not, altogether, the writer of this passage. I can work as hard and as happily as I like at this writing without the more general *doubt* that might accompany, even if ever so subtly or faintly, any writing wholly my own. Or perhaps it is not so much doubt as the *tension* that this thing may not even come into existence, or that if it falters its way into existence it may not deserve to survive. Whereas there is no doubt that this French sentence before me must be written, in English, and be written in this way: now I can apply myself to doing it.

In this sort of writing, there is no blank page to worry about, when you sit down to write. Someone else has already written what you are about to write, someone else is giving you closely specific "guidelines"—in other words, the original text.

It is also a kind of writing you can do when you are blocked in your own writing. Roland Barthes is quoted by Kate Briggs in her fine book on translation, *This Little Art*, saying, in his lecture course on the novel: "I would advise a young writer who is having difficulty writing—if it's friendly to offer advice—that he should stop writing for himself for a while and do translations, that he should translate good literature, and one day he will discover that he is writing with an ease he didn't have before." This was, in fact, exactly my situation—blocked in my own writing—when I began translating Maurice Blanchot for the first time.

2) In translating, then, you are at the same time always solving a problem. It may be a word problem, an ingenious, complicated word problem that requires not only a good deal of craft but some art or artfulness in its solution. And yet, though the problem is embedded in a text of great inherent interest, even importance, it always retains some of the same appeal as those problems posed by much simpler or more intellectually limited word puzzles in the daily or Sunday paper or in a slim book picked up at a train station—a crossword, a Jumble, a code.

Margaret Jull Costa, writing about translating the work of Javier Marías, in one of the Sylph Editions Cahiers series on translation and writing, discusses a particular problem she struggled with, and then concludes: "This, of course, is the kind of nerdy fiddling that all translators spend hours over—and actually enjoy." Eliot Weinberger, in his contribution to a very useful collection of essays called *In Translation*, edited by Susan Bernofsky and Esther Allen, calls us translators "the geeks of literature." Nerd, geek.

Example of nerdy fiddling: Here is not a complicated problem but a simple one. I must translate the final sentence of the passage about the steeples of Martinville and Vieuxvicq in *Swann's Way*. After the young narrator, sitting up next to the coachman, has borrowed a piece of paper from the doctor and written his piece about the steeples, he says, in one of Proust's wonderfully brief, simple sentences: "And then I began to sing." That was how I translated it. But before making that decision, I considered the alternative: "And then I began singing." The choice made me think harder than I'd ever had before about the difference between the effect of "to sing" and that of "singing." Although the two were so close, I had to ask myself in what way they were different, and which was more effective. We commonly use either form—"I began to realize" or "he began digging"—but I decided that if you are about to begin something, "to sing" sounds more like a beginning than the present participle, "singing," which by its nature implies continuing action. Rhythmically, too, the sentence read better with the closing iambs of "began to sing."

Further along in the same essay, Jull Costa observes something related but a little different: "What I say here is certainly not intended as a lament about 'difficult' writers . . . because I really enjoy dealing with 'difficulties.'" Nerdy fiddling with difficulties, or simply with choices.

3) A third pleasure, or convenience, is that translating is a kind of writing you can do not only when you are fresh, energetic, and in a positive frame of mind, but also when you are tired or cross, for the very reason that you are not under the pressure of invention. You can still be methodical when you are tired. I do not have to summon to this writing all the forces that I would summon to my own. I can puzzle out this one puzzle on a public bus with commotion all around me.

You can consult dictionaries and find alternative words when you are in a bad mood. This activity may even improve your mood.

4) Then there is the pleasure of company versus solitude: When you are translating, you are working in partnership with the author; you are not as alone as you usually are when writing your own work. You sense the author's hovering presence, you feel an alliance with him, and a loyalty to him, with all his good and his less good character traits, whether, like Proust, he is neurotic and difficult, and at the same time generous and funny, or, like Flaubert, tender toward his family and at the same time full of contempt for a great many people and types of people. Perhaps it is that you overlook his less admirable qualities in admiration for what he has written; or your judgment of him is tempered by your awareness that you have a degree of power over his work—to do well or ill by him in the small arena of the translation.

You may also have company in the shape of a cotranslator or an informant—the native-language speaker who will guide you away from subtle mistakes.

5) Related to this is the fifth pleasure: You are to some extent disappearing from yourself for a little while, as you do any time you become wholly absorbed into an activity. You leave yourself behind for hours at a stretch, and this is not only a relief but an adventure. To quote Eliot Weinberger, again, from the same essay: "For me, the translator's anonymity . . . is the joy of translation. One is operating strictly on the level of language, attempting to invent similar effects, to capture the essential, without the interference of the otherwise all-consuming ego." (He does caution, though, at another point,

that the ego can assert itself again: "Translators sometimes feel they share in the glory of their famous authors, rather like the hairdressers of Hollywood stars.")

If you are also a writer, you are all too much involved with your own sensibility, what you will invent, what your mind will turn up unexpectedly, what your vocabulary will be. The source of what you do will be your own self, just as, more physically, the source of a singer's voice is her own self, her own body, muscles, vocal cords.

And when you are not writing, you are also inescapably present with yourself, self-involved to a greater or lesser degree.

But when you are translating, your own self is set aside, you are subsumed into the author and the work you are translating.

6) So that is pleasure number 6, that in this activity you are entering another person—you are speaking in his or her words, you are writing what he or she wrote. You become a sort of shadow person, for a time, insubstantial. In this, you are like an actor. It is restful. When I am translating Proust I am no longer quite myself; I am here, but hidden in the shadow or subsumed within the identity of this other writer. I am only part of the whole of what I usually am. And it is a relief from myself. Weinberger, again: "The introspective bookworm happily becomes the voice of Jack London or Jean Genet."

You develop the ability, if you did not have this before, to be both yourself and another, or multiple others, at the same time.

Some translators concentrate on one author: more, and less, well-known translators come to mind—Ann Goldstein on Elena Ferrante; Rosmarie Waldrop on Edmond Jabès; Don Bartlett on Karl Ove Knausgaard; Michael Hofmann on, by turns, Joseph Roth and Peter Stamm, with intervals of Franz Kafka, Hans Fallada, and many others; I, for a few years at a time, on Maurice Blanchot, Pierre Jean Jouve, and Michel Leiris, with a number of others interspersed. Other translators translate always a different writer and so identify with many in succession.

7) You are entering not only the author but another culture for longer or shorter periods of time. Translation is a very deep sort of armchair travel—all your thoughts are taken up with the culture of, say, Normandy of the 1830s; or with Paris high society at the turn of the twentieth century. Don Bartlett, as Knausgaard, studies literature in the Norwegian Hanseatic town of Bergen or, earlier, hides his precious supply of beer on New Year's Eve behind a bank of snow; Rachel Careau, as the peculiar and inimitable Roger Lewinter, makes a mystical discovery in a Geneva flea market or closely observes a (Swiss) spider; Susan Bernofsky, as Robert Walser, retreats into a mountaintop asylum and writes in a graphite script so small it is for many years taken to be nonsense. You are traveling, and you are, inevitably, always learning—and you have the stimulation of both.

This sojourn in another language, and in another culture and another history, is one I thirst after because it relieves me, for a while, of my own culture and the present; there is no doubt that I like the experience of having my mind engaged in this other place and time and in this other way of thinking for long periods of an ordinary American day.

———

8) You not only enter that other culture, but remain to some extent inside it as you return to your own, so that even in your U.S. life, things you experience may jump out at you in French: you may open a can of *pois chiches* to add to your salad at lunch, or you see deer *brouter* in a nearby field, or you find that your closet is simply too *exigu*, or twilight descends and the time of day appears to you to be *entre chien et loup*. You think, at the Columbia County Fair, that perhaps this farmer, before walking to the exhibits, will knot the corners of his handkerchief and place it on his head, to protect himself from the sun—as do the farmers arriving at the great agricultural fair in *Madame Bovary*.

9) As a result of often stepping outside it, or spending long weeks outside it, you come to acquire greater perspective on your own native culture, with its particular history. You are always in it and of it, but you do not take it for granted. You appreciate the individuality of any culture, but you also notice—with no bias, you hope—what is superior about each; your own culture is not superior in every respect. You also like to imagine what it is that the French like about your own country. If I enjoy their sometimes rigid codes of conduct, they probably enjoy our greater casualness and freedom from constraint. I enjoy the impression I receive in France that every acre, even every square meter, is valued and used; they probably enjoy the vastness, and carelessness, of many places in the United States. I relish the history that goes so far back behind every settlement in France; they probably enjoy the relative youth of ours.

You are, in any case, not inhabiting exclusively and constantly your own country and culture, but are looking outward with a wider perspective, more constantly aware of the international.

10) Because, however, you are always drawing on the resources of your own language for such a variety of different styles and sensibilities, or—if you translate a single author— a style and sensibility and personal history quite different from your own, you become more and more knowledgeable about your own language and its resources as you work— from author to author, or book to book, year to year, decade to decade. Translating continuously feeds my own writing by, among other things, enriching my English and developing my capacities in English. The problems upon problems that pose themselves, in translating, require me to become ever more ingenious in my home language; working within these constraints requires me to become more adept.

I am not quite as much of a Francophile as some translators from the French. My own language is always primary for me, my first and greatest love among languages. French will almost always seem foreign to me. After all these years, I still can't fully assimilate the fact that one entire word, and a complex one, consists only of the letter *y*, that insect-like letter, that sort of stick bug or praying mantis. How strange, I continue to think—though it is true that, as I learn other languages, languages entirely new to me, French feels more comfortably familiar, like coming home.

Although I constantly hunger for the sounds and sights and grammars and oddities and cultural references of other languages, I continue to revel in my own language, the deep and rich associations I have with its words, phrases, sentences; the richness and enormous extent of the English vocabulary, the flexibility and malleability it gains, for instance, from the fact that the formal, abstract Latinate vocabulary is paralleled by the blunt, informal, emotional, concrete Anglo-Saxon. I look forward to the unexpected unknown word that will inevitably come along to offer me its surprise. (Recent examples have been: *swinking*, *scrag*, and *ineliminably*.)

I want to take the always slightly mysterious French sentence and transform it into something every word, and nuance, of which will be thoroughly *home* to me, which is what English is to me—the home language. It is the decipherment and then the transformation that satisfy me. So, much as I may love many, many sentences of Proust's or Flaubert's, I am out to annihilate them, for the moment, to replace them by something fine in my own language, what Virginia Woolf described so succinctly, in a 1937 talk on craftsmanship, as "the right words in the right order"—in English.

11) But, for translators who are also engaged in writing of their own, here is another great pleasure: Just as you can enter another person and speak in his voice, you are also no longer confined to writing in your own style and with your own sensibility, but can write in the style of Proust, for instance, with his elaborated syntactic pyramids, and then, a few years later, in the style of Flaubert, with his clipped clauses and fondness for semicolons. You are at the same time clothing yourself, for a while, in the sensibility of the original author: Proust's affectionate portrait of the grandmother in *Swann's Way* becomes my own affectionate portrait of her, in Proustian sentences. Flaubert's moment of compassion for the dying Emma becomes my own compassion, in English, though I may privately feel more sympathy for the often de-

rided Charles, quietly meeting his end in the sunlight, on a garden bench, as he is being called in to lunch.

This phenomenon, of slipping into the style of another writer, gives you great freedom and joy, in your manipulation of language. You are ventriloquist and chameleon.

And while you comply with this alien style, while you fit your own prose into it, you may also, positively, react against it, in your hours off, your away hours: it was while I was translating, with such pleasure, Proust's very long and ingenuity-taxing sentences that I began, in contrary motion, to write the very shortest stories I could compose, sometimes consisting only of the title and a single line.

12) I search for the reasons why I continue to want to translate, or rather, what impels me to continue translating. I suspected, but wasn't quite ready to admit, that the fact was I really *wanted to write this book* in English, whatever it was: I wanted to convey those strange moments of Blanchot's *L'Arrêt de mort* in English, I wanted to construct those complex sentences of Proust's *Du Côté de chez Swann* in English, I wanted to tell the story and make the wry comments, in English, of *Madame Bovary*; I was charmed, and moved, by this story of Peter Bichsel's, and wanted to see it in English prose, though as nearly as possible, somehow, in just the way he wrote it.

In her contribution to the anthology *In Translation*, Clare Cavanagh, translator of Wisława Szymborska (pronounced "veeswava shimborska") and others, expresses, in relation to translating poetry (which she calls "impossible"), what may be at the heart of the translating impulse: "You see a wonderful thing in front of you, and you want it. You try reading it over and over, you see if you can memorize it, or copy it out line by line. And nothing works; it's still there. So if it doesn't already exist in English, you turn to translation; you try remaking it in your own language, in your own words, in the vain hope of getting it once and for all, of finally making it your own. And sometimes you even feel, for a while at least, for a day or two or even a couple of weeks, that you've got it, it's worked, the poem's yours. But then you turn back to the poem itself at some point, and you have to hit your head against the wall and laugh: it's still there."

Over the years, on the other hand, there were certainly quite a few books I did not love and that I did not want to write, especially early in my translating career, when I was obliged to take on whatever translation work came my way in order to earn my living. There was still pleasure in the work, but it was the pleasure of solving the word problem, and, more generally, the satisfaction of supporting myself honorably.

But two recent experiences—of translations I did *not* do—have convinced me that maybe it really is true that if a book or story in another language excites or inspires me, I want to write it myself in English.

One case: I hungered to translate Gerard van het Reve's *De avonden* (*The Evenings* in English, now at last translated by Sam Garrett), once I discovered it—a darkly humorous Dutch classic from 1947 portraying ten days in the postwar life of a fraught family triangle of mother, father, and resentful live-at-home grown son, in which, for instance, a plate of pickled herrings, green from having been left too long, its onions black, nevertheless makes an appearance at the dinner table. I tried translating a sample few pages, thinking it would not be too difficult, since it was concrete and repetitious, but my beginner's Dutch comprehension simply wouldn't have caught some of the subtleties in it.

The second case was the arrival in my house of Michel

Leiris's *Phantom Africa* (*L'Afrique fantôme* in the original), published in an English translation by Brent Hayes Edwards, reminding me how much I had been tempted, many years ago, when the book was just waiting for a translator, to translate it. I did not take it on, mainly because of its sheer size: it is 720 pages long and weighs just under three pounds. (I weighed it.) But how interesting was this very long and personal journal cum anthropological document. Why was I not content just to read it, why did I want to transform it myself into an English text?

It is not that I think my translation would be better than that of the present translator, though in the case of certain books, I suspect—or I know—that mine would have been better. (And perhaps this—here's a last-minute thought— would be another pleasure of translating: creating a translation superior to an existing loathsome betrayal of the original and thus, triumphantly, getting rid of the travesty.) No, it is simply the desire to *do it myself*. Is this yearning similar to that of any half-talented musician, such as I am, to play this Goldberg variation myself, even though my playing is so much worse than that of any of the pianists I could listen to in a recording? Similar to that of the earnest, slightly tense-looking woman who sets up her easel on the bank of the Seine and paints Notre Dame for the ten-thousandth or hundred-thousandth time, producing yet another not terrible but not really good painting—the joy of *doing it herself*.

13) Another pleasure, in the course of the translation, in the thick of it, or even after one version has been published: You can share your translation conundrums with others. You may present your problem to friends over dinner.

The one I took out to an Indian restaurant was this: If

Proust could structure a quite short sentence with subordinates in such a way as to include four prepositional phrases in a row in the middle—three of them with "of"—and four verbs one after another at the end, three of them completing subordinate clauses, could I do the same? I couldn't, though I went into contortions trying. The sentence I took with me in order to get help with it from friends, help that I didn't get, though the dinner was enjoyable, was, in my eventual (compromise) translation:

> A man's voice which he tried to distinguish from among the voices of those of Odette's friends whom he knew asked:
>   "Who's there?"

You write to an old friend from high school who is now a plantswoman, can read French, and may know what Proust meant by the *vigne vierge* in the Bois de Boulogne that turned red in the fall. You have many exchanges with her about Boston ivy, English ivy, Virginia creeper, and others. (At another point in the novel, however, "wild vine" seemed the right translation for it.) Or you receive speculations from strangers: an elderly gentleman living outside Oxford who has read an article of yours in which you present a problem from the translation believes that it is not a ray of light on which the titmouse is bobbing, but the ray of a plant, because he has seen it out his back window. In this case, he may actually prove to be correct, whereas most suggestions, or corrections, offered confidently by non-translators—as I'm sure most translators have experienced—are *not* useful.

And many translators, I'm sure, regularly share conundrums with spouses or partners who can't help and who often can't even begin to understand what the problem is, but who must, out of loyalty, or compassion, or because they live in the same house, listen patiently to the translator as she goes into great detail about the problem she is up against, or the triumph she has experienced in getting this meaning into "the right words in the right order." I can see, across our bowls of breakfast cereal, that friendly, open expression combining willingness and bafflement.

14) And there is another pleasure, for someone like me who am not really a scholar—and that is the pleasure of scholarship, or one aspect of scholarship, or what perhaps just *reminds* me of scholarship: the very painstakingly thorough research into the material in the book I am translating.

Sometimes the research has been botanical, or avian, as in the instances I just mentioned. Sometimes, as in the case of my recent translation of a slim volume of Proust's letters, the research has been biographical or historical. But most often, for me, the research is into a single, even quite common word, such as *soir*, usually but not always meaning "evening," and the sources I consult are just a few, and mainly dictionaries. If I was mystified that the word *soir* in French sometimes means afternoon and sometimes evening and sometimes even later, the answer might lie in the fact that it is derived from a Latin word that means a point in time later in the day, like the Spanish *tarde*—also not a fixed time—so that *soir* really has the elastic meaning of "later in the day," whether afternoon, evening, or even later.

As I translate, I learn. I could make that a separate pleasure, but for now I'll let it remain part of the pleasure of being, or acting, the scholar.

15) I was quite new to the writings of Maurice Blanchot when I began translating *L'Arrêt de mort* (*Death Sentence*) many years ago; I was suffering a prolonged dry spell in my own writing, and this was a good way to occupy my writing time and mind until I could write my own work again—as Barthes advised. And I was not a deeply dedicated lover of Proust when I embarked on translating *Du Côté de chez Swann*, but came to it by chance, being invited to translate it. But in both cases I passed almost immediately from the outside, being the respectful admirer of this writer, though not the ardent fan, to deep inside this writer, so far inside that I could not see the outside, and still can't see the outside. It was from inside that I traveled through the book sentence by sentence and physically came to know each atom of each word, rarely stepping back to look at the whole.

Related to this may be yet another pleasure of translating, one that I have experienced but had not articulated to myself until I read a comment by a reader/writer/translator on the *Words Without Borders* website, that he had started translating Spanish poetry in order to learn, from the inside, how the poems worked. So that is another pleasure: seeing more closely, from the inside, how a particular work of literature is put together. You are obliged to stay with it sentence by sentence, or line by line, and consider every word: you come to know it very well.

When I translated *Madame Bovary*, I saw more clearly, more exactly, the art and artfulness of Flaubert's work in that novel—his care with transitions and handling of point of view, for instance—and although I still didn't love the book the way I had always loved his *Bouvard et Pécuchet*, I became a dedicated admirer of it.

---

16) Another pleasure may be the better solution to a problem that comes later, on second or third consideration. Proust was a great reviser, as we know. I had many afterthoughts, too, about the choices I had made, usually taking a perfectly good solution and trying to bring it even closer to the original, attempting to magically reproduce the original. Here is one instance, from the Proust translation: The phrase *catastrophe diluvienne* occurs in an early passage about the comfort of sitting before the hearth when the weather outside is bad, and for months I thought "catastrophic deluge" was a perfectly good translation for it, and really quite a forceful little phrase. And it is. I like the way it reproduces Proust's *c-d* sequence, for instance. But I was reconsidering it one day—always a little risky—and realized that I could both move closer to Proust's original and write a phrase I found more interesting and rhythmically pleasing by translating it much more literally—perhaps verging on the overly mannered—as "diluvian catastrophe," and both my desires for this translation were satisfied: to stay close to the original and to write it well.

Rereading a passage of my translation months or years later is always both painful and pleasurable: in the case of something I have got right, that I'm happy with, I relish and savor this phrase and that as I never would a phrase in my own writing. But I also wince when I read, yet again, a problem not perfectly solved. The compromise involved in any translation can be painful.

17) Another pleasure is hearing from readers who are grateful for your work, especially if your work makes available a book never before translated that now delights or moves them. I recently heard from a high school pal of mine that he loved the Proust *Letters* that had just come out, and because

of it was now listening to César Franck again. Or if your work makes available to readers a classic that was previously obscured by a less than wholly faithful or readable translation (quite a few people, in the case of *Swann's Way*).

This pleasure is purer, less selfish, than that of hearing that your own (nontranslation) writing has delighted someone, because the good translation is truly a service, at the same time that it is a personal pleasure. You have opened the way, you have given access, to the work of another writer. In certain cases, you have introduced a wide new readership to a writer you admire.

18) Yet another pleasure (I keep finding them), which I discovered as I was reading for enjoyment a translated novel, is—after so many years of translating—detecting through the English what the original might have been. Usually, this is because the translation has remained very close to the original and is also, at certain moments, not quite natural English, though not necessarily for this reason unpleasant. This occasional strangeness can become part of the style of the work in English and create quite a charming effect, as in, for instance, a translation of one of Georges Simenon's Maigret novels. We have the style of the novel as it is—in Simenon's case, the short sentences, the short paragraphs, the prevalence of exclamations and exclamation marks, sentences and phrases trailing off into ellipses, fragments repeating information (as Maigret thinks it over). And then we have the occasional unobtrusive locution or expression that sounds—to me, anyway—more French than English, or at least not quite English, and that points me back to the French.

For instance (and I'm guessing, since I do not have the French in front of me—but that's what I do when I'm reading), if a bartender removes the head of foam from a glass of beer "*with the help of* a wooden knife," this might be, more naturally, in French, "*à l'aide de*." "I'm listening, madame" might be "*Je vous écoute, madame*"; "*She . . . had underlined* with a glance the inappropriateness of Mejat's laughter" might be "*Elle avait souligné*"—"underline" could also have been translated "emphasized" or "stressed"; "it wouldn't surprise me"(not unnatural in English, either) could be "*il ne m'étonnerait pas*" (a little more common in French); "in other words" might be "*c'est-à-dire*" (more frequent in French, and also possibly translated "that is"). I can't guess exactly which idiom in French produced "A whole other kettle of fish, that one!" but the tagged-on "that one" is certainly more characteristic of French than English—perhaps "*celui-là*" or rather, since a woman is in question, "*celle-là*." One last example, exceptionally, falls perhaps into the category of discordant idiom, and that is the exclamation of an old wife of a customs officer who lives in a mussel-farming village near the coast: "I say!" This may possibly be, in French, "*Ma foi!*" In any case, to my ear, the very characteristically British exclamation is a bit out of place.

19) So perhaps we have here almost a nineteenth pleasure—not just reading bits of the original *through* the English translation, but, in fact, for moments, reading both at the same time, the English primary but the French now and then echoing in the background.

20) Another pleasure, experienced quite a long time after I identified the third pleasure of translating (that you can do the work even when tired or cross), was this: it is not only

that you can translate when you are tired or cross, or upset, but that if you have a long habit of translating, this activity has become such a comforting, satisfying, and familiar one that, as soon as you sit down and begin translating, if you are upset, you immediately calm down and are comforted.

21) The last pleasure I have identified is a little perverse but one that should probably have been obvious to me long ago, and it is this: the pleasure of reading a foreign text, coming upon a problematic phrase, especially one you have wrestled with many times in the past, and *not* being responsible for translating it.

A final observation will not describe a last pleasure, but perhaps the silver lining to a translation cloud. One frustration in translating is the restraint you need to show, having to remain faithful to this text, write this story using this sequence of sentences, find words for these words, solve this problem, refrain from shifting into your own style or, worse, expressing your own ideas. And there is usually not an exact equivalent of the original, or if there is, it is awkward, or unnatural, and can't be used; translation is, eternally, a compromise. You settle for the best you can do rather than achieving perfection, though there is the occasional perfect solution.

But I have the theory that, for me, at least, and perhaps for others, too, the frustration of this constant compromise may create a certain pent-up energy that is later released in the relatively free territory of your own writing, or, if you are not also a writer, maybe in your tennis game or your morning run. Perhaps all that richness of language and variety of syntax that we could not use in the translation comes tumbling out in our own prose, or if that is not, precisely, what comes tumbling out, surely our own new composition, or our tennis or our running, is electrified, or galvanized, by this release.

The French, in their outward forms at least, are extremely courteous—and outward forms can be a significant factor in harmonizing human relations. The French have a greeting or kind wish for every occasion throughout an ordinary day. Eating a sandwich with a friend by a French riverside, one year, I was surprised that more than one stranger, strolling past in the sunlight between us and the water, said to us, with simple civility: *bon appétit!* At that point, we became more aware of how, all day long, it was *bon* this and *bon* that— *bonjour, bon après-midi, bonne nuit, bonne chance, bonne fin de séjour, bon voyage.* One *bon* that we had not noticed before issued now and then from a waiter as he delivered the next course: *bonne continuation!* And so I will conclude my catalog of pleasures by saying to my fellow translators, and to all of us in general, hoping to absorb and retain the courtesy of the French: *bonne continuation!*

2020

PROUST

MARCEL PROUST

A LA RECHERCHE
DU TEMPS PERDU

I

DU CÔTÉ DE CHEZ SWANN

★

GALLIMARD

Reading Proust for the First Time:
A Blog Post

I know approximately, but not exactly, when I first read Proust. I was living in France at the time. I was probably twenty-four or twenty-five. I bought the little cream-colored two-volume Gallimard edition of the first book of the novel—*Du Côté de chez Swann*. I still have this edition, and I know exactly how much of it I read because I did then what I still do, all these years later, when I'm reading a book in another language that I don't know as well as I'd like to: I wrote neatly, with a well-sharpened pencil, along the top and sometimes the bottom margins of the page, the English translations of the words I didn't know or wasn't sure of.

I know exactly where I stopped in the book—about two-thirds of the way through, I'm sorry to say. But that is also consistent with the way I read then, and still read, in the case of many books, even the most interesting and even the most significant to me personally. When I first encountered Beckett, for instance—the book was *Malone Dies*—I was startled and fascinated by it, but I did not finish reading it. What seems to interest me, in these cases, is the form, the technique, the approach to composing a piece of fiction, rather than the impact of the whole work, which I could receive only by reading it to the end.

I can also see which of Proust's words I didn't know or wasn't sure of at that time. Some are by now familiar: *assouvir*, *effroi*, *atterré*. But others I still have trouble remembering: *fourbe*, *charmille*, *stercoraire* (unhelpfully glossed by me then as "stercoraceous, stercoral").

It was from this two-volume edition that I chose to work when I began my translation of the book into English, about twenty-five years later. There was a more definitive French edition available, and further along in the project I put my old edition aside and continued the work using that text, but in the beginning I worked from the older books for reasons partly sentimental and partly aesthetic. I enjoyed returning to the pages that a younger self had labored over, as though working alongside her; and these small-format, lightweight, handsomely designed volumes with their off-white, textured pages—I don't know if the paper is rag or not, but you can see variations of color and material in its weave—and their dark, deep, clearly imprinted type, are a pleasure to hold and read.

I did not finish reading the book before I began to translate it, nor did I go back to the beginning and read it all the way through, since it was by then a long-standing habit, or practice, not to read a book before beginning to translate it. So two-thirds of the book was a very distant, surely buried memory, and the last third was entirely new to me.

What is hard to determine is what sort of influence reading Proust for the first time had had on me as a young writer. Clearly I was interested enough to read two-thirds of the book without giving up. Also, I tended then, and still tend, to absorb fairly quickly and thoroughly the "writing lesson" offered by whatever I was reading—the lesson in form, structure, phrasing, word choice, sensibility, and so on, what could be learned from another writer. I may have learned from Proust that there is almost no limit to how extensively or deeply one can explore a single perception or emotion, even a fleeting one. (A lesson continued and extended when I began to translate Maurice Blanchot, not long after.) I must have learned great patience in writing, particularly in finding the right expression for a subtle thought. I must have learned that although plot has a role to play in a novel, it does not have to be primary, and in fact the novel is almost always more interesting when plot is not primary. (I was at about the same time reading American detective novels translated into French, again to improve my understanding of the language, so I had the contrasting example before me of novels in which plot was primary.) And another thing I must have picked up was, paradoxically, the importance of economy, of finding the exact expression of a thought, of not groping after the right words. I say paradoxically, of course, because one might not associate economy with the stupendous length of the entire seven-volume *In Search of Lost Time*, and even of *Swann's Way* alone, as well as of many sentences within it. But although Proust was so expansive, he was also, always, economical, never saying more than was necessary to the full expression of his thought.

2013

Introduction to *Swann's Way*

Many passages from Marcel Proust's *Swann's Way* are by now so well-known that they have turned into clichés and reference points and occupy a permanent place in contemporary Western culture. Scenes and episodes are familiar even to many who have not actually read the book: say "Proust" and they will immediately think "madeleine" and "tea," if not "cork-lined room." Yet confronting the book itself is an entirely different, and individual, experience. One will have one's own way of visualizing the narrator's childhood bedtime scene with his mother, his visits to his hypochondriac aunt, his teasing of the servant Françoise, his embrace of the prickly hawthorns, his vision of the three steeples, and his first piece of serious writing. Swann's agonizing love affair with Odette and the narrator's youthful infatuation with Swann's daughter, Gilberte, will be colored by the personal associations of each reader, who will likewise have unexpected memories, recalled by unexpected stimuli, that will enable him or her to identify with the narrator in the most famous scene of all, in which the taste of a tea-soaked madeleine suddenly incites his full recollection of his childhood in the village of Combray and, from this, leads to the unfolding of all the subsequent action in the four-thousand-page novel.

One will find, too, that the better acquainted one becomes with this book, the more it yields. Given its richness and resilience, Proust's work may be, and has been, enjoyed on every level and in every form—as quotation, as excerpt, as compendium, even as movie and comic book—but in the end it is best experienced, for most, in the way it was meant to be, in the full, slow reading and rereading of every word, in complete submission to Proust's subtle psychological analyses, his precise portraits, his compassionate humor, his richly colored and lyrical landscapes, his extended digressions, his architectonic sentences, his symphonic structures, his perfect formal designs.

Swann's Way is divided into three parts: "Combray," "Swann in Love," and "Place-Names: The Name." "Combray," itself divided into two parts, opens with the bedtime of the narrator as a grown man: he describes how he used to spend the sleepless portions of his nights remembering events from earlier in his life and finally describes the episode of the madeleine. A second and much longer section of "Combray" follows, containing the memories of his childhood at Combray that were summoned by the taste of the "*petite madeleine*" and that came flooding back to him in unprecedentedly minute and sensuous detail. This first part of the book, having opened at bedtime, closes—itself like a long sleepless night—at dawn.

"Swann in Love," which jumps back in time to a period before the narrator was born, consists of the self-contained story of Swann's miserable, jealousy-racked love for the shallow and fickle Odette, who will one day be his wife; the narrator with whom we began the book scarcely appears at all.

The third and last part, "Place-Names: The Name," much shorter than the rest of the volume, includes the story of the narrator's infatuation, as a boy, with Swann's daughter, Gilberte, during the weeks they play together on the chilly lawns of the Champs-Élysées and ends with a sort of coda that jumps forward in time: on a late November day, at the time of the writing, the narrator, walking through the Bois de Boulogne, muses on the contrast between the beauties of the days of his childhood and the banality of the present, and on the nature of time.

The story is told in the first person. Proust scholars have identified a handful of slightly different *I*'s in the novel as a whole, but the two main *I*'s are those of the rather weary, middle-aged narrator as he tells the story and the narrator as a child and young man. The first person, however, is abandoned for shorter or longer intervals in favor of what is in effect an omniscient narrator, as when, in "Combray," we witness conversations between his aunt Léonie and the servant Françoise that the boy could not have heard; and most remarkably during nearly the whole of "Swann in Love."

Not only is the story told in the first person, but the protagonist is referred to several times in the course of *In Search of Lost Time*, though not in *Swann's Way*, as "Marcel," and the book is filled with events and characters closely resembling those of Proust's own life. Yet this novel is not autobiography wearing a thin disguise of fiction but, rather, something more complex—fiction created out of real life, based on experiences and beliefs of its author, and presented in the guise of autobiography. For although Proust's own life experience is the material from which he forms his novel, this material has been altered, recombined, shaped to create a coherent and meaningful fictional artifact, a crucial alchemy—art's transformation of life—which is itself one of

Proust's preoccupations and a principal subject and theme of the book.

The episode of the madeleine, for instance, was based on an experience of Proust's own, but what Proust apparently dipped in his tea was a rusk of dry toast, and the memory that then returned to him was of his morning visits to his grandfather. The scene of the goodnight kiss was set not in a single actual home of Proust's childhood, but in a melding of two—one in Auteuil, the suburb of Paris where he was born, and the other in Illiers, a town outside Paris where he spent many summers. Similarly, the characters in the novel are composites, often more perfectly realized ideals or extremes, of characters in his own life; the annoying Mme Vinteuil is based closely on a certain Mme X of Proust's acquaintance, but to avoid offending her by too blatantly describing her, Proust attributed her habit of incessantly painting pictures of roses to another character, Mme de Villeparisis.

What is introduced in this inaugural volume of *In Search of Lost Time*? As Samuel Beckett remarks in his slim study *Proust*, "The whole of Proust's world comes out of a teacup, and not merely Combray and his childhood. For Combray brings us to the two 'ways' and to Swann, and to Swann may be related every element of the Proustian experience and consequently its climax in revelation. . . . Swann is the cornerstone of the entire structure, and the central figure of the narrator's childhood, a childhood that involuntary memory, stimulated or charmed by the long-forgotten taste of a madeleine steeped in an infusion of tea, conjures in all the relief and color of its essential significance from the shallow well of a cup's inscrutable banality."

Through Charles Swann, the faithful friend and constant dinner guest of the narrator's family, we are led, either directly or indirectly, to all the most important characters of

In Search of Lost Time. As Proust himself says, describing the book in 1913, in a letter to his eventual publisher, Bernard Grasset, "There are a great many characters; they are 'prepared' in this first volume, in such a way that in the second they will do exactly the opposite of what one would have expected from the first." Nearly all, in fact, are introduced in *Swann's Way*: the young protagonist, his parents, and his grandmother; Swann, his daughter, Gilberte, and Odette, who is both the mysterious "lady in pink" early in the book and later the lovely Mme Swann; Françoise, the family servant; the narrator's boyhood friend, the bookish Bloch; and the aristocrat Mme de Villeparisis. Stories are told about them that will be echoed later by parallel stories, just as the story of the young protagonist's longing for his mother is echoed within this volume by the story of Swann's longing for Odette and the narrator's, when he was a boy, for Gilberte. Stories are begun that will be continued, hints are dropped that will be picked up, and questions are asked that will be answered in later volumes; places are described that will reappear in greater detail. "Combray," which contains some of the most beautiful writing in the novel, sets the stage for the rest, and in its first pages introduces the principal themes that will be elaborated in subsequent volumes: childhood, love, betrayal, memory, sleep, time, homosexuality, music, art, manners, taste, society, historic France. The later volumes, in turn, give "Combray" an ever-richer meaning, and reveal more fully the logical interrelation of its parts. As Proust himself, again, in the same letter, says: "And from the point of view of composition, it is so complex that it only becomes clear much later when all the 'themes' have begun to coalesce."

In the narrator's recovery of his early memories through the tasting of the tea-soaked madeleine, for instance, we first learn of Proust's conception of the power of involuntary memory: the madeleine is only the first of a number of inanimate objects that will appear in the course of *In Search of Lost Time*, each of which provides a sensuous experience that will in turn provoke an involuntary memory (the uneven cobblestones in a courtyard, for instance, or the touch of a stiffly starched napkin on the lips). The incident of the madeleine will itself be taken up again and revealed in a new light in the final volume.

In the narrator's early passion for his mother and Swann's for Odette, we are introduced to the power of love for an elusive object, the obstinate perversity with which one's passion is intensified, if not in fact created, by the danger of losing the beloved. The narrator's infatuation with Gilberte in the present volume will be echoed by his more fully developed passion, as an adult, for Albertine in a subsequent volume. In the very first pages of *Swann's Way*, the notion of escape from time is alluded to, and the description of the magic lantern that follows soon after hints at how time will be transcended through art. The wistful closing passage in the Bois de Boulogne introduces the theme of the receding, in time, and the disappearance of beloved places and people and their resurrection in our imagination, our memory, and finally in our art. For only in recollection does an experience become fully significant, as we arrange it in a meaningful pattern, and thus the crucial role of our intellect, our imagination, in our perception of the world and re-creation of it to suit our desires; thus the importance of the role of the artist in transforming reality according to a particular inner vision: the artist escapes the tyranny of time through art.

In one early scene, for example, the young protagonist sees the object of his devotion, the Duchesse de Guermantes, in the village church. He has never seen her before; what he has loved has been his own image of her, which he has created from her name and family history, her country estate, her position and reputation. In the flesh, she is disappointing: she has a rather ordinary face, and a pimple beside her nose. But immediately his imagination goes to work again, and soon he has managed to change what he sees before him into an object once again worthy of his love. Similarly, later in the novel Swann finds that his love for Odette is wonderfully strengthened, even utterly changed, the moment he realizes how closely she resembles a favorite painting of his: he now sees the painting, as well, when he looks at her. The power of the intellect, the imagination, has come to work an alchemical change on the inadequacy or tediousness of the real.

Proust began writing *Du Côté de chez Swann* when he was in his late thirties, sometime between the summer of 1908 and the summer of 1909, as near as we can make out from references in his letters and conversations. His mother, with whom he had lived, had died in 1905, and following a stay of some months in a sanatorium, he had moved into an apartment in Versailles while friends searched for a suitable place for him to settle. This place turned out to be an apartment at 102, boulevard Haussmann, which was already familiar to him since the building had been in the possession of his family for some years; his uncle had died in the apartment and his mother had often visited it. The building is now owned by a bank, but one can still view Proust's high-ceilinged bedroom with its two tall windows and marble fireplace. In this room, of modest dimensions, Proust spent most of the rest of his life—slept, rested, ate, received visitors, read, and wrote. It was here that most of *À la Recherche du temps perdu* came into being.

In a sense, the book had already been in preparation for several years before it began to take the form of a novel. It was never destined to be composed in a neatly chronological manner in any case, and elements of it had been emerging piecemeal in various guises: paragraphs, passages, scenes were written and even published in earlier versions, then later reworked and incorporated into the novel. The famous description in *Swann's Way* of the steeples of Martinville, for example, had had an earlier incarnation as an article on road travel; and versions of many scenes had appeared in Proust's first, unfinished, and unpublished novel, *Jean Santeuil*, which juxtaposed the two childhood homes that Proust would later combine to form the setting of the drama of the goodnight kiss.

Proust had been projecting a number of shorter works, most of them essays. At a certain point he realized they could all be brought together in a single form, a novel. What became its start had, immediately before, begun as an essay contesting the ideas of the literary critic Charles Augustin Sainte-Beuve, a work that he conceived as having a fictional opening: the mother of the main character would come to his bedside in the morning and the two of them would begin a conversation about Sainte-Beuve. The first drafts of this essay evolved into the novel, and at last, by midsummer of 1909, Proust was actually referring to his work in progress as a novel. Thereafter the work continued to develop somewhat chaotically, as Proust wrote many different parts of the book at the same time, cutting, expanding, and revising endlessly. Even as he wrote the opening, however, he foresaw the conclusion, and in fact the end of the book was completed before the middle began to grow.

A version of the present first volume, *Du Côté de chez*

Swann, was in existence by January 1912, and extracts including "A Ray of Sun on the Balcony" and "Village Church" were published that year in the newspaper *Le Figaro*.

Although one possible publisher, Eugène Fasquelle, had announced that in his opinion "nothing must interfere with the action" in a work of fiction, Proust nevertheless submitted to him a manuscript of the book in October 1912. At this point, admitting that his novel was very long but pointing out that it was "very concise," he proposed a book in two volumes, one called *Le Temps perdu* (Time Lost) and the other *Le Temps retrouvé* (Time Found Again), under the general title *Les Intermittences du coeur* (The Intermittences of the Heart). He had not yet found the title *Du Côté de chez Swann*.

He received no answer from Fasquelle and, in November 1912, wrote to the Nouvelle Revue Française, a more literary publisher that had developed from the literary journal of the same name, founded by André Gide, and was later to take the name of its director, Gaston Gallimard. By now Proust was considering three volumes.

In December 1912, Gallimard and Fasquelle both returned their copies of the manuscript. Fasquelle, and other publishers, too, Proust wrote in a letter to a friend, would not undertake to publish a work "so different from what the public is accustomed to reading." Gide later admitted to Proust: "The rejection of this book will remain the most serious mistake ever made by the NRF—and (since to my shame I was largely responsible for it) one of the sorrows, one of the most bitter regrets of my life."

At the end of December, Proust approached another publisher, Ollendorff. He offered not only to pay the costs of publication but also to share with the publisher any profits that might derive from it. Ollendorff's rejection came in February and included the comment: "I don't see why a man should take thirty pages to describe how he turns over in bed before he goes to sleep." At last Proust submitted the manuscript to the energetic young publisher Bernard Grasset, offering to pay the expenses of publishing the book and publicizing it, and Grasset accepted.

By April 1913, Proust was beginning to work on proofs. He said in a letter to a friend: "My corrections so far (I hope this won't continue) are not corrections. There remains not a single line out of 20 of the original text. . . . It is crossed out, corrected in every blank part I can find, and I am pasting papers at the top, at the bottom, to the right, to the left, etc." He said that although the resulting text was actually a bit shorter, it was a "hopelessly tangled mess."

During this time, he made final decisions about titles. Ideally, he would have preferred simply the general title, *À la Recherche du temps perdu*, followed by "Volume I" and "Volume II" with no individual titles for the two volumes. However, his publisher wanted individual titles for commercial reasons. Proust decided the first volume would be called *Du Côté de chez Swann* and the second probably *Le Côté de Guermantes.* He explained several times what these titles meant, that in the country around Combray there were two directions in which to take a walk, that one asked, for example: "Shall we go in the direction of M. Rostand's house?" (His friend Maurice Rostand had in fact suggested the title of the first volume.) *Du Côté de chez Swann* would, most literally translated, be the answer: "in the direction of Swann's place" or "toward Swann's."

But the title also had a metaphorical signification. *Chez Swann* means not only "Swann's home, Swann's place," but also "on the part of Swann, about Swann"; that is, the title refers not just to where Swann lives but to the person Swann is, to Swann's mind, opinions, character, nature. And by extension the first volume concerns not just Swann's manner of living, thinking, but also Swann's world, the worldly and artistic domain, while *Le Côté de Guermantes* (now the third volume of the novel) concerns the ancient family of the Guermantes and their world, the domain of the aristocracy. And it is true that the character Swann gives the volume its unity. (By the end of the novel, the two divergent walks are symbolically joined.)

Proust's friend Louis de Robert did not like the title, and Proust mentioned a few others—rather idly, as it turns out, since he was not really going to change his mind: "Charles Swann," "Gardens in a Cup of Tea," and "The Age of Names." He said he had also thought of "Springtime." But he argued: "I still don't understand why the name of that Combray path which was known as 'the way by Swann's' with its earthly reality, its local truthfulness, does not have just as much poetry in it as those abstract or flowery titles."

The work of the printer was finished by November 1913—an edition of 1,750 was printed—and the book was in the bookstores November 14. Reviews by Lucien Daudet and Jean Cocteau, among others, appeared. Not all the reviews were positive. The publisher submitted the book for the Prix Goncourt, but the prize was won, instead, by a book called *Le Peuple de la mer* (The People of the Sea), by Marc Elder.

A later edition was published in 1919 by Gallimard with some small changes. A corrected edition was published by Gallimard in its Bibliothèque de la Pléiade series in 1954 and another, with further corrections and additions, in 1987.

The first English translation of *Du Côté de chez Swann* was done by Charles Kenneth Scott Moncrieff, a former military man—a captain wounded and decorated in World War I— and already the translator of the Anglo-Saxon poem *Beowulf* and the eleventh-century *Chanson de Roland*. In 1921, Scott Moncrieff left his job at the London *Times* to devote himself full-time to translation, embarking on an English version of the entire *À la Recherche du temps perdu*, which he called *Remembrance of Things Past*. He was to intersperse this work, over the next nine years, with other translations, including works by Stendhal and Pirandello. What was advertised as the "first installment" of the Proust opus, *Swann's Way*, was published by Chatto and Windus in 1922, the same year Proust died. Scott Moncrieff himself died in 1930, in the midst of working on the final volume, which was completed by Stephen Hudson.

In 1981, nearly six decades after the publication of Scott Moncrieff's *Swann's Way*, came Terence Kilmartin's revision of *Remembrance*. Based on a corrected edition of the French, his work brought the translation closer to the original, cut many of Scott Moncrieff's gratuitous additions and embellishments, and corrected most of his misreadings, though it did not go as far as it could have in eliminating redundancy and cutting the fancier flourishes, and it also introduced the occasional grammatical mistake or mixed metaphor; in addition, Kilmartin's ear for the sounds and rhythms of English was not as sensitive as Scott Moncrieff's. After Kilmartin's death and the publication of the still-more-definitive 1987 Pléiade edition, the translation was further revised by D. J. Enright, an English poet and scholar, and so another edition, incorporating most of Kilmartin's changes and the further revisions of Enright, was published in 1992 under the corrected general title of *In Search of Lost Time*.

The two revisions of Scott Moncrieff's *Swann's Way* retain so much of his original work that they cannot be called new translations.

Thus, there existed, until the 2002 Penguin edition, only one other English translation of *Du Côté de chez Swann*, and that was *Swann's Way* as translated by James Grieve (Australian National University, 1982), an Irish-born writer and professor of French literature in Canberra and eventually, also, translator of the second volume of the Penguin edition. Grieve's approach was not to follow as closely as possible the order within the sentences of the original French, as had been Scott Moncrieff's, but to study the text for its meaning and then re-create it in a style that might have been that of an author writing originally in English. He therefore brought to his version a greater degree of freedom in word choice, order, and syntax.

If Proust has been reputed by some to be difficult reading, this can be attributed perhaps to several factors. One is that the interest of this novel, unlike that of the more traditional novel, is not merely, or even most of all, in the story it tells. (In one letter, Proust himself describes the work as a novel, but then, having second thoughts, qualifies that description with typical subtlety and precision by adding that, at least, "the novel form" is the form from which "it departs least.") In fact it does not set out to tell a linear, logically sequential story, but rather to create a world unified by the narrator's governing sensibility, in which blocks of a fictional past life are retrieved and presented, in roughly chronological order, in all their nuances. A reader may feel overwhelmed by the detail of this nuance and wish to get on with the story, and yet the only way to read Proust is to yield, with a patience equal to his, to his own unhurried manner of telling the story.

Another factor in Proust's reputed difficulty for Anglophone readers in particular may be that in the Scott Moncrieff translation, which was the one most commonly read, before the existence of the Penguin edition, by readers of Proust in English, Proust's own lengthy, yet precise, expatiations were themselves amplified by a certain consistent redundancy that makes the translation at all points longer than the original. For example, Proust's single word "strange" is rendered in English by Scott Moncrieff, for the sake of euphony or rhythm, as "strange and haunting"; "uninteresting" becomes "quite without interest"; "he" becomes "he himself." Multiply these individual choices through a long novel and one adds considerably to its bulk.

At the same time, Proust's prose was heightened by Scott Moncrieff, by the replacement, throughout, of Proust's plain words by more colorful ones; and he was given, regularly, a more sentimental or melodramatic turn. The effect of all these individual choices was to produce a text that, although it flows very well and follows the original remarkably closely in word order and construction, is wordier and dressier than the original. As with many of the first translations of seminal literary works, it somewhat misrepresents the style of the original, which was, in this case, essentially natural and direct, and far plainer than one might have guessed.

Proust did not believe that great length was desirable in itself. He categorically rejected sentences that were artificially expanded, or that were overly abstract, or that groped, arriving at a thought by succession of approximations, just as he despised empty flourishes. When he describes Odette as having a *sourire sournois*, or "sly smile," the alliteration is there for a purpose, to further unite the two words in one's mind. As he proceeded from draft to draft, he not only added material but also condensed. "I prefer concentration," he said, "even in length." And in fact, according to one meticulous

count of the sentences in *Swann's Way* and in the second volume of the novel, nearly 40 percent of the sentences in these
two books are reasonably short—one to five lines—and less
than one-quarter are very long—ten lines or more.

Proust felt, however, that a long sentence contained a
whole, complex thought, a thought that should not be
broken up. The shape of the sentence was the shape of the
thought, and every word was necessary to the thought: "I
really have to weave these long silks as I spin them," he wrote
to one friend. "If I shortened my sentences, it would make
little pieces of sentences, not sentences." He wished to "en-
circle the truth with a single—even if long and sinuous—
stroke."

Many contemporaries of Proust's insisted that he wrote
the way he spoke, although when *Du Côté de chez Swann*
appeared in print, they were startled by what they saw as the
severity of the page. Where were the pauses, the inflections?
There were not enough empty spaces, not enough punctuation marks. To them, the sentences seemed longer when
read on the page than they did when they were spoken in his
extraordinary hoarse voice: his voice punctuated them.

One friend, though surely exaggerating, reported that
Proust would arrive late in the evening, wake him up, begin
talking, and deliver one long sentence that did not come to
an end until the middle of the night. The sentence would
be full of asides, parentheses, illuminations, reconsiderations,
revisions, addenda, corrections, augmentations, digressions,
qualifications, erasures, deletions, and marginal notes. It
would, in other words, attempt to be exhaustive, to capture
every nuance of a piece of reality, to reflect Proust's entire
thought. To be exhaustive is, of course, an infinite task: more
events can always be inserted, and more nuance in the narration, more commentary on the event, and more nuance

within the commentary. Growing by association of ideas, developing internally by contiguity, the long sentences are built up into pyramids of subordinate clauses.

These sentences are constructed very tightly, with their many layers, the insertion of parenthetical remarks and digressions adding color and background to the main point, and delaying the outcome, the conclusion of the sentence, which is most often a particularly strong or climactic word or pair of words. They are knit together using a variety of conscious and unconscious stylistic techniques that become fascinating to observe and analyze: repetition, apposition, logical contrast, comparison; extended metaphors; nuanced qualifications within the metaphors themselves; varieties of parallel structures; balanced series of pairs of nouns, adjectives, or phrases; and lavish aural effects—as in the alliteration of this phrase: *faisait refluer ses reflets*, or the ABBA structure of vowel sounds in this one: *lâcheté qui nous détourne de toute tâche*; or the cooing of the dove at the end of this paragraph: *Et son faîte était toujours couronné du roucoulement d'une colombe.*

And yet Proust's economy prevails, and extends even to his punctuation, with, in particular, a marked underuse of the comma. The effect of this light punctuation is, again, that the whole thought is conveyed with as little fragmentation as possible, and that it travels more quickly from writer to reader, has a more noticeably powerful trajectory. The punctuation, of course, in part determines the pace in the breath span of the prose. If, as occasionally and conspicuously happens in *Swann's Way*, a sentence is chopped into a succession of short phrases separated by commas that halt its flow, the prose gasps for air; whereas the very long sentence, relatively unimpeded by stops, gives the impression of a rush to yield the thought in one exhalation. In my translation I attempted to stay as close to Proust's style as possible, in its every aspect, yet without straying into an English style that was too foreign or awkward; with particular attention to word order and word choice, his punctuation, too, could often be duplicated in English, and commas that might have seemed necessary could quite happily be eliminated or reduced.

One last comment concerning word choice: Often the closest, most accurate, and even most euphonious equivalent to a word in its original language may be a word in translation more commonly used decades ago than it is now: for instance, the French *chercher* means both "to look for" and "to try," so its perfect equivalent in English is our "seek," still current today but rare and more specialized than its equivalents. Or, to go further back in time, for the French *corsage*, the part of a woman's dress extending from the neck to the hips and also known as the "waist" or "body" of the dress, the perfect equivalent is "bodice," which in fact means the same thing. I have chosen to use both of these and many other close equivalents. Other perfectly identical English equivalents have simply receded too far into the past by now and will be too obscure to be understood. A couple of centuries ago, we referred, in English, to a "piece of water" just as Proust does to *une pièce d'eau*, and meant, as he did, an ornamental pool or pond. And then there are some borderline cases, some perfect equivalents that may not convey as much to the contemporary reader as a close approximation, so that what one gains in exactness one loses in expressive power; some of these I have reluctantly bypassed, such as "parvis," identical to the French, which means the area in front of a sacred building, and is the name neatly given by Proust to the part of the garden outside Françoise's "temple," and for which I have substituted "temple yard"; but others, such as "aurora," I have used because they were too perfect to give up.

My translation of *Du Côté de chez Swann* originated in the following way. A project was conceived by the Penguin UK Modern Classics series in which the whole of *À la Recherche du temps perdu* would be newly translated on the basis of the latest and most authoritative French text, edited by Jean-Yves Tadié (Gallimard, 1987). The translation would be done by a group of translators, each of whom would take on one of the seven volumes, overseen by a general editor. I was invited to join the group of professors, poets, translators, and critics in the fall of 1995, and I chose to translate the first volume. Between 1996 and the delivery of our manuscripts, the tardiest in mid-2001, we worked at different speeds and levels of efficiency in our different parts of the world—one in Australia, one in the United States, the rest in England—with some breaks for other work.

After a single face-to-face meeting in early 1998, which most of the translators attended, we communicated with one another and the general editor by letter and email, although time constraints, distractions, and other commitments did not allow for the sort of ongoing discussion at a deeper level that would have been so fascinating. We agreed, often after lively debate (and occasionally with some dissenters), on certain practices that needed to be consistent from one volume to the next, such as retaining French titles like "Duchesse de Guermantes" and leaving the quotations that occur within the text—from Racine, most notably—in the original French, with English translations confined to the notes. (A particularly extended correspondence involved how to translate Proust's term for the early-morning, winding, very slow "milk train"—*le tortillard*. And at the moment, I can't remember how it was resolved.) There was also a general consensus that a degree of heterogeneity across the volumes was inevitable and perhaps even desirable, and that philosophical differences would exist among the translators. As we proceeded, therefore, we worked fairly independently and decided for ourselves how close our translations should be to the original—how many liberties, for instance, might be taken with preserving Proust's long sentences. As he reviewed all the translations, the general editor, Christopher Prendergast, kept his editorial hand light.

I had translated over thirty books from the French when I began work on *Du Côté de chez Swann*. I felt more exhilaration and more trepidation beginning this than I had felt embarking on more comfortably private projects—a biography of Alexis de Tocqueville or Maurice Blanchot's *L'Arrêt de mort*, for instance. I knew that whatever the merits of other books I had done, this one by Proust was the most highly regarded, and the work I did on it might eventually come under close scrutiny. And yet I proceeded in much the same way I always have with a translation.

One difference from previous translations was that I found myself exploring each French word and each English word more thoroughly than ever before; there was no doubt that this book deserved whatever care I could put into it. Another difference was that, as I became aware of Proust's less obvious stylistic habits, how he was incorporating alexandrines into his sentences or building parallel structures, with liberal use of assonance and alliteration, I began trying to do the same when I could. If I failed to produce, for example, the hexameter that Proust had so beautifully involved in a certain phrase, by just how much would I have changed his thought? A single sentence would thus sometimes require the sort of writing and rewriting, fiddling and refining, that might have gone into translating a piece of verse.

This meant that my translation proceeded at a very slow pace, and, since the manuscript was over 550 pages, went on for a long time. But the publisher would finally brook no more delay. Then, like the distant steeples of Martinville, the end was suddenly in front of me.

The Penguin UK translation appeared in October 2002, in six hardcover volumes and as a boxed set. A paperback edition soon followed, for which the translators were permitted to make some minor revisions, far fewer than we would have liked. For copyright reasons, only the first volumes subsequently appeared in American hardcover and paperback editions over the following several years—the rest of the volumes had to wait until 2019, which then seemed impossibly distant but is now already past. For my American editions, I was permitted as many revisions as I liked—which was fortunate, since a translator always has afterthoughts.

The Child as Writer: The "Steeples" Passage in *Swann's Way*

The following passage is taken from close to the end of the "Combray" section of *Swann's Way*. (After it comes the self-contained love story, "Swann in Love," and then the coda-like "Place-Names: The Name.") The "Combray" section includes many of the most famous scenes in Proust's *In Search of Lost Time*, including the opening insomniac confusions, the tasting of the madeleine, and the bedtime drama of the mother's goodnight kiss. The extract presented here shows the young narrator for the first time translating his rapture over a thing of the outside world into a piece of writing.

A number of thoughts are inspired by this passage. First is the curious (and amusing) observation that whereas many novels contain a child who wants to grow up to be famous, particularly a famous writer, or is sad that he will never be one, this—*In Search of Lost Time*—is among the few novels in which the child in question will have his wish granted and will in fact grow up to be a famous writer. And as we read this, what is also interesting is our perspective: we the readers know that the child on whom this young narrator is based has indeed grown up to be a famous writer; yet neither the fictional nor the real child knows this; and even Proust the author, as he writes it, cannot be at all sure (though he may suspect it), since he is still, at this point, spurned by artistic circles in Paris as a superficial dandy. So we the readers are the only ones who know—we know more than Proust himself, in this case.

The child, as Proust narrates it, worries that he has no ideas, that there is an empty hole where the future subjects of his writing should be, that he would live and die just like "other men" and "was simply one of those who have no aptitude for writing." But then, as confidence returns, he believes that his all-powerful father will be able to arrange things so that he will indeed be a successful writer in the future: "Perhaps my lack of talent, the black hole that opened in my mind when I looked for the subject of my future writings, was also merely an illusion without substance, and this illusion would cease through the intervention of my father, who must have agreed with the government and Providence that I would be the foremost writer of the day."

A second interesting thing here is the quoted passage that is presented as the young narrator's first piece of serious writing. For one thing, it is not very different from the description that preceded it, in the adult narrator's words, and the fact that it is not very different draws our attention to it more pointedly. In what ways is it different and why should Proust want to, in effect, duplicate a passage—write it twice over with only slight variations? Is he first presenting the scene as it "really" was, so that we can compare the reality to the child's depiction of it? Yet, of course, the adult narrator's description of it is no more "real" than the child's.

Which brings up at least two more questions. Do we

worry about verisimilitude in this novel? Proust is such a master of convincing prose that we accept a great deal without question. How likely is it, really, in fact, that anyone could write such a lovely description with a pencil and scrap of paper in the fading daylight while seated on the hard seat of a carriage that is jolting along at a fast clip not over a paved road but over the little stones and ruts of a dirt track?

And, further, how likely is it that a child could write such a sophisticated and polished description at all, even under more peaceful circumstances and even if, as Marcel says, he himself as an adult touched it up a bit before presenting it? Young Marcel's age is somewhat variable, anyway, in the first volume of the novel: it seems, throughout, to be an amalgam of different ages. Would a child of thirteen or, say, seven do all of the following: wait for his mother's kiss in the hallway; enjoy his private lust in the little room that smelled of orris root; be allowed to sit with the adults at dinner for a short time only; read Bergotte and discuss him with his friend Bloch and with Swann; tearfully embrace the hawthorns in his new jacket and rip the curlpapers out of his hair; write a highly polished description of the steeples; dread the approach of bedtime once again, and with it the separation from his mother?

Lastly—or not lastly, since there are surely many more interesting thoughts buried in these pages—there is the central question Proust is addressing here: the mystery of how a written thing first begs to be written and then comes into being. How a simple object seems to call out to us (Proust reiterates the examples of roof and stone); how we are urged to do something about our feeling, at first not knowing what; how a "pretty sentence" relieves us of that urge; how we feel exhilaration afterward. And how, more generally, our expressive reaction to the excitement of inspiration may be the inarticulate *Zut, zut, zut, zut* of the adolescent striking the vegetation with his furled umbrella, which we witnessed in an earlier passage; or, in this passage, the highly articulate written description; or, most primitive, age-old, and perhaps equally satisfying, the different medium of song: "I began to sing." The boy himself does not yet see that his responsiveness to an ordinary object will make the "success" of the successful writer and that he need not be discouraged that he has not found an appropriately great subject for his future literary work.

> How much more distressing still, after that day, during my walks along the Guermantes way, did it seem to me than it had seemed before to have no aptitude for literature, and to have to give up all hope of ever being a famous writer! The sorrow I felt over this, as I daydreamed alone, a little apart from the others, made me suffer so much that in order not to feel it anymore, my mind of its own accord, by a sort of inhibition in the face of pain, would stop thinking altogether about poems, novels, a poetic future on which my lack of talent forbade me to depend. Then, quite apart from all these literary preoccupations and not connected to them in any way, suddenly a roof, a glimmer of sun on a stone, the smell of the road would stop me because of a particular pleasure they gave me, and also because they seemed to be concealing, beyond what I could see, something which they were inviting me to come take and which despite my efforts I could not manage to discover. Since I felt that it could be found within them, I would stay

there, motionless, looking, breathing, trying to go
with my thoughts beyond the image or the smell. And
if I had to catch up with my grandfather, continue on
my way, I would try to find them again by closing my
eyes; I would concentrate on recalling precisely the
line of the roof, the shade of the stone which, without
my being able to understand why, had seemed to me
so full, so ready to open, to yield me the thing for
which they themselves were merely a cover. Of course
it was not impressions of this kind that could give me
back the hope I had lost, of succeeding in becoming a
writer and a poet some day, because they were always
tied to a particular object with no intellectual value
and no reference to any abstract truth. But at least
they gave me an unreasoning pleasure, the illusion of
a sort of fecundity, and so distracted me from the tedium, from the sense of my own impotence which I
had felt each time I looked for a philosophical subject
for a great literary work. But the moral duty imposed
on me by the impressions I received from form, fragrance or color was so arduous—to try to perceive
what was concealed behind them—that I would soon
look for excuses that would allow me to save myself
from this effort and spare myself this fatigue. Fortunately, my parents would call me, I would feel I did
not have the tranquillity I needed at the moment for
pursuing my search in a useful way, and that it would
be better not to think about it anymore until I was
back at home, and not to fatigue myself beforehand
to no purpose. And so I would stop concerning myself with this unknown thing that was enveloped in
a form or a fragrance, feeling quite easy in my mind
since I was bringing it back to the house protected

by the covering of images under which I would find it alive, like the fish that, on days when I had been allowed to go fishing, I would carry home in my creel covered by a layer of grass that kept them fresh. Once I was back at the house I would think about other things, and so there would accumulate in my mind (as in my room the flowers I had gathered on my walks or objects I had been given) a stone on which a glimmer of light played, a roof, the sound of a bell, a smell of leaves, many different images beneath which the reality I sensed but did not have enough determination to discover had died long before. Once, however—when our walk had extended far beyond its usual duration and we were very happy to encounter halfway home, as the afternoon was ending, Doctor Percepied, who, going past at full speed in his carriage, recognized us and invited us to climb in with him—I had an impression of this kind and did not abandon it without studying it a little. They had had me climb up next to the coachman, we were going like the wind because, before returning to Combray, the doctor still had to stop at Martinville-le-Sec to see a patient at whose door it had been agreed that we would wait for him. At the bend of a road I suddenly experienced that special pleasure which was unlike any other, when I saw the two steeples of Martinville, shining in the setting sun and appearing to change position with the motion of our carriage and the windings of the road, and then the steeple of Vieuxvicq, which, though separated from them by a hill and a valley and situated on a higher plateau in the distance, seemed to be right next to them.

As I observed, as I noted the shape of their spires,

the shifting of their lines, the sunlight on their surfaces, I felt that I was not reaching the full depth of
my impression, that something was behind that motion, that brightness, something which they seemed
at once to contain and conceal.

The steeples appeared so distant, and we seemed
to approach them so slowly, that I was surprised when
we stopped a few moments later in front of the Martinville church. I did not know why I had taken such
pleasure in the sight of them on the horizon and the
obligation to try to discover the reason seemed to me
quite painful; I wanted to hold in reserve in my head
those lines moving in the sun, and not think about
them anymore now. And it is quite likely that had I
done so, the two steeples would have gone forever to
join the many trees, rooftops, fragrances, sounds, that
I had distinguished from others because of the obscure pleasure they gave me which I never thoroughly
studied. I got down to talk to my parents while we
waited for the doctor. Then we set off again, I was
back in my place on the seat, I turned my head to see
the steeples again, a little later glimpsing them one
last time at a bend in the road. Since the coachman,
who did not seem inclined to talk, had hardly answered anything I said, I was obliged, for lack of other
company, to fall back on my own and try to recall my
steeples. Soon their lines and their sunlit surfaces split
apart, as if they were a sort of bark, a little of what
was hidden from me inside them appeared to me, I
had a thought which had not existed a moment before, which took shape in words in my head, and the
pleasure I had just recently experienced at the sight

of them was so increased by this that, seized by a sort of drunkenness, I could no longer think of anything else. At that moment, as we were already far away from Martinville, turning my head I caught sight of them again, quite black this time, for the sun had already set. At moments the bends of the road would hide them from me, then they showed themselves one last time, and finally I did not see them again.

Without saying to myself that what was hidden behind the steeples of Martinville had to be something analogous to a pretty sentence, since it had appeared to me in the form of words that gave me pleasure, I asked the doctor for a pencil and some paper and I composed, despite the jolts of the carriage, and in order to ease my conscience and yield to my enthusiasm, the following little piece that I have since found again and that I have not had to submit to more than a few changes:

"Alone, rising from the level of the plain, and appearing lost in the open country, the two steeples of Martinville ascended toward the sky. Soon we saw three: wheeling around boldly to position itself opposite them, the laggard steeple of Vieuxvicq had come along to join them. The minutes were passing, we were going fast, and yet the three steeples were still far away ahead of us, like three birds poised on the plain, motionless, distinguishable in the sunlight. Then the steeple of Vieuxvicq moved away, receded into the distance, and the steeples of Martinville remained alone, illuminated by the light of the setting sun, which even at that distance I saw playing and smiling on their sloping sides. We had taken so long approaching them that I was thinking about the time we would still need in order to reach them, when suddenly the carriage turned and set us down at their feet; and they had flung themselves so roughly in front of us that we had only just time to stop in order not to run into the porch. We continued on our way; we had already left Martinville a little while before, and the village, after accompanying us for a few seconds, had disappeared, when, lingering alone on the horizon to watch us flee, its steeples and that of Vieux-vicq were still waving goodbye with their sunlit tops. At times one of them would draw aside so that the other two could glimpse us again for an instant; but the road changed direction, they swung round in the light like three golden pivots and disappeared from my gaze. But a little later, when we were already close to Combray, and the sun had set, I caught sight of them one last time from very far away, seeming now no more than three flowers painted on the sky above the low line of the fields. They reminded me, too, of the three young girls in a legend, abandoned in a solitary place where darkness was already falling; and while we moved off at a gallop, I saw them timidly seek their way and, after some awkward stumbling of their noble silhouettes, press against one another, slip behind one another, now forming, against the still pink sky, no more than a single black shape, charming and resigned, and fade away into the night." I never thought of this page again, but at that moment, when in the corner of the seat where the doctor's coachman usually placed in a basket the poultry he had bought at the market in Martinville, I had finished writing it,

I was so happy, I felt it had so perfectly relieved me of those steeples and what they had been hiding behind them, that, as if I myself were a hen and had just laid an egg, I began to sing at the top of my voice.

2004

[October 1914?]

Madame,

Please permit me to appeal to you and the Doctor for tomorrow Tuesday regarding the noise (early). I had to go out today in extremely dangerous health conditions and I very much dread tomorrow. — If in a little while I am better I would be happy to talk to you about Clary. I have learned through some friends very dear to him one thing which I tell you in *confidence* for it is a very delicate subject but one which makes me very happy because I believe that this may be for him a great consolation: I mean an awakening of a profoundly religious life, *an ardent* and profound faith.

Your very respectful

MARCEL PROUST

About Clary, I ask you not to speak of this at least for the moment.

Proust in His Bedroom: An Afterword to Proust's *Letters to His Neighbor*

Most of the letters in this collection, published by New Directions in my English translation in 2017, were written to Proust's upstairs neighbor, Mme Marie Williams. At first they were exclusively concerned with the noise that was disturbing him. Then, as a certain fellow feeling established itself between the two correspondents (Mme Williams, too, was something of a recluse), the correspondence extended to other subjects—literature, music, the war—though regularly reverting to the problem of the noise. The pretty Mme Williams was a talented harpist and a fan of Proust's writing, and she was a gifted writer herself, so that the two sometimes seemed to be in friendly competition—judging from Proust's remarks about her letters and from the small fragments that he quotes in his own—as to who wrote in a more elaborately graceful style. It appears that, despite living in the same building, and despite the twenty-three letters Proust sent to her—perhaps even more that have since been lost—the two may never have met.

As for her husband, the American dentist Charles D. Williams, to whom Proust wrote three courteous notes (one accompanying a bouquet of flowers), he was described by Proust's housekeeper and faithful companion, Céleste Albaret, as "a sports enthusiast" who "went off every Saturday with his chauffeur to play golf." She added that in Proust's opinion, the dentist and his wife formed a rather "disparate" couple.

As we read Proust's letters to Mme and Dr. Williams, it is helpful to picture the room in which he wrote them, and him in the room. Although one would imagine that the room would be preserved as a museum, even furnished with Proust's own furniture (which exists), that is not the case. Proud though the French are of one of their premier authors, the apartment at 102, boulevard Haussmann in which he lived for nearly twelve years and in which he wrote most of *In Search of Lost Time*, was, last I checked, now part of the premises of a bank. Some years ago, it was, at least, possible to visit the room during the summer by appointment on Thursday afternoons. One was shown around by a bank employee, with interruptions when she had to go off and answer a banking question.

I was surprised that although the drawing room, in particular, had a comfortably and gracefully solid, old-fashioned appearance, the apartment as a whole was not maintained as a full museum, with Proust's furniture or close approximations. His outstanding fame, and the fame of his peculiar habits, the fame of the bedroom itself, locus of his creation, and of the very cork on the walls, would seem to require some sort of acknowledgment beyond this minimum, and most reasonably a transformation into a museum. Yet it was used by the bank for entirely nonliterary or nonhistorical purposes.

But my initial surprise and disappointment evolved into something more complicated. A space of ongoing work, in the world, continues to have an active life. The bank that owns Proust's apartment now shares it with Proust in a sort of agreeable compromise. The bedroom, and more generally the apartment, is neither wholly a museum nor merely an impersonal, unhistoried office space. The bank admires Proust, honors him, and allows for him, without entirely yielding to him; a woman who otherwise worked on banking matters took time each Thursday, in season, and by special appointment, to discuss Proust with pleasure and enthusiasm, sometimes leaving the visitor for a few moments or longer to take care of a banking matter and then returning to say something about, for instance, the cork.

There was something of a personal discovery in visiting the apartment this way, as though you really came to do business at the bank and then found within the bank not only the apartment but the very bedroom of a writer you greatly admired. Paradoxically, all this made the presence of Proust's own living quarters all the stronger, perhaps because of the effort one made to visualize the apartment within the bank premises; perhaps because any discovery of one's own is more exciting than an effect arranged by someone else; perhaps because the contrast was so striking that the original apartment sprang back into one's mental picture: it was so much not-there that it kept returning, whereas if it had been reproduced in a simulacrum it would be there, but only through impersonation—and only statically, not dynamically.

Proust's bedroom was unpopulated for much of the day, unless it was being used for a meeting with a client or among bank officials. A portrait of Proust hung on the wall, but the talk in the room would have been about financial matters, and though financial matters greatly interested the generous, extravagant, reckless, impulsive Proust—he writes to his neighbor Mme Williams that he is (this was several months before the start of World War I) "more or less completely ruined"—his spirit would probably not be present. It might drift in for a moment if those taking part in the meeting paused to recall him and his life's work. And French bankers and their clients would conceivably have a strong interest in and respect for Proust.

When I visited, the room gave the impression of being rather small, perhaps because of its very high ceiling, which Céleste estimated to be some fourteen feet high. Yet Proust described it as "vast" when he made the difficult decision to rent the apartment. In fact the room measured nine and a half paces by six, as I, without measuring tape, estimated it, which translates to roughly twenty-one feet by fifteen, or over three hundred square feet. Maybe it seemed small also because it was so relatively empty, containing only a sideboard, a bookcase, a small table in the center, and four small chairs.

According to the bank employee and guide, certain structural parts of the room were the same as they had been in Proust's time: what he would have gazed at daily were the two tall windows; two of the four doors; the moldings around the tops of the walls; the parquet floor with its herringbone pattern; and the fireplace with its thick white marble mantel. Besides the portrait on the wall, there were only a few outward signs that this room had anything to do with Proust: a short row of volumes of the Proust Society's quarterly journal occupied part of one shelf in the otherwise empty glass-fronted bookcase, one that had not belonged to Proust; and, on the top of the sideboard, which also had not belonged to Proust, a small sign announcing "Proust's bedroom" alongside a stack of brochures about the actual Proust Museum, which was elsewhere—in the house of "Tante Léonie" out in Illiers-Combray, one and a half hours from the city.

When Proust lived in it, when he rested, slept, ate, wrote, read, inhaled his smoking Legras powders, drank his coffee, and entertained visitors there, it was crowded with furniture. We learn from a description by Céleste that there was, for instance, a large wardrobe between the two windows, and, in front of the wardrobe, so close that its doors could not be opened, a grand piano. Between the grand piano and the bed, an armchair as well as three small tables which Proust used for three different purposes. Other pieces of furniture—a bookcase, a work table that had belonged to Proust's mother, a different sideboard—stood at various spots against the walls. Céleste had to squeeze her way in and out.

My guide pointed out the corner in which Proust's bed had been placed, along the wall opposite the windows, and where he wrote a great deal of the novel. Standing between the head of the bed and the wall, an Oriental screen protected him from drafts and helped buffer him from the sounds that came from the adjoining building, on the other side of the wall.

Noise from construction within the building or from next door was a continuing menace for Proust during his years here, as we can see from *Letters to His Neighbor*. The tenant on the entresol below, one Dr. Gagey, was having work done on his apartment when Proust first moved there, in the last days of 1906, as we know from the complaints, sometimes humorous, in his other, voluminous letters. Just as the work on Dr. Gagey's apartment was ending, relief in sight, work began in the building next door, where one Mme Katz was installing a new bathroom just a few feet from Proust's head. (Kafka, at about this time, was recording the same sorts of complaints in his diaries, though he liked to turn them into small stories about what fantastic things these neighbors might be doing.)

After the death of his mother, Proust had made the decision not to continue living in the too-large, memory-haunted family apartment. The apartment at 102, boulevard Haussmann was just one possible choice of residence among many that he had investigated by proxy, with the help of a host of friends and without moving from his temporary rooms in a hotel at Versailles. It is therefore surprising to realize that he was in fact a quarter-owner of the building at the time, his brother owning another quarter and his aunt the remaining half.

When he moved in, he considered the apartment to be no more than a transitional residence. It was the first he had ever lived in on his own, but it was a familiar part of his past: his mother had known it well, since his uncle had lived and died here—Proust had in fact visited him on his deathbed, in the same room that was to become his own bedroom. Later, through inattention, and without fully realizing the consequences, Proust allowed his aunt to buy his own share and his brother's, and thus had no say in the matter when she in turn decided, in 1919, to sell the building to a banker, who intended to convert the premises into a bank, obliging him to move out against his will, and thereafter, in fact, to move twice more. This was only three years before his death. In Céleste's opinion, it had hastened his decline.

To give a context to the room in which Proust wrote his many letters and the apartment in which the room was situated, it is helpful to have some sense of the geography of Proust's building. The French system of numbering is different from the American or English: what the French call the first floor is the floor *above* the ground floor, the second floor is two floors above street level, etc. Proust's apartment

was on what the French would call the first floor, the dentist's practice on the second, the dentist's apartment on the
third. But, complicating this numbering system, in the case
of Proust's building, was the entresol, that low-ceilinged
half-floor that can lie between any two floors but is generally
situated between the ground floor and the first, in which case
we in English more commonly call it the mezzanine.

When there is an entresol, the floor above it may in fact
be called the second floor, and this is what Proust calls it at
least once in this collection of letters, as do the editors of
the French edition. Other sources, including Céleste's memoir, call it the first. (There is no disagreement about where
Proust lived, just some inconsistency about how to number
the floor.) I will adhere to the traditional French system in
discussing the apartments and inhabitants of 102, boulevard
Haussmann.

However, to clarify matters for American or British readers: there was, at that address, first the ground floor, which in
those days was entered from the street through a two-paneled
carriage entrance (the same that Proust mentions indignantly
in one of his letters, Letter 13). This level contained, at least,
an apartment occupied by the concierge Antoine and his
family. One flight up, there was the entresol, under Proust's
apartment, occupied by Dr. Gagey, his wife, and their daughter. Another flight up was Proust's apartment. Above it was
the practice of the American dentist Charles Williams, on
the street side directly above Proust's head, as well as, in the
back, his laboratory. Since this latter workplace was located
away from the street, looking out on the courtyard, Proust
was not bothered by the footsteps of the several assistants
who worked there.

Above Dr. Williams's practice was the apartment occupied by the Williamses and their small son, who was about

four years old when they moved in. There were another two floors above the Williamses' apartment, but it is not clear who lived in them, though on the top floor, under the roof, there would usually have been small independent rooms connected by a narrow corridor, the bedrooms of the servants who worked in the apartments below. There was a back stairway that Proust referred to as the service stairs or "small" stairs. This was used by the building's servants, and by the concierge when he brought up a message for Proust, discreetly tapping at the kitchen door to avoid the disturbance of ringing the doorbell, and for other deliveries, including the milk, brought daily by the neighborhood *crémerie* for Proust's coffee. Somewhere in Proust's apartment, probably near or next to the kitchen—though it is not clear from the simplified floor plan of the apartment included in the French edition of these letters exactly where—was a bedroom for the use of a servant, and this was where Céleste slept after she moved in, sometime in 1914.

There have of course been changes in the layout of the rooms since the time Proust occupied them. There is now a door at the head of Proust's bed. The corridor outside his bedroom, across which he used to step, in the direction of the courtyard, on the way to his dressing room and bath, now extends into the building next door. The other door out of his bedroom, the door he assigned to be used by visitors and his housekeeper, now opens into a generous room with a massive conference table in the center and a fireplace at either end. Here, too, very little is original: the fireplaces, the parquet floors, and the windows. But a change in the wood of the floor marks the line where a wall used to stand, separating Proust's large drawing room from the small anteroom outside his bedroom where his guests would wait to see him.

These rooms line the street side of the apartment. In back of them, toward the courtyard, there are other original vestiges: the marble surface of the stairs and landing by which visitors used to approach the apartment; the shaft for the present small elevator (though it is now a different elevator) that occupies the center of the stairwell; the oeil-de-boeuf window through which Céleste would look out into the stairwell to see who was coming up. Proust's visitors stopped and waited on the landing outside the front door of the apartment, but there is no longer a wall or door there, only open space and two white pillars. Nowadays, from a spot that was once inside the apartment, you can watch the stairwell as men in shirtsleeves and ties and women in suits, carrying folders, walk up from the landing that would have opened into the apartment of Dr. Gagey and on up to the next floor—the floor where Dr. Williams had his practice and his laboratory of assistants—or come trotting back down, talking finance. Visitors now coming up to the first floor (or second, as we would call it) to do business with the bank will see, when they walk into what used to be Proust's apartment (crossing what used to be the entryway, where his gloves and handkerchiefs sat in a silver salver), an open area with a sofa and armchairs, and they may sit there to talk. This was in fact Proust's dining room, though the walls are gone and he employed it not as a dining room but as a storeroom. He had inherited a great deal of the contents of the family apartment and did not want to part with much of it, but he could not find places for it all in the other rooms, so he filled the dining room until it was "like a forest," according to Céleste. An imaginative financier with a little information might be haunted, sitting next to the lone potted plant, by the lingering ghostly presence of a crowded accumulation of heavy fin de siècle furniture and bric-a-brac, imbued with Proust's personal associations.

There is no longer a balcony on the front of the building, though Proust describes stepping out onto one from his bedroom and actually enjoying a rare contact with sunlight. The apartment is no longer a silent set of rooms whose closed shutters and drawn curtains create an eternal night, but is now dazzlingly well lit, with its high ceilings, spacious windows, fluorescent lights, and glowing computer screens, prosperous and busy.

A fourth reference to Proust within his former bedroom is not immediately obvious: the walls are lined with cork. But this is a marbleized, decorative cork that has been put on the walls since Proust's time and is not even obviously cork unless you look closely. It is a sort of compromise cork, a stand-in for Proust's. In Proust's time, the bank officer explains, the walls were more crudely covered in thick slabs of raw bark off the cork trees that grow in the South of France, painted over in black so as to protect Proust's lungs from the material's crumbling or disintegration—though Céleste has described it as being the color of honey. The famous cork was suggested to Proust by his close friend the poet Anna de Noailles, another noise-phobe, who used it in her own home.

The extant contents of Proust's bedroom are in the Musée Carnavalet, the city museum of Paris. They are down a hallway and not far from the re-created bedroom of Anna de Noailles—an arrangement that seems both comforting, as though the two friends can now call out to each other from their bedrooms at night, and also chilling, as though there has been a degree of violation in this public exposure of their most private places of rest and creation (the comtesse also wrote in bed). Here, too, square tiles of cork line the walls of Proust's room, a plain tan cork that the literature of the museum describes as an exact replica of Proust's (leaving us in doubt as to which cork is the correct one). In the museum at Illiers-Combray are displayed a few more objects from Proust's apartment, among them the dishes he ate from, the coffee maker used by Céleste to prepare his special coffee, and several shelves of his books.

Because they are the real thing and not replicas or approximations, Proust's bedroom furniture—the brass bedstead, the bedside table and lamp, the desk, the sideboard, the chaise longue, two armchairs, and the Oriental screen—are haunted by his presence, especially those with signs of wear: most of all, because so intimately associated with the human body, the places on the upholstery where the nap of the fabric has been worn down to the thread, not only by Proust himself but perhaps even more by others, too, presumably his mother, his father, his brother, visitors to the family, and Proust's own visiting friends. The eloquent mark of use is here like the dip in a stone step before a church door, for instance the church door at Illiers-Combray.

Because of his illness, Proust spent most of his time in bed, heavily dressed in—according to one account—socks, long underwear, and two sweaters, with a hot-water bottle at his feet that was renewed three times a day. A blanket folded in four hung over the large door to the room to protect him from drafts and noise. Both shutters and curtains were closed over the double-paned windows, so that sounds from the street were muffled. The chandelier that hung from the ceiling was never illuminated. A candle was kept burning, since he lit his powders using a folded paper rather than striking a match. He generally woke "for the day" at nine in the evening, and had his only meal at that time—coffee and a croissant that Céleste would bring to him when he rang.

But sometimes, after he had been awake for some hours, though still in bed, Proust would decide on impulse to go out and see a friend. In the dark bedroom, the only light would come from his bedside lamp and the fire in the fireplace, if it was winter. He would cross the short hallway outside his room to get dressed. His suit was made to measure and his patent-leather boots were bought at the Old England shop. He tended not to wear out his shoes, since he put them on only to go out, was transported by taxi, and walked on carpet and parquet floors (though just once, in wartime, he returned home on foot with shrapnel on his collar). He would arrive at the friend's house, wake him up, and start talking.

Or, from time to time, when he felt well enough, Proust liked to have a friend come visit, as long as that friend followed certain rules: no cigarettes, of course, and no perfume. Proust describes the composer Reynaldo Hahn coming in, playing the piano for a little while, then leaving "like a hurricane" (or, at other times, "like a whirlwind"—as Proust puts it apologetically in Letter 23).

One can pause to listen, via YouTube, to the composition by Reynaldo Hahn mentioned in the note to Letter 23, "Le Ruban dénoué," twelve waltzes for two pianos. As performed by two Italian pianists in a lamplit chamber concert in Rome, it is at times dynamic and forceful, more often gentle. The audience, visible in the background, is so absolutely still that for a while you might think the video has been manipulated and they have been frozen visually. From this, you may stray over to Anne Sofie von Otter singing another composition of Hahn's, a three-minute song. Her voice is liquid, effortless. In contrast to his style of entering and leaving Proust's building, Hahn's compositions tend to be calm, balanced and elegant, intimate, moderate in tempos and dynamics, and characterized by uncluttered simplicity, charm, and sentimentality. Hahn himself, though a singer and gifted interpreter of his music, apparently smoked and talked too much.

Many friends have described visiting Proust in the room, among them the writer Maurice Rostand, who says of the place: "Everything was left lying around, his aspirins and his dress shoes; books were piled up in pyramids; ties were strewn alongside catalogs, invitation cards to the British embassy lay next to medical prescriptions." (In his actions, however, Céleste asserts that he was neat and quick.)

Céleste, in her memoir, remembers that the predominant color of the room was blue, and the lamp next to his bed cast a green light because of the shade. She describes the room as perpetually dark as night and densely smoke-filled when Proust had been burning his powders. The smoke from these powders would sometimes drift under the doors and out into the rest of the building, and the neighbors might complain.

And it has to be said that in other ways, too, Proust was in his own turn guilty, on occasion, of disturbing other tenants in the building. He describes to a different correspondent how another longtime close friend, Robert de Montesquiou, came by in the early hours of the morning and, in his emotion, kept stamping on the floor "without pity" for the Gagey family sleeping downstairs (whom Céleste describes in her memoir as *plutôt des couches-tôt*, or "rather early-to-bedders").

Or, several times, Proust, a great lover of music, and not well enough to go out to concerts very often, would hire musicians to come play for him in his bedroom. Once, at 1:00 a.m., impulsively and without prior warning, he sent for the Poulet Quartet to come play César Franck's Quartet. Before beginning, the musicians (in the room lit only by candles) hung cloths over the opening of the fireplace to stop the sound from traveling (though one would think that was hardly effectual). When they reached the end of the piece, at two in the morning, Proust induced them (for a handsome sum) to start over and play the whole piece again.

But on the whole, Proust was well liked by his neighbors, for the same qualities so evident in his letters to Mme Williams: his grace, eloquence, thoughtfulness, sympathy, gestures of gratitude. Evidence of these good relations is not hard to find: an inscription in a copy of his Ruskin translation, *La Bible d'Amiens*, to his "good neighbor," one Arthur Pernolet, who occupied the apartment above him before the arrival of Dr. Williams, and whom Proust knew already before he moved in; the helpfulness of Mme Gagey when the time came for most (or all?) of the tenants of the building to move out—she supplied Proust with the results of her own research into suitable apartments; and the fact that a year after they were no longer neighbors, having scattered to other buildings, the *couche-tôt* Dr. Gagey came to Proust in answer to a request for a consultation: oddly enough—and perfectly symbolic—Proust had put something in his ear to block the ambient noise; it had got stuck, and the ear was infected.

As the vast resources of the internet allow us to walk along a Paris street that is almost unchanged from the 1920s and gaze up at—or even float over—the building in which one of Proust's friends died, and as it allows us within a few seconds to begin listening to one of Reynaldo Hahn's compositions, or to leaf through the caricatures of the very popular singer Thérésa, with whom Hahn was infatuated, so it also reveals more of the life of Proust's building: the wartime activities of Dr. Gagey, who was commended in 1915 for his ambulance service "in circumstances often difficult and always perilous"; and the legacies of the former upstairs neighbor, Proust's friend Pernolet, who, after his death, also in 1915, left funds to at least two Paris museums for the acquisition of paintings. Follow every reference in these letters, and Proust's world opens out before us.

Proust, so very solitary, as he says in many of his letters, and devoting most of his waking hours to his work, was also intensely gregarious and an uninhibited talker. When he was feeling well enough, he liked to talk without pause, and the person he talked to the most, because she was always available, was Céleste, an intelligent and responsive listener. He often rang for her after she had gone to bed, and she would come as she was, in her nightgown and robe, her hair down her back, as she says. He would talk to her for hours at a time, sitting up in bed leaning against two pillows, while she stood at the foot of the bed.

Gide describes, in his journal, Proust's style of talking: "His conversation, ceaselessly cut by parenthetical clauses, runs on." The diplomat and Proust fan Paul Morand enlarges upon this: the Proustian sentence, as Proust spoke it in conversation, was "singsong, caviling, reasoned, answering objections the listener would never have thought of making, raising unforeseen difficulties, subtle in its shifts and pettifoggery, stunning in its parentheses—that, like helium balloons, held the sentence aloft—vertiginous in its length . . . well constructed despite its apparent disjointedness . . . You listened spellbound."

This style, so natural to him in conversation, pours out

also in his letters—letters, as his friend Robert Dreyfus put it, "in which he always wanted to say everything, as in his books, and in which he succeeded by means of an infinity of parentheses, sinuosities, and reversals." It is the same style that is evident, though more strictly controlled, in the extended, balanced periodic sentences of his finished, published work (or, perhaps one should say, his work that is never quite finished but brought to a certain point and then ended). Here is an example from Letter 23, with Proust's characteristic paucity of punctuation and his multiple enclosed subordinate clauses: "My friend Reynaldo Hahn who for the 1st time in 15 months was returning from the front and who entered in disarray may have occasioned some noise which would so ill have recompensed that which you are sparing me."

Another example of the missing punctuation can be seen in Letter 14: "I am quite unwell as I write but I thank you deeply for the letter that has brought me I assure you a vision more enduring than a bouquet and as colorful." And, later in the same letter: "Not to mention the innumerable 'mature roses' of two poetesses my great friends whom I no longer see alas now that I no longer get up Mme de Noailles and Mme de Régnier"—note the interpolated comment and at least five, by my count, commas missing which would be present in a more standard syntax.

We are told that Proust wrote with prodigious speed. This, too, is apparent from the letters—his sprawling handwriting, his tendency to abbreviate, the occasional omitted word, and perhaps, though not necessarily, the missing punctuation.

Yet, at the same time, his natural syntactical agility is always evident, as in Letter 13, where he includes in one fairly short sentence a rather elaborate, and in this case indignant, parenthetical remark ("as I have been accused") that manages to enclose within it yet another clause ("it seems"): "I have been so ill these days (in my bed which I have not left and without having noisily opened or closed the carriage entrance as I have it seems been accused of doing) that I have not been able to write." Here he exemplifies, in a rougher, more urgent way, his declaration concerning his published writing that a sentence contains a complete thought, and that no matter how complex it may be, this thought should remain intact. The shape of the sentence is the shape of the thought, and every word is necessary.

Perhaps the most extreme example, in this collection of letters, of his complex syntax and lack of punctuation, as well as his colorful and fertile imagination, comes in Letter 25, which is mainly devoted to the cathedral of Reims so heavily damaged by bombardment in the first autumn of the war. Here we approach the precision, the rhetorical heights, and the luscious imagery of *In Search of Lost Time* (and with a reference to a Ruskin title covertly slipped in): "But I who insofar as my health permits make to the stones of Reims pilgrimages as piously awestruck as to the stones of Venice believe I am justified in speaking of the diminution to humanity that will be consummated on the day when the arches that are already half burnt away collapse forever on those angels who without troubling themselves about the danger still gather marvelous fruits from the lush stylized foliage of the forest of stones."

The acute understanding of psychology and social behavior displayed so richly in the novel is another continuing thread in the letters, and is especially apparent in Letter 20: "I always defer letters (which could seem to ask you for something) to a moment when it is too late and when consequently, they are no longer indiscreet."

And the gentle touches of humor, so prevalent in the

novel, also have their place in the letters, as in the continuation of Letter 20: "Considering how little time it took to do the work on Ste Chapelle (this comparison can only I think be seen as flattering), one may presume that when this letter reaches Annecy, the beautifications of Boulevard Haussmann will be nearly done." (With, later in the same letter, his comparison of the various noises that surround him to his lullaby.)

How revealing letters can be, in the era when they were written by hand and not often copied over, especially not by the suffering Proust, who much of the time, according to him, had barely the strength or energy to write even a short note. Unrevised, a letter may show the thread of the thought as it develops: "When it has subsided," Proust writes of one of his attacks, in Letter 24, and then realizes it may not subside, and so goes on to add what has just occurred to him: "if it subsides."

The letters, written over a span of years and in different moods and physical conditions, show different aspects of his personality and character. He may be gracious and flattering, as in Letter 11: "At least I would have the joy of knowing that those lovely lucid eyes had rested on these pages"; or flowery and eloquent, as in Letter 15: "My solitude has become even more profound, and I know nothing of the sun but what your letter tells me. It has thus been a blessed messenger, and contrary to the proverb, this single swallow has made for me an entire spring." Or, in contrast to his poetic descriptions, he may suddenly deploy, with cool adeptness, in Letter 26, a metaphor taken from the world of chemistry: "Already I carry around with me in my mind so many dissolved deaths, that each new one causes supersaturation and crystallizes all my griefs into an infrangible block."

He is meticulous and particular in his requests as to when

and where his upstairs neighbors might nail shut their crates, in Letter 18: "Or else if it is indispensable to nail them in the morning, to nail them in the part of your apartment that is above my kitchen, and not that which is above my bedroom. I call above my bedroom that which is also above the adjoining rooms, and even on the 4th"; but he is equally fastidious in describing the nature itself of disturbance from noise (as he continues the sentence): "since a noise so discontinuous, so 'noticeable' as blows being struck, is heard even in the areas where it is slightly diminished."

And in Letter 19, too, he goes into detail about the effect of noise: "What bothers me is never continuous noise, even loud noise, if it is not *struck*, on the floorboards, (it is less often no doubt in the bedroom itself, than at the bend of the hallway). And everything that is dragged over the floor, that falls on it, runs across it." I think we readers, peering over Mme Williams's shoulder, may find his precision amusing, but he himself, though so likely at other times to see the humor in a situation, here seems in deadly earnest. And the same earnestness must be present in another letter, Letter 21, as he describes one of his weekly torments (again, with a somewhat eccentric placement or omission of commas): "Yet tomorrow is Sunday, a day which usually offers me the opposite of the weekly repose because in the little courtyard adjoining my room they beat the carpets from your apartment, with an extreme violence."

Proust's style, in these letters, then, is a mix of elegance and haste, refinement and convolution, gravity and self-mockery, marked by abbreviations and mistakes, very little punctuation, and no paragraphing to speak of, or almost none, as he shifts from topic to topic.

My approach to translating this style was to attempt to reproduce it, not supplying missing punctuation or correcting mistakes, but at the same time trying to retain as much of its grace, beauty, sudden shifts of tone and subject, and distinctive character as I could. It was a pleasurable challenge to attempt to reproduce his non sequiturs, his flowery constructions, his literary references, and his exact instructions for lessening the intrusions of noise. One is bound to feel compassion—as his neighbors did—for the beleaguered Proust, pushing ahead, against all odds and in the worst of health, with his vast project; it is certainly impossible, in any case, for anyone with neighbors of his or her own to blame him for being so fussy about the noise.

One particular challenge in the translation was to create a passable version of Proust's pastiche, in Letter 20, of the sonnet by Félix Arvers. This poem became so famous in its day that Arvers has been dubbed a "one-poem poet," so famous that it inspired a well-known American poet to translate it. One would not immediately associate Henry Wadsworth Longfellow with Proust, and yet, for a time—not at the same time—they were both concentrating their attention, and their literary abilities, on Arvers's "My Secret." We may gain yet another idea of the original from reading Longfellow's version, from which I had hoped to steal some phrases but managed only to take the last line:

MY SECRET

My soul its secret hath, my life too hath its mystery,
A love eternal in a moment's space conceived;
Hopeless the evil is, I have not told its history,
And she who was the cause nor knew it nor believed.
Alas! I shall have passed close by her unperceived,
Forever at her side, and yet forever lonely,
I shall unto the end have made life's journey, only

Daring to ask for naught, and having naught received.
For her, though God hath made her gentle and endearing,
She will go on her way distraught and without hearing
These murmurings of love that round her steps ascend,
Piously faithful still unto her austere duty,
Will say, when she shall read these lines full of her beauty,
"Who can this woman be?" and will not comprehend.

By way of coda: After these letters were, not so long ago, brought into public view from where they had been residing in the Museum of Letters and Manuscripts in Paris, and after some excerpts from them in the original French were published in *Le Nouvel Observateur* online on October 10, 2013, an unexpected response added a few more details to our understanding of Proust's life and activities.

A person by the lyrical name of Lerossignol—"the nightingale"—writes an online comment to the article. He is the grandson of a florist who had a shop in the seaside town of Houlgate, on the stretch of the Normandy coast aptly known as the Côte Fleurie (the Flowery Coast); Houlgate is a neighboring town to Cabourg, where Proust liked to vacation and which was transformed into Balbec in Proust's novel. This was the shop that Proust patronized in the years 1908 to 1913 when sending flowers to, among others, Mme Williams. Monsieur Lerossignol writes that the family archives in his possession include records of the shop's transactions, which mention Proust's sending flowers to the Williamses; Monsieur Lerossignol has therefore known the name for a long time and was aware that the couple must have been acquaintances of Proust's. But only now, with the publication of the present letters, does he know who they were. He would like, incidentally, to correct one statement in the commentary that accompanies the extracts—that in those days etiquette required that a man send flowers not directly to a married woman but to her husband. He can attest from his family records that this was not always the case, and he knows in which cases Proust sent flowers to the husband and in which, in fact, directly to the wife. With regard to the Williamses, however, he adds, Proust was always very correct. Monsieur Lerossignol goes on to remark that Proust, despite his illness, did venture into the family flower shop; his grandmother counted thirty-two visits before 1912.

From the invoices of Proust's orders, it is possible to know the names of those with whom he associated while staying at the vast Grand Hôtel de Cabourg, before his health worsened to such an extent that he confined himself permanently to Paris. Monsieur Lerossignol has had the idea of organizing a tour of the still surviving villas of those to whom Proust sent flowers in Houlgate ordered from Au Jardin des Roses (In the Rose Garden), the shop owned by M. Lerossignol's grandparents, who were also named Lerossignol.

2017

LEARNING
A FOREIGN LANGUAGE:
SPANISH

AVENTURAS DE TOM SAWYER

MARK TWAIN

Reading *Las aventuras de Tom Sawyer*

I'm not sure why I want to learn Spanish just now. It may have something to do with the fact that I have recently finished a long, hard translation from French and want to take a break from that language, yet remain in some foreign language. It certainly also has to do with the fact that there are so many Spanish speakers in the United States. I want to be able to communicate with them, or at least understand them. I hear this from friends and acquaintances, too: "It has become necessary," says one, even though he is fairly isolated on a hilltop in a rural area and boards dogs for a living. A family member studied Spanish to help with his work in a city hospital. I used to go into the bodega on the corner of my block in Brooklyn nearly every day and was frustrated that I recognized only a few words, always the same ones: *Domingo, entonces, yo quiero*. I would like to be able to read Borges's *Ficciones*, Rulfo's famous novel *Pedro Páramo*, which I'm told does not have a good English translation, maybe some Unamuno and some stories of Cervantes's, but most of all his enormous *Don Quixote* that always stands before me like a Mount Everest (perhaps I will die on its slopes). I knew a little Spanish, some of the basics, from having tried to study it decades before, when I was a teenager. So I decided to take some lessons; I took them from my son's Spanish teacher, along with another mother. We had six lessons before the teacher went away for the summer, but now I have continued studying on my own.

My method of studying Spanish is to read *Las aventuras de Tom Sawyer* without looking up any words in the dictionary. Now and then, as a "treat," in order to find answers to persistent grammar or usage questions, I consult another book I found at a library sale, *Spanish Omnibus for All Levels: A Comprehensive Survey for High School and College* by Martel and Alpern. It is excellent—clean, clear, and attractive, with interesting lists and small black-and-white illustrations including portraits, engravings, maps, and cartoons.

I did not really "pick" *Tom Sawyer* to read. I don't have many books in Spanish in the house, since up to now I knew so little Spanish, and this book has sat on the bookshelf alongside several other books by Mark Twain for years. It's an old paperback. The cheap paper is brown with age and the type is uneven, but it is a nice size and shape, and pretty well bound. It has crude black-and-white line drawings at the start of each chapter and a color illustration on the cover of two boys in a rowboat. It was first published in Mexico in 1958; this edition is from 1974. It was translated into Spanish by one Sara Gómez. After a few Spanish lessons with the teacher, I remembered the book and took it off the shelf, wondering if my Spanish had improved enough to read it, since, after all, it is a children's book. The first sentence in the book is the single word "Tom!" with an upside-down exclamation mark before it. The second sentence I didn't understand. Nevertheless, I began to read the book, found that I could make out more or less what was happening, enjoyed it, and didn't want to stop.

So for the past few months, off and on, I have been reading *Las aventuras de Tom Sawyer*. By now I have read a little
over half the book (136 out of 252 pages). I am reading
it better and faster as I go along, because of course I understand more and more. I am learning quite a number of
the words as I read them, though some are still mysterious.
As soon as I am pretty sure what a word means, I write it
down in a little notebook. I carry the notebook with me, and
sometimes I review the words when I have to sit and wait for
something.

I had decided right away not to look up any words in
the dictionary, and again I am not quite sure why. Stopping
constantly—every few words—would certainly have taken
most of the fun out of the reading; but also, this way of reading soon turned into a challenge to myself, and then into an
exercise in learning words purely from their contexts, which
is of course how children learn their native language; and it
has been interesting to see how that works.

The book is a good choice for this exercise, for several
reasons: it is a tale full of adventures, written in concrete
language, with a minimum of philosophy and description;
it was written with children in mind, so it is simpler in its
language and ideas; it is a story I know very well from having
read it in English at least twice and seen the good (old) and
the mediocre (more recent) movie versions several times, so
I always know roughly what is happening and what is about
to happen; I like the story and appreciate it in a different way
through the screen of Spanish, as though these boys really
were native Spanish speakers and lived in a *pueblo*; and perhaps because, since it was originally written in English, the
phrases, sentences, and paragraphs are composed in a more
familiar, English-language pattern. (I suspected this might
be a helpful thing back when, in France, I used to read Série

Noire detective novels translated into French from American English.)

I have a book called *Latin for Americans* that I bought, probably also at a library book sale, because I liked the title and because I'm interested in Latin, though I haven't yet done much with it. This book advises one to try reading just this way: "Read through a Latin sentence, trying to get the meaning of each word as you come to it. Sometimes an English word derived, or formed, from the Latin word, will give you the clue; sometimes you will have to guess from the rest of the sentence."

Part of the reason this exercise—learning from the context, without looking a word up—works pretty well to teach me the language is that it provokes a little minor frustration and also arouses my curiosity. It is frustrating to be engrossed in a story and suddenly not to know exactly what is happening and miss some of the action. It is then especially satisfying to figure out, if I can, what the mystery words are and fill in some of the picture. And it would not be a "treat" to consult the grammar review if my strong curiosity had not already been aroused. Because I am consistently denying myself the dictionary, it now seems an amazing resource: I have only to open the book (I will not) and instantly find the Spanish for all these English words, or vice versa.

There are always a number of words I don't know and may never understand, and I have to put up with that. Besides reviewing the words in the notebook from time to time, I sometimes try to make up sentences using them, which is an excellent way to learn a word so you don't forget it. But I don't do this very faithfully. Writing the words down in the first place helps me remember them. Some I wouldn't remember if they simply occurred in a list; I recognize them only if they reappear in a helpful context. But many, out of all the words I write down, I retain simply because they are repeated so often—they reappear over and over in the course of the book so now I know them and I don't think I'll ever forget them: *grito*, "shout"; *anteojos* ("in front of the eyes"), "eyeglasses."

A recent acquaintance told me he had spent six years studying Spanish in his grammar and high school classrooms and still knew only a little. Naturally I compare that with my experience now, and think children would learn very fast if they could do it more or less this way and benefit from the following: an interesting story; freedom to work independently; their own aroused curiosity; and constant reinforcement of vocabulary. Especially important would be the aroused curiosity, how much better they would learn if they were actually eager to know the answers before they were given them. In this way they would advance very quickly with comprehension, at least. Conversation would have to have a similarly provocative and amusing immersion program. Perhaps they could start their foreign language at the age when they love mysterious ciphers and code-breaking, at, say, age eight or nine. In any case, as I discovered with the traditional way of learning to ride a bicycle, the traditional classroom Spanish lesson seems a very ineffectual method as it is now, and years of classroom Spanish lessons seem a colossal waste of children's time. (Here is what I discovered about the best way to teach a child to ride a bicycle: using an undersized, borrowed bicycle and a gentle slope.)

I am beginning to understand better how I figure out an unknown Spanish word. Sometimes it is exactly the same in Spanish (*plan* = plan). Sometimes it is almost exactly the same (*temblar* = tremble). Sometimes it is a cognate of an English or a French word and close enough to guess (*esparció* = scattered; the cognate is *sparse*); *abrigo* = shelter; the cognate is the Fr. *abri*). When it is not recognizable, then I can often understand it from the context. Sometimes a single context is sufficient because no other word would fit (*copo de nieve* = snowflake, in the passage quoted below, since I already knew that *nieve* = snow). More often, at least two contexts are needed in which the word is used in different ways. One example would be *hoja*. The first time I read it was in the phrase *hoja de papel*, "*hoja* of paper." Several choices would have made equal sense, paired with "paper" in that context, so I didn't yet know what *hoja* meant. Then I saw the word again in the context of a woods or a tree; and a third time when Huck rolls a dry *hoja* around something else to make a kind of cigarette: then I knew that only one meaning would work as well with paper as with a tree and a cigarette, and I had the word: "leaf."

Another example would be *rodillas*. When Tom gets down onto his *rodillas* before climbing into bed, I didn't know exactly what they might be, even when I understood that he was saying his bedtime prayers. But then, many pages later, when he wades into the water up to his *rodillas*, only one word would work in both contexts: "knees."

One last example would be these two contexts occurring some pages apart: an *hilo* of water; an *hilo* of ants. Stream? Context gradually narrows the possibilities—or rather the superimposition of contexts narrows them. Or logic poses the question: What form is it that both water and ants can take? You do not understand a word, and you wait for another context to come along that will explain it to you. Then, at last, after you have tolerated a lot of incomprehension, like a child, your understanding of the word arises of itself within you. The "answer" to what the word is does not get pasted onto you from outside, as from a dictionary. It comes from within you and so is deeper and more inherent.

Sometimes I read straight on without going back, but often, when I learn one word, it explains the meaning of other words that came just before it, so I look back, and, one by one, each newly acquired word gives me the clue to the next one. Knowing Tom had gotten onto his knees before climbing into bed gave me the answer to another word: *rezar* = pray. And another, later: *arrodillarse* had to mean "kneel." Reading a sentence several times over is often enough to teach me most of the mysterious words.

I have wanted to see if my comprehension has improved at all and have been looking for opportunities (*oportunidades*) to eavesdrop on conversations in Spanish, most recently in a bus terminal. There I found an old woman who, helpfully for my purposes, was talking to herself in Spanish in the ladies' room. I had just missed the phone conversation she had been having at a pay phone, which would have been even better, since I could have stood very close to her at the next phone as long as I liked. Families on the subway are usually sitting too far away for me to hear them over the rumble of the train. At the ATM, I could ask the machine to continue in Spanish, ditto for the telephone, in the case of certain electronic information—bus schedules, for instance. Playing an episode of *NYPD Blue* (but not as good as I remembered it to be) I could click on "Language" and opt to see it again in Spanish. I haven't done any of this yet. When presented most recently with a calm, quiet chance to converse with a native Costa Rican, I found myself completely tongue-tied and realized afterward that the language difficulty was adding itself onto another difficulty—this particular relationship was a little tricky and required a tactful approach, so that even in English I would choose my words carefully. My most successful attempt at conversation so far was with a friend who was also practicing her Spanish.

I have written down in my notebook 518 words by now. This means that, starting with the rudiments of a language and reading a simple, familiar adventure story, one can increase one's vocabulary relatively painlessly by 518 words (most of them permanent acquisitions) in 136 pages, and at the same time go from a very sketchy knowledge of the language to a somewhat more fluent understanding of it. Those rudiments could include a basic vocabulary of the most common words and perhaps the present-tense conjugations of common verbs. I read recently that in English, a mere 43 words account for half of all words in common use, and that just nine (*and*, *be*, *have*, *it*, *of*, *the*, *to*, *will*, *you*) account for a quarter in almost any sample of written English (my source is a very entertaining exploration of the English language, *The Mother Tongue: English and How It Got That Way*, by Bill Bryson). In another grammar I found at a secondhand bookstore, *A Practical Key to the Kanarese Language*, by F. Ziegler (published by the Basel Mission Book Depot, Mangalore, 1953), the beginner is presented with a vocabulary of 162 "indispensable" words: common verbs, adverbs, adjectives, prepositions, numbers, parts of the body, family members, and common objects such as the knife and the umbrella. One could draw up or find the same sort of list for Spanish, including such essential words as *algo*, "something," and learn it before embarking on this experiment. In the passage below, for instance, certain of these essential words can be identified because they occur so many times: *un*, *la*, *en*, *y*, *las*, *más*, *de*, *los*, *se*, *con*, *una*, *el*, *como*, *del*, etc. I've chosen the passage more or less at random—it is the latest I've read—to illustrate how this practice of learning-from-context works for me.

The three boys—Tom Sawyer, Huck Finn, and Joe Harper—have snuck away from home and are staying on an island in the Mississippi River within sight of their town, pretending to be pirates. Their families think they have drowned and are arranging a funeral for Sunday. The boys are planning to show up at the funeral and surprise everyone. But Sunday is still a few days off, they are a little homesick, and a storm is descending on them.

First, I will offer the passage in Sara Gómez's Spanish translation, with words italicized that I had not seen before or could not guess when I came to them:

Hubo una pausa. Un *resplandor* espectral convirtió la noche en día y mostró *nítidas* y distintas hasta las más diminutas *briznas* de hierba, y mostró también tres caras lívidas y *asustadas*. Un formidable *trueno* fué *retumbando* por los cielos y se perdió, con sordas repercusiones, en la distancia. Una *bocanada* de aire frío *barrió* el bosque, agitando el follaje, y esparció como *copos* de nieve las cenizas del fuego. Otro *relámpago cegador* iluminó la selva, y tras él siguió el *estallido* de un *trueno* que pareció *desgajar* las *copas* de los árboles sobre las cabezas de los muchachos. Los tres se *abrazaron*, aterrados, en la densa oscuridad en que todo volvió a sumergirse. *Gruesas* gotas de lluvia empezaron a *golpear* las hojas.

—Rápido! . . . A la tienda!—ordenó Tom.

Se irguieron de un salto y echaron a correr, *tropezando* en las *raíces* y en las lianas, cada uno por su lado. Un *vendaval* furioso rugió por entre los árboles, sacudiendo y haciendo *crujir* cuanto encontraba en su camino. *Deslumbrantes relámpagos* y *truenos ensordecedores* se sucedían casi sin intermitencia. Y después cayó una lluvia torrencial, que el *huracán impelía* en líquidas sabanas al *ras* del suelo. Los chicos se llamaban recíprocamente a gritos, pero los *bramidos* del viento y el *retumbar* de los *truenos* ahogaban por completo sus voces. Sin embargo, se juntaron, al fin, y buscaron abrigo bajo la tienda, ateridos, temblando de espanto, *empapados* de agua, pero *gozosos* de hallarse juntos en medio de su angustia.

Next, here is the passage with English supplied for the parts I understood and some explanation of how I came to understand some of them using basic vocabulary and Spanish study along with cognates and context:

Hubo una pausa.
> [*Hubo* seems familiar from basic Spanish study: probably past tense of *haber*, "have."]
>> There was a pause.

Un *resplandor* espectral
> [cognate is *spectral*; I also see *splendor* but can't figure out a connection]
>> A spectral *resplandor*

convirtió la noche en día
> [cognate is *converted*]
>> changed night into day

y mostró
> [cognate is *demonstrate*]
>> and showed

nítidas y distintas
> [cognate is *distinct*; have no idea about *nítidas*]
>> *nítidas* and distinct

hasta las más diminutas *briznas* de hierba,
> [cognates are *diminutive* and *herb* (Fr. *herbe* = grass); don't know about *briznas*]
>> even the most diminutive *briznas* of grass,
> [a few sentences later I will return to this and

decide *briznas* must be "blades" and then
remember the French cognate *brin*, "blade"]
 even the most diminutive blades of grass,
y mostró también
 and also showed
tres caras lívidas y *asustadas*.
 [cognate is *livid*; don't know about *asustadas*]
 three pale and *asustadas* faces.
Un formidable *trueno* fué *retumbando* por los cielos
 ["formidable" is the same]
 A formidable *trueno* went *retumbando* through
 the heavens
y se perdió, con sordas repercusiones, en la distancia.
 [cognates are *perdition* and Fr. *perdre*, "lose";
 repercussions; and *distance*; Fr. *sourd* meaning
 "deaf," and *sourdine*, "mute" on a musical
 instrument, make me think *sordas* could mean
 "muted" or "muffled"]
 and lost itself, with muffled echoes, in the
 distance.
Una *bocanada* de aire frío *barrió* el bosque,
 [cognates are *air* and *bosky* meaning "wooded";
 in *bocanada* I see *boca*, "mouth," and *nada*,
 "nothing," but I don't know if that's relevant]
 A *bocanada* of cold air *barrió* the woods,
agitando el follaje,
 [cognates are *agitated* and *foliage*]
 shaking the foliage [leaves],
y esparció como *copos* de nieve las cenizas del fuego.
 [*esparció* has "sparse" buried in it and it is what the
 wind does; *copos* I knew had to be "flakes" because
 of the context; the comparison to snowflakes told
 me what *cenizas* was; I had encountered it before,

knowing it was related to the fire, but not exactly
what it was]
    and scattered like snowflakes the ashes of the
    fire.
Otro *relámpago cegador* iluminó la selva,
    [don't know what the first two are, but soon will
    know one of them; cognates—*illumination* and
    It. *selva* from the second line of Dante's *Inferno*:
    Nel mezzo del camin di nostra vita, mi trovai
    in un' selv' oscura; I don't know much Italian,
    though I took a class in that once, too, but I once
    memorized (inaccurately) the first two lines of the
    poem]
        Another *relámpago cegador* lit up the woods,
y tras él siguió el *estallido* de un *trueno*
    [don't know those two words, but soon will know
    the second, when I look back]
        and after it followed the *estallido* of a *trueno*
que pareció *desgajar* las *copas* de los árboles
    [cognates: *appear* and *arbor*; I think *copas* has to
    be the only part of the tree I haven't learned yet—
    not the trunks, branches, or leaves, so maybe the
    tops]
        which appeared to *desgajar* the treetops
sobre las cabezas de los muchachos.
    [I've learned all these words in "basic vocabulary"
    study]
        over [or on] the boys' heads.
Los tres se *abrazaron*, aterrados,
    [I've learned *brazo* for "arm," so *abrazaron*
    must be "put their arms around each other" or
    "embrace" (which is a cognate, in fact); another
    cognate may be *terrified*]

>The three put their arms around each other, terrified,

en la densa oscuridad en que todo volvió a sumergirse.
>[cognates: *dense, obscurity, revolve* ("return"), *submerge*]
>>in the dense darkness into which everything had been once again submerged.

Gruesas gotas de lluvia empezaron a *golpear* las hojas.
>[cognates: Fr. *gouttes* ("drops")]
>>*Gruesas* drops of rain began to *golpear* the leaves.

—Rápido! . . . A la tienda!—ordenó Tom.
>[cognates: *rapid, order*]
>>"Quick! . . . To the tent!" Tom ordered them.

Se irguieron de un salto y echaron a correr,
>[*irguieron* had stumped me, earlier in the book, but if you're sitting down and you consistently do this before you start running or walking, it must be "stood up"; *salto* is "jump," cognate being *saltimbanco* and Fr. *sauter*; cognates for *correr* are Fr. *courir* and Eng. *courier*]
>>They jumped to their feet and began running,

tropezando en las *raíces* y en las lianas, cada uno por su lado.
>[*tropezando* sounds a little like "tripping," though I would be suspicious because *o* to *i* isn't a usual shift, but then it is confirmed by *raíces* (cognate Fr. *radice*, "root"; Eng. *radish*) and lianas; *lado* means "side," but I'm guessing that, as with the troublesome French word *côté*, "side" can also mean "direction"]
>>tripping over the roots and vines, each in his own direction.

Un *vendaval* furioso rugió por entre los árboles,

> [I see some sort of "wind" in *vendaval* because
> of *viento*, "wind," maybe a gust of wind; cognate
> *furious*; maybe *rage* for *rugió*]

A furious gust of wind raged through the trees,

sacudiendo y haciendo *crujir* cuanto encontraba en su camino.

> [is *crujir* related to "crux"?; is there some idea
> of crossing or bending?; cognate for *encontraba*
> would be "encounter" but I know already that it
> usually means "find"]

shaking and bending any it found in its path.

Deslumbrantes relámpagos y *truenos ensordecedores* se sucedían casi sin intermitencia.

> [after a number of paired repetitions, I catch on
> to the fact that *relámpagos* and *truenos* must be
> "lightning" and "thunder," especially clear in this
> sentence where they follow each other almost
> without "intermittence," so I can note them down
> and go back and look at earlier instances; the *lum* in
> the adjective *deslumbrantes* may be related to light,
> and it may mean "blinding" since the adjective after
> "thunder" seems to mean "deafening"; I would
> put a question mark in my notebook; cognate for
> *sucedían* is *succeed* in the sense of "follow"]

Blinding flashes of lightning and deafening
thunder followed one another almost without
interruption.

Y después cayó una lluvia torrencial,

> [cognate is *torrential*]

And afterward fell a torrential rain,

que el *huracán impelía* en líquidas sabanas al *ras* del suelo.

[is *huracán* really "hurricane" or just "storm"?; cognate for *impelía* may be *impel*, so this may mean "send"; I am pleased to find *sabanas* again in a metaphor after learning it in an early scene in Tom's bedroom; more cognates may be Fr. *ras*, "level," and Eng. *soil*]

> which the storm sent in sheets of liquid across the ground.

Los chicos se llamaban recíprocamente a gritos,

[cognate: *reciprocal*; *gritos* I learned earlier in the book; the other words are basic vocab]

> The boys called out to each other, shouting,

pero los *bramidos* del viento y el *retumbar* de los *truenos*

[whatever noises wind and thunder make—there are too many choices for now; I need to see another use in another context]

> but the *bramidos* of the wind and the *retumbar* of the thunder

ahogaban por completo sus voces.

[I learned *ahogar*, "to drown," a few pages earlier, when that is what the townspeople think has happened to the boys; cognates—*completely*, *voices*]

> drowned out their voices completely.

Sin embargo, se juntaron, al fin,

[cognates: *embargo*, *join*, *final*]

> Yet they found each other at last,

y buscaron abrigo bajo la tienda,

[cognates: Fr. *abri*, "shelter"; I already knew *tienda*, though I didn't know why it also meant "shop" or "store," although it occurs to me now that the connection may go by way of the canvas cover or awning]

> and sought shelter under the tent,

ateridos, temblando de espanto, *empapados* de agua,
>[cognates: *terrified, tremble*—I hesitate over the
>dropping of the *r*, but then remember the name
>of a literary magazine, *Temblor*, itself named after,
>I think, an earth tremor; I learned *espanto* earlier
>in the book when the boys witness a graveyard
>murder committed by Injun Joe (who is called,
>in Spanish, "Joe el Indio"); *empapados* is almost
>certainly "soaked" but I'm not sure enough yet]
>>terrified, trembling with fear, *empapados* in
>>water,

pero *gozosos* de hallarse juntos en medio de su angustia.
>[cognates: *joined, middle, anguish*]
>>but *gozosos* to have found each other in the
>>midst of their anguish.

Now I will join the English parts to make what looks temporarily like a poem:

There was a pause.
A spectral resplandor
changed night into day
and showed
nítidas and distinct
even the most diminutive briznas of grass,
and also showed
three pale and asustadas faces.
A formidable trueno went retumbando through the heavens
and lost itself, with muffled echoes, in the distance.
A bocanada of cold air barrió the woods,
shaking the foliage,
and scattered like snowflakes the ashes of the fire.
Another relámpago cegador lit up the woods,

and after it followed the estallido of a trueno
which appeared to desgajar the treetops
over the boys' heads.
The three put their arms around each other, terrified,
in the dense darkness into which everything had been once
     again submerged.
Gruesas drops of rain began to golpear the leaves.
"Quick! . . . To the tent!" Tom ordered them.
They jumped to their feet and began running,
tripping over the roots and vines, each in his own direction.
A furious wind raged through the trees,
shaking and bending any it found in its path.
Blinding flashes of lightning and deafening thunder
     followed one another almost without interruption.
And afterward fell a torrential rain,
which the storm sent in sheets of liquid across the ground.
The boys called out to each other, shouting,
but the bramidos of the wind and the retumbar of the
     thunder
drowned out their voices completely.
Yet they found each other at last,
and sought shelter under the tent,
terrified, trembling with fear, empapados in water,
but gozosos to have found one another in the midst of their
     anguish.

After some rewriting and guessing at the words, here is a
version in English prose, no doubt sprinkled with mistakes:

There was a pause. Then a spectral gleam changed
night into day, showing, detailed and distinct, even
the tiniest blades of grass, and at the same time revealing three faces pale with astonishment. A formidable

clap of thunder rumbled through the sky and vanished, with muffled echoes, in the distance. A gust
of cold air barreled through the woods, shaking the
foliage and scattering the ashes of the fire like snowflakes. Another brilliant flash of lightning lit up the
woods, and after it followed the rumble of a clap of
thunder, which seemed to crack the treetops over the
boys' heads. The three of them grabbed each other,
terrified, in the dense gloom into which everything
was once again sunk. Fat drops of rain began pelting
the leaves.

"Quick! . . . Get to the tent!" Tom ordered.

They jumped to their feet and ran, tripping over
roots and vines, each in a different direction. A furious wind raged through the trees, shaking and bending those that it found in its path. Blinding flashes of
lightning and deafening peals of thunder followed one
another almost without interruption. And then a torrential rain came down, driven by the storm in sheets
of water across the ground. The boys kept shouting
back and forth to each other, but the howling of the
wind and the rumbling of the thunder completely
drowned out their voices. Still, they found each other
at last and sought shelter inside the tent, terrified,
trembling with fear, soaked in water, but overjoyed to
be together in the midst of their anguish.

Now, at last, I look at Twain's original—this is my des-
sert. I have been wanting to compare his original with my
guesses and deductions all along but first needed to attempt
the experiment of translating the translation. I'm guessing
that Twain's original will be livelier and more idiomatic than
my rather formal and colorless version.

There was a pause. Now a weird flash turned night into day and showed every little grass-blade, separate and distinct, that grew about their feet. And it showed three white, startled faces, too. A deep peal of thunder went rolling and tumbling down the heavens and lost itself in sullen rumblings in the distance. A sweep of chilly air passed by, rustling all the leaves and snowing the flaky ashes broadcast about the fire. Another fierce glare lit up the forest, and an instant crash followed that seemed to rend the treetops right over the boys' heads. They clung together in terror, in the thick gloom that followed. A few big raindrops fell pattering upon the leaves.

"Quick, boys! go for the tent!" exclaimed Tom.

They sprang away, stumbling over roots and among vines in the dark, no two plunging in the same direction. A furious blast roared through the trees, making everything sing as it went. One blinding flash after another came, and peal on peal of deafening thunder. And now a drenching rain poured down and the rising hurricane drove it in sheets along the ground. The boys cried out to each other, but the roaring wind and the booming thunderblasts drowned their voices utterly. However, one by one they straggled in at last and took shelter under the tent, cold, scared, and streaming with water; but to have company in misery seemed something to be grateful for.

Here is what I have noticed, comparing the two: Twain's understanding of "weird" is an earlier one than ours and closer to "spectral." "And showed" is more dynamic than my present participle "showing." The Spanish translation omitted "that grew about their feet," as translations sometimes do omit material, either by accident or because the translator feels that the material is already implied by the rest of the sentence. "Lost itself" is more vivid (and closer to the Spanish) than my "vanished." Twain's "sweep" of air is more unusual than my "gust" and "snowing the flaky ashes broadcast" more vivid and unexpected than "scattering the ashes . . . like snowflakes." "Go for the tent" is a little less familiar to us, but sounds better, than "Get to the tent." I seem to have misunderstood "making everything sing." On the other hand, I like my "fat drops of rain" and "pelting"—though that word may not be correct—better than Twain's choices. The classics are never "improved" in their own language, are they? They remain intact, with whatever faults they may have. But privately we may toy with changes. Borges, I was told recently by someone who met him once—but for all I know this may be a familiar story—used to pass the time, in his blindness, by making slight alterations to, and improving upon, passages of Shakespeare. The example given was a string of *no*s in, I think, a speech of Lear's: "No, no, no, no." Shakespeare had given Lear four *no*s, but Borges felt there should be five. I don't know if this revision of his took place in the English original or in Spanish translation.

2004

TRANSLATING FROM
ENGLISH INTO
ENGLISH

An Experiment in Modernizing
Laurence Sterne's *A Sentimental Journey*

Laurence Sterne's *A Sentimental Journey through France and Italy by Mr. Yorick* was first published in 1768, unfinished, cut short by Sterne's death from tuberculosis. His earlier, more famous book, *Tristram Shandy*, had been attacked by some for its ribaldry, its perceived licentiousness, its cynicism—"a scandal coming from a clergyman," as Virginia Woolf reported it in her introduction to the neat, small-format 1928 World's Classics edition of *A Sentimental Journey*—and his aim in writing the latter was in part to change his readers' perception of him, to portray himself as sensitive, humane, decent. Yet inevitably, since this work reflects its author so closely, it is as unconventional in spirit and form as the earlier book, artfully and painstakingly contrived to give the impression of having been dashed off, of being coolly casual, what Woolf calls "semi-transparent." She found it "modern" more than ninety years ago, in the liberties it took "with grammar and syntax and sense and propriety and the long-standing tradition of how a novel should be written." We find it modern, still, today.

What had been bothering me, as an incongruity, an imbalance, was that whereas artwork of the eighteenth century and further back, to the beginning of discovered painting, is readily available, at least in reproduction, and enjoyed by the general public, not just scholars or specialists, and likewise the music of the eighteenth century and earlier—though as one goes back through the centuries, the numbers of listeners does drop off—the great works of literature before, say, Jane Austen, are mostly unread, even by writers. Here, too, of course, the further back in time we go, the smaller the readership becomes. There are shelves and shelves full of fresh and surprising language and convivial company that are ignored by writers and completely unknown to most of the same people who may crowd New York's Metropolitan Museum of Art and who then, on their way out of town, may hear a little Vivaldi from the loudspeakers of the Port Authority Bus Terminal or Penn Station. The language of earlier writing is certainly a barrier, and yet some adventurers learn Arabic, Hebrew, and Swahili, and many more learn French, German, and Spanish. But those avid language-learners don't as readily try to cross the barrier to James Boswell's English, or John Donne's, or further back to Chaucer's or Beowulf's (at which point the English is admittedly a more or less foreign language). But maybe the barrier is something other than the language; maybe it is the sensibility or the worldview that changes too much, as we travel back in time, for us to understand it, or, if we understand it, to feel any sympathy for it.

But if the language is indeed one barrier, my idea was to see what would happen when I tried to "translate" what struck me as quite a modern text in its eccentricity of form, its sense of humor, its featuring the author as main character, its intimacy with the reader, and its irony, into an English that would present fewer problems, fewer oddities to a present-day reader. This exercise was a deliberate experiment—unlike most so-called experimental writing—but it was never meant to be more than a bridge. I thought—as, years later, I hoped, trying the same sort of thing, to bring new readers to the children's classic dog story, *Bob, Son of Battle*—that if I made some Sterne easier to read, perhaps a few readers would be drawn to the original. I attempted only a few pages, and they were published; I never intended to "translate" the entire book.

I am calling a "translation" what in other contexts or for other purposes might be termed a new version, sometimes simplified, sometimes abridged. I'm thinking of "easier" editions of such children's classics as *The Secret Garden*, or an edition I have of *Robinson Crusoe* in words of one syllable. One of the aims of these versions is the same, to make a good book accessible to a larger, or different, audience.

The 1993 simplified *Secret Garden* is at several removes from the original: it is a so-called *novelization* based on a *screenplay* of the *movie* of the novel by Frances Hodgson Burnett, first published in 1911. The style of the original book is changed—sentences are shorter and simpler in this version, repetitions are avoided, except for a monotonously frequent "Mary" as the first word of a sentence ("Mary Lennox lived in India." "Mary was cared for by an Indian woman." "Mary ran, shrieking and muddy, back to the bungalow."). Burnett's original description of the spoiled young Mary—"She was the most disagreeable looking child ever seen. . . . She had a little thin face and a little thin body, thin light hair and a sour expression"—becomes: "Mary Lennox was a sour little girl. Her skin was pale as powder and her frame as thin as a twig." Not just the style and language of the original novel are changed in the later version, but some of the facts and plot turns of the story. Mary's father does not hold "a position under the English Government," as Burnett narrated, but is a British general, and the cholera that kills Mary's parents and her ayah in the original becomes an earthquake. Because the earthquake occurs abruptly, we miss the ominous whispering and mysterious absences of familiar servants that signal the presence of the disease. What frightens Mary in the original story is not a sudden crash, but the utter silence when she awakens in the morning—again, more effectively ominous. And, significantly, in the novelization, the opening scene shows Mary reacting with anger toward the flowers she is trying to form into a little makeshift garden, whereas in the original, she, who is otherwise so selfish, is shown loving and caring for flowers, which foreshadows what is so central to the later parts of the story—the resurrection by Mary, Dickon, and Colin of the overgrown garden in England.

As for the 1867 version of *Robinson Crusoe* in words of one syllable, "adapted to the use of the younger readers," as the author, Lucy Aikin, writing under the pen name Mary Godolphin, advises in her preface, its aim was to provide them with a piece of literature more interesting and inherently appealing than the isolated sentences then found in grammar books. It is in fact written with such considerable grace that its self-imposed constraint is hardly noticeable. It is also radically abbreviated. Whereas the original deploys eight substantial paragraphs, digressive and full of subordinate clauses—and including large portions of two paragraphs declaiming upon the superiority of the "middle station of life" (also described as "the upper station of low life") as compared to the "miseries and hardships" of the working class and the "pride, luxury, ambition and envy" of the upper classes—to bring the hero on board ship, Godolphin's simplified version accomplishes this in the first, short paragraph, as follows:

> I was born at York on the first of March in the sixth year of the reign of King Charles the First. From the time when I was quite a young child, I had felt a great wish to spend my life at sea, and as I grew, so did this taste grow more and more strong; till at last I broke loose from my school and home, and found my way on foot to Hull, where I soon got a place on board a ship.

Within three more short paragraphs, a storm comes up and the ship founders, though in this first shipwreck, as opposed to the later one that throws Crusoe onto his island, those on board are rescued. The limitation of using only words of one syllable is fascinating to watch in action. Conveniently, Crusoe's birthplace is the one-syllable York and his first point of embarcation on this ill-fated voyage the one-syllable Hull. And, of course, much of the basic vocabulary of English is monosyllabic—for instance, Godolphin has at her disposal the words *sail, squall, wind, leak, pumps, stem to stern, no hope, save our lives, fire off guns, in need of help, rough, rope, wild sea, oars, shore.* Finding substitute locutions for certain of the most common disyllabic words—such as *around, over, under,* and so forth—will demand some ingenuity. But of course a similar sort of ingenuity is required in any translation into English from another language (an extreme example being that of the twentieth-century French writer Georges Perec's novel *La Disparition*, composed entirely without using the letter *e*, which was translated into the ingenious, equally *e*-less English version *A Void* by Gilbert Adair). Exceptions to the constraint, explained in the preface, are made only for a couple of proper names, most importantly Crusoe's friend Friday.

Daniel Defoe's 1719 original, with ellipses where I am (greatly) abbreviating it here, covers somewhat the same material as follows:

> I was born in the year 1632, in the city of York. . . . Being the third son of the family, and not bred to any trade, my head began to be filled very early with rambling thoughts: my father . . . had designed me for the law; but I would be satisfied with nothing but going to sea. . . . It was not till almost a year after this that I broke loose. . . . Being one day at Hull, where I went casually and without any purpose of making an elopement that time . . . I consulted neither father or mother any more . . . But leaving them to hear of it as they might . . . on the first of September, 1651, I went on board a ship bound for London: never any young adventurer's misfortunes, I believe, began sooner, or continued longer than mine.

To my ear, Godolphin's words of one syllable succeed in capturing something of the tone of the original, whereas the novelization of *The Secret Garden* is a far more lusterless attempt. Then again, the objectives of the two books were different: in the case of the novelization, to exploit the ready-made audience that had been captivated by the movie; in Godolphin's, to rewrite a great story so as to make it available to beginning readers.

As I set about translating the opening pages of *A Sentimental Journey*, several things surprised me. For one, I found I had to work hard to understand the text at certain points where I had passed right over difficulties on earlier readings. A phrase of Sterne's that bewildered me, "where Nature (take her altogether) has so little to answer for," by degrees became understandable to me in the following steps: (1) where nature (taken altogether) . . . ; (2) where nature (regarded as a whole) has so little to defend; (3) . . . can be accused of so little; (4) where nature (considered as a whole) can be accused of so little. Despite my best efforts, I have probably still misconstrued some sentences.

In addition, I became more specifically aware of differences between the English of Sterne's time and that of ours. For instance, Sterne would employ more inversion ("said I") and a more complex sentence structure with more subordinate clauses ("before whose tribunal I must one day come").

I also realized that I had to proceed in stages, with intervals between drafts, because what seemed to be a comfortably modern version compared to Sterne's prose would, when next I read it, though it was a little more modern than Sterne's English, seem once again not of our time. This is, of course, what happens with translation from a foreign language, too: we think that just because we have now caused the passage to exist in English, as it never existed in English before, it is a successful, living English text; we need time and distance to see that it isn't yet fully alive or perhaps even wholly idiomatic.

I discovered that translating Sterne's vocabulary, diction, and style could do only so much to make the text "twentieth-century friendly." There were still differences in culture and mentality that could not be changed and would continue to seem odd, difficult, and foreign to our time—for instance, the personification of nature ("her"), as quoted above. I might have predicted this.

Most glaringly, of course, doing this translation raised

the question—as happened later with *Bob, Son of Battle*—of whether it ought to be done at all. In the interests of "normalizing," for the sake of readability, I was eliminating some of Sterne's nicest moments: some lively verbs ("skipping out of [the carriage], and pulling off my hat"); some unusual (to us) and colorful adjectives ("the whole army of peregrine martyrs"); and most of the dashes Sterne uses so freely in place of a variety of other punctuation, what Woolf calls the punctuation "of speech, not writing," which brings "the sound, the associations, of the speaking voice in with it." Punctuating conventionally rather than with dashes has the effect of smoothing out the flow of the text. Similarly, wasn't a lot of Sterne's particularity being evened out into something bland? An extreme example of the impossibility of translating an English text into easier English would be Joyce's *Finnegans Wake*. Although inventive translations have been done into other languages, to change the English would be to lose most of the character of the book.

Maybe I could have avoided sacrificing so much of Sterne's eccentricity. I don't know yet; I'll see what I think when I come back to read it in a few years. It was interesting to explore, however, the limits of what was possible in translating English of one century to another—at what point the original was simply left too far behind for this translated work to be considered still the same work by the same author.

To give an idea, I'll quote the first paragraphs of the book in my translation, followed by the same in Sterne's original. Sterne jumps right into the story, beginning—and this is the sort of thing that strikes me as so modern—with an exchange between the narrator and someone identified only as "the gentleman," in a place that is unidentified. The "rights" he refers to—evidently the subject of their conversation—are also unidentified. The narrator seems to me likeable, in his modesty about his clothing, for instance. The section is very brief, as are all the sections that immediately follow. The section headings are also eccentric, the first having none, and then "Calais" being followed by "Calais. The Monk," "Calais. The Monk," and "Calais. The Monk." The footnote is Sterne's.

"They manage this sort of thing better in France," I said.

"Have you been to France?" asked the gentleman, turning to me quickly with a most courteous sort of triumph.

"Strange," I said, thinking it over. "The fact is that simply by sailing twenty-one miles—it isn't any farther from Dover to Calais—one acquires these rights. I'll have to look into it."

So, giving up the argument, I went straight back to where I was staying, packed half a dozen shirts and a pair of black silk pants—"The coat I have on will be good enough," I said, looking at the sleeve— and took a seat in the Dover stagecoach. Since the packet boat sailed at nine the next morning, by three that afternoon I was sitting at dinner eating a fricas-seed chicken, so undeniably in France that if I had died that night of indigestion, no one in the whole world would have been able to suspend the effect of the *Droits d'aubaine*:* my shirts and pair of black silk pants, suitcase and all, would have gone to the king of France. Even the little picture I have worn for so long would have been torn from my neck, though I told you, Eliza, that I would carry it with me to my grave.

* All possessions of foreigners dying in France (except the Swiss and the Scottish) are seized by virtue of this law, even if the heir is present. Because the profits of these contingencies are retained by the one who collects them, there is no redress.

So ungenerous! To seize what is left behind by an unwary passenger lured by your subjects to their coast! I swear, Your Majesty, it's not right. And it makes me very sad that I should have to argue with the king of such a civilized and courteous nation, one so renowned for sentiment and fine feelings.

But I have barely set foot in your country.

CALAIS

When I had finished my dinner and drunk a toast to the health of the king of France, to convince myself that I felt no resentment toward him, but, on the contrary, honored him very much for the humanity of his attitude, I felt an inch taller for being so generous.

Here is the original, complete with longer and shorter dashes:

——They order, said I, this matter better in France.——
—You have been in France? said my gentleman, turning quick upon me with the most civil triumph in the world.——Strange! quoth I, debating the matter with myself, That one and twenty miles sailing, for 'tis absolutely no further from Dover to Calais, should give a man these rights—I'll look into them: so giving up the argument—I went straight to my lodgings, put up half a dozen shirts and a black pair of silk breeches— "the coat I have on, said I, looking at the sleeve, will do"—took a place in the Dover stage; and, the pac- quet sailing at nine the next morning—by three I had got sat down to my dinner upon a fricassee'd chicken

so incontestibly in France, that had I died that night of an indigestion, the whole world could not have suspended the effects of the *Droits d'aubaine**—my shirts, and black pair of silk breeches—portmanteau and all must have gone to the King of France—even the little picture which I have so long worn, and so often told thee, Eliza, I would carry with me into my grave, would have been torn from my neck.—— Ungenerous!—to seize upon the wreck of an unwary passenger, whom your subjects had beckon'd to their coast—by heaven! SIRE, it is not well done; and much does it grieve me, 'tis the monarch of a people so civilized and courteous, and so renown'd for sentiment and fine feelings, that I have to reason with——

But I have scarce set foot in your dominions—

CALAIS

When I had finish'd my dinner, and drank the King of France's health, to satisfy my mind that I bore him no spleen, but, on the contrary, high honour for the humanity of his temper—I rose up an inch taller for the accommodation.

*All the effects of strangers (Swiss and Scotch excepted) dying in France, are seized by virtue of this law, though the heir be upon the spot—the profit of these contingencies being farm'd, there is no redress.

I have righted inversions ("I said" instead of "said I," moved interpolated phrases so as to unite separated parts of the sentence, restored whole words ("stagecoach" rather than "stage"), substituted English spelling for French ("packet boat" rather than "pacquet"), modernized certain vocabulary ("quoth" becoming "said," "thee" becoming "you"), up-dated certain usages (we would not say "an indigestion" but "a case of indigestion" or "a bout of indigestion" or simply "indigestion"), punctuated conventionally rather than with dashes, and more.

In changing the text for contemporary consumption, of course, I am taming it, forcing it into a conventional mode, attenuating Sterne's personal presence, in fact doing what the first translators of innovative authors such as Kafka did when presenting him in English. In the case of Kafka, only as one translation succeeded another over the years, or de-cades, did the English translations dare to move closer to the strangeness of Kafka's original German.

2000

BOB

SON OF BATTLE

By ALFRED OLLIVANT

A Thrushwood Book

GROSSET & DUNLAP
Publishers, NEW YORK

Translating *Bob, Son of Battle:*
The Last Gray Dog of Kenmuir

INTRODUCTORY

I do certain things backward. I follow an impulse to embark on a project without questioning my motivations or the wisdom of the project until I'm well on my way. I dive in without a plan, or without planning very far ahead, which leads to my spending a lot of possibly "wasted" time on things but may also take me to some interesting places. I probably do not want to think ahead for fear of not going on with the project at all. Thus, for instance, I may begin reading, taking notes, or even translating, without asking whether I should. (One result is that I have many unfinished projects at different stages of development.) And so it was with this "translation" of Alfred Ollivant's *Bob, Son of Battle* from one kind of English to another, as I felt instinctively that it was a worthwhile thing to do and only later woke up to its inherent difficulties and at the same time began figuring out some of the more complicated reasons why I thought I should do it.

A Swiss writer I admire, Peter Bichsel, remarked in the course of one story that when he was three years old, he was the same person he is now, his fingers then should not be called "little fingers"—they were the same fingers; his anger then was the anger of the same person that he is now. This helps me to see children in a slightly different way—they are indeed a species apart from grown-ups, but they are also the people they will be later, though still developing.

I notice my own complete suspension of disbelief during a dream, a film, or a novel, including Ollivant's *Bob, Son of Battle* even as I was working on it. From this comes the thought that the suspension of disbelief experienced by children, by these young developing people, must be even more powerful. For them, imaginative literature is not read at arm's length, with objectivity. It is experienced emotionally. They live through it, but "safely," and can return, after closing the book, to their own lives. They have experiences, even difficult ones, safely, in their reading.

Like a dream, a well-told, convincing story is experienced, at the time of the reading, as though it were real, and is added to the sum total of a child's life experiences. As the essayist Guy Davenport said of Wittgenstein, we read to multiply our experiences.

Another observation, a recurring one: that we forget so much more than we remember. We forget most of what we read, and we forget most of what we experience. I come from a long line of thrifty women and men, so this bothers me: If we forget most of our experience, then how can we make good use of it? One answer, anyway, must be that it serves to change us, develop us. In the case of children, the most powerful imaginative literature must, even more forcefully, develop their imagination, their capacity for emotion, their empathy, and maybe also their intelligence, their courage, their resilience, and their sense of right and wrong.

Ollivant's book was for me, as a child, one of those powerful works of the imagination. It is not perfect, it is not irreproachable. But it has done certain things very well, well enough to have had a lasting effect on its readers. The reason that I embarked on "translating" it was that I saw it disappearing from sight and did not want it to disappear.

If Ollivant's book was not faultless, neither is my version of it. So, when I compare examples of Ollivant's sentences or phrases to my version, you may prefer the original; I sometimes do, myself.

THE BOOK

Ollivant's 1898 children's classic was long declared to be— and still is, by some—one of the great dog stories of all time, if not the greatest. One reviewer, E. V. Lucas, writing in *The Northern Counties Magazine* soon after the book was published, felt that this was the first time "full justice" had been done to a dog as a character in fiction. He declared that "*Owd Bob* is more than a dog story; it is a dog epic."

Bob, Son of Battle is set in the county of Cumbria, in Northern England, in the wild Daleland country close to the Scottish border, within a sheepherding community. The plot centers upon the rivalry between two sheepdogs—the noble Owd Bob, last of a long line of champions, gentle and patient, and the pugnacious, ill-tempered, ugly mongrel Red Wull—along with their masters and the boy who is caught in the middle, the son of one man but devoted to the other. Depicted in the most extreme terms, throughout, is the contrast between the character of the good master, James Moore, with his good dog, Owd Bob, and that of the violent father, M'Adam, with his mongrel, Red Wull, though both dogs and both masters are extraordinarily adept at the exacting skill of herding sheep.

Other important elements in the story are the unfolding

mystery as to which dog is killing sheep during the night; the death of not just one, but two loving mothers, one during the novel and one recollected; the yearly sheepherding trials and the competition for the coveted Shepherds' Trophy; the strong ties that form between a man and his dog, of which there are many examples in the book; the sheepherding culture in general; the vividly evoked, sparsely populated landscape of moors, lakes, and streams; the life of the village, including the tenant-landlord relations of the time; and, more generally, that slice of English society in the late nineteenth century with its rigid class hierarchy.

At the heart of the book, however—the most moving and complex aspect of the story, for me as a child and no doubt for many—is the difficult relationship between the boy David and his bereaved, hard-drinking father, and alongside this, perhaps even more compelling, the close bond between that father, a lonely, embittered little man, and his mongrel, generally regarded by the villagers as a brute and a renegade. For a part of the power of the book lies in the complicating strain of good, and even heroism, that runs through the malevolent or monstrous, both within the man and within the dog.

MY FIRST READING OF IT

I first read *Bob, Son of Battle*, as I'll call it, since that is the title by which I knew it, when I was ten or twelve years old. But I never forgot the story or the experience of reading it. It was deeply moving to me, like certain other books I read in my childhood at about that age, such as *The Garden Behind the Moon*, *The Yearling*, *The Hobbit*, *Hans Brinker, or the Silver Skates*, the novels of C. S. Lewis, *The Secret Garden* and others by Frances Hodgson Burnett, *Five Children and It* and others by E. Nesbit, two by George MacDonald, Oscar Wilde's *The Happy Prince*, Kate Seredy's *The Good Master*, Johanna Spyri's *Heidi*, and many more.

THE BOOK SEEMED TO HAVE BEEN FORGOTTEN

Even though I had never forgotten *Bob, Son of Battle*, I began to think that not many people knew it anymore. The story had had a strong hold on generations of readers after it first appeared, was published in the hundreds of thousands of copies, was made into a movie no fewer than four times, and is still in print in several editions, and yet it appeared now to be sinking into oblivion. It was not commonly mentioned in lists of classic children's books, in fact I saw its name nowhere. I had been asking my friends, acquaintances, and colleagues, including enthusiasts of sheepherding trials, if they had read the book, but they had not even heard of it. I was sure few children had ever opened it. I wondered if that was because the language of the book was simply too hard to read nowadays. As a child, I was moved to tears by it despite this, impelled by the power of the story. So were other children in those years, the 1950s, as well as both earlier and later (the *Reader's Digest* condensed version of 1968 retains the difficult dialogue). I thought that perhaps only the rare child would make the effort now, and so I felt my choice was clear: do nothing, and a good book would gradually be forgotten; or "translate" the text into easier English, however much of a betrayal that might be, and give it a new life.

THE LANGUAGE OF THE BOOK

The language in which the book is narrated is of an earlier time, with more complex constructions and more sophisticated vocabulary; and the speech of the characters is mostly in Scots and Northern English dialect. And though this was evidently not an insurmountable obstacle to earlier readers, those of today, particularly children, were less patient, I thought, less tolerant of "difficult" words, and more easily distracted; they might not expect to persist in reading their way through and beyond baffling sentences in pursuit of an exciting story.

On one website, the book is advertised as appropriate for the fourth-grade reading level, ages nine and up. But a few features of the book make it hard going even for some adults. Ollivant's style, though generally clear and vivid, even graceful, includes a few features, such as a fondness for inversion, that make for confusing reading; his vocabulary is very much of his time (*reckoned* for "believed"), or is sometimes impenetrably British for an American reader (*chaff* for "tease"), or a little sophisticated for today's child (*élan, epithet, antipathy, wraith*). It includes the vocabulary of professions or functions that have disappeared from, or were never a part of, our culture, such as that of the drover. The story may rely on references that few readers now would understand ("for the gray dog had picked up the puppy, like a lancer a tent-peg"). But the most serious obstacle to an easy immersion in this dramatic, emotionally charged story is the prevalence of Cumbrian dialect in most of the dialogue, along with Scots dialect in the speech of David's father. There is possibly only one character, the local pastor, who speaks in more or less standard English.

Here is a sampling of comments from some reviewers,

both baffled and enthusiastic, on a couple of book-buying sites, most assuming the dialect to be exclusively Scottish:

"It is a hard book to read because of the scottish dialect. (There were some portions of dialog that I could neither say nor understand at all.)"

"It was the book that changed my whole world as a child when it came to reading. After reading it, I started to read more, and more, it was to me what Harry Potter was for my children's generation."

"I read this when I was a kid. I remember struggling with the Scottish dialect, but still liked the book."

"12-year-old me . . . who hunted down and read every dog book in existence, rated this one as the best of them all."

I CONCEIVE THE PROJECT

I did not want the book to disappear, so I had an idea that seemed straightforward enough before I attempted it: I would do a kind of translation of it. I would go through it converting the dialect to standard English and simplifying whatever other difficulties the prose style presented, just enough so that almost everything could be understood more easily.

I did not realize just how many subtle difficulties the project would pose, once I started it. The questions that arose included: How old a reader should I aim for; how easy should I make the prose; which vocabulary would be too daunting, and were there true equivalents that were any easier; would the disturbing material in the book, such as alcoholism or the graphic depictions of dead sheep and dogfights, be acceptable to cautious parents?

ALFRED OLLIVANT AND HOW THE BOOK CAME TO BE WRITTEN

The story of how Alfred Ollivant came to write the book is in itself unusual. He was born in Sussex, England, in 1874, into an upper-middle-class British family part of whose lineage extended back to a village in Cumberland, as it was known then, the county in which the novel is set. Many of the men in the family were career military officers, and he himself was planning to follow their example. After attending Rugby School, he had been groomed at the officers' training school at Woolwich, where he did well. He had graduated as a senior gunner with a prize in horseback riding, and was, like his father, his older brother, two first cousins, and an uncle who had fought in the Indian uprising of 1857, headed for a career in the British army. After he received his commission in the Royal Artillery, at the age of nineteen, he was spending several weeks at home on leave, gathering what he would need to take with him when he joined his artillery unit, when, "out hacking," as his granddaughter reports, he had a bad fall from his horse; in the words of a friend of his, he "took a toss on a hard road." In this fall he severely injured his spine. His injury was complicated by tuberculosis, and his recovery was to be long and slow; for the first fourteen years, he was an invalid under the care of doctors and live-in nurses.

Evidently, Ollivant did not immediately realize that he would have to give up his hopes for a military career, since he did not formally resign his commission for another two years. He must then have seen that if he recovered at all, he might never be strong enough for life in the army.

OLLIVANT READS ROBERT LOUIS STEVENSON

Because of his injury, Ollivant had to spend his days lying flat on his back, in what one commentator called a "mattress grave." There was very little he could do but read. He was one day making his way through Robert Louis Stevenson's 1887 *Memories and Portraits*, a collection of short pieces recalling events of Stevenson's youth, when he came upon a true story, in "Pastoral," told by an old shepherd.

When he was a young man, Stevenson used to take long walks over a hill called Allermuir, in the rolling Pentlands to the southwest of the city of Edinburgh, and there he often encountered this shepherd, whose name was John Todd. Although the old man was generally impatient with city people out walking in the countryside, and looked sourly upon the world in general, he and young Stevenson grew to be friends. Stevenson would walk with Todd and watch him at his work. On one of their walks, the old shepherd told him the story of a fine sheepdog he had known, young, talented, quick to learn. It was not his, but one belonging to another shepherd.

But this dog, as may happen to even the best of them, had turned into something shepherds dread, and that was a sheep-killer. As John Todd told Stevenson, it would go roaming far away from its own master's land and flocks, find a sheep from another flock, and kill it. The way Todd discovered it was this: as he was resting one day under a bush, near a small pool used for bathing sheep, he saw a young collie come skulking down the hillside, as though secretly. He knew the dog. What was it doing so far from home, and why did it look so guilty? John Todd watched as it came to the water's edge and then plunged in, washing from its mouth and head the evidences of its crime, the "maculation of sheep's blood," as Stevenson describes it. Now Todd had to tell the owner of the dog what he had seen. And that was the end of that young sheepdog—"for alas!" as Stevenson continues, "he was that foulest of criminals under trust, a sheep-eater." The guilty dog "was had out to a dykeside and promptly shot," because once a dog turns into a sheep-killer, it will never change.

The germ of *Bob, Son of Battle* was evidently planted at that moment. Young Ollivant, no more than twenty or twenty-one at the time, a dog-lover from his childhood and well acquainted with the north country of England, was moved and impressed and formed the idea of writing a similar tale himself. Slowly healing, often in pain, lying flat on his back with a writing board fixed across his chest, most usually out in the garden—for the doctors had prescribed large doses of fresh air—and now and then losing pages to the wind, he began work on what he had planned as a short story but which grew into a novel. It took him three years to write it—seven drafts in all. As one of Ollivant's early critics commented, "Literature owes a great deal to enforced idleness, whether the writer be sick or in prison."

PUBLICATION OF *OWD BOB*

When he was finished writing the novel, Ollivant sent it to publishers in both the United States and England. It appeared in 1898, when he was only twenty-four, and was called *Bob, Son of Battle* in the United States, while in England, its full title was *Owd Bob—Being the Story of Bob, Son of Battle, the Last of the Grey Dogs of Kenmuir*. The English publisher asked him to rewrite the book and change several parts of it. In the English version, the book starts with M'Adam lying drunk on the kitchen floor with his old dog

Cutty Sark. In the American version, it starts with the farm-hands of Kenmuir at work in the barnyard. Red Wull as a puppy comes into M'Adam's life differently in the English version: M'Adam finds him out in the hills, crouching in the grass by the side of his dead mother. In the American version, a man passing through town is offering him for sale in the local tavern. The most important scenes, though, and the end of the story, are the same in the two versions.

ITS SUCCESS, DIFFERENT EDITIONS OF THE BOOK, AND CRITICAL RECEPTION

In England, the book attracted little attention at first, while in America, it was a success almost right away, described by one newspaper, within a few months of publication, as "probably the greatest literary sensation of the year." A decade or more later, it was acknowledged as a classic in England, too. It continued to be bought and read by hundreds of thousands of people, adults and children alike. It was made into a British silent film in 1924; a talkie under the title *Owd Bob* (aka *To the Victor*), in 1938; the Technicolor *Thunder in the Valley* (aka *Shepherd of the Valley, Bob Son of Battle*), in 1947; and a more recent production also called *Owd Bob*, set on the Isle of Man, in 1997. Because of its decades of popularity, many hardcover and paperback editions of the book exist, and also other versions: one heavily abridged and rewritten in *Famous Dogs in Fiction*; a drastically shortened picture book for young children; a Dell comic book giving the author's name as Oliphant; and a few others shorter and sometimes simpler than the original. Movie memorabilia exist in the form of "lobby cards" from the 1947 movie as shown in Mexico (*Hogares sin madre*—No Mothers in the Home); and at least

one Lon McCallister Bob Son of Battle Rare Signed Auto-
graph Photo Dixie Cup lid has been offered for sale on the
internet.

Thirty years after the book's publication, in 1928, William Lyon Phelps, a Yale professor and speaker on the lecture
circuit, wrote, in an article about dog literature, "The two
most remarkable dogs I ever met in fiction are both in *Bob,
Son of Battle*—the hero, Bob the Gray Dog of Kenmuir, and
the villain Red Wull. Their continued rivalry has an epic force
and fervor. It is the eternal strife between the Power of Light
and the Power of Darkness." He commented that wherever
he spoke, touring the United States, he had only to mention the name of the book to evoke "a wave of delighted
recognition."

OLLIVANT AFTER BOB, SON OF BATTLE

As for Alfred Ollivant, he wrote several more books during his
years as an invalid and afterward, publishing novels, poems,
and articles for journals. He did eventually walk again, marry,
and have a child, as well as travel, especially to Switzerland
for the mountain air, but he was not in good health. He died
of tuberculosis in 1927, at the age of fifty-two, leaving a wife
and a ten-year-old daughter.

THE QUALITY OF THE BOOK

An overview by one J. P. Collins, published in 1920 in *The
Bookman*, described it thus: "The gamut of emotion in *Owd
Bob* rings true throughout . . . [The author's] prose beats
with a compelling power; if the dialect is serrated, it cuts

through every obstacle; and as for the picturing of mood and landscape and storm, it shows a master's touch."

The book is solid in its construction and offers variety: chapter openings vary from the long, historical view to the close-up, dramatic scene. Suspense is maintained throughout, complex characters are developed in relation to twists of the plot and they in turn influence, by their natures and actions, the progress of the story. The setting of the action is evoked through detailed descriptions and references to features of the landscape; Ollivant is good at close observation of detail, whether in a person, animal, or landscape, so that all are vividly present.

Stylistically, the writing is graceful and economical, much of the time. There is a refreshing mix of long, complex sentences and brisk shorter ones. The dialogue is expressive and dramatic. Ollivant is finely attentive to the sounds of the language, as in this well-balanced sentence, with its parallel structure and alliteration, which appears during a description of one of the sheepherding trials: "Sheep should be humored rather than hurried; coaxed rather than coerced."

A minor flaw, as I see it, is that the men who gather in the local tavern, functioning as a sort of Greek chorus, never seem to talk or think of anything else but the central elements of the plot, namely Owd Bob's prowess and fine character, the contrast between the upstanding James Moore and the weaselly M'Adam, and so on. The scenes are well done, but Ollivant does not involve the men, for the sake of realism, in talk of mutton prices, sheep diseases, or taxation.

Occasionally, though not often, there is a touch of sentimentality in this book as in other, later ones of Ollivant's. I did not change this formulation of his: "spring already shyly kissing the land." But I did take the liberty, further along in the book, of modifying his description of cottages "cuddled in the bosom of the Dale" to "huddled in the shelter of the Dale"—still a personification, but one degree less sweet.

Besides the more complex central characters, there are a host of minor characters, colorful, one-dimensional figures who nevertheless act true to type and are marked by convincing individuality. Admirably, too, a number of the dogs in the book, besides the central two, are deftly characterized in the course of the story or during the scenes of the competitions, so that they stand out individually and even memorably, making the climactic fight toward the end of the book all the more moving.

THE CHARACTERS IN THE BOOK, COMPLEX AND LESS COMPLEX: M'ADAM AND MOORE

As for Ollivant's characters, the book purports to be about the good dog, Owd Bob, of a "sad-eyed, silver-coated" breed, as one commentator described it, along with his master, James Moore, but the focus, the emotional center of interest of the book, is very much the other master, Adam M'Adam, and his dog, Red Wull, also called the Tailless Tyke. The book is titled after the one, and begins and ends with that one, and yet the other takes over much of the space of the pages. It is the good people who are relatively bland and featureless, not quite real, and the troubled one who, with his internal struggles, captures our imagination. To quote William Lyon Phelps again, this time writing in 1910, on M'Adam: "This bitter and lonely wretch is a real character, and his strange personality is presented with extraordinary skill." And about his dog: "Red Wull is the hero of a hundred fights . . . The death of the Tailless Tyke is positively Homeric."

The reviewer E. V. Lucas describes the "steady enmity

on the one side and steady tolerance on the other . . . Adam M'Adam [being] the steady enemy, and James Moore the forgiving object of his hatred." He felt that "Mr. Ollivant's greatest claim to distinction [was] the creation of this man" and that "the little man's reality is extraordinary."

Part of the mastery of the character depiction is the complexity of M'Adam, the embattled Scot, as he sees himself, surrounded by his enemies, the English, and the stark contradictions within his character: his distrust of other men and his tenderness for the wife he has lost; his bond with his dog and his jealousy of his son's attachment to Moore; his love of the poetry of Robert Burns and his loss of faith in God. He is strong, courageous, a hard worker, expert at handling his sheep; he has some sense of honor and chivalry. There are several moments in the story when it seems possible that with just a little love and patience, and help from others, the troubled man might have changed; a possible turning point comes, and then the opportunity vanishes in a misunderstanding. Fate was against M'Adam—things had not gone his way. And the same is true of Red Wull, who was, as the preface to the *Reader's Digest* edition of the book put it, "a splendid worker for all his evil temper," loyal to his master, loving and defending him and craving his affection and attention. It is Red Wull, too, who saves a child from drowning and rescues a woman astray in a blizzard. It was not really the fault of that fierce and courageous tiny puppy—"a little tawny beetle of a thing," as Ollivant describes him early on, with "a natural attitude of grisly defiance"—that he grew up to be what he was.

Ollivant chose to depict James Moore, his family, and his dog, on the other hand, as impossibly good. "In the duel between these men there is no comparison," writes Collins, "for the stunted misanthrope, McAdam, outweighs his neighbour in intensity and grip. James Moore is simply a type of magnanimity, like a speaking shadow out of some old morality play; but the widowed hermit with the idolatrous belief in a hound that plays him false, is passionately real in every snarl. Like Shylock and Milton's Satan, Adam is so far supreme from the dramatic standpoint that you forget the moral claim of his antagonist."

E. V. Lucas remarks of Moore that "a blemish or two would have saved him." The reviewer admits that his sympathies lie with Adam M'Adam. He finds Moore's goodness "boring"; "the rectitude of James Moore and the almost clockwork merits of Owd Bob are insipid." Perhaps Ollivant himself was more drawn to the tragically twisted character.

In fact, we come to know M'Adam and his inner life, his mind and emotions, much better than we do those of James Moore, and M'Adam's mind, with his strong biases, his defiance of God, his love of Burns's poetry, and his loyalty to his native Scotland, is not just more complex but richer and more interesting than the mind and heart of James Moore as far as we are allowed to glimpse them.

THE STEREOTYPING OF WOMEN

Another touch of sentimentality shows up, perhaps, in a weakness that Ollivant corrected in later work: his tendency to idealize women. He accepted some of the conventions of his time, and he was young—his attitude, as displayed in his later writing, was to change. In *Owd Bob*, the female characters, without exception, are gentle moral guides, tidy and clean in their persons and housekeeping, kindhearted and understanding, the younger girls modest, demure, sometimes mischievous or silly, and the older women compassionate and motherly.

In his later books, this tendency is rarely in evidence: Ollivant gives us fully developed women and girls—ambitious, courageous, humorous, and physically bold. In fact, his thoroughly enjoyable 1918 novel *Boy Woodburn*, published within a couple of years after the birth of Ollivant's only child, is the story of a girl by that name who, an expert horseback rider, disguises herself as a male jockey, rides in the Grand National at Aintree, and wins, on a horse acquired by her father from a "gypsy." If that plot sounds familiar, I strongly suspect that Enid Bagnold, aged about twenty-nine when the book appeared, and working during the war as either a nurse in England or a driver in France, was inspired not only by Ollivant's plot but also by the character of Boy Woodburn's strong mother, when she came to write her own book *National Velvet* (1935) many years later.

SCENES THAT REPEATED

Is the book a little overheavy on certain types of scenes? M'Adam alone drinking, M'Adam and his son confronting each other, the men as they gathered in the tavern?

But then, I was reading very slowly, as I translated, about six pages an hour, because I was working on the text, struggling to find equivalents for certain vocabulary, stopping to look words up in the dictionary, compiling one glossary of dialect words and another of difficult words, as well as making a list of topics that might require a note, and also stopping to research those topics. I would get pleasurably lost in that research, staring at old pictures of cattle drovers on their way to London or reading old newspaper articles about high-society weddings. So a scene that might have flown by if I had been reading along at my usual pace was likely to seem slower and more repetitious because I was paying so much attention to it.

"TRANSLATING" THE BOOK INTO MORE STANDARD AND SIMPLER ENGLISH

The aim of a translation, most generally, is to make a work available to another group of readers, and this was also my aim in the case of this more unusual translation. I am used to the practice of writing in English something that exists in another language. But it is actually harder, I have found now, over the course of three experiments, to convert one kind of English into another kind.

I did not know exactly what to call what I was doing. I was not translating Ollivant's Victorian English into contemporary English, since I was touching it as little as possible; I was not Americanizing it, since I wanted to leave it British. There were passages that I did not change at all, so would it be right to call this "a new version"? The term "adaptation," for what I was doing, bothered me, because what was I adapting it to? No single term seemed quite right. In the end, "version" seemed close enough, since a version does not necessarily have to be extremely different from the original.

COMPROMISE

I did not, in fact, feel that I was a traitor, as I labored over the million little decisions any translation involves; I was doing my best to serve the original. I was not betraying the original, but my version was probably paler, or tamer. But translation does involve compromise, a willingness to accept trade-offs and imperfection. As I have worked on translations from other languages, the challenge has almost always been to reproduce every feature of the original as closely as I could, while still writing expressive English. In the project of translating from Ollivant's English, the challenge was to replace the more difficult language with a clear, readable, more contemporary text, without losing the style of Ollivant's book, the feel of the time in which it was written, or the place where the story was set. I would be making as few changes as I could, preserving the grace and rhythm of the original. Many sentences or parts of sentences in the narration, though few in the dialogue, would remain intact. I would attempt to preserve the force and character of the speech, and even the word order where possible, and merely convert the dialect into standard English, leaving a word or two of the colloquial speech—easy enough for the reader, for instance, would be "ye" for "you" or "ay" for "yes"—to give a flavor of the original. I might also retain some ungrammatical constructions: "I didn't know yo' was theer" became "I didn't know you was there." It is not that the reader couldn't figure out the original sentence, but that the original would be more daunting.

After some hesitation, I also decided to change the names of some of the characters very slightly to make the reading less cumbersome and to rid the page of some of its many apostrophes: M'Adam would become McAdam and the farmhand Sam'l would become Sammel. If these changes were trivial or entirely unnecessary, as perhaps they were, this is an example of the problem I faced, of where to draw the line between necessary and unnecessary changes. Lastly,

I gave the book a new title, one that combined the American and the English.

CHANGING THE DIALECT TO STANDARD ENGLISH: NORTHERN ENGLISH

Burnett's *The Secret Garden* introduces the broad Yorkshire speech of Dickon and his family and explicitly points to the problem it poses to outsiders, because it is new to the main character, Mary, who has come to England from colonial India. She likes it and teaches herself to speak it. In *Bob*, the dialect is simply there, as a natural part of the locality; it is up to the reader what to make of it.

We might know some words, like *summat* ("something"), *nowt* ("nothing") or *ken* ("know"), from *The Secret Garden*, for example. We can guess at some words; they read, often, like a phonetic spelling of a familiar word with a different pronunciation, or nearly: *feyther* ("father"), *welly* ("really"), *thowt* ("thought"), *doon* ("down"), *owd* ("old"), *ghaist* ("ghost"), *oot* ("out"), *tak* ("take"), *larn* ("learn"), *guid* ("good"), *git* ("get"), *masel* ("myself").

But others are quite unlike the standard equivalents: *wame* for "belly," *maun* or *mun* for "must," *ony gate* for "at any rate, anyway," *cobby* for "headstrong, obstinate," *wambly* for "wobbly," *wag* for "to lurch or sway," *gradely* for "fine, excellent."

There are Scottish and Northern English dialect words that I've seen elsewhere, before, but forgotten the meaning of, like *willie-waught* ("a draft of ale").

(In fact, of course, I have actually encountered all these words before, since I have read the book before, but it was part of an experience I can no longer completely reach in memory.)

We encounter also *waesucks* ("alas"), *hafflins* ("half"), *snash* ("insult"), *stirk* ("ox"), *corbie* ("crow"—similar to the French *corbeau*), as well as phrases and whole sentences quite impenetrable: to "dree one's weird" (to "endure one's fate"); or "It's no cannie ava!" ("It's not clever at all!"); or—spoken by one of James Moore's farmhands when he catches Adam M'Adam skulking about the farmyard, "Noo, rin whoam" ("Now, run along home"). A longer piece of that speech is: "But theer! yo'm sic a scrappety bit." Another representative sentence: "Tis but yon girt off" ("It has only wandered off somewhere"—I think).

There is also, now and then, a bit of British slang, as, for instance, *moke* for "donkey"; or *wigging* for "scolding."

ADAM M'ADAM'S SCOTTISH DIALECT

Adam M'Adam is a transplant from over the border in Scotland and uses words not always understood even in the north of England, such as *fash* for "worry, trouble, bother," *gin* meaning "if," *haud* meaning "hold," *ilka* for "every," *forbye* for "besides," *aiblins* for "maybe," *gey* for "very," and *fecht* for "fight." To him, *naethin' ava* means "nothing at all." Speaking to his dog, Red Wull, as he often does in the book, he says about his son David: "I've tholed mair fra him, Wullie, than Adam M'Adam ever thocht to thole from ony man." Meaning: "I've endured more from him, Wullie, than Adam M'Adam ever thought he would have to endure from any man." Another example of M'Adam's speech: "Aiblins his puir auld doited fool of a dad kens mair than the dear lad thinks." This I translated into more standard English as "Maybe his poor old fool of a dad knows more than the dear lad thinks."

SPECIALIZED VOCABULARY

Then, adding to the difficulties, there is a good deal of specialized and regional vocabulary: from sheep husbandry (*drench, husk, hoose, wether, gimmer, tup, hogg*); from farm or rural life (*lurcher, brace*); from features of the landscape of Cumbria (*fell, ghyll, tarn, spinney, mere, dell, eminence, covert, beck, knowe, march,* and *scaur*); and the weather (*sea fret*—a wet mist or haze coming inland from the sea). We have vocabulary from professions or functions which have disappeared from our culture, for the most part, such as that of the drover—one who drives livestock over very long distances to market. Or from industry of the past: at one point, in response to a remark of M'Adam's, James Moore's face is described as "hard as the nether millstone." Or from heraldry: in one highly dramatic moonlit scene, after a sheep-killing, we see Red Wull emerged from the shadows, "a huge dim outline as of a lion *couchant.*"

There are unfamiliar terms related to customs that may have for the most part disappeared, such as the *minute-bell*, which was a bell tolled to give notice of a death or funeral. As M'Adam watches David go off in the rain, after the death of James Moore's wife, "there began the slow tolling of the minute-bell in the little Dale church." I changed this very slightly, substituting an "explanation" for the unfamiliar term: "There began the slow tolling of the funeral bell, once every minute, in the little Dale church."

If I chose not to retain a word, I would often supply

the definition instead: in place of *scaur* I might write "steep, rocky place." For *fell*, I might instead write "stretch of open country"; for *ghyll*, I might substitute "ravine."

The first sentence of the book, in the original, reads: "The sun stared brazenly down on a gray farmhouse lying, long and low in the shadow of the Muir Pike; on the ruins of peel-tower and barmkyn, relics of the time of raids, it looked; on ranges of whitewashed outbuildings; on a goodly array of dark-thatched ricks."

I thought the two architectural terms *peel-tower* and *barmkyn* might stop a reader from diving into the book. More words I thought too difficult were *brazenly*, *ranges*, *a goodly array*, and *ricks*, so, after undoing an inversion and making other changes, the first sentence in my version reads: "The sun stared boldly down on a gray farmhouse lying long and low in the shadow of the sharp summit of Muir Pike; it shone on the ruins of a fortified tower and a rampart, left from the time of the Scottish raids; on rows of white-washed outbuildings; on a crowd of dark-thatched haystacks."

UNFAMILIAR WORDS AND NAMES

Then, there were nondialect words unfamiliar to me, such as *humorsome* meaning "whimsical," *ahint* meaning "behind," or *lightsome* meaning "shining, glowing, radiant, or luminous."

The "Royal Stand-backs" was the name given to an imagined army regiment of cowards: last onto the field of battle, and first off. A *cateran* was a member of a band of brigands and marauders in the Scottish highlands.

FAMILIAR WORDS USED IN UNFAMILIAR WAYS

The book also included a number of familiar words that Ol-livant used in ways now mostly strange to us. *Faculty*, for instance, once meant "trade" or "occupation"; *traffic* could also mean "trade," or "business." *Pertness* could also mean "high-spiritedness," or "impudent boldness."

Some sentences might be misunderstood now for this reason, as in the case of *crack* in the following: "For no man can lose in a crack the friend of a dozen years and remain unmoved." *Crack*, here, means "moment," as in "the crack of dawn." I had used the latter phrase for years, but did I ever stop to think what *crack* meant? I may have assumed it meant something like "sudden appearance." After I became alert to this meaning, I spotted it again, used in this way, in a magazine article: "Attendance was not required at every meeting, or even expected, but at the crack of each opening hour I could be found loosening my coat on the threshold of that month's designated spot."

Some of Ollivant's vocabulary is distinctly that of an ear-lier time—he was, after all, born in 1874, nearly 150 years ago. Because of the intervening years, certain meanings of words have become less common, an example being *reckoned* for "thought, felt, or considered," as in: "Parson Leggy, who was reckoned the best judge of a sheep or sheep-dog 'twixt Tyne and Tweed." Ollivant sometimes uses *without* to mean "outside," as in a scene where Moore's daughter attempts a visit to M'Adam: "There she . . . lifted a warning finger at her companion, bidding him halt without." In this sentence, one could change the less familiar *bidding*, *halt*, and *without* so that the sentence read, "asking him to stay outside."

Another example, from a scene depicting one of the sheepherding trials, is the word *hedge* meaning to "press thickly" or "crowd": "By this time there was a little naked space of green round the bridge-head, like a fairy circle . . . Round this the mob hedged."

At times, Ollivant's vocabulary is too British for an American to understand, as in his use of *chaff* for "tease." David is often found visiting Moore's farm: "On these occasions he loved best to sit on the window-sill outside the kitchen, and talk and chaff with Tammas and the men in the yard." Phrases occur in nonstandard or variant forms, such as "you live on me" ("you live off me") and "the two on you" ("the two of you").

STANDARD BUT RARE

I would also come upon standard English words less often encountered, such as *titivate* (nothing to do with *titillate*) or *hobbledehoy*. One day I would encounter *affray*, the next, *fleer*. And then, *meed*, *wang*, *ruck*, *swag* (when used as a verb), or *scud*. I looked up each word—I had to, so that I could "translate" it; and I established an extensive glossary to keep track of the words I was finding, along with their meanings. To help with this, I used several Scots-English dictionaries online, and some Cumbrian word-lists.

Other words were somewhat familiar to me, but not common—unknown, for instance, to my dinner companions one evening, sophisticated and seasoned writers and readers all, when I tried out a couple of them: *anent* and *asseverate*. More of those borderline words, which we encounter now and then but wouldn't be able to define, might include *debouch* (not *debauch*), *worsted*, and *inanition*. On some days

I know what *contumely* means—or, I should say, when encountered in certain contexts—on other days, or without a context, I don't.

And finally, there are those words that are well understood by adults but that a child today is not likely to understand: *infamous, conclave, crux, surly, surmise, vigilance, sardonic, taunt, gibe, immolate, aghast, élan, epithet, antipathy, wraith, smithy, erstwhile, hearken, paean, mortification, dallying, wizened, derelict, musketoon, impugn*, and so on.

OTHER DIFFICULTIES: INVERSIONS

Ollivant's style, though generally clear and vivid, includes one stylistic feature more common to the time in which he was writing the book, the mid-1890s, and that is the use of inversions. This could make for a momentary awkwardness in the reading of a sentence. I tended to turn the inversions around to make the sentence easier.

Some were not difficult—"But what cared he?" became "But what did he care?" "Dared hardly contemplate" became "Hardly dared to imagine." "Sometimes he could restrain himself no longer" became "Sometimes he could no longer restrain himself." But other instances of inversion could be quite challenging, such as: "Then had there been done something worse than sheep-murder."

The placement of an adverb might feel like an inversion of the more natural order, as in the opening of a paragraph describing David's changed relations with Moore's daughter Maggie: "David had now a new interest." English word order is so flexible that there are no fewer than three alternatives that seemed to me easier: "David now had a new interest," "Now David had a new interest," and "David had a new interest now." Of course, these sorts of changes were not vitally necessary, or would not have been had they not been embedded in narration, and dialect dialogue, that presented other difficulties.

COMBINATION OF DIFFICULT SENTENCE STRUCTURE AND UNFAMILIAR VOCABULARY

There were sentences that combined two types of difficulties, a complex construction with a couple of unfamiliar words. In one of the climactic scenes, we have the sentence: "Up and down the slope the dark mass tossed, like some hulk the sport of the waves."

I try to imagine how a child might read this. She might understand the first part—"up and down the slope the dark mass tossed"—since she knows there is a fight going on—in fact it is the fight to the death, at the end of the book. What happens then, when the young reader does not understand *hulk*—not in the sense Ollivant meant it, as "ship"—or *sport*—again not in the sense he meant it, as "plaything"—and then comes to *waves*, which presumably would bewilder her when combined with the rest of the sentence: Ollivant is comparing the whirling mass of fighting dogs to a boat being tossed by rough waves. I imagine she would simply accept the words into her brain without trying to fit them together in any way. Does she enjoy the words in themselves, and the vague image of waves doing something to this dark mass, or does she skip over the words and go on without responding? How do our brains deal with passages in which some of what we read we don't understand?

CHANGING A COMPLICATED SENTENCE

Here is another example of a sentence that combined more than one difficulty—a somewhat complicated idea expressed in sophisticated vocabulary: "The heat of the Dalesmen's enthusiasm was only intensified by the fever of their apprehension." I thought *apprehension* would be beyond some readers, especially when used within the illness metaphor— "fever of their apprehension"—and then further combined within the overall image: heat intensified by fever. The following, although not much changed, might be easier: "The Dalesmen's enthusiasm was all the stronger because of their feverish anxiety."

During this project, I kept putting myself in the place of the less experienced reader. At a certain point, however, I became confused: as I progressed through the book, I saw more and more difficulties in the vocabulary and sentence structures and found myself changing more and more of the language. Then I had to step back and reevaluate what I was doing. I was heading down an impossible path: by the standards I was establishing, I would have to recast every sentence, every phrase. So I tried to return to a middle path, changing only the most difficult things, allowing some of the less difficult to remain.

Deciding when to leave in a "difficult" word also clarified for me which of these difficult words were not essential to understanding the story—for instance, I could leave in difficult adjectives, adjectives one doesn't have to know. The last part of the opening sentence reads: "on ranges of whitewashed outbuildings; on a goodly array of dark-thatched ricks." The adjectives *whitewashed* and *dark-thatched* could be left. Confronting the difficulties also led me to observe at which points the story was exciting enough to allow for the inclusion of a "difficult" word. My working principle, concerning vocabulary and sentence structures, then became to simplify the more complex sentence structures and allow a few difficult words when they occurred in a familiar, "easy" context, so they would not be daunting.

REFERENCES, BURIED ALLUSIONS OR QUOTES, AND EPITHETS

Ollivant's story includes references or embedded quotations that today's reader, brought up in a different culture, would be less likely to recognize. For instance, there is the word *Bedlam* when used to refer, not generally to "chaos" but specifically, historically, to London's Bethlem Royal Hospital for the insane. Or there is *Taffies*, for which I could not find any meaning except possibly that of "Welshmen," if I am correct in making that deduction from the nursery rhyme: "Taffy was a Welshman, Taffy was a thief; Taffy came to my house and stole a piece of beef." There are also occasional traditional epithets that readers, if they are not local, will not understand: for instance, Yorkshire being "the county of the broad acres" or the "land of the Tykes."

One type of reference is to figures or places in the Bible, both common and less common: M'Adam is once indirectly compared to Judas Iscariot, and at another point described thus: "He stood entirely alone; a son of Hagar, mocking." He himself calls James Moore's daughter a Jezebel. Owd Bob, as he is keeping watch at the bottom of the stairs while James Moore attends his wife in her dangerous childbirth upstairs, is described in this way: "The dim light fell on the raised head;

and the white escutcheon on his breast shone out like the snow on Salmon," Salmon being a low hill mentioned in the Bible as a source of firewood for burning the nearby city of Shechem.

My solution was to explain indirectly, and as unobtrusively as possible, within the text, what the name or phrase referred to. I would not ordinarily do this in a translation from another language, since my ideal is not to add anything that was not in the original text. I learned only a few years ago that it is called "stealth-glossing," a term that is satisfyingly melodramatic and precise at the same time.

So I have amplified the text here and there with a little description of local color that I did not want either to leave mysterious or to omit: for instance, I identified the rivers in the phrase "'twixt Tyne and Tweed"; and added a few words to the mention of a peewit, so that "whistled a shrill, peculiar note like the cry of a disturbed peewit" became "like the cry of the black-and-white moorland lapwing when startled from its nest"; and added a more substantial phrase to suggest the work a drover does: whereas the original reads, in a list of the men in the tavern, "and one long-limbed, drover-like man—a stranger," I have written: "and a long-limbed fellow, a stranger, who had the look of a drover, that is, one of those hardy and solitary men whose profession it is to drive animals to market over long, lonely distances." *Cairngorms*, from the Scottish Highlands, might be mysterious, so I stealth-glossed them thus, in the description of Red Wull: "Two yellow eyes, glowing in the darkness like cairngorms" becomes "glowing in the darkness like two smoky quartz stones from the Cairngorm mountains."

Since the author now and then offers a comment or an explanation, I felt somewhat justified in intruding occasionally myself, to identify a Biblical reference, for instance, or a quotation from Robert Burns, plentiful in the book. Sometimes the quotation is embedded in the narrative or in M'Adam's speech—a scrap of Biblical text so thoroughly assimilated into everyday language that it is hardly noticeable, such as the phrase "without respect of person," a veiled quotation from 1 Peter 1:17: "And if ye call on the Father, who without respect of persons judgeth according to every man's work." I did not identify buried or assimilated quotations when to do so would have been too pointed or clumsy.

There are allusions to bygone customs or recreations, as in this description of Owd Bob and Red Wull when he is still small: "for the gray dog had picked up the puppy, like a lancer a tent-peg." I read all about lancers, originally cavalrymen armed with lances, and their sport with tent pegs, a game once very popular in the military and still played in various places around the world. I decided not to explain the metaphor, or leave it as it was, but to substitute a different metaphor, one that I thought conveyed somewhat the same image. I compared Owd Bob's move to a swallow snatching an insect out of the air. That was a rare instance of replacing some of Ollivant's text by my own.

MORE ON THE STEREOTYPING OF WOMEN

If I wanted the book to be attractive to modern readers, another, much trickier problem was what to do about the stereotyping of women and the occasional glimpse of sentimentality. I wanted both the characters and the author to be sympathetic. After thinking it over, I decided to take the liberty of changing very slightly a few instances of stereotyping.

I would adjust, here and there, the attitude of the author to the main female character in the story, to the women in general, and even to the boy David.

I should say that in a translation from another language, I would not tamper with the text in this way; I would not adjust the author's attitude, feeling ethically bound to present the book as it was in the original, complete with the author's textual errors or personal prejudices. But my rules were a little different here.

Owd Bob was described early in the book by old Tammas as having "the brains of a man and the way of a woman"—apparently a common formula at the time (it appears twice more). I replaced it more elaborately than usually, since its implication did not make sense to me: that all men are smart and all women are subtle in their manner of coaxing others to do as they wish. This belief is put in the mouth of a character, not advocated by the author; now I'm not sure I would make the change. But I did change it to: "As clever as any person and as gentle as the spring sunshine." The men at the trials, when they begin acting foolish, are compared to "so many giddy girls." I changed this, perhaps unfairly, to "a gang of brainless boys." There are very few such explicit declarations of gender bias in the book, but the attitude is inherent in Ollivant's portrayal of women and girls. The fact that his attitude was so radically different by the time he wrote *Boy Woodburn* might somewhat justify my changes.

As for the portrayal of James Moore, I doubt that I did anything to render him less bland; that would have been going too far in rewriting the original. I do remember portraying David as having "strong fingers" rather than "big fingers" to tip the characterization of the boy just a little more toward the sympathetic.

EPITHETS

I thought of adding epithets whenever certain stock characters reappeared, such as "gloomy" for Sammel Todd, the farmhand, or "glum" for Sexton Ross, or "kindly" for the "lady of the manor." There was, in favor of it, both a certain literary tradition (Homer's "wine-dark sea") and euphony, and the fact that it would help the reader to remember these characters. The epithets would be applied to the name only when the character reappeared after an interval. In the end I never did this, however, because it would have strayed too far from Ollivant's own intentions and writing style.

TYPING WITHOUT CHANGING

There was rarely a paragraph that did not seem to need changing. Yet sometimes, one sentence would follow another in which everything could be left as Ollivant had written it. I was "translating" by typing the text out verbatim. Uneasy, I had to remind myself what the point of the project was, that it included leaving the text alone whenever I could.

UNANTICIPATED PROBLEMS

It was when I encountered the difficult words in the narration and began deliberating over them that I came face-to-face with at least three stubborn and unexpected questions. The first was: How difficult could I allow the words in this book to be? Where would I draw the line between moderately difficult and too difficult to include, or, quantitatively, how many difficult or incomprehensible words should I leave in my version? The second problem: Those "difficult" words simply did not have exact equivalents. There really was no such thing as a true synonym. The third problem was that I could not always define or give even an approximate equivalent for words I thought I knew. I found myself turning constantly to the dictionary to look up words I had been familiar with almost all my reading life, like *gaunt, bedraggled, aghast, haggard,* or *dismay.* I had to know more exactly than ever before what they meant, so that I could substitute for them a simpler word, or perhaps two that, together, would create something like the same image or convey the same meaning.

PROBLEM #1: HOW DIFFICULT SHOULD I ALLOW THE TEXT TO BE?

How old a reader was I directing the book toward, a child of ten or twelve, but also an adult? If so, just how easy should I make the prose? And which vocabulary would be too daunting? If readers did not know *haggard,* they would probably not know *gaunt.* Would they know *conspirator, clad, mangled, mutilated, lacerated*? If they did not know *glower,* they might not know *scowl.* Did I have to rely on the less emphatic *frown* all the time? Speaking of *emphatic,* what is a simple word for *emphasis—stress*?

PROBLEM #2: THERE ARE NO TRUE SYNONYMS

It was at this point, searching for equivalents, that I realized yet again how particular all these words were, and that they had no exact equivalents. Any substitute I chose carried with it a slightly different shade of meaning. *Show* was close enough to *evince*, and *crowd* to *throng*, and *notice* to *remark*, but was *rugged* the same as *craggy*, *hit* the same as *smite*, *again* the same as *afresh*, *closely packed* the same as *serried*, *unfriendly* the same as *hostile*, *scold* the same as *reprove*, *polish* the same as *burnish*, *coolly* the same as *dispassionately*, *shine* the same as *luster*?

PROBLEM #3: WORDS I KNOW
BUT CAN'T DEFINE

In the course of this debate, I found that my working understanding of familiar English vocabulary wasn't quite specific enough when it came to translating a word into something simpler. I knew the word *bedraggled*, functionally, from years of reading and use; I understood it to mean rather disheveled, in rumpled and perhaps torn clothing. But I did not know that it also involved being wet, as though having been dragged through the mud. I knew that a *blunderbuss* was a gun, but not precisely that it had a short, large-caliber barrel and was flared at the muzzle. I learned, from looking it up, that a *hulk* was not just a ship, but one that was large, old, heavy, unwieldy.

I had recently learned more about bracken—which, in this novel, is trampled and soaked in blood during a climactic fight between Red Wull and Owd Bob. I had become familiar with it when comparing earlier English translations of *Madame Bovary*, in which Emma Bovary rides through it with her first lover, Rodolphe. I subsequently saw some actual bracken myself on an autumn walk in the woods. Before that, I had guessed from my reading, wrongly, that it was some kind of rough ground cover, a sort of heather, low-growing and a little prickly, not, as it is, a type of coarse fern. In another novel by Ollivant, bracken appears again, thigh-high to the main character.

How (even if slightly) inaccurate one's understanding of words is: after decades of reading, writing, and translating, I still did not know, until I looked it up, that a wayfarer was usually on foot; or that *gutter* was not restricted in meaning to what runs alongside a road or at the eave of a roof, but could be any furrow or groove. It was a little shocking to think that even those of us who are "literary," whose lives are involved nearly every day with reading and writing, may be using and understanding certain words, perhaps many words, somewhat *approximately*.

DEFINING WORDS: DICTIONARIES

I discovered how inexact my definitions were because I looked up many words in various online dictionaries, hoping there might be lists of useful synonyms that I could access quickly. Looking up a word this way was much quicker than picking up a printed book and turning the pages, and it was perfectly adequate most of the time. One disadvantage was that I had to learn to ignore the ads inviting me to websites for help with heroin addiction or Huntington's disease, or for losing belly fat, or an item about a scandal that might bring down the White House, or about a Mormon "plan of happiness," or simply the question "What's your football fantasy?"

MISGIVINGS

Because I plunged into this project of "translating" *Bob, Son of Battle* without considering it from all angles, several misgivings occurred to me as I went ahead with it, and I had some doubts about what I was doing. I went on, anyway.

MISGIVING #1: THE LOSS OF THE DIALECT ENTAILS LOSS OF COLOR AND TEXTURE

With the standardization of the dialect, and the simplification of some of Ollivant's sentence structures and vocabulary, there would inevitably come—no matter how hard I tried to retain as much of the interest as possible of his style—a diminution of color and texture, particularly in the loss of the vivid regional speech and the nuance of the descriptions, with their naming of local features. As I made these changes, I was experiencing what I had found once before, when I attempted to put the first chapter of Laurence Sterne's *A Sentimental Journey* into modern English, because part of the interest of Sterne's prose lay precisely in the words and constructions he chose to use, and they could not be traded out without harming the sense and spirit of the work.

There was no question that what M'Adam yells after David, who has gone off into the rain with his overcoat—"Tak' it aff at onst, ye muckle gowk"—was more interesting (if less comprehensible) than my rendering of it—"Take it off at once, ye great fool."

MISGIVING #2: YOU DON'T HAVE TO UNDERSTAND EVERY WORD OF A BOOK ANYWAY

What threatened to undermine the whole project, once I realized it, was the idea that it is perfectly all right to read a book that is full of mysterious words and sentences, references and quotations; that I did not in fact need to do what I was doing. I could have left it alone, a treasure to be discovered intact.

Reading without understanding every word is in fact how we readers learn new words. Difficult words are "good" for children, and children don't mind them, or children actually like them. Children may like the dialect, as Mary did in *The Secret Garden* and as did one adult acquaintance of mine who read Ollivant's book when she was a child—she enjoyed learning the dialect or just sounding it out without understanding it.

One may even—as I learned from the experience of another person I talked to about this, which startled me—be moved by words one doesn't understand at all.

Richard Henry Dana, Jr., in *Two Years Before the Mast*, deliberately used a quantity of specialized sailing language that we lay readers would surely not understand, even though part of his aim in writing the book was to show us, from the inside, what the life of a sailor was like. In fact, I think that is why he used that language without explaining it, to bring us right inside the scene in which the sailors (including Dana) were doing their work.

HOW CHILDREN READ: YOU CAN READ RIGHT THROUGH DIFFICULT SPEECH, BUT I WAS AFRAID READERS WOULD ABANDON THE BOOK

Of course, in an exciting book, mysterious words are, or were when I was a child, tolerable to a capable young reader, because they don't generally occur in formidable clusters but are scattered through a narrative otherwise clear enough, and the formidable clusters can be skipped over. Because the story is so powerful, you can read right over these hard words and puzzling expressions and not mind, because you are so eager to know what happens next. That is what I must have done when I first read *Bob, Son of Battle*. In fact, this is the way we learn words, whether quite accurately or not—from reading or hearing a new word in a context in which we understand what it means, either exactly or approximately. One correspondent, after reading about my project, reminded me that children as they grow up are constantly surrounded by language they don't entirely understand, the language of the adult world.

As I was learning foreign languages through reading alone, a few years ago—first Dutch and then Norwegian—I acquired new words sometimes with but usually without the dictionary, from reading them in their contexts. I realized I was more likely to remember them because (1) they were repeated in the story (in a Dutch detective story, for instance, the recurring word *betuignis*, "witness") and (2) they were an integral part of the story that was unfolding, so that after I finished the book I was likely to associate the word with a part of the plot.

I realized at a certain point, as I worked on *Bob, Son of Battle*, that there was actually a close connection between this project, of making Ollivant's book easier to read by translating unfamiliar words, and the project of learning Norwegian solely through reading page after page on which almost all the words were unfamiliar: the aims of the two projects were in fact diametrically opposed.

I still spend too much time regretting some of the ineffective educational methods used with my two sons in various school courses. One was those isolated lists of vocabulary words, twenty each week if I remember rightly, which one teacher used to assign. This was part of a teaching approach—sheer memorization—that looked impressively rigorous but was actually useless. Far superior was a vocabulary-building workbook used in another school that taught a more limited number of words each week by presenting them in various contexts, including word games and exercises, and ending always with a crossword puzzle.

ANSWER TO MISGIVINGS #1 AND #2

But do as many children today still read patiently through language they don't understand? Not everyone will keep going when they come to a hard sentence. They may give up, put the book away, and never return to it. So this became my answer to both of those misgivings: the book in my version might have less color and character, and perhaps there were children and adults who would have read the original, or were reading it, but this version would at the very least bring more readers to a good book and perhaps lead them back to the original *Owd Bob*, to enjoy the speech of Cumberland and Scotland and every word of the story as it was first written.

MISGIVING #3: THE DARKNESS OF THE STORY

I have almost always approached any translation I undertake without reading the text beforehand. There are several reasons for this, but a primary one is to keep my own interest stimulated and thus my prose more alive. I do not know what is ahead on the next page. I kept to this principle in working on *Bob, Son of Battle*. But the problem with working this way, in this case, was that a great many years had passed since I had last read the book, and although I remembered its larger themes and more important characters, I did not remember it in detail.

And so, as I went along, I was surprised by how dark a

story it is, how many scenes there are of violence between father and son, or between dog and sheep, or between dog and dog, or that portray the crowd turning against the individual, or the individual blind drunk on the kitchen floor. A children's book? A book suitable for children? I was struck by another misgiving: here I was, working to bring back into view, mainly for children, a book that would then prove hardly suitable for children.

ANSWER TO MISGIVING #3: THE EXPERIENCE OF THE CHILDREN WHO HAD READ IT

Yet, many children have read the book without apparent harm. One acquaintance of mine in England, a book reviewer, editor, and commentator, read it with her father when she was seven; it was their favorite book. A retired Oxford professor wrote to me that when he was a schoolboy, the book was read aloud to the student body every Sunday evening, to their great enjoyment, by their headmaster. Yet another English correspondent, an elderly Quaker, told me that he had absolutely loved the book at age fourteen but had since then met not a single soul who had heard of it.

ANOTHER ANSWER TO MISGIVING #3: OTHER CHILDREN'S BOOKS WITH DIFFICULT MATERIAL, DIFFICULT SITUATIONS, DIFFICULT ADULT CHARACTERS

But as I review, in my mind, the children's books that left the deepest impressions on me as a child, many or most of them included or even hinged upon difficult material. I did not particularly gravitate toward these themes, since the books I remember are for the most part classics of children's literature. Perhaps the material was not usually as graphic as sheep-killing and recurrent physical combat, but certainly there was a heavy presence of such dark topics as bereavement, loneliness, estrangement within families, death, and poverty. Important characters in the books, both children and adults, were emotionally cold or cruel, deceitful, cowardly, jealous, as well as kind, honest, compassionate, courageous. Usually, of course—in contrast to the case of *Bob, Son of Battle*—the resolution of the story was a positive one. In some, the protagonists return safe from hazardous adventures, but in many others, more important for the emotional effect of the story, adults who have been estranged or hostile warm to the child or another protagonist, or a child's own failings of character—cowardliness, recklessness, meanness, selfishness—gradually weaken and disappear under beneficent influences.

Some of these stories I remember better than others, and some I have dared to reread; not others, for fear that my remembered impressions will be diminished or lost.

CHILDREN IN DIFFICULT CIRCUMSTANCES

Among these books full of dark material, there are some in which children are placed in difficult circumstances: in Twain's *Tom Sawyer* (published in 1876), Tom, a resilient, spunky lad with a conscience and an affectionate nature, and in the care of a loving aunt, is an adopted child, disobedient and naughty a good deal of the time. His friend Huck Finn, loyal, imaginative, and smart, has a situation similar to David's in *Bob, Son of Battle*—living alone with a violent, alcoholic father, though this father, unlike Adam M'Adam, is never shown in a gentler, more thoughtful moment.

In *The Garden Behind the Moon* (1895), by Howard Pyle, the protagonist, David, is an isolated, lonely boy picked on by the other children for being simpleminded, what the children call a "moon-calf." But he dares to walk over the water along the path of light from the moon and discovers another world in which he is not a simpleton but a hero.

The children in *Hans Brinker, or the Silver Skates* (1865) are poor. Poverty is also a burden for the families in *Five Little Peppers and How They Grew* (1881), by Margaret Sidney, as well as in Louisa May Alcott's *Little Women* (published in two volumes, in 1868 and 1869). Sara Crewe in Burnett's *A Little Princess* (1905) loses her wealth and is relegated to the status of school servant, living in a bare attic room and treated with scorn by the other children. Death haunts a number of the books: in Johanna Spyri's *Heidi* (first appearing in serial form in 1880 and 1881), the spirited little heroine is orphaned at the age of five and left abruptly in the care of a grandfather she has never met before. Mary, in *The Secret Garden*, loses her parents and her Indian nanny and is sent to live in her uncle's house in England. In the same book, her cousin Colin has been abandoned emotionally by his father and left in the charge of the servants. Kate, in *The Good Master* (1935), by Kate Seredy, is a motherless girl whose father cannot control her and who is sent to live in the country with relatives she hardly knows.

Some of these children are in difficult situations because of the adults in their lives. How many indifferent or unfriendly adults, in these novels, are won over by good, patient, understanding children? The grandfather in Burnett's *Little Lord Fauntleroy* (first appearing in serial form in 1885 and 1886); the grandfather in *Heidi*; in *The Secret Garden* not only Colin's father but also the old gardener and, to some extent, the housekeeper and the family doctor. In *Hans Brinker*, the ill-natured doctor shows a kindlier side and relents, and the disabled father is restored to health, while the family's poverty is also reversed. In *Rebecca of Sunnybrook Farm* (1903), by Kate Douglas Wiggin, the stern, elderly aunt is softened by the charming and imaginative little girl.

There are adults who do not change. The mother in Marjorie Kinnan Rawlings's *The Yearling* (1938) has been embittered by the loss of a succession of children, and she remains a hard woman, though, crucially to the depiction of her character and our sympathy for her, she displays some rare moments of kindness. In *Bob, Son of Battle*, of course, one of the continuing questions is whether a moment of tenderness in M'Adam's heart will lead to a more understanding relationship between him and his son, but it is not to be. Huck Finn's father, too, does not change.

There are understandable reasons for the hardness of the adults in these stories. Most often the reason is bereavement and subsequent grief—M'Adam has lost his beloved wife, as has the doctor in *Hans Brinker*, Colin's father in *The Secret Garden*, and the mother her children in *The Yearling*. In the case of the English grandfather in *Little Lord Fauntleroy*, he is angry because his son has abandoned his family title and heritage, gone off to America, and married "beneath him"; after his son's death, the positive influence of his little grandson causes him eventually to accept both the boy and his mother.

Then there are children whose own difficult characters are important to the plots of the novels. In *The Good Master*, Cousin Kate, the city girl, wild, reckless, and spoiled, is gradually tamed by the loving, cheerful, and orderly family of her aunt and uncle and by life in the country, often believed, at that time, to be an especially wholesome environment. Her evolution is somewhat similar to that of Mary in *The Secret Garden*, who arrives from India a scrawny, sallow, willful child and who is "cured" by the no-nonsense country ways of the Yorkshire people and, most important, by the effect of the garden and tending it in the healthy outdoor air, as is her counterpart and cousin, Colin.

Complexity of character has an important effect in this: Mary and Colin's selfishness combined with their vulnerability and openness to change; the surliness of the old gardener, who has a soft spot only for a little robin and is reluctantly won over by the children; in contrast, the sunny natures of the boy Dickon and his sister Martha. As for the mother of Dickon and Martha, like mother figures in some of the other books, she is portrayed as goodness itself—patient and resourceful, selfless and even-tempered despite the demands of her many children and her dire poverty. In most of the books I'm thinking of here, mothers seem to be either absent or faultless. In *Bob, Son of Battle*, they are both.

The theme of the curative powers of rural life appears not only in *The Secret Garden* and *The Good Master*, but also in *Heidi*, whose protagonist feels trapped in the confining walls of the city, free and happy on the open mountainside. I wonder about the possible influence of this notion on young readers—though perhaps they have to be predisposed to welcome it.

EVEN IN FANTASY LITERATURE, COMPLEX CHARACTER PLAYS A VITAL ROLE

I see, as I look at other children's books, how important complexity of character is, even in fantasy literature. Bilbo Baggins, the main character in *The Hobbit* (1937), by J.R.R. Tolkien, is an example, displaying, as he does, the conflict between his preference for a life of routine, including a substantial afternoon tea in his comfortable armchair (which appeals to the "Baggins" side of his heritage), and what he is eventually called upon to do, in his high adventure, which develops to the full his intelligence, courage, and resourcefulness (stimulating his mother's, or the "Took," side of his heritage).

Profoundly moving to me, as a child, was the portrait of the boy Edmund in *The Lion, the Witch, and the Wardrobe* (1950), by C. S. Lewis—his weak, deceitful nature, vulnerable to corruption by the evil White Witch. The other children are solidly good: the older brother, Peter, the responsible leader; the older sister, Susan, the "motherly" one; and the younger sister, Lucy, bright, thoughtful, and compassionate. Is it too much to claim that when a child reads this book at an impressionable age, it is the troubled Edmund who interests her the most, in part because of his weakness, in part because of the struggle that is taking place inside him between good and evil?

In other fantasies, for instance in MacDonald's *The Princess and the Goblin* (1872), the emphasis may be more on the incidents of the adventure itself, the great and potent danger hidden within the tunnels of the mountain, and less on the characters of the protagonists: the balance tips toward adventure.

Dramatically, the bad or the evil is a more powerful element. The good is a known, safe quantity, in a sense finished, or uncomplicated; the weak or troubled character is not only dangerous, but also unpredictable, and therefore of higher interest; he or she also carries the potential to change for the better. Edmund, after several more books in the series, becomes a good, strong person. Part of the dramatic tension in *Bob, Son of Battle* lies in the question of whether Adam M'Adam will show his gentler side for long enough, or at the right moment, for David to recognize it.

There were other books I liked but was not profoundly moved by, and perhaps this absence of moral tension was the reason. Among them I could mention the Laura Ingalls Wilder books published between 1932 and 1943—*Little House in the Big Woods*, *Little House on the Prairie*, and others—which portrayed hardships in pioneer family life but were in the end relatively bland, with characters that did not capture my imagination; and two books in the category I could describe as "struggling single mother with brood of lively children": *Little Women* (though the father is alive, he is almost entirely absent); and *Five Little Peppers and How They Grew*, in which a poor family headed by the widowed mother "Mamsie" struggles to get along but does so with unfailing cheerful industry.

It is more and more clear to me that, when we are still growing up and are most impressionable, these stories allow us to enter fully, as a dream does, into another reality that includes experiences otherwise far beyond us in our own lives. When I was a few years older, I lived yet other lives when I read *The Greengage Summer* (1958), by Rumer Godden (beautiful stylist); and the series of Jalna novels by Mazo de la Roche.

ANSWER TO MISGIVING #3: WAS THE BOOK AIMED AT CHILDREN?

One question might remain unclear, about Ollivant's novel: whether he even intended it for children. I responded completely to the book, when I was a child. It is regarded, by long tradition, as a classic for children. But his family are firm in saying that it was not meant for children. It may have been co-opted for the children's market because of its subject matter: dogs are central to it, and two children are among the main characters, growing up neighbors and coming to love each other. Whereas a book may appeal to both children and adults, the marketing people in the publishing world may be the ones who direct the book to one readership or the other.

The Secret Garden is another book that we think of as intended for children, but its first publication, under the working title *Mistress Mary*, was in serial form in an American magazine aimed at adults. In book form, published first in New York, then in London, it was marketed to both adult and juvenile audiences.

There are many examples of "crossover" books—for instance, in our own time, the Harry Potter series and Philip Pullman's epic fantasy *His Dark Materials.* Many adults revert to the company of their childhood favorites—some of which stand up under adult scrutiny while some don't. Anna Sewell, who, like Ollivant, was injured while still young and eventually confined to her bed for long periods, wrote *Black Beauty* (1877)—another book we recommend to children— for an adult audience, with, she said, "a special aim . . . to induce kindness, sympathy, and an understanding treatment of horses." Wittgenstein was reading it on his deathbed.

Perhaps we should remember that there was more of an overlap, one hundred years ago and earlier, between the occupations and interests of adults and children. Adults enjoyed playing parlor games like blindman's buff, while children were given responsibilities we now think of as adult—at the age of twelve, a boy might be hired as cook for a crew of sailors on a months-long voyage; at fourteen, John Quincy Adams served, in Russia, as secretary to the American dip-

lomat Francis Dana; George Washington, at the age of sixteen, worked as a surveyor. Children as young as five are still
expected, in many families, to look after their younger sib-
lings. Sailors, in *Two Years Before the Mast*, played hopscotch
on the beaches of California.

OTHER ADAPTATIONS OR RETELLINGS OF
CHILDREN'S BOOKS: *TREASURE ISLAND*

In answer to my misgivings about my project, I had to remember that my own version of *Bob, Son of Battle* was actually just one more of a number, down the years—evidence of
the book's popularity. Many other popular children's books
have also appeared in simplified or shortened versions. I have
two altered versions of Robert Louis Stevenson's *Treasure
Island* in my library, though not the original.

The opening of the original—one rather long sentence
full of information—is as follows: "Squire Trelawney, Dr.
Livesey, and the rest of these gentlemen having asked me
to write down the whole particulars about Treasure Island,
from the beginning to the end, keeping nothing back but the
bearings of the island, and that only because there is still treasure not yet lifted, I take up my pen in the year of grace 17—,
and go back to the time when my father kept the 'Admiral
Benbow' inn, and the brown old seaman, with the sabre cut,
first took up his lodging under our roof."

In an abridgment that I remember reading to my son
and admiring for its skilled writing, the opening sentence is
broken up into parts. "The bearings of the island," probably judged to be too unfamiliar in its nautical specificity, is
replaced by something blander, and the graphic and pretty
phrase "not yet lifted"—more unexpected than "dug up"—is

also generalized: "Squire Trelawney, Dr. Livesey, and the rest of these gentlemen have asked me to write down the whole story about Treasure Island, from the beginning to the end, keeping nothing back except how to find the island, and that only because there is still some treasure there."

The version in the inexpensive, large-print Stepping Stones Classic paperback summarizes the second part of the sentence: "To begin my story, I must go back to the time when my father kept the Admiral Benbow Inn. I still re-member the day when a strange new guest turned up at our door." It takes care of more content thus: "Squire Trelawney and Dr. Livesey have asked me, Jim Hawkins, to write down the story of Treasure Island. I will tell you everything, just as it happened. The only thing I won't tell you is where the island is. That's because there is still treasure buried there." Again, the opening long sentence is broken up into several shorter, simpler sentences and some "nonessential" material is omitted. The simpler version, though blunt and shorn of Stevenson's beauties, is not badly written.

ROBINSON CRUSOE

The most interesting project of adaptation I have seen goes beyond merely simplifying or abridging a classic in order to reach a wider market of readers, and this was the project of one Lucy Aikin, under the pen name Mary Godolphin, who, interested in early childhood education, produced, in 1867, a version of *Robinson Crusoe* in words of one syllable, which was followed over the next few years by similarly monosyllabic versions of other books including *Aesop's Fables*, *The Pilgrim's Progress*, and *The Swiss Family Robinson*. (Only the titles of the books and the proper names have more than one syllable.) These versions necessarily omit some of the material in the original, but the constraint under which they are written does not, to my ear anyway, noticeably harm their effect.

In Godolphin's version, *Robinson Crusoe* opens:

> I was born at York on the first of March in the sixth year of the reign of King Charles the First. From the time when I was quite a young child, I had felt a great wish to spend my life at sea, and as I grew, so did this taste grow more and more strong; till at last I broke loose from my school and home, and found my way on foot to Hull, where I soon got a place on board a ship.

The original begins (and I'm skipping some of it):

> I was born in the year 1632, in the city of York, of a good family, though not of that country, my father being a foreigner of Bremen, who settled first at Hull; he got a good estate by merchandise, and, leaving off his trade, lived afterwards at York; from whence he had married my mother, whose relations were named Robinson, a very good family in the country, and from whom I was called Robinson Kreutznaer . . . I had two elder bothers . . . Being the third son of the family, and not bred to any trade, my head began to be filled very early with rambling thoughts: my father, who was very ancient, had given me competent share of learning . . . and designed me for the law; but I would be satisfied with nothing but going to sea.

And after some years and another few pages of quite small print, the boy goes off to sea without his family's permission.

In a brief preface, Mary Godolphin acknowledges that she has not produced an original book, but adds that she is filling a need by providing "youngest readers" with monosyllabic reading matter that is more than merely "a few short, unconnected sentences . . . chiefly in spelling books." She is offering a story that, as she says, has always aroused "deep interest" in the "minds of the young." And indeed, when I compare her *Robinson Crusoe* to a page of an early reader I have here in the house, an old one, from 1894, the difference is easy to see, though the sentences in the reader—here, an exercise for teaching contractions—have their own poetry: "It is not dark now. The flowers do not hang their heads. The birds are not hidden. The rain does not fall. The hay has not been spoiled." I would add that these classics as rewritten by Mary Godolphin might also be enjoyed by adults who have difficulty reading, or reading English.

I also see a similarity between these adaptations of classic literature, still in their own ways eloquent despite missing so much of the content and language of the originals, and early translations of powerful classics such as *Madame Bovary* or the works of Kafka. First translations into English often somewhat misrepresent the original in order to soften its strangeness for the Anglophone readership. Yet the works are so powerful that they survive this misrepresentation.

A NEW THOUGHT ABOUT COMPASSION FOR THE DIFFICULT CHARACTER

As I was imagining why both children and adults found *Bob, Son of Battle* so compelling, I thought of the sustained suspense of several ongoing plots: the competition, each fall, for the Shepherd's Trophy; the mystery of which dog was killing the sheep; and the question of whether M'Adam would find some path to reconciliation with his son. In the course of this, I was also trying to figure out where my sympathy for "the little man" came from or would come from, given the many, many scenes in which he behaved badly.

It was certainly, in part, that we witness him in times of vulnerability, or sorrow, and at moments when he displays gallantry or bravery; for instance, after begging a favor from James Moore, late in the story, he humbly shakes Moore's hand on it in thanks. But the question also led me to what seemed like a completely new thought, of a different sort of interaction between character and reader: that it might be the compassion shown by *another character* in the book that demonstrates to the reader a way to feel compassion for a difficult one. It may be the compassion of James Moore's wife, and of James Moore himself, and of the "lady of the manor" for M'Adam that demonstrates a way for the reader to attempt the same compassion, especially as M'Adam responded to those overtures with more gentleness than usual. And—if it's not hoping for too much, being naively optimistic—by extension it might show the reader a way to attempt compassion in real life for a difficult person.

Perhaps I thought of this because we in the humanities seem, now, to be asked to justify our existence within a culture increasingly prone to adopt a business model, a culture that challenges us to answer: What is the use of reading or studying fiction? One answer is that in reading fiction we can endure tragedy—loss, death, disability—at a safe remove, and then return to our own life, intact, but more experienced emotionally. Another is that the reading of fiction may teach, or encourage, empathy. But then, of course, we may be asked, further, to justify the practical advantages of empathy in the business world.

THE UNEXPECTED PLEASURES OF THE PROJECT, EXPLORING AND LEARNING ABOUT THE CULTURE OF THE BOOK, AND THE EXPANDED EDITION I NEVER PREPARED, WITH ENDNOTES I NEVER INCLUDED

As I worked on the book, I was investigating and learning many things about the book's subject matter and wider culture that were new to me—about the geography of the setting, the local customs, the work of raising sheep, and so forth. I thought of including some minimal notes in the back of the book to explain many things that might be unfamiliar to today's readers, but in the end, I did not, mainly because to do this would have given the book a scholarly sort of cast that I did not want it to have. However, with enough time—maybe another lifetime—I would have liked to produce an edition of the book that included extensive notes on all the following topics, starting with:

Cumbria, formerly known as Cumberland: a county in the northwest of England, one of the most sparsely populated in the UK, bordered by Scotland, North Yorkshire, Northumberland, County Durham, Lancashire, and the Irish Sea; it is very mountainous, and contains the Lake District and England's highest mountains (every peak in England over 3,000 feet); it has a history of invasions, migration and settlement, battles and skirmishes between the English and the Scots; it was the birthplace of the following: William and Dorothy Wordsworth, Thomas De Quincey, Samuel Taylor Coleridge, Beatrix Potter, and Stan Laurel (of Laurel and Hardy); and going on to include:

the Scottish raids;

the border between Scotland and England: long a de facto border and legally established in 1237; thus, one of the oldest still existing borders in the world; for centuries, until the Union of the Crowns, the region that straddled the border was a lawless territory in which cattle rustling, arson, and pillaging were common and which suffered from repeated raids in both directions by the Border Reivers (reiving = plundering or raiding), who were active until the seventeenth century; tribal or clan loyalty was to blood relatives and families, and these families might extend across the border;

the art of thatching ricks;

the sheepdog culture: this topic would also include what I learned about sheepherding, and that the job of a sheepdog is more complex than we laypeople can know or imagine: it must not only understand its master's orders and even sometimes read its master's mind, but also use its own wits and judgment; without a dog, a shepherd would not be able to control his or her flock; one of the minor pieces of information that startled me, in what I learned, was that Australian kelpies—and other sheepdogs, I'm sure—when they find themselves at the rear of a flock of sheep tightly massed in an enclosed space and they need to get to the front of the flock, have been trained to run right over the backs of the sheep to get there; another surprising fact was that in the landscape in which a flock is driven to pasture by dog and shepherd, every hollow, dell, rise, and escarpment has been named, for the reason that the shepherd must be able to order his or her dog into these places;

sheep-shearing;

sheep-counting and old local sheep-counting systems, derived from a Bryonic Celtic language; two of the systems used in Cumbria were: yan, tyan, tethera, methera, pimp; sethera, lethera, hovera, dovera, dick; and: yan taen tedderte, medderte, pimp; haata, slaata, lowra, dowra, dick.

shepherds' crooks: you could use a shepherd's crook as

support when walking over rough terrain; to catch a sheep by the neck or legs; to separate out one sheep from the flock; to extricate a sheep or lamb from a tangle of shrubbery; or as defense against a predator; shepherds did not buy their sticks, but made them themselves or acquired them from older shepherds or from "stick dressers"; the craft of creating the sticks is a highly developed one, and competitive; a Border Stick Dressers' Association was formed in 1951 on the English side of the Scottish Border; the crook itself, on the end of the stick, may be shaped from wood or from the horn of an animal—ram, goat, or cattle; hazel wood makes the best shepherd's stick because it is both stout and pliable;

plank-bridges;

the three rivers: the Derwent, which flows through the Lake District; the Tyne, one branch of which rises on the Scottish border, one in Cumbria; and the Tweed, which flows primarily through the Scottish Borders region of Scotland and forms for seventeen miles the border with England;

Cutty Sark, also spelled Cuttie Sark, the name of M'Adam's first dog and a term in the Scots language meaning a short shirt or chemise; it was the name of a character (a witch) in Robert Burns's 1790 poem "Tam o' Shanter"; there was a famous clipper ship of the same name built in 1869, but the whiskey was not created until 1923; as for the name Tam O'Shanter itself, it was later adopted not only for the hat, but also for an early twentieth-century brand of tobacco advertised as "favorite dark flake" and sold for eleven pence an ounce;

Burns's "Cottager's";

drovers: engaged in the work of driving livestock such as cattle, sheep, geese, and turkeys to market over very long distances, sometimes on horseback and usually with the help of one or more dogs; "drove roads," as they were called, were particularly wide and punctuated by dogleg bends where there was shelter for man and animals in times of heavy rain or snow; drovers were generally viewed as so reliable and responsible that a wealthy family would sometimes entrust their son to a drover's care for a journey into London; once the drover, with his dog and his herd or flock, had reached, for instance, the market in London and needed to stay there for some time, he might send his dog back home by itself along the same route; the dog's meals at each inn on the return journey would have been paid for in advance on the way down;

Burns's "Willie Brew'd a Peck o' Mault" ("we are na fou, we're nae that fou");

tail docking of dogs;

peewits and their distinctive cries;

the name "Wull";

petticoats;

market cross: a cross made of wood or stone, often elaborately carved; it stood in the center of a marketplace, in a market town; the custom of erecting these crosses dates back to the seventh century and many of them, hundreds of years old, still stand in British towns and in former British colonies;

the patriotic song of Scotland, "Scots wha hae wi' Wallace bled!," for hundreds of years the unofficial national anthem, lyrics by Robert Burns;

Burns's poem "To a Mouse, on Turning Her Up in Her Nest with the Plough, November, 1785," which contains those very famous and often misquoted lines, "The best-laid schemes o' mice an' men / Gang aft agley";

Cerberus;

the knob-kerry; also called "knobkerrie," a stick with a round knob at the end; it is carried by David at one point in the novel, but was originally used as club or missile by

South African tribesmen; the word was imported from the Afrikaans *knopkierie*, from the Middle Dutch *cnoppe* and the Khoikhoi *kiri*; the Khoikhoi people were also known as Khoekhoe, Khoisan, and Hottentot;

fairy circles;

Burns's poem "My Wife's a Winsome Wee Thing," whose last stanza begins: "The warld's wrack we share o't, / The warstle and the care o't . . ."

WHERE MY RESEARCHES TOOK ME

I learned that some schools were identified, at one time, by the master's name—as, for instance, the school where Ollivant's father was educated: "Mr. Pritchett's," in the village of Old Charlton.

I observed that newspapers of the 1930s and '40s, on their society pages, when enumerating the guests at a fashionable seaside hotel, would list them in the following order of social prominence: titled nobility, military, men of the church, medical doctors, gentlemen and ladies.

I spent much time trying to track down the previous owner of my secondhand copy of one of Ollivant's books: it had been given to him as a prize for winning a contest in a film magazine. But my searches led to nothing, or rather, they did not lead definitively to this particular Charles Taylor, though someone else out there was also looking for a man of that name who lived in the same town. I most often came upon men of that name from that region detained for debt. Still, I learned more than I had known before about early cinema in England, had a taste of English life in 1916, and visited a town called South Normantown that I had never heard of before. I was left with the unexpected fact that a popular film magazine chose to give a book as a prize for winning a competition—this would not happen today.

I stumbled upon other odd pieces of information: for instance, an online bookselling page for *Boy Woodburn* offered an author bio in German for, not Ollivant, but one Baron Geo. Fr. Ompteda, born about ten years before Ollivant. There was a striking resemblance, however: Ompteda, too, trained to be an officer, fell from a horse, had to resign his commission, and then turned to writing. He translated the collected works of Guy de Maupassant, among other works.

Researching Ollivant himself and his family, I read, online, an 1889 handbook written for the students and parents of England's two best-known and most prestigious military academies, Sandhurst and Woolwich: *The Military Career: A Guide to Young Officers, Army Candidates and Parents.* From it I learned such things as that applicants must be no less than 5 feet, 5 inches in height and that the average height of cadets on entering Woolwich was 5 feet, 8.2 inches; on leaving, 5 feet, 9.7 inches. I learned what the Woolwich cadets were to bring with them upon entering school, including three nightshirts, nine pocket handkerchiefs, a razor strop, a Bible, a prayer book. The first-year students, it seemed, would share a room with up to three others, and share a servant as well. They might add to their rooms, to make them more comfortable, such items as a carpet, a kettle, tea-things, etc. No firearms or dogs were to be kept by the students. It was not desirable that they should have large sums of money at their disposal. The infantry supplies, when the graduates went off to take up their commissions, included, besides the elements of the uniform and such equipment as a portable iron bedstead, portable washstand, portable bookshelves, and so on, as part of their "plain clothes" dress, lace shoes, dress shoes, slippers, tennis shoes, cricket shoes, cloth spats, four pairs of gloves and a glove-stretcher, and more mysteriously named items such as a "housewife" (sewing kit) and a "traveling maud"—which may be the same thing, but which I so far can't identify.

OTHER PLEASURES: COMING TO KNOW THE OLLIVANT FAMILY

Learning more about Ollivant's family and English society of that time, I became, as usual, so interested in the subject that I went far down various paths of digression not strictly useful for my project. I researched the family going back many generations, into the 1600s; established a genealogy to which I could refer; learned that John Blunt not only is the name of the character in one of Ollivant's other novels but also was that of his maternal grandfather, and that his paternal grandfather was a bishop in Wales who maintained a household including eleven servants; witnessed, in the laconic eloquence of a census form, Ollivant as head of a household in 1911 with, as his only company, a live-in nurse and a maidservant; learned from probate documents how much money Alfred Ollivant's father left upon his death, how much Alfred Ollivant himself left, how much was left, for comparison, by others on the same page of the book—a commercial traveler, a "gentleman," a police constable, a meat purveyor, an accountant, an engine fitter, a corporation waterman, and a second lieutenant; read contemporary American newspaper accounts of Ollivant and his books; read society columns about weddings attended by Ollivant and/or his wife, including lists of wedding gifts; learned that Ollivant and his wife, who had socialist leanings, made it known, when they became engaged, that they were not to be given any gifts; read newspaper lists of the guests in seaside hotels that included one or another Ollivant.

I eventually went in pursuit of Ollivant's grandchildren, the three children of his only child, Rachel, because I thought I might learn more from them personally about the author; after some searching, I made contact with them by a piece of luck through an ad for a rental cottage in the southeast of England. After corresponding with one granddaughter, I eventually, on a trip to England, was welcomed at the dairy farm she owned with her husband. There I met, also, her brother and two of Ollivant's great-grandsons. I shared a family dinner at a long farm table, looked through family scrapbooks, and heard family lore; and late in my visit learned, to my amazement, that under one of their pastures lay some ancient archaeological remains that they were choosing, for the time being, not to unearth.

There, I also experienced a moment of utter contentment that I still look back on with pleasure: standing in borrowed Wellington boots in the vast cow barn next to the house, sipping from a glass of delicious homemade sloe gin, I watched the swift and slippery birth of a calf, as handled by one of Ollivant's great-grandsons—and thought afterward that the sloe gin would not have been the same without the birth of the calf into the bed of straw, nor the birth of the calf without the sweet sloe gin in my hand, and that even the generosity of the borrowed Wellingtons played its part in the experience.

I corresponded also with the second granddaughter, who lives in France, came close to meeting her, and thereafter continued to receive her holiday newsletters.

THE POWER OF SUSPENSE AND
SUSPENSION OF DISBELIEF

Having to read very slowly like this, as I worked on *Bob, Son of Battle*, gave me the leisure to think about the traditional elements of fiction, especially suspense and the suspension of disbelief, even as I was experiencing them myself.

As I typed on, I tried to remember how the story ended. I knew one part of the outcome but had forgotten others. It was harder, of course, for me to get caught up in the story as I worked on it, because I was working on it so slowly. But I did get caught up, and, as the evening wore on, I would want to get through just one more page before I stopped, and then one more. As I came closer to the end of the novel, the action became more suspenseful, and I had to force myself not to look ahead.

I became acutely conscious, at certain moments in the plot, that on the other side of this page, when I turned it, I would find out what happened. Reading became very physical: my action of turning the page, made of paper, made of wood pulp, and resting my eyes on the indented black type at the top of the next page, would give me the answer to the question in my mind; I was hanging on it. I had forgotten, for the moment, that this story never took place, that it was invented, and by someone very young.

The question I was hanging on, when I realized how complete was my suspension of disbelief, was which dog had been killing the sheep by night. The answer had been close at various times before, in the story, and now we were *really* about to be told what it was, the page in my hand, the answer there on the other side. And then I was satisfied, I had the answer—only to be deceived. For the *real* answer was a few pages further on.

Away from the book, the next day, when I had only fourteen pages to go and was awaiting the answers to a few more questions about "what was going to happen," I realized that the story still had reality for me, the characters seemed to be there still, about to go on with the action. I could tell myself that none of this had really happened, that these characters did not exist, but I still believed in them. I don't know if the events of the book seemed all the more real because I had experienced them as a child.

The continuing power of suspense was strong even when I reached the stage of reading proofs and making small corrections, despite the fact that I now knew the story. The words would not disappear from the page nor the action go on without me if I stopped reading, and I needed to stop, to make changes in the text, yet I still felt, at a highly dramatic moment, that somehow I might affect the outcome if I did. In some part of me I must have believed that the story could turn out differently, this time, that it still hung in the balance.

Tears came to my eyes during one scene, and again when I came back to work the next day. I would say to myself, But this did not really happen, and then feel pained again, as though it had. How powerful is this thing, the suspension of disbelief—how powerful fiction and its illusions! We read, at the end of the novel, that M'Adam sits cradling in his lap the great head of Red Wull, who is no more. We believe it, even though, really, before Ollivant conceived them, there was no M'Adam and no Red Wull. What are we crying for? But once the words are written, and read, and imagined in our minds, they are real to us.

2014

Chap 1.

Cape Cod.

In the western hemisphere of our planet, about half way from the Equator to its northern pole, reaching out into the Ocean toward the sun-rising and forming the southeastern portion of the State of Massachusetts, is the peninsula of Cape Cod.

It is not the oldest land on the globe, yet, consisting of materials of the azoic age, it can claim, even with the geologist, a great antiquity. How long it stood, high and dry, before the historic period, or the age of man, are known not. The great waves of the Atlantic beat upon its sandy shore and the fine woods, far inland, resounded with the war of the breakers on Mallabar, long, long before the nations of the Old world flourished and decayed, or the red men roamed the forests of the New.

From Memoir to Long Poem:
Sidney Brooks's *Our Village*

By a curious chain of events involving uncles and nephews, childlessness, estrangement, and happenstance, I was led to read the memoir of an ancestor of mine. Perhaps this could have come about another way, but the chain began with the ancestor himself, Sidney Brooks, born in 1813 in Harwich, Massachusetts, a Cape Cod town of fishermen, sailors, ships' captains, and farmers, with a meetinghouse, a general store, eventually a bank, a dance hall, and a library. Sidney grew up there and remained there all his life, apart from an occasional few years away—to attend school and college, for instance. He had no children of his own and, at his death, left his papers, including his memoir, to his sister Roxanna, who in turn passed them down to her son Henry Brooks Davis, my father's grandfather. The papers passed from Henry to his middle son, Malcolm. At some point, probably in the 1930s, Malcolm had a serious quarrel with his own son, also called Malcolm, which led to a permanent estrangement, so that when the older Malcolm neared the end of his life and began disposing of his things, he handed down the family papers, not to his son, but slantwise to his nephew, my father. Among the papers was Sidney's memoir, handwritten and contained in three notebooks and titled *Our Village*. My father, when he grew old, in turn passed a portion of these family papers to the place with the most interest in them, Harwich's historical society. The historical society, after a few more years, caused the memoir to be painstakingly transcribed into a typescript, including Sidney's cross-outs and errors and reproducing the pagination of the notebooks. It then had this memoir published in book form and offered for sale in its gift shop and by mail to its membership.

The interest of the historical society was, of course, in the history of Harwich as revealed in the memoir, which included mention of many townspeople and details of such events as the advent of a minister, enlistments in the Civil War, and a fatal accident on the town common involving the careless firing of a defective old cannon.

My own interest in reading it, when I acquired a copy, was a little different: to know in more detail the earlier history of my family; and to learn more generally about how people lived in the nineteenth century, something that has always interested me, partly out of plain curiosity and partly out of an idealism that causes me to consider certain earlier customs and habits as possibly more wholesome, useful, and sustainable than some of our own, and to be prepared, also, to adopt them for myself. This was a narrative perfectly suited to engage me: an account of earlier times, yes, but one whose protagonists were my own forebears and their sometimes eccentric family members. The book also contained rapturous descriptions of the landscape around Harwich and little stories about the townspeople.

As I read and took notes, I also became more and more captivated by Sidney's character and sensibility and by the style in which the memoir was written. He was frank, forth-

right, generous, and compassionate. He was a firm abolition-
ist, like many in the town, and lived according to his moral
convictions as a devout Christian. He was dedicated to education; he founded, designed, and had built a secondary
school in the town and presided over it for many years before
moving up to Boston, for several years, to direct a "school
ship," moored in the harbor, for street boys or delinquents.
The school he founded in Harwich is now the premises of
the same historical society that holds his papers.

He had an affectionate nature, and, as a writer, he paid
loving attention to his world and the world of his memories:
no detail was too small to include. He described exactly and
in closely observed detail not just his fellow townspeople, his
pupils, the teachers in his school, and his family, but also, extensively, the natural surroundings of the town including the
native flora, which he took care to document, collect from
the wild, and plant on the school grounds; he portrays also
such natural phenomena as the temporary pools that formed
after a rain, architectural features of the different houses, including the fireplaces, and such village sounds as the hum of
the spinning wheels, the ringing of the blacksmith's anvil,
and the clack of the looms coming from the attic chambers
along the main street.

In the late 1860s through the late 1870s, as he was composing the memoir, looking back in time, he missed the
simpler days of his childhood and the purer, healthier, less
despoiled landscape. There were fewer buildings, he tells us:
there were, fifty years before the time of his writing, only
eight houses in the village, and the four of them east of the
meetinghouse "were all grandfather's children, and their
children were all cousins." It was more peaceful then: "The
Sabbath-day quiet of those times can hardly be conceived."
Of course, we, now, looking at the busy intersections of

Harwich and the lines of cars heading in and out of the center, would find his own 1870s landscape far purer and less despoiled. And whereas he also remarks that in the days of his childhood, "people were not as busy as they now are and far more social," our response would be, of course, that we have become even busier in the intervening 150 years since he wrote, and in certain ways, at least as regards how we play, pray, or make music together, or simply converse face-to-face, even less social. We can long for the days of his old age as he longs for the days of his childhood.

He chose his words carefully, and composed his phrases and sentences with natural grace. It was the grace of a well-educated man who cared deeply about the form of a piece of writing, but also, I can guess, one whose ear for rhythm and the sounds of words had been developed by hearing his father read aloud, on countless Sundays, most usually from the King James translation of the Bible (accompanying himself, most strangely, by using the kitchen wall as his instrument and producing a sort of sustained tone, or drone, from it by the stroking of his hand). Even though the text of the memoir was not a finished piece of writing, still residing, as he left it, in his notebooks as first set down, with its misspellings, omitted words, missing punctuation, passages inadvertently repeated, and the whole never restructured or revised, it was still, phrase by phrase, remarkably smooth and pleasing to read.

As I read on in the book, I began, involuntarily, to hear its phrases as lines, or pieces of lines, in a poem; the idea gradually impressed itself upon me that this memoir had the potential of being transformed into a long narrative poem, that its inherent nature was, really, to be a narrative in verse, that its sentences would lend themselves to being selected and separated out into poetic lines. Although I could not, and still cannot, say exactly why the memoir would be more effective as a poem, I can think of a few reasons, the primary one being that the memoir would be read at a different pace and its words and images absorbed in greater isolation; they would be given the space to sound and reverberate on their own. I finished reading the book, marking every passage that I thought might go into a poem and even sketching out, on the empty spaces on the page, possible lines. Soon after I finished reading the book, I began converting parts of it into sections of a long poem.

I have by now "translated" about seventy pages' worth of material from Sidney's memoir. Some of this version has been published. I will continue going through the memoir looking out for more "eligible" passages to be incorporated into the long poem, and I will also rethink and revise what I have already done.

The project raises a few questions, and one is to what extent I am the author of this long narrative poem and to what extent Sidney Brooks is its author. Of course, in one sense it is a collaboration, involuntary on Sidney's part. And maybe that is the only way to think of it: the words, phrasing, sentiments, ideas, memories, reflections, and choices of subject matter are his. The notion that this material could be a poem, and the work of forming it into a poem, are mine, as are the ultimate selection and arrangement of the material in this form, taking from Sidney's own selection and sometimes superceding or revising his arrangement. Whether this cooption and distortion on my part is ethically sound is another question that could be asked, but I myself have no doubt that there is room on the shelf for both Sidney Brooks's original memoir and my poetic version of it, and I may even conjecture that he would not have minded a broader reading public for his words and thoughts.

One resemblance this conversion had to the sort of translation I was used to working on, from a foreign language, was that the original text, in this case, too, was given—I did not have to invent the material. In this case, even the English words were given, and, wanting to preserve them, I could concentrate on other aspects of composing the poem: identifying the passages that appealed to me, selecting material from within them, rewriting them just a little, as necessary, putting the selections into a logical order, deciding on line breaks, arranging the lines on the page, deciding on last words in lines, deciding on last words in stanzas.

I did not feel bound to use every word of the memoir, of course, but took only what moved me and what I thought would work well in the poem. I also selected within the sentences, if necessary, using only parts of them. I changed the order of the material within the book and sometimes within a sentence. I made other changes, too, moving a word or cutting a repetition, but insofar as possible I left the language as it was, since Sidney's own words and phrases were what I had found so pleasing and expressive of his nature and personality and what he observed. As for whether some sorts of material simply didn't belong in a poem, in theory I didn't think so; I believed that any material could find a place in a poem, even a dry fact or pedestrian language, depending on how it was used.

But, in fact, some material did not immediately reveal its potential. For instance, near the end of the memoir there is a series of accounts of the ministers who came and went from Sidney's church: this was important to him but seemed to me, at first, too dryly factual to include. Then I had second thoughts. With extensive cutting, the accounts might work, highly abbreviated, as a sort of incantation, thus: Mr. Mills, who died among us; Rev. Litchfield, who came the year Aunt Naomi was born; Blind Kimble, who had sufficient use of one eye and prayed for us in his dark room; Rev. Underwood, who had an excellent wife and a large family of boys; Dr. Storrs, whose thundering eloquence startled the bats above the ceiling; Mr. Cobb, a young man full of zeal; Mr. Crocker, a graduate of Harvard; Mr. Pell, who was afraid the Lord would not find him on Resurrection morning, the cemetery being so overgrown; Mr. Avery, who went I know not whither.

If one advantage of the project was that I did not have to invent the material or even supply the English words, for the most part, one disadvantage was that although I was practiced in writing prose, I was not practiced in writing lineated verse, particularly in how to decide on line breaks. This was something I would have to think consciously about. I had not turned to reference books or poetry handbooks, and perhaps I preferred not to, so as to come at it with my own thoughts. I was already, anyway, in the habit of paying attention, when reading a poem, to how the lines were broken and found myself approving or disapproving, liking or disliking them, of identifying, when I noticed them, what I believed were wise or unwise line choices.

Whenever I think about how to achieve good line breaks, I remember how, once, when I was teaching for just a semester at the same college where John Ashbery had a more regular position, and we were both, along with a third faculty member, reviewing with a student her completed project, a collection of poems, I took the opportunity, in the midst of our discussion, to turn to John Ashbery and ask him—sure that his answer would benefit the student as well as satisfy my own curiosity—how he would advise deciding where to break a line, in a poem. I was hanging on his answer, since here, I believed, was one of the most interesting of our living poets, and what would he say? I expected him to talk about phrasing, or breath, or units of meaning, or the power of the final word in a line, or the play with a shift in meaning from one line to the next, or conversational style versus formal style, or something else quite specific. I was looking for reliable and consistent rules, guidance from an authority. But his answer was brief, something to the effect of "Wherever it feels right." Well, now, what to do with that? Especially if your "feel" for the line break is so uneducated, so unpracticed, so untrustworthy?

There were several ways to go on thinking about it, after that answer. I could imagine what else he might have said but hadn't, and begin making my own rules. When asked about line breaks in her poems, in a *Paris Review* interview, Rae Armantrout wandered a bit, at first, looking for how best to articulate what her rules or guiding principles might be. She sounds a little like Ashbery, at the start: "Part of it is intuition, what I think sounds good." But then she goes on:

> Partly I write in a short line because I first learned my line from William Carlos Williams. But that's not really a good enough explanation, because lots of other poets started with Williams and ended up someplace completely different. So I must have stayed with that line for some other reason. I like to build in surprise so the movement from line to line is unpredictable. I'd *like* each line to be of some interest in itself. I want to create a sense of starting out and not knowing where you'll end up . . . I want to re-create that experience for the reader, too, of having to stay alert to the turns . . . Look out, what's coming next.

Or I could take Ashbery's answer as, really, the best and only answer, and here is how it might work: you would simply have to keep attempting your own line breaks, trusting your instincts and then listening again to what you had done, examining your line breaks, reexamining them. You would also, when you were not writing your own poems, study the line breaks of other poets, especially poets you unquestionably admired. You would then return to examine your own, and in that way inculcate in yourself a feel for line breaks, until you could confidently, without worrying, break the line "wherever it felt right."

Another way, I thought, to go on from that answer of Ashbery's was to both attempt the line breaks "wherever it felt right" and then, also, observing your own "instinctive" sense of where to break the line, try to derive some rules for yourself, your own rules. Or, before attempting that, you could try to learn and formulate more explicitly, from your instinctive reaction to the line breaks of the poets you were reading, what it was you liked about the good ones and disliked about what seemed to you the bad ones, and thus derive rules. You could read interviews with poets you admired and listen to what they said about the poets they in turn admired (as, later in the interview, Armantrout remarks about Robert Creeley: "you get those whiplash linebreaks"; I'll go and see what she means). Of course, different poets would break lines in different ways, and you would want to be able to evaluate those various different ways, not just a single way. I could start by studying line breaks as Ashbery himself handled them, though his approaches might change over the many years he wrote poems.

In any case, in the end, there was no real choice, for me, but to break the lines instinctively, since no one was guiding me. When I had been at it for some weeks, converting passages of the memoir into lines of poetry, I found that I preferred, mostly, to keep phrases intact, as they naturally occurred, and also to keep intact parts of sentences that belonged together, even long ones, rather than to break them in the middle, in a sort of wraparound conversational mode, as Ashbery himself does in some of his poems. For instance, his "City Afternoon" begins with that sort of line break:

> *A veil of haze protects this*
> *Long-ago afternoon forgotten by everybody*
> *In this photograph, most of them now*
> *Sucked screaming through old age and death.*

Here, the continuation of one phrase, "forgotten by everybody / in this photograph," into the next line actually changes, slightly, its meaning: the "long-ago afternoon" is not forgotten by everybody in general, as we understand it if we stop at the end of the first line, but by everybody "in this photograph." And that is one available effect of breaking a line in the middle of a phrase—you offer one meaning and then modify it slightly in the next line. But this does not happen in the first two lines of the poem—having read the word "this," we need to suspend our comprehension until we reach its noun, "long-ago afternoon." But here, one interesting effect of the interrupted phrase is the tension it creates between what is unfinished—the suspended phrase— and what is finished, the line.

In most of the poems in this book (*Self-Portrait in a Convex Mirror*, 1975), however, he breaks the line so that it keeps intact the natural phrases. In a stanza at the end of "As One Put Drunk into the Packet-Boat," for instance, eight of the nine lines break at a place in the sentence that keeps the

natural phrases intact, but one line does not, breaking between an adjective and the noun it modifies, and it is worth
puzzling over why he chose to carry that phrase over into
the next line:

> *And a sigh heaves from all the small things on earth,*
> *The books, the papers, the old garters and union-suit buttons*
> *Kept in a white cardboard box somewhere, and all the lower*
> *Versions of cities flattened under the equalizing night.*

Perhaps he wanted to put a little extra stress on "lower,"
as the last word in a line has a little extra stress, or attention,
just as the words occurring together on the line have stress,
or gain attention, as a group together. Or perhaps he broke
in the middle the phrase "all the lower / Versions of cities"
in part, also, for variation, which is often another important
trait of a good poem. Or perhaps simply because it made a
pleasing group of words in itself: "Kept in a white cardboard
box somewhere, and all the lower." Or for the sake of the
next line, which works so well this way, as a unit: "Versions
of cities flattened under the equalizing night."

I felt that to employ very frequently the conversational,
wraparound mode of line break, if at all, would not suit Sidney's more deliberate, nonconversational style of writing, or
his more formal, though gentle, nature. But I did occasionally, as Ashbery did in the above stanza, allow a phrase or
clause to continue over onto the next line, as in the following
verse, separating subject from verb, for instance. Later in the
memoir, Sidney repeats what he has said about how quiet
the village was on Sundays, but amplifies it a little, perhaps

forgetting that he has written a version of it already. This I converted, retaining intact the natural phrases, except for one, in the following way:

> *The profound Sabbath-day quiet of those times*
> *can hardly be conceived.*
> *No church bell was within hearing,*
> *for there was none on our houses of worship.*
> *No carriages were in the streets,*
> *for the only transportation then*
> *was mostly by ox-cart, and the oxen too*
> *claimed their day of rest.*
> *As if to break the utter silence,*
> *a cock crowed at mid-day*
> *and was answered by another and another*
> *from the far-off hamlets.*

In this example, I like the sound of the line "was mostly by ox-cart, and the oxen too." The fact that the roosters can be heard from one hamlet to another—here, where I live, also in a rural village, that could be a distance of over three miles—gives a clear idea, purely through an image, of how very quiet it was.

I had just concluded, skimming through, that in this slim book, in any case, Ashbery always capitalized his first lines, when I turned the page and saw one whole poem, "As You Came from the Holy Land," in which all the lines begin with lowercase letters and, in fact, there is no punctuation at all, which has the curious effect, at least for me, of giving an equal stress to every word, in a sort of continuous staccato.

But, as for punctuation, without having put the question

to myself, I was already retaining Sidney's, keeping intact whole sentences and capitalizing not at the beginning of each line but only as I would in prose, at the beginning of a sentence. It simply felt more natural to me; perhaps, being a prose writer by habit, I was more comfortable retaining this aspect of writing conventional prose.

The verses might barely read as poetry rather than prose, in some passages, but I did not mind that. Some lines would naturally be quite long, if there was not a good breaking point, while some would be naturally very short, and this would provide variation, as in the following sequence:

> *Every man in the town was a farmer.*
> *Whatever his vocation,*
> *farming was his avocation.*
> *The carpenter, the storekeeper, and the fisherman*
> *had each his field of corn;*
> *and every one who attended exclusively to farming,*
> *and the squire and the minister,*
> *his pair of oxen.*
> *And so the squire, the storekeeper and minister,*
> *the fisherman, carpenter and doctor,*
> *when not called away professionally,*
> *came, in haying time,*
> *into the meadows.*

Now, reading this over, I think I might change, for reasons of rhythm, "professionally"—which has so many quick syllables within the one word, and only one accent—to "by his profession," which has two natural accents, better spaced. And in fact that is another consideration in creating the lines of this poem: how the stresses fall on the syllables; in other words, the rhythms within the lines.

I went back and changed line breaks often. I worried when there were too many lines of the same length following one another; I worried that the lines would become, rhythmically, too mechanical, although, of course, from the examples I was looking at, having lines of more or less equal length should be no problem in itself. In a group of lines of the same length, the variety or interest is provided by many other things, including the word choices or the differences in rhythm.

This attempt to turn *Our Village* into a poem certainly led me to some further considerations about what a good poem was, or about aspects of what made a poem good; or, easier to consider, since there are many kinds of good poems, in what ways a less-than-good poem was failing. Besides the line breaks, I thought yet again about the vocabulary of a good poem, and the phrasing, the imagery, the sentiments expressed, and so on. In fact, studying the conversion of this piece of prose into poetry could, if I let it, lead right into the question that comes up fairly regularly in my life: What *is* the difference between prose and poetry? The question has interesting answers, and leads to a fruitful discussion, but the various answers are long and complicated, since there are so many different kinds of poems and prose to take into account.

When some pages of this poem were eventually published, a poet friend of mine wrote to me in response, saying he liked its "leisurely pace," and particularly the end. I had used, for the last lines, something that Sidney Brooks had actually written quite early in the memoir:

> *It was given to me, in the nineteenth century,*
> *to spend a lifetime on this earth.*

Along with a few of the sorrows that are appointed unto
*   men*
I have had innumerable enjoyments;
and the world has been to me, even from childhood,
a great museum.

He told me it reminded him of the last lines of Pound's
"Provincia Deserta," which he sent to me. I looked here and
there in my books of Ezra Pound for the whole poem and
then found it in an appendix to *A Walking Tour in Southern*
France: Ezra Pound among the Troubadours, a collection of
Pound's notes and jottings from 1912 transcribed and edited
by the translator and Pound scholar Richard Sieburth. There
is some verse in the book, but it is mostly prose, a good deal
of it fragmentary. In a curious reversal, from the direction of
my project, much of the fragmentary prose gives the impression that a poet is writing poetry in lines of prose.

The Pound poem is not long, about two pages, in three
extended stanzas with short lines. Its closing is a little briefer,
and its lines shorter, than Sidney's, but the tone of both is
elegiac:

So ends that story.
That age is gone;
Pieire de Maensac is gone.
I have walked over these roads;
I have thought of them living.

Maybe, I wondered, it was what came before the very
end of the Brooks poem that reminded my friend of Pound.

We shall soon sleep
in the dust with our fathers.

As the centuries roll by,
the same bright sun and azure sky by day
and the glorious constellations by night;
the same hills and valleys and rivulets and gray old ocean
that now form our lovely landscape
will remain and greet the eyes
of the coming generations of men and women
and of little children playing in our streets.

The part I have acted,
the scenes I have witnessed,
the friends I have walked with,
the bright days, the rising and setting suns,
the silvery moonlight, the fields and woods,
the roads and by-paths,
the lovely hillsides and lowly vales,
the sweet songs of birds
and the roar of the ocean
will be remembered and reviewed
thousands and millions of years
after I have left
the shores of time.

The repetitions of "I have" at the end of the Pound poem
echo many that come before, especially "I have walked," "I
have looked," and "I have seen," as in:

I have lain in Rocafixada,
     level with sunset,
Have seen the copper come down
     tingeing the mountains,
I have seen the fields, pale, clear as an emerald

Now, looking at the Pound poem, I see another possibility for the Brooks poem, when I return to work on it. I could indent some of the lines, as Pound does here; not every line needs to start back at the left margin. This indenting is comfortable to the eyes, in the pattern it forms on the page. It is more relaxed, with more white spaces. It is also more comfortable to read: the eye drops straighter down to the next line, rather than moving all the way to the left. And it is a sort of compromise between an entirely new line and a continuation of the line you are reading. You read it a little differently, I think: there is a pause and then the continuation as though spoken in an undertone. Indenting like this might even solve the problem that kept recurring, for me, when I was unsure whether to start a new line or continue on the same one. Some of the longer lines above, for instance, could be altered to read:

> *the friends I have walked with,*
> *the bright days,*
> > *the rising and setting suns,*
>
> *the silvery moonlight,*
> > *the fields and woods,*
>
> *the roads and by-paths*

Or, maybe more logically:

> *the silvery moonlight,*
> *the fields and woods,*
> > *the roads and by-paths*

I look again at the Ashbery book, now curious to see whether he does this at all. In fact, hardly at all, is the answer.

He does it, by my count, five times in the entire book of thirty-five poems. In two instances, there is only a single word on the indented line below, once "forgotten" and once "endeth." Another instance, two words, creates an image of color, like Pound's "copper . . . / tingeing the mountains." It is this, in "Farm II," in which all beginnings of lines are capitalized and no punctuation occurs until the period at the end:

> *You can't walk out too far that way any more*
> *They say the children are demolishing*
> *The insides of the woods*
> > *burnt orange*
> *That it's spectacular*

Another poet to consider, finally, one more properly to have considered first, really, is the New York City native Charles Reznikoff, one of the group of Objectivists influenced by Pound and William Carlos Williams, others being Louis Zukovsky, George Oppen, Carl Rakosi, Lorine Niedecker, and the Englishman Basil Bunting. Trained as a lawyer, Reznikoff soon abandoned the practice of law in favor of working for his father's hat company (he apparently composed poems while waiting to meet with buyers in Macy's department store) and other jobs. In addition to his poems, novels, translations, and family memoirs, Reznikoff undertook a mammoth project: to compose a book-length poem from material derived from transcripts of trials covering the thirty years from 1885 to 1915—a "recitative," as he called it, of American life. This long work, more than 580 large-format pages in the most recent edition, the 2015 reissue, is called *Testimony*. He later went on to compose another, called *Holocaust*, based on the transcripts of the Nuremberg trials.

For *Testimony*, Reznikoff selected from a great deal of material—"several hundred volumes," he said, adding deprecatingly, "not many as law cases go." According to Eliot Weinberger in the book's introduction, Reznikoff read as many as one hundred to one thousand pages to find material for a single poem, often not a very long one. This is almost beyond my understanding. His way of proceeding was different from mine with *Our Village*: he selected the material and then did not quote verbatim from it, for the most part, but rewrote the facts in his own way, sometimes revising extensively. He generally omitted explicit expressions of emotion, allowing the facts to convey it, in keeping with the formulation that he often quoted: that poetry should be precise about the thing and reticent about the feeling. Whereas Sidney Brooks was consistently and beautifully precise about the thing, he was not reticent about his feelings, a quality that I admired in him and retained in the verses. He had a vocabulary full of specifics, but he also employed such general words as *lovely*, *beautiful*, and *sweet*:

> Solitude was sweet to me
> and the Sabbath day when there was no meeting
> was my chosen time for rambling
> in Grandfather's woods on the east of the village.
> . . .
> Here I reflected on all I read,
> thought of the past, which seemed then farther behind me
> than that period does to me now,
> laid scenes of future, great undertakings
> and tried in vain to understand the longing and aspiration
>   in me
> for something I could not define
> and have never yet found.

Reznikoff, in *Testimony*, also chose to omit commentary, whereas, again, Brooks includes it and I have retained it in the verses. In the following, he introduces the story he is about to tell of the death of old George Weekes, a town character called the "Indian Preacher" (he was not a Native American but perhaps preached *to* the "Indians") whose mind was addled and who tended to wander far from the home of the relative with whom he lived.

> *The last end of a good man*
> *is generally peaceful,*
> *and he comes down to his grave*
> *"like a shock of corn fully ripe."*
> *But again the best man may be brought to grief in old age,*
> *and his sun obscured before it sets,*
> *going down in clouds and darkness and tempest.*
> *No one now living knows precisely*
> *the nature of George Weekes' delinquency*
> *or the grief that made him a crazy man.*

Sidney Brooks describes how the winter day darkened early while the snow began to fall, supplementing the facts as he knew them by what he imagined:

> *The east wind caused him*
> *to draw his garments more closely about him*
> *and the snowflakes to light on them,*
> *first one by one, then more thickly,*
> *until the rising wind*
> *drives them full in his face*
> *and blinds and smothers him.*
> *. . . The surly northeaster*

was howling through the trees
and the snow was fast encasing their trunks

Old George tries to find shelter in a nearby house, but the children are home alone and won't open the door to him. He retraces his steps through a small valley, and there Brooks imagines the rest:

His strength failed.
A strange sleep came over him
and he was still.
The snow, covering him deeply,
became his winding sheet,
and the wind . . .
moaning among the boughs
of the rocking pines,
. . . sung his funeral dirge.

This account of George Weekes's death is not unlike the material of Reznikoff's *Testimony*, which offers one grim story after another, some merely of theft or betrayal, but many more ending in death, usually violent death—in drunken brawls, farm or railway accidents, suicide, murder. Among the shortest, for example, is the following:

It was early in the morning,
drizzling,
and because of the fog
still dark.
The old woman began to cross the railroad tracks
slowly.
No sound of whistle or bell

or glow of headlight—
and the speeding engine struck her.

I notice the line breaks there: longer lines followed by a single word or two, evidently for reasons of emphasis and rhythm.

Unlike *Testimony*, Sidney Brooks's memoir includes, as a part of village life and life in general, not only accounts of death, insanity, poverty, debt, betrayal, delinquency, illness, but also portrayals of what was equally a part of village life as he knew it, the manifold pleasures of childhood, play, the local flora and fauna in all their particularity, the affectionate family circle, harmonious relations of other kinds, love and friendship, the landscape in all its smallest parts, known and cherished for their associations—places, for instance, "where we had rode the horses to water and picked up button pears."

This passage about Sunday, the day of rest in a community united in its Christian faith, includes animals and landscape:

Even on the Sabbath,
there is some necessary work to be done,
Grandfather's cattle and our own
to be driven to water across the fields to the south,
down the long slope of the hill to the Maple Swamp,
"Old Brindle" leading the way,
the oxen and other cows marching
in their regular order.
The water that sinks into our fields from the rain and snow
gushes up through the soft peat of the swamp, pure,
sparkling among the tussocks, never freezing.
The cattle find the spring-holes
and are left to return of their own accord,
after browsing in the swamp and neighboring woods.

Sidney's beloved younger sister Harriet, at the age of fifty-nine, dies at home of cancer and is laid on a bed of ice downstairs in the "east room" of the house where she had lived with her two unmarried sisters. Her family stay with her as long as they can, even after she is carried into the cemetery vault—which remains open for a few days, for reasons I can imagine but don't know with certainty, as they visit her there, before at last the vault is closed.

But, balancing this account, which includes details such as Harriet's right breast, at the end, having become "as hard as stone," is the description of her at the age of three. On this day, his little playmate is industriously imitating her elders at her own chosen "work," which is to carry sand in a hat from the middle of the road onto the front step of the house, creating a layer three inches deep. Harriet has dressed herself, this day, in Sidney's outgrown clothes because "she took a fancy to that attire / and mother was too busy to apply force," and she presents a sight, with her "flaming red," curly hair, that Sidney relishes as much as the grown-ups who are working at their various tasks nearby: his mother "trimming up the hop vine and herbs and planting in the garden," his father "busy between the store and the farm," and Uncle Jonathan "morticing posts and splicing rails near the wood-house."

The appeal of the memoir at first, for me, was, as I said, to enter an earlier time in which things were done differently, in which the culture, habits, customs, economics, and social relations were not like ours and in some of their aspects more wholesome and a possibly useful model. Another attraction of the memoir, as I also said, was the company of the observant Sidney himself, and his gentle, perceptive, and honest depiction of the life around him. What made me embark on the project of converting the memoir into a poem was in part, I have not yet said, the satisfaction of bringing into finished form something that needed, as I saw it, some revising; of being at liberty to take a text that was often lovely in itself and perform operations on it: cut and move material, eliminate a repetition, introduce some silence after an eloquent word, while preserving, in their best settings, the parts that appealed to me most.

I will end with the example of one of my favorite brief accounts in *Our Village*, a portrait of the friendship between two old men.

In Sidney Brooks's day, old people tended to live out the remainder of their lives in their own homes or in the home of a relative or perhaps an acquaintance or neighbor paid to look after them. They lived on, year after year, as best they could, passing their time as they liked. They were generally free to wander, like George Weekes, even if demented. They contrived ways to get around and helped to the extent that they were able, like another old man, Sidney's Uncle Eben. He was paralyzed down one side of his body, and had been placed, Sidney says, in "a snug boarding place . . . with Mrs. Wilson Kelley." Uncle Eben used a chair as a crutch to get around, leaning on the top of it as he walked, sitting on it when he was tired, and for many years could also be found by the kitchen window, or on a patch of grass in warm weather, or in the woodshed in winter, sawing and splitting the "small wood" with his good arm.

As for the two old men in the following small poem, they had come to an agreement with Sidney's brother Obed, who was in charge of the general store owned by their father. They had agreed, like some others in the town, to deed him some of their property in exchange for his sustaining them from the provisions of his store, with food and cloth, after they were no longer able to work. I don't know how common this sort of arrangement was, nor whether the benefit was in fact mutual or weighted toward one party or the other.

For the moment, I am giving individual titles to some parts of the poem, and I have called this section "Our Old Patriarchs." It has some of the suddenness and incompleteness of many of the Reznikoff poems in *Testimony*, along with the implied promise that we also find in them, in the opening factual information, of something dramatic or climactic to come, a promise that, in Reznikoff's poem, is sometimes fulfilled, sometimes not. In this case, Sidney's account simply stops short with the "picture that often occurred." (I don't think the "uncles" are blood relatives of Sidney's; I think he addresses them thus out of respect.)

OUR OLD PATRIARCHS

Our brother Obed had married Clementine Guignon,
a native of France, buoyant and bright,
and fitted up for her in good style
a cottage in the woods,
called Pine Grove Cottage.
He had, at that time, the entire control
of father's stand of business.

Our old patriarchs,
such as Seth Nickerson, and Uncle Joe Phillips,
and Uncle Andrew Clark, and others,
who had grown too infirm to work,
gave him a deed of some of their property
in exchange for a living out of his groceries
and his coarse broadcloth to keep them decent and warm

and his cotton goods,
for their wives had now ceased to spin and weave.

And so this was a picture that often occurred:
Uncle Seth and Uncle Joe, eighty years old,
would creep along the Brewster road,
rolling a wheelbarrow by turns,
in which to carry home their pork and molasses,
and talking together like two children,
and stopping to talk with me.

2020

TRANSLATING
PROUST

Loaf or Hot-Water Bottle: Closely Translating Proust (Proust Talk I)

The first volume of Proust's *In Search of Lost Time* has been called, in English, *Swann's Way* for almost all of its life in English. At various times, as I worked on my translation of the book, I called it *Swann's Way, By Way of Swann's, The Way by Swann's,* and *Along the Way by Swann's.* (Nabokov, in his lectures on the book, proposed, as title, *The Walk by Swann's House.*) This translation was published first by Penguin UK in England in the fall of 2002 as *The Way by Swann's* and then, in 2003, by Viking Penguin in the United States as *Swann's Way,* and finally as a Viking paperback under the same title.

An entire, if short, essay could be devoted to the problem of how to translate the title. Other essays arising from this translation project might concern Proust's famous long sentences; C. K. Scott Moncrieff's style of translating; Scott Moncrieff himself; other first translations of classics, such as Willa and Edwin Muir's of Franz Kafka and Constance Garnett's of the Russians; nineteenth-century questions about the novel form and the fact that Proust hesitated to call this a novel (just as Leo Tolstoy denied that *War and Peace* was a novel and Nikolay Gogol declared that *Dead Souls* was a poem); and Proust's various strategies for expanding his sentences. But in this essay I'm going to write almost exclusively about close translation—how I proceeded in my translation of what is again being called *Swann's Way*.

First, a little necessary background—and I'll offer it in a sentence that, if not constructed with Proustian elegance, is at least long and contains subordinate clauses. It came out that way when I wrote it, as though I wanted to put all the information in one long, unbroken sentence, as in fact Proust wanted to do.

After having worked as a translator from the French quite consistently for thirty years or so, pausing briefly to work on my own stories and stopping for an extended time once only, as far as I can remember, to finish a novel, continuing to enjoy translating most of the time, working on a range of books of all degrees of excellence and nonexcellence, of interest and no interest, since this was how I earned most of my living and was therefore not in a position to choose, most of the time, what I wanted to translate, books ranging from a sentimental biography of Marie Curie to histories of China and art catalogs, and including several innovative novels by Pierre Jean Jouve, a volume of travel essays by Michel Butor, several books of fiction and literary philosophy by Maurice Blanchot, I was thinking, one day, though not for the first time, that sooner or later I would like to give less attention to translation and more to my own fiction, when, in the early afternoon, the phone rang.

The call was from Penguin UK asking if I would like to be part of a team of translators that was to do the whole of Proust's *In Search of Lost Time* for the Penguin Classics series, each translator taking on one volume. I immediately knew that I wanted to do this, but it was a large commitment of time. After a little hesitation, considering both selfish and unselfish motives, I said I would, and I also opted, since I was given the choice, to translate the first volume, *Du Côté de chez Swann*—the only one, as it happened, that I had read even in part. I wasn't able to start work on it right away, because I was finishing another translation, a book titled *Fibrils*, by the early surrealist and ethnographer Michel Leiris, the third volume of his four-volume *La Règle du jeu* (*Rules of the Game*), an exploration of self and language that he called an autobiographical essay. In fact, the immensely long and complex sentences in that book were good preparation for translating Proust.

At the time I was invited to join this translation, I, like many people I have since questioned, had read only a small portion of Proust's four-thousand-page novel. Even good readers—and good writers—have told me that when they tried to read it, they got sleepy. Many fall asleep thirty pages into *Swann's Way* and never return to it. Advocates and enthusiasts of Proust say the action in the novel really picks up after the first book. But of course others say that some of the most beautiful writing is in this first volume. I owned the revised Scott Moncrieff translation but had not read it; I had read about two-thirds of *Du Côté de chez Swann* in French, carefully underlining the words I didn't know and writing the English in the top and bottom margins. But this reading was some decades before, back in the 1970s.

I had a number of questions for myself early on in this project. After the first—whether to do it at all—the second was how to proceed. This book was certainly exceptional—would I do it differently from the way I had done almost all the other translations? After just a little debate, however, I decided I would embark on it, at least, in the same way; I did not know whether some different method would evolve or if the experience itself would be different.

When I approach a translation I don't generally read the book first, I translate more or less "blind," looking only a paragraph or a page ahead, sometimes not even that. The book and the work of translating are both much livelier experiences for me if I don't know exactly what's coming up next, if, as I work my way forward, I watch how the book unfolds. Many orderly people can't imagine working this way, but the fact is that a number of other translators do—I seem to remember that William Weaver, for instance, followed the same procedure in his numerous translations from the Italian. And so I was not going to go back and reread *Du Côté de chez Swann*, or even finish reading it before I began translating.

These same orderly people would object to another choice I made: I did not want any further knowledge of Proust himself or his life to influence the way I read the book. I decided not to seek out, ahead of time, biographical material or critical writings that discussed his style and his themes, that gave the sort of overview that might come between me and the words on the page. I wanted to confine myself to a rather raw, naive reading of the text as I wrote my first version in English. Then, when I had a working draft, I would begin to read around the text and let other influences affect it. So I was in the curious situation of knowing relatively little about Proust and about the novel as a whole—and deliberately keeping myself in ignorance.

I would also not look at other translations—to me, this went without saying, though, again, there are translators who proceed very differently and sit down with previous versions open in a row in front of them from the very start. Once I read something, it's very hard for me to get it out of my head. I did not want to absorb the tone, rhythm, diction of Scott Moncrieff before establishing my own. Also, if I looked only at the original text without the influence of other interpretations, I might see something they had not seen; or, to put it another way, if I looked at their interpretations too soon, I might miss something in the text, having been too influenced by them to see with my own eyes. And so I did the first draft—amounting to about 550 pages in manuscript—without looking at the other translations.

By "other translations," I mean, really, just two: the first translation of *Swann's Way*, by C. K. Scott Moncrieff; the first revision of it, by Terence Kilmartin; the further revision by D. J. Enright; and, lastly, the independent translation by James Grieve, published in 1982.

Scott Moncrieff's translation, over the eighty years during which it was virtually the only one (since Grieve's was not widely distributed or known), was, by most of its readers, considered a masterpiece and much loved, and so completely identified with Proust's own work that it seemed, to them, to *be* Proust, the only possible English version. Some people would become incensed, or at least distraught, at the thought of any tampering with it, beginning with the title for the whole novel, *Remembrance of Things Past*, which Scott Moncrieff took from a Shakespeare sonnet and which, though it is a lovely title in itself, does not reflect the content of the book and did not seem right to Proust himself. Scott Moncrieff's translation and the later revisions of it do have problems, however, and, much as I came to admire Scott Moncrieff's work, I found myself disagreeing with most of his choices.

For a long time, there was a misconception that Richard Howard was translating the whole of the Proust novel, or had translated it. In fact, Howard began the project back in

1988 but did not continue. The first pages of his projected translation appeared in *The Paris Review* in 1989, and they were useful to me for comparison.

Another early question that haunted me was whether a new translation was needed at all.

This was a real worry, for a while, until I came to know the translations and revisions better. If, I thought, the Scott Moncrieff version was faithful to the structures of the sentences and beautifully written (according to some, anyway), and if it had then been twice revised on the basis of corrected originals, so that textual faults were set right and at the same time Scott Moncrieff's more extravagant flourishes of style and departures fixed and his most extreme archaicisms or preciousnesses or squeamish euphemisms cleaned up, then wouldn't one have the ideal English version? Well, no. One problem is that neither Kilmartin nor Enright—as far as I can see from a number of close comparisons along the way— was as good a stylist as Scott Moncrieff, so that although the latest version is undoubtedly more correct than Scott Moncrieff's, the newly rendered passages are not always up to the standard of writing of the original translation. The text throughout could also be brought much closer to the French. There is still a great deal of "padding" in the revised versions. And not all the archaicisms have been eradicated— you will still come upon expressions such as "I bethought myself"—nor all the mistakes corrected.

For instance, one entire sentence, though a short one (four words), was omitted from the Scott Moncrieff translation as well as both revisions. The context is the description of a family dinner that includes Swann and takes place in the days when the narrator is a child. His frustrated grandfather keeps trying to get Swann to tell a certain story and is foiled

by the actions of two annoying female relatives. Proust remarks: "These efforts were fruitless."

In another spot Kilmartin, in his revision of Scott Moncrieff, shortened a sentence slightly and in doing so gave it
a structure that is grammatically wrong. Scott Moncrieff's
original reads: "Wait until you hear me say 'Good morning, Françoise,' and I touch your arm before you give it to
her." Kilmartin's: "Wait until you hear me say 'Good morning, Françoise,' and tap you on the arm, before you give
it to her." (The day I discovered that was a day of minor
excitement. A translator's excitement is, after all, a strangely
localized thing—and hard to convey because it arises from
minutiae so tedious to explain.)

One more example of a change for the worse, I think, in
the revision is the rendering of the exclamation "*Zut, zut, zut,
zut*," translated by Scott Moncrieff as "Damn, damn, damn,
damn" and awkwardly changed by Kilmartin to: "Gosh,
gosh, gosh, gosh."

In the midst of the second draft, I began to read a little about
Proust's life, and his style, and consistently checked my work
against the other translations. Sometimes a puzzling passage
was clarified or a guess seconded. I wanted to check to make
sure I hadn't gone wrong, but I was also simply curious to
see how the other translation had solved a problem, especially a tricky one. Often another version made me confirm
that mine felt right to me, or it induced me to improve it.
Sometimes I found a word I hadn't thought of using—in
Scott Moncrieff, say, *housetop* for *roof*. (After all, one is always
on the lookout for more vocabularies.)

Interestingly, the Scott Moncrieff and my version were

almost entirely different at every point in every sentence, even though our aims were so similar. Only every page or so would they coincide exactly in a phrase or short sentence such as: "'No, I don't know them,' he said," or "where there was a waterfall," or "Sometimes we went as far as the viaduct." Now and then, Scott Moncrieff had a closer, more literal version of a phrase, one that I had thought of and rejected as too literal, and when I read it in print I saw that it worked and restored it.

I'm not certain whether I even asked myself that other important question early on: Did I intend to do a close translation or a free translation? I have always opted for a close translation—except, say, in the case of the Marie Curie biography, whose language in the original was so coy and sentimental that I really had to make changes in the style. A close translation is both harder and easier: harder because the confines are so tight, but easier for that same reason—you don't have as many options. I prefer the narrow constraints. And since you make the rules yourself, you can, in the end, depart as far as you need to in order to create a text that reads well in English.

In the first draft I kept extremely close, intentionally, even to the point of oddness, because what you think you can't do—what you think won't work in English—actually may work, and unless you try it you won't know. Many very close, even completely literal, solutions did work. But there were also oddities in the first draft that I couldn't keep, so I took them out, though I liked them: for instance, for *désorbité*, meaning "out of one's element, removed from one's familiar surroundings," I had *disorbited*. That had to go, but I enjoyed it while it lasted. In the second draft, I began moving away from the very closest versions, but only as far as necessary to make a good piece of writing.

Another aim of a translation done so long after Scott Moncrieff's—nearly eighty years—should be, one would think, to achieve an idiom that is at least closer to the idiom of our time. And another early question to myself was: What kind of diction or language would it be written in? Would my version sound very contemporary? Was that even possible? I would pose the question to myself from time to time, almost idly, as if wondering what the weather would be. I did not really make a decision, but found that as I began translating, the question answered itself—the diction more or less chose itself.

The fact is that the goal of making a close translation determined the diction in at least two ways that I can see now: First, staying close to the word choices of the original, which are often plainer, simpler, or blunter than what Scott Moncrieff chose, and insofar as possible adding nothing that was not in the original, necessarily produced a text that was sparer and plainer than Scott Moncrieff's, and therefore more contemporary to us in its style. (Of course this implies, interestingly and correctly, that Proust himself, though writing at the same time as Scott Moncrieff, was writing in a style more akin to the style of our time than Scott Moncrieff was.) But second, staying close to the sentence structures of the original, which are often elaborate and full of dependent clauses, can't be done without using a diction that is somewhat more formal than what we might commonly see in our own contemporary fiction, since the writing of our time favors shorter, simpler sentences than the writing of the past; we may be impatient with having to hold a part of a sentence in our mind while we hear another, subordinate part or several layered subordinate parts.

There are a number of short and simple sentences in *Swann's Way*, beginning with the first: "For a long time, I went to bed early." But a great many have a monumental architecture and delayed gratification. Malcolm Bowie in *Proust among the Stars*, discussing the syntax, makes the point that some confusion is part of the experience of reading Proust: "The temporality of Proust's sentence is insistently heterogeneous," he says. "Moment by moment, the flow of time is stalled, and unpacked into its backward- and forward-looking ingredients. The reader who does not hesitate is lost."

Like any translation, this one involved me in the pleasure and absorbed concentration of attempting a hard word puzzle. I would say to myself, Here is the challenge: See if you can end this sentence on the word *dove* (or *alone* or *path* or *sleep*) without using the passive voice. Or, see if you can include three words beginning with the letter *p* in the last phrase of the paragraph. See if, for *oiseuse*, you can find a word in English beginning with *o* and ending in the *z* sound that means the same thing and, if possible, has the same derivation. Handily, for this last problem, there was the perfect solution, *otiose*, which I would never, I'm sure, use in my own writing, partly because I can't remember what it means. I associate it wrongly with *odious*, whereas it actually means, like the French, "at leisure" or "idle."

Otiose is a borderline case—a word used in contemporary English prose but not very commonly. It's acceptable, not too obscure, but many readers will probably have to look it up. I don't mind that, of course.

In this project I consulted five dictionaries regularly and several others occasionally. The oldest was one I had found in the now defunct very extensive secondhand bookstore called Editions in the Catskills. This is a two-volume French-English dictionary published in 1885, when Proust was fourteen years old. It is based on the dictionary of the Académie française and various English-language dictionaries including Noah Webster's and Samuel Johnson's. It includes a definition, in French, of the French word, which is useful because it tells me what this word meant to the French at that time, when Proust was entering what this dictionary defines as his adolescence. (The definition was the same then as ours now, the period extending from puberty to manhood, but that period, then, was understood to last from age fourteen to age twenty-five.)

I also used my French-French dictionary, the *Petit Robert*, far more than I had ever done before, and this was one of the ways that this project did in fact turn out to be different from previous translations.

Whereas I have always had the habit of reading the etymologies of English words to get to the heart of them—to find, for instance, that within the word *gregarious* is the root *grex, greg* meaning "herd"; if you are gregarious, you like to mingle in the herd—now I found I was often reading the etymology of a French word as well, trying to get to know it better, trying to see, perhaps, if what I chose for the English could have the same concrete origin as the French. Sometimes I might even translate into English, not the word itself, but the word's origin: *alors*, "then," comes from the Latin *illa hora*, "at that hour." So I felt I had the option of translating *alors* as "at that hour," though I'm not sure I ever did. Whether I did or not, knowing the derivation gave me a clear sense of just how specific *alors* is, compared to *then*.

Being aware of the etymology of a word, French or English, seemed to give me more options in my choices of equivalents. For instance, there is the French *s'entasser*, meaning "to pile up" or "to heap up." Usually I would favor an Anglo-Saxon monosyllable like *heap*, but in at least one case I chose to translate *s'entasser* as "accumulate"—whose derivation is the Latin *ad* + *cumulare*, "to heap up." (A "cumulus" cloud is one that appears to be heaped up.)

Reading so many etymologies, I became much more aware of Latin as a direct ancestor of French and a constant presence within the language, especially the Latin, originally, of those Roman soldiers who occupied, married, and settled in Gaul. And, too, I found that, paradoxically, whenever you go minutely, microscopically into a single word, you enter some large place, some area of history or culture you had never entered before. You think about the relation of *boulevard* to the word it was derived from, *bulwark*. You wonder why *losange*, meaning a lozenge or diamond shape or rhombus and derived from a Gaulish word, changed gender from feminine to masculine in the eighteenth century. And why, in the twelfth century, the French abandoned the Latinate word for rooster—*jal*, from *gallus*—in favor of the onomatopoeic word *coq*.

The surprises I had translating this book have in part resulted from looking more closely than ever before at a single word, looking into the histories and meanings of individual words in both languages. In translating you become very aware of synonyms, because you are always looking at every possible way of saying something. But how far apart most so-called synonyms really are; eventually, what leap out are the differences. *Anyway* is different from *in any case*, because a *way* is different from a *case*. *For instance* is different from *for example*, because an *instance* is different from an *example*. No choice is simple, even one that seems obvious.

Then there are the differences between the French and English so-called equivalents. The commonest equivalent of *toujours* is "always"—though you can sometimes use "ever" or "forever." But the differences emerge when you look more closely: *toujours* is a shortened form of *tous les jours*, "all the days," "every day," whereas *always* is a shortened form of "all ways," "in every manner," or "by every route." One word refers to time and the other to manner; they came to their meanings by different routes. *Toujours* also has the constant presence within it of *jours*, "days," and since *jour* can also mean "daylight" and "light," *toujours* also has the constant presence of "light." *Toujours* also has the advantage of its built-in rhyme—it has a pleasing sound.

And in fact the sound of his words plays such a large part in the effect of Proust's work that this becomes an important aspect of translating him. The obvious translation of *gens* is "people." But *gens* is a quick word—think of *jeunes gens*, "young people"—and close in sound to *genre*, meaning "kind" or "sort," and to *gentil*, meaning "nice." Our English *people* is longer and more ungainly, and close in sound to *feeble* or *pebble* or *peephole* or *peeper*—what you hear in the swamps in the spring. The associations of the two words are very different, yet in the case of *gens* we usually do not have any alternative.

Another way in which this translation was a different experience was that I became more specifically aware of the different features of my practice of close translating—what I can identify, after the fact, as my "rules":

First, at the level of the individual word, I want to give the closest equivalent whenever possible: for *disait*, "said," I will almost always use *said*, not *remarked*, *began*, *murmured*, *took the opportunity to say*, or *assured him*. Scott Moncrieff will often replace a plain or a neutral word with a more expressive or loaded word: for *tenu*, "held," he has "squeezed"; for *petit*, "little," he has "tiny"; for *intérêt*, "interest," he has "fascination"; for *vidés*, "emptied," he has "purged"; for *regardait*, "looked," he has "peeped."

What he is doing in this last case, and what he does to some degree throughout his translation, is to bring his understanding of the context into his choice of the word. He knows that Aunt Léonie is looking *over the tops of her glasses* at her guests as she makes fun of Swann, and so he supplies the word *peep*. But that is giving the reader of the English more than the reader of the French, who is given the more neutral word *look* to form his or her own image of Aunt Léonie.

Because of the close relationship between French and English, there are many words that are identical, of course. Some are perfect equivalents, and lovely in their own right, like "lacustrine" for *lacustrine*. James Grieve rejected *lacustrine* in favor of *lakeside*, and when I read Grieve's choice I worried: Was mine too obscure? Then I opened a book of John Ashbery's poems and happened on the title "These Lacustrine Cities" and was reassured that at least one writer in English, having the choice of all possible words, chose that one.

There are other perfect equivalents, though, that a translator must hesitate to use, which is maddening, because although they are the same words as the French and mean the same, they are so unfamiliar to a reader that they may express very little, such as *aurora*, meaning, as the French *aurore* does, the pink or rosy or yellow-gold light in the sky just before the sun rises.

Many words, of course, used to have the same meaning in English as in French and no longer do—you encounter them throughout a Henry James novel. One meaning of the French *solitude* is a solitary or secluded or isolated place, and that is what our English *solitude* once meant, as well. Here is Jack London, in his short story "In a Far Country" (1899): "Beyond his bleak skyline there stretched vast solitudes, and beyond these still vaster solitudes." In *A Passage to India*

(1924), E. M. Forster uses the word *dispose* in the same way as the French do, to mean "arrange." In my 1885 dictionary, I find these equivalents.

Failing the identical word, you sometimes find a pleasing, expressive cognate that is close in sound to the French, such as *tumble* for *tomber*, "to fall," but that is rare.

The second "rule" of close translating would be not to add any material that is not in the original. A difficult word for a translator is the French *oubli*, which means "forgetting," "forgetfulness," "failure of memory," "oblivion"—we don't have a good equivalent for those two syllables. In one passage, for *oubli*, Scott Moncrieff has "waters of Lethe," Lethe being the river in Hades whose waters cause forgetfulness of the past. He has added a mythological reference that is not in the original. This is an instance of the extravagant Scott Moncrieff that was not corrected by Kilmartin. In another spot—also uncorrected—he adds a metaphor: for *l'entrée des Enfers*, "the entrance to the Underworld," he has "the jaws of Hell."

Another kind of addition is the insertion of words whose only function is rhythmical or syntactical: If you're going to change the original for the sake of rhythm, or stress, or to reproduce some element of the original syntax, you would rather add to the text, of course, than subtract from it. However, if you are a conscientious translator, you won't want to add new material, so your only recourse is to duplicate, to repeat material, to, in effect, "pad" the text. You may double an adjective, as in Scott Moncrieff's "strange and haunting" for Proust's "strange"; or you may add filler words like *rather*, *perhaps*, or *quite*, which have the effect of attenuating or diluting the original. Scott Moncrieff will sometimes add a false or redundant specificity—*himself* in "he himself" or *peculiarly* in "peculiarly gentle." Or he will add emphasis: "for

me so painful" becomes "so exquisitely painful to myself"—
and here he is adding also a nuance of pleasure, not in the
original, to the pain.

In more substantial additions—where Scott Moncrieff
again brings his prior knowledge of the context into his
choice—"crow" becomes "solitary crow" because he already
knows it's alone; or the single word *confidence* in the original becomes "newfound confidence." Arguably, he is not
adding a new idea, but he is making the passage wordier
than the original, and sometimes redundant. Translations in
general do tend to be longer than their originals in part for
this reason.

The third rule would be not to subtract anything from
the French, especially by condensing: at one point, Proust
talks about "the place surrounding" a certain woman of
whom the narrator is daydreaming; I would rather not substitute the word *setting* even though *setting* means "the place
surrounding" a thing or "the place in which" the thing is.

More obvious may be not to leave out words or images.
In one of his many scenes of harmonious family life, Proust
describes a family walk on a Saturday evening after church.
For *nos pas solitaires*, "our solitary steps," Scott Moncrieff has
"our steps in the silence." Here he is both adding and sub-
tracting. Solitary steps in the evening that incite the dogs to
bark does suggest silence, but one doesn't have to spell it out.
Perhaps he was bothered by a family having "solitary" steps.
And yet that contradiction is interesting.

The fourth rule would be to retain repetitions: repeat
words that Proust repeats, rather than introduce variations.
Sometimes Scott Moncrieff seems to want to avoid Proust's
deliberate repetitions, which he may hear as inelegant. In one
long sentence, one of the famous ones about the afternoon
falling piece by piece with the ringing of the church bells,

Proust uses the word *bonne*, "good," for the smell of the air—*la bonne odeur de l'air*—and then eight lines down the page uses the word again in *bon dîner*, "good dinner"—*pour lire jusqu'au bon dîner qu'apprêtait Françoise*, "to read until the good dinner which Françoise was preparing." Scott Moncrieff translates *bon dîner* as "good dinner," but *la bonne odeur de l'air* as "the fragrance of the air." Proust's style is natural and unaffected, and, surprisingly, often plain and blunt. There is something I find strong and elemental about the repetition of the word *good*, which I would not want to lose.

The fifth rule would be to respect the structures of the sentences as Proust created them: to retain each sentence intact, whether it is long and full of dependent clauses or short and simple. Inevitably, a frustrated reader of Proust in English would ask me please to break up the sentences for easier reading. This would have been to falsify the experience of reading Proust.

The sixth would be to retain the same order of elements in a sentence, so that they unfold for the reader in the same order. Often this means sacrificing something else: *au marché de Martinville* would be most literally translated "at the Martinville market"; by changing that to "at the market in Martinville" you reproduce the rhythm and the word order of the French and end with the word "Martinville."

I tried, whenever possible, to begin and end sentences and especially paragraphs with the same word or at least phrase that Proust did. So my seventh rule would be to begin a sentence or paragraph with the same word or words as in the original. For instance, in one passage about the walks the family took, Proust begins two consecutive sentences with the word *jamais*, "never": *Jamais dans la promenade du côté de Guermantes nous ne pûmes remonter jusqu'aux sources de la Vivonne . . . Jamais non plus nous ne pûmes pousser jusqu'au terme.* "Never, in our walk along the Guermantes way, could we go as far as the sources of the Vivonne . . . Never, either, could we go all the way to the end point that I would so much have liked to reach, all the way to Guermantes." I had second thoughts about this. The "never, either" reads a bit strangely, and so at one point I revised it away and followed Scott Moncrieff's compromise—"Nor could we go all the way to"; later I reread the French and decided I couldn't let the repetition "Never . . . Never" go, even if "Never, either" was strange.

The eighth rule, then, would be to end a sentence or paragraph the same way as in the original: preferably the very last word should be the same. Better to end, say, given a choice, with *Martinville*, as the original does, than *market*.

Ninth would be rather a tall order, but often possible: to reproduce the play of sounds, especially the alliteration and the assonance, as much as possible.

Of course the book is filled with it: *faisait refluer ses reflets*; or the ABBA structure of this phrase: *lâcheté qui nous détourne de toute tâche*; or this sort of symmetrically balanced construction, which occurs over and over again: *j'éprouve la résistance et j'entends la rumeur des distances traversées* (with, in addition, the rhyming pair *résistance/distances*). This sort of soundplay is particularly noticeable at the ends of paragraphs, especially at the end of a long sentence that is building by the accumulation of words and images. One extreme example, though it's a short, simple sentence in this case, comes at the end of a pretty description of Françoise's scullery as a Temple of Venus: *Et son faîte était toujours couronné du roucoulement d'une colombe.* (Note the *t*'s, *ou*'s, *r*'s, *c*'s, and the echo in *couronné/roucoulement/colombe*.)

Where Proust describes the water of the Vivonne river

as filling, like some distant port, *du rose et de la reverie du couchant*, I have the option of reproducing the alliteration with "the rose and reverie of the sunset" rather than translating *rose* more literally as "pink." Sometimes I go a little further than Proust does in one passage as compensation for not being able to go as far as he does in other passages: where he talks about a certain street with *ses particularités curieuses et sa personnalité revêche*, I add one more term of alliteration by rendering the phrase as "its curious peculiarities and its cantankerous personality." Some sounds just naturally come out right because of the cognates—something that would not happen often with English and Farsi, for example—so that without any effort on my part *au marché de Martinville* will have accents on the same vowel sounds in English: "at the market in Martinville."

The tenth rule would be not to normalize something that seems odd at the moment—the "solitary steps" mentioned earlier, or the cooing separated from the dove. Or the metaphors that Scott Moncrieff regularly turns into (less radical) similes: in Proust a balcony floats in front of a house; in Scott Moncrieff's version it only "seems" to float.

My last rule came from something I discovered fairly late in the translation, partway through the second draft—that even Proust's punctuation could be followed quite closely. After punctuating "by ear" or by instinct in the first draft, unthinkingly, I began to look at Proust's punctuation per se, to see if I could follow it more closely and in particular if I could punctuate as lightly as he does. It is possible much more often than one would imagine. Here is just one instance of this: after I was finished revising the translation for the American edition, I reread the opening of the sentence discussed above, "Never, in our walk along the Guermantes way, could we go as far as the sources of the Vivonne," com-

pared it to the original, and realized that I could have removed two commas that were not in the French and were
not necessary. This latest revision would have to wait for a
future edition: "Never in our walk along the Guermantes
way could we go as far as the sources of the Vivonne." Yet
the challenge of matching Proust's punctuation was not just
a game. The absence of pauses in certain long sentences reproduces some sense of Proust's rapid and breathless manner
of speaking and is deeply native to his style, as one can see
from reading his letters.

Perhaps the eternal weighing of options that is always involved in a translation project is best illustrated by an example of the debate that went on over a fairly simple sentence,
this one involving food.

The word *boule* means, most simply, "ball," but in the
following context may mean "loaf of bread" and may mean
"hot-water bottle," and would make sense in either meaning, because it is something comforting and warm that the
servant Françoise makes or prepares for the young narrator.

Françoise has just been furiously slaughtering a chicken
down in the scullery, calling it "filthy beast, filthy beast,"
and Marcel is horrified by her cruelty and wishes the family
would fire her immediately. But then he selfishly asks himself:
*Mais qui m'eût fait des boules aussi chaudes, du café aussi par-
fumé, et même . . . ces poulets?* The closest translation of this
was, I thought: "But who would have made me such warm
loaves, such fragrant coffee, and even . . . those chickens?"
Actually, still more literal, and possible, would be: "But who
would have made me loaves so warm, coffee so fragrant, and
even . . . those chickens?" (This was an instance in which the

more literal version would have worked, though in the end I did not opt for it.)

Proust has used a plain verb—*faire*, "make"—for all three elements. He has also begun a parallel structure with *des boules aussi chaudes, du café aussi parfumé*, but departed from it with: *et même . . . ces poulets*. These are three things Françoise makes for Marcel. There is something very elemental about the idea, simply, of making. But Scott Moncrieff preferred to replace *make* by his own verbs, a different verb for each noun, enriching the sentence significantly; at the same time, he also completed the parallel structure of the sentence: "But who would have baked me such hot rolls, boiled me such fragrant coffee, and even—roasted me such chickens?"

There's something nice about those verbs, the alliteration of *baked* and *boiled*, and the heartiness of *roasted*; you get a better sense of the delicious food. This is an example of the good writing in Scott Moncrieff's translation. However, Proust could have given each food its own verb and chose not to. He could also have created a completely parallel structure; he has many throughout the book. I can only guess at his reasons: maybe he wanted to draw us up short with the uneloquent "those chickens," which also better describes, from the narrator's point of view, the creatures as they are at the moment—being put to death rather than coming to the table as a savory dish. One reason I believe so strongly in staying as close as possible to the original author's choices rather than overinterpreting or "improving" him is that we as translators should not presume to have understood everything he was trying to do; by presenting his text as he presented it, to the extent possible, we offer Anglophone readers the chance to read and interpret without our meddling.

Now, Kilmartin evidently objected to "boiling" the coffee, so he took it out and replaced it with "made," which I think is rather weak, because although he is restoring one of Proust's verbs, he is not restoring the other, and the parallelism of Scott Moncrieff's version, nice in itself, is disrupted, since the three particular cooking verbs—*baked*, *boiled*, and *roasted*—become *baked*, *made*, and *roasted*: "But who would have baked me such hot rolls, made me such fragrant coffee, and even . . . roasted me such chickens?" This, too, is a good example of Kilmartin's approach to revision, which in part corrects deviations in the original Scott Moncrieff translation but is not as well written and often stops short of completely restoring the Proust original.

Whereas Scott Moncrieff and his revisers translated *boules* as "rolls," James Grieve opts for "hot-water bottles" and his version is longer: "But, then, who would there have been to fill those nice hot-water bottles, to make me such fragrant coffee and even—to roast me those chickens?" He also keeps Scott Moncrieff's full parallel structure and follows Kilmartin's lead in his uneven mix of particular and general verbs. There are two other votes for "hot-water bottle": one in a nice footnoted French edition of the "Combray" section of *Swann's Way* edited by Germaine Brée and Carlos Lynes, Jr., the other in my *Harrap's* dictionary: "hot-water bottle" is given as the equivalent, while the only reference to bread is a military term, "ration loaf." But then I find, in the *Petit Robert*, the phrase *boule de pain*—"ball of bread."

Now, I was already leaning away from the "hot-water bottle" solution and toward the "loaf" solution because of the other two terms of the sentence. Also, our local baker, across the creek, sold what he called a *boule* that was a round loaf. At last I telephoned him to discuss it—he already knew I was working on the Proust translation because he had baked me some *petites madeleines* for an event at the public library. He told me that *boule* is a common term for a shape of bread, like *baguette* or *ficelle*. I asked him if it could be used to refer to a roll, since Scott Moncrieff and Kilmartin translated it by "hot rolls," and he said that it was definitely not a roll but a loaf, and that in the 1970s in San Francisco you used to be able to order a "*boule* of soup"—soup served in a hollowed-out round loaf that you would eventually eat. (A few weeks after that conversation, I found offered on the menu, in a restaurant in Connecticut, chili served in what was called by the inventively Frenchified name of "bread boulé.")

Somewhere in the course of these explorations, a person I was talking to about it suggested that since English-speaking readers now know the word, the perfect equivalent for *boule* would in fact be the same word, *boule*. But there is an interesting problem involved in this solution: the word may be identical to the French, but the context is different, so the word changes, too. (Even the fact that it is a French word in a translation from the French changes the effect of a word.) To Proust, the word would refer to a common sort of loaf, consumed by the broadest spectrum of society, including those who, in America, at one time, bought Wonder Bread and Freihofer, but also those who bought Arnold's and Pepperidge Farm, and then those who, more recently, bought fresh-baked baguettes and ficelles from small upscale bakeries. The word *boule* imported into a book in English, however, would refer only to an elite, effete item.

So the only equally universal English equivalent would be *loaf*. In order to retain the idea of "ball," I could call it a *round loaf*—it would not be an awkward insertion here since Proust is already waxing a bit lyrical: "such warm loaves" would become "such warm round loaves."

And at this point I thought I was done with the problem.

However, fresh doubts were raised by an assiduous graduate student who was reading the translation for a project of his own, and so I consulted two native Frenchmen of a certain age. One of them said it could be either a loaf or a hot-water bottle, but that Proust had made great use of hot-water bottles and called them *boules* as a shortened, affectionate form of the standard term *bouillottes;* my other informant declared that a *boule* was definitely a hot-water bottle, preferably the kind made out of metal that he himself had grown up with, and in the end he clinched the decision in favor of the hot-water bottle by pointing out something I had not thought of, that Françoise would not have made her own *boules* but would have bought them at—where else?—the *boulangerie.* (The word *boulangerie* does indeed come from the Picard word *boulenc*, "one who makes bread in the shape of a ball.") So that is just one example of how, in the course of a translation, as you explore all the possibilities before making a final decision, you go a considerable distance in a circle before ending up not far from where you started but much better informed.

2003

Hammers and Hoofbeats: Rhythms and Syntactical Patterns in Proust's *Swann's Way* (Proust Talk II)

Translating Proust led me to think about the terms *parataxis* and *hypotaxis* more explicitly than I had before. The present essay is more or less paratactic in its overall structure though hypotactic within its two parts. The first part is about sounds and numbers in Proust's life and prose, the second, not entirely unrelated, is about the structures of Proust's more complex sentences.

Parataxis comes from the Greek for "arrangement side by side" and according to some definitions allows the elements to be connected by conjunctions, as in this example from Hemingway (1927): "There was a big sea running and waves broke and the wind blew the spray against the car." Or they can be side by side without conjunctions, the most famous example being *veni, vidi, vici*, "I came, I saw, I conquered," purportedly written in a letter "home" from the battlefield by Julius Caesar (ca. 47 B.C.).

The opposite of parataxis, *hypotaxis*, from the Greek for "arrangement under," means constructed in a relationship of dependent clauses, as in this sentence from Henry James, written about seven years before Proust began composing *Swann's Way*:

> The same secret principle, however, that had prompted Strether not absolutely to desire Waymarsh's presence at the dock, that had led him thus to postpone for a few hours his enjoyment of it, now operated to make him feel that he could still wait without disappointment.
>
> —*The Ambassadors* by Henry James;
> Harper's Modern Classic edition, 1930

A translator tends to think very much in terms of sentences and particularly types of sentences because for a translator a sentence is, among many other things, a construction and a problem in construction. The terminal points consisting of the initial capital letter and the closing period are welcome ones, since the problem won't usually extend beyond them; we are presented with one problem, one sentence, at a time. The problem to be solved may not be hard: the two-word sentence *Il frappa*, "He knocked," takes about four seconds—I measured this—to read, understand, and translate. But one line later may come a sentence that will take much longer to solve: "A voice which he tried to distinguish from among the voices of those of Odette's friends whom he knew answered: 'Who's there?'" This problem sentence may take two or more hours of deliberation at home alone and then further conversation with friends over dinner in an Indian restaurant, conversation that is ultimately not helpful.

As I went deeper and deeper into Proust's sentences, in the second and later drafts of my translation of *Swann's Way*, I became more specifically aware of just how Proust put his sentences together, how he worked with alliteration and assonance, syllable counts, parallel constructions, balance and imbalance, numbers; what the difference was, for instance, between the phrases that stood alone and those that were constructed of balanced pairs; the difference between the simple sentences and the compound and complex, and between the paratactic and the hypotactic. Along the way I discovered an extremely useful book-length study by Jean Milly of Proust's syntax called *La Phrase de Proust* (Proust's Sentence), which revealed even more: the verse forms embedded in the sentences; the less obvious duplications, including oppositions, disjunctions, and exclusions; and even some intriguing play with anagrams whereby, for instance, in the passage about the steeples of Martinville, the word *clocher*, "steeple," is surrounded by what Milly calls an "anagrammatic environment" consisting of words that repeat the sounds of *clocher*, such as *chemin*, *couchant*, *flèche*, *rapprocher*, *cocher*, and *écorce*.

At the same time that I was discovering the structural surprises of his sentences, I was deeply immersed in the world of the past that Proust was describing, the world of his childhood and of the years before his childhood, when the fictional Swann falls in love with Odette, and, later, the years of Proust's young manhood. Although, as I worked, I myself was hearing the sounds of, first, twentieth- and, then, twenty-first-century traffic passing under my windows, I was at the same time imaginatively reentering a world in which the sound in your ears, when you went along a road in a vehicle, was not the steady hum of an engine but the clip-clop of horses' hooves.

Thinking about the rhythms and sounds of Proust's prose and then about the environments in which he grew up, I began to relate the two and think more specifically about the sounds that surrounded him, and the rhythms of these sounds. I began to wonder just how much of an effect these rhythms had on the rhythms of his prose.

Proust took piano lessons when he was a child and his family held concerts in the house. As an adult, he kept a piano in his room while he was writing *In Search of Lost Time* and he listened, in the evenings, to symphony concerts via the *théâtrophone*, a direct telephone connection to the concert halls. In the "Swann in Love" section of the novel, the sonata by Vinteuil is the anthem of Swann's love. What were the other environmental sounds in his life, the rhythms both musical and nonmusical? What were the sounds that surrounded Proust from, say, age seven to seventeen, from about 1878 to 1888?

Some of the sounds then were different from the sounds now, some the same.

The sounds in the city (either in his parents' apartment or in his uncle's house in Auteuil), outdoors: birds warbling and chirping in the garden, voices in the garden calling and shouting, laughing, occasionally singing, sung music and instrumental music; his own piano lessons and practice, and his brother Robert's; musical instruments being practiced in different apartments in the neighborhood; voices practicing scales and songs and arias (some of the same sounds that you hear now in a bourgeois neighborhood, and that you hear in Hitchcock's *Rear Window*); people calling their pets; dogs barking—I don't know what the laws were then regulating pets or other animals roaming free in the streets, about 1885; cats meowing or caterwauling in the middle of the night; people whistling; footsteps on sidewalks; tradesmen calling their wares through the streets; horses' hoofbeats, trotting and walking; carriage wheels rattling on cobblestone and grinding over dust and dirt over stone (i.e., the steady sound of wheels under the regular rhythm of the hoofbeats either pacing or trotting); in the carriage, the creaking of the wood and leather along with the hoofbeats and wheels. Carillons from churches; church bells sounding the hours, tolling for deaths, pealing for weddings. Think of Proust's description of the tears he continues to shed inside himself even now that he is an adult: they are, he says, "like those convent bells covered so well by the clamor of the town during the day that one would think they had ceased altogether but which begin sounding again in the silence of the evening."

Proust would have heard many of the same sounds in the small town of Illiers, the model for Combray, where the family went to visit Aunt Amiot, the model for Tante Léonie, during the holidays and summers, including dogs barking like the dogs in *Swann's Way* as the family return from their walk on Saturday evening:

> From gates far apart, dogs awakened by our solitary steps sent forth alternating barks such as I still hear at times in the evening and among which the station boulevard (when the public gardens of Combray were created on its site) must have come to take refuge, for, wherever I find myself, as soon as they begin re-sounding and replying, I see it, with its lindens and its sidewalk lit by the moon.

Other sounds in a small town might have been: the bell at the garden gate announcing a visitor; a grocer's boy, as in the "Combray" section of *Swann's Way*, hammering crates on a summer's afternoon when the aunt was "not resting"; or a blacksmith at his forge. The surroundings in those days were, on the whole, quieter: a village could be so quiet that a hammer striking several streets away might sound as if it were next door. A cock crowing in the next village might be heard in this one. The sounds Proust heard made more of an impact on him, literally.

Indoors, he would have heard, in both city and country: the rustle of women's dresses (remember the young narrator in *Swann's Way* dreading the very thing he longs for most: "But this goodnight lasted so short a time, she went back down so soon, that the moment when I heard her coming up, then, passing along the hallway with its double doors, the soft sound of her garden dress of blue muslin, hung with little cords of plaited straw, was for me a painful moment"); there would have been the ticktock of a pendulum clock and its chime; the rattle of silverware and clinking of glasses and chinking of pottery at the table; the stirring of tea in a tea-cup; the banging of pots and pans in the kitchen; the cook beating batter, scraping a mixing bowl, chopping vegetables; the sound of a rug beaten on a line outside. There would have been the whistling of the family; voices conversing, voices reading aloud—a continuous sound with variations, as in this description of the narrator's mother:

> With this inflection she softened as she went along any crudeness in the tenses of the verbs, gave the im-perfect and the past historic the sweetness that lies in goodness, the melancholy that lies in tenderness, directed the sentence that was ending toward the one that was about to begin, sometimes hurrying, some-times slowing down the pace of the syllables so as to bring them, though their quantities were different, into one uniform rhythm, she breathed into this very common prose a sort of continuous emotional life.

And finally, at Illiers, there would have been the particular sounds associated with a walk in the countryside: the various cries and calls of the birds; the flapping wings of birds taking flight, passing overhead, or landing; all the different volumes and levels of wind in the trees; multiple footsteps of people out walking, in regular or irregular patterns and softened by the surface of dirt or grass; farmers calling and shouting at their animals or fellow laborers, maybe shepherds calling or whistling to their dogs; others calling dogs and children and each other; on country roads, wagons or carriages passing with the sound of rolling wheels, hoofbeats, again, walking or trotting, the creaking leather of the carriage or harness or saddle, the crack of a whip; the regular swish of scythes through wheat or hay; church bells tolling in the distance; the sound of carillons, this time in the midst of a relative silence rather than the din of a city; cicadas trilling and frogs croaking; cows lowing and sheep bleating; people chanting or singing while at work in the fields.

I laboriously cataloged and enumerated these sounds for myself—though not even exhaustively—because I was trying to discover whether Proust's acoustical environment was much richer and more rhythmical than ours is today. Rhythm being an ordered interruption or division of continuous sound, I wanted first to contemplate what might have been the sources of Proust's sense of rhythm, and then to observe the ways in which he employed rhythm in his very deliberate sentences.

Surely one major difference between his acoustical environment and ours today is that in his childhood and youth and later, up to the advent of the automobile, Proust would have heard more punctuating noises, either regular or irregular, and fewer steady ambient noises, whereas we today are surrounded by steady ambient noise, mainly because of the prevalence of electric power and the combustion engine: we hear the computer or refrigerator or oil furnace always humming in the background, often highway traffic either whispering (in the distance) or humming, thundering, roaring (nearby). Because of unceasing vehicle traffic in a large city, there is an unremitting steady background din, with no chance for the convent bells to be heard in the evening.

Some of the sounds surrounding Proust were more rhythmical, more distinctly punctuated, and some less so, more continuous. A hammer striking is predominantly rhythmical, while certain meandering birdsongs, like that of the nightingale, are more melodic.

Different sounds have different beats:

One: Many cooking sounds are rhythmical; they tend to have the rhythm one-one-one-one at equal intervals: mixing with a wooden spoon, pounding a chicken cutlet.

The beating of a rug also has a rhythm of one-one-one-one, but slower.

Hammering has a rhythm of one-one-one-one, unless it is *one*-two, *one*-two.

Two: A horse trotting before a carriage would have a brisk *one*-two-*one*-two rhythm. This is presumably a sound Proust would have heard a great deal throughout his youth and on into adulthood, when he lamented the coming of the automobile.

Three: I had more trouble thinking of sets of threes in the sounds surrounding him—aside from those in music and musical prose, where sets of threes are so important. Certain repeating birdsongs come in sets of threes. The sound of a dog lapping water from a bowl may come in sets of threes and fours.

Four: A horse walking would have a leisurely *one*-two-*three*-four, *one*-two-*three*-four rhythm. The horse's head nods in time to its walk, on the first and third beats.

Continuous: Then there are the sounds that are not broken into rhythmical beats, that are continuous, though with variations: carriage wheels turning, over a dirt track or stones; a grindstone turning, briefer; the noise inside a water-powered mill would be continuous, loud and unvarying. In fact, it is in the nature of a wheel—whether carriage wheel or mill wheel—moving steadily to produce a steady stream of sound because it is an endless surface. The wind, which can be continuous for shorter or longer periods before it rises or falls; a babbling brook, with barely perceptible variations; a powerful high waterfall would be continuous without any real variation.

How do these rhythms, these beats, these numbers show up in the sentences of *Swann's Way*?

1. The number one stands alone, has no counterbalance, no forward motion, no continuation. It is the teacher's single rap of the ruler on the desk. It is the briefest Proustian sentence, such as the single-word exclamation "What?" or "Oh!" And perhaps one could argue that by contrast to longer sentences, his very brief two-word statements or questions also have the effect of a single beat: "He knocked," or "Who's there?"

2: Two is the number of balance, or, to take the French cognate (and false friend), *la balance*, meaning the old-fashioned scale with its two pans. It is the number of thesis and antithesis, question and answer, not only in speech but also in games—tennis, checkers, chess; it is the back-and-forth swing of the pendulum in a pendulum clock.

The following sentence, in which Proust is commenting about the frescoes of the Virtues and Vices of Padua, is typical of his handling of pairs, or doubles—and the balance that pervades the novel. It is five lines long and punctuated by commas and one semicolon (doubles are italicized here):

> But later I understood that the *startling strangeness*, the *special beauty* of these frescoes was due to the large place which the symbol occupied in them; and the fact that it was represented, *not as a symbol*, since the thought symbolized was not expressed, *but as real*, as *actually experienced* or *physically handled*, gave something *more literal* and *more precise* to the meaning of the work, something *more concrete* and *more striking* to the lesson it taught.

Notice the doubling within the doubling in the last part of the sentence.

Another passage in which the pairs multiply comes in the middle of a long paragraph about the narrator's bedridden, hypochondriac Tante Léonie's views of her own health condition (alliteration boldfaced):

> *Les uns, les pires et dont elle s'était débarrassée les premiers, étaient ceux qui lui conseillaient de ne pas "s'écouter" et professaient, fût-ce négativement et en ne la manifestant que par certains silences de **d**ésapprobation ou par certains sourires de **d**oute, la **d**octrine subversive qu'une **p**etite **p**romenade au soleil et un **b**on **b**ifteck saignant (quand elle gardait quatorze heures sur l'estomac deux méchantes gorgées d'eau de Vichy!)*

lui feraient plus de bien que son lit et ses médecines.
L'autre catégorie se composait des personnes qui avaient
l'air de croire qu'elle était plus gravement malade
qu'elle ne pensait, qu'elle était aussi gravement ma-
lade qu'elle le disait.

Some of the beautifully balanced alliteration in that passage can be reproduced in the English translation, mostly through the grace of the Latinate cognates:

One group, the worst, whom she had got rid of first, were the ones who advised her not to "listen to herself" so and subscribed, if only negatively, and manifesting it only by certain disapproving silences or by certain dubious smiles, to the subversive doctrine that a little stroll in the sun and a nice rare steak (though two wretched sips of Vichy water would lie on her stomach for fourteen hours!) would do her more good than her bed and her medicines. The other category was composed of the people who appeared to believe she was more gravely ill than she thought, that she was as gravely ill as she said she was.

Notice also Proust's willingness to repeat for effect: "*plus gravement malade qu'elle ne pensait, . . . aussi grave-ment malade qu'elle le disait*"; "more gravely ill than she thought, . . . as gravely ill as she said she was." Notice also that sentence number one describing the first category of people is long and complexly structured, whereas sentence number two describing the second is markedly shorter—two lines as opposed to five. Many of Proust's sentences are actually quite short and provide a necessary variation and contrast to the longer ones.

3: Three is the number of beginning, middle, end; or thesis, antithesis, synthesis. It presents three equal elements, as in *veni, vidi, vici*; or it posits two and concludes with a third. Whereas the number two suggests balance and sometimes, as in the case of the pendulum, indefinite continuation, the rhythmic use of three, followed by silence or a pause, suggests conclusion or finality—which is why it is such a vital and useful element in descriptive and dramatic prose.

One example occurs at the very end—appropriately—of the same long paragraph detailing Tante Léonie's attitude toward her illness. It is yet another good example, also, of Proust's use of both exact repetition and close parallel structure. It is another short sentence. (The alliteration, in this case, indicated in boldface, is in the translation, not the original—as, by compensation, I attempt to make up for the many instances in which the alliteration in the original can't be reproduced in the translation.)

> *En somme, ma tante exigeait à la fois qu'on l'approuvât dans son régime, qu'on la plaignît pour ses souffrances et qu'on la rassurât sur son avenir.*

> In short, my aunt required that her visitors at the same time **c**ommend her on her regimen, **c**ommiserate with her for her sufferings, and en**c**ourage her as to her future.

Sometimes patterns of twos and threes are combined, as in this fragment of a sentence taken from the passage about the steeples of Martinville, in which, again, Proust also makes use of parallel structure, alliteration, and, here, assonance:

en constatant,
en notant

> *la forme de leur flèches,*
> *le déplacement de leurs lignes,*
> *l'ensoleillement de leurs surfaces*

As I observed,
as I noted

> the shape of their spires,
> the shifting of their lines,
> the sunlight on their surfaces

4: Four takes the number of balance—two—and doubles it. It is the number of walking and marching: left, right, left, right. It is the outset of something that will continue, maybe indefinitely.

In *Swann's Way* the number four appears in lists: for example, looking again at the passage about the steeples of Martinville, the young narrator tells us that if he, jolting along next to the driver in the carriage careening down the winding roads that presented constantly changing perspectives, had not written down a description of the steeples, they would have gone to join forever those other elements of his surroundings that had made an impression on him but that he had forgotten: trees, rooftops, fragrances, sounds.

When his mother unexpectedly indulges him after he has been so disobedient as to wait up for her in the hallway, in the famous scene of the goodnight kiss, she offers to read to him and brings out the four books by George Sand that his grandmother was going to give him on his saint's day: *La Mare au diable*, *François le champi*, *La Petite Fadette*, and *Les Maîtres sonneurs*.

Then there are the four adjectives he attributes to the word *Parma* in the following passage, part of his reverie over the train timetables in which he describes his daydreams about different destinations. Notice, once again, Proust's willingness to repeat something like a list, though in this case, mysteriously, slightly changing the order:

> Because the name of Parma, one of the towns I had most wanted to visit, ever since I had read *La Chartreuse*, seemed to me compact, smooth, mauve, and soft, if someone mentioned a certain house in Parma in which I would be staying, he gave me the pleasure of thinking I would be living in a house that was smooth, compact, mauve, and soft, that bore no relation to the houses of any real town in Italy, since I had composed it in my imagination using only that heavy syllable, *Parme*, in which no air circulates, and the Stendhalian softness and tint of violets with which I had permeated it.

The strong quality of balance in Proust's sentences, the predominance of balanced elements, may serve to slow down the forward motion of the story, rocking readers back and forth as they amble along, instead of sending them hurtling forward. Now, how does he use these elements to build up some of those complex and, incidentally, hypotactic, sentences?

The translator, or at least this translator, works within the single sentence, solves it—up to a certain point, in any case—and then goes on to the next. I had two reasons not to break up any of Proust's longer, more complex sentences: First, my aim was to present the text as nearly as I could in the way it was presented originally to its native readers (complicated as that concept really is—and I know I'm simplifying here what could be said to involve the whole vast question of how to approach translation). And second, Proust specifically declared that he did not want the long sentence to be fragmented: that no matter how complex, a thought should remain intact within one sentence. It can also be argued that Proust's formal and more complex syntax actually allows more room for grace and richness.

The paratactic sentence—in which the elements are set side by side, either connected or not connected—is much easier to follow because each part of the sentence is completed, and understood, as it goes along. Here are some more examples of parataxis taken from the same story by Hemingway, "Che Ti Dice La Patria?," with elements connected by the conjunction *and*, of which he was very fond: "A big car passed us, going fast, and a sheet of muddy water rose up and over our wind-shield and radiator. The automatic windshield cleaner moved back and forth, spreading the film over the glass. We stopped and ate lunch at Sestri. There was no heat in the restaurant and we kept our hats and coats on." Our understanding of the sentence keeps almost exact pace with the unfolding of it. There are present participial phrases modifying the action ("going fast" and "spreading the film") but no subordinate clauses.

In the hypotactic sentence, in which one or more dependent clauses hangs off the main clause, our understanding must hold the beginning of one clause in suspension—or, in the case of Proust and certain other stylists, sometimes more than one clause—and read other material in the sentence before we can complete that clause, as in the following sentence about Swann's behavior in his love affair with Odette, which also contains an inversion. This sentence was a particularly thorny one to translate. I'm satisfied with my solution, which, as usual, I was determined to keep very close to the original, though it is at the same time rather awkward English—perhaps really too awkward. However, I couldn't resist chopping up the latter half of the sentence with commas in the same extreme way that Proust does.

S'il arrivait après l'heure où Odette envoyait ses domestiques se coucher, avant de sonner à la porte du petit jardin, il allait d'abord dans la rue où donnait au rez-de-chaussée, entre les fenêtres toutes pareilles, mais obscures, des hôtels contigus, la fenêtre, seule éclairée, de sa chambre.

If he arrived after the hour when Odette sent her servants to bed, before ringing at the gate of the little garden he would first go into the street onto which looked out, on the ground floor, between the windows, all alike but dark, of the contiguous houses, the only one illuminated, the window of her room.

I can imagine, if it is not too fanciful, that all those commas are slowing down the sentence to reflect Swann's cautious steps around to the back of the house.

A particular kind of hypotactic sentence structure, whether in a long or a short sentence, is one of those aspects of Proust's prose that cause difficulties for some readers. It is the structure in which there are pyramids of subordinate clauses, or—perhaps a better image—Russian dolls of nesting clauses, each containing another inside it, so that the reader cannot leave behind what came earlier in the sentence but must hold multiple beginnings of clauses in suspension in order to complete, one by one, each clause and eventually the sentence.

These days, we generally don't write very elaborate hypotactic sentences. The writing of our time favors shorter, simpler sentences like (though this was written almost a hundred years ago) Hemingway's: "There was no heat in the restaurant and we kept our hats and coats on." Many of us are impatient with having to hold one part of a sentence in our mind while we hear another, subordinate part or several layered subordinate parts, à la Henry James (1843–1916) or Nathaniel Hawthorne (1804–1864), before we are released from the grip of the succession of dependent clauses and allowed to receive the whole sentence into our understanding. (It must be said that there are other readers who relish this syntactical experience.)

Objecting to what he called the notational style, which he felt did not permit the nuances of a thought to be expressed, Proust allowed his sentences to grow by *irradiation*, or *deflagration*, by which he meant an explosion with a sort of chain reaction. The sorts of nuances Proust was talking about may perhaps be well illustrated by two examples from our own Anglophone literature, the first taken from the American Hawthorne, who died not long before Proust was born, and the second from the Scot James Boswell, who lived in the previous century, and, in fact, died not long before Hawthorne was born.

The following construction, which is still perfectly readable, was common in its time. It comes from Hawthorne's *Our Old Home, and English Note-Books*, published in 1863.

It is the dedicatory note to his friend Franklin Pierce, four-teenth president of the United States:

> Only this let me say, that, with the record of your life in my memory, and with a sense of your character in my deeper consciousness as among the few things that time has left as it found them, I need no assurance that you continue faithful forever to that grand idea of an irrevocable Union, which, as you once told me, was the earliest that your brave father taught you.

In the following layout, I have tried to show the patterns of dependent clauses and phrases:

(1) Only this let me say,
    (2) that,
        (3) with the record of your life in my memory, and with a sense of your character in my deeper consciousness
            (4) as among the few things
                (5) that time has left
                    (6) as it found them,
    (2) I need no assurance
        (7) that you continue faithful forever to that grand idea of an irrevocable Union,
            (8) which,
                (9) as you once told me,
            (8) was the earliest
                (10) that your brave father taught you.

One's understanding of this sentence keeps pace with its unfolding, except in two spots where the clause is interrupted or suspended ("that, with the record of your life in my memory" and "which, as you once told me"), where one must wait before completing the thought. The sentence has one main clause, the inverted imperative "Only this let me say" ("Let me say this") with—even though it is not very long—no fewer than seven dependent clauses, as well as some prepositional phrases. It has also about eleven different ideas in it, either stated or implied, implied sometimes by a single adjective. Here are the eleven ideas that I can find:

1. I keep a record of your life in my memory
2. I have a sense of your character in my deeper consciousness
3. I have a shallower and a deeper consciousness
4. your character has remained the same over time
5. few things have remained the same over time
6. I know that you continue faithful to the idea of an irrevocable Union (because I remember your life and have a sense of your character)
7. a Union may or may not be irrevocable
8. the idea of an irrevocable Union is a grand one
9. this idea (of an irrevocable Union) was the earliest idea your father taught you
10. you told me this
11. your father was brave

The following example, published about eighty years earlier, is from James Boswell's introduction to *The Journal of a Tour to the Hebrides with Samuel Johnson* (1785). It is shorter—three lines long—but has three suspensions in it. The conventions of its punctuation at that time were a little different from what they are now: the comma between "remarkable" and "that" would be appropriate to German syntax. We would not have a comma before the parenthesis or at the end of the parenthetical content, or, probably, the commas around "and lively correspondence." Boswell is talking about the invented word *equitation*:

> It is remarkable, that my noble, and to me most constant friend, the Earl of Pembroke, (who, if there is too much ease on my part, will please to pardon what his benevolent, gay, social intercourse, and lively correspondence, have insensibly produced,) has since hit upon the very same word.

The way this sentence would expand through what Proust called deflagration would be the following. One would start from the bare bones of the sentence—and it is often the bare bones of the sentence, in other words the main clause, that the translator or reader needs to locate and keep firmly in mind, in elaborated prose such as Proust's. The main clause of this sentence is very short: "It is remarkable." Adding a little flesh to the bare bones, the main idea of the sentence is:

1. It is remarkable that the Earl of Pembroke has hit upon the same word.

Now, one would expand it from the inside thus (additions in italics):

2. . . . that *my friend* the Earl of Pembroke
3. . . . that my *noble* friend the Earl of Pembroke
4. . . . that my noble *and to me most constant* friend the Earl of Pembroke . . .
5. . . . has *since* hit upon the same word . . .
6. . . . has since hit upon the *very* same word . . .
7. . . . the Earl of Pembroke *who will please*

> *to pardon what his social intercourse and*
> *correspondence have produced*

8. . . . who *if there is too much ease on my part* will
   please to pardon . . .
9. . . . what his *benevolent, gay,* social intercourse,
   and correspondence, have produced . . .
10. . . . what his benevolent, gay, social intercourse,
    and *lively* correspondence, have produced . . .
11. . . . have *insensibly* produced . . .

In many of his sentences, Proust seems to favor the sort of complex pyramidal hypotactic sentence of the Hawthorne and Boswell examples above, a grammatical suspension in which we are presented with the beginning of a clause or phrase and asked to wait for its completion, but he makes it more difficult in at least two ways: a clause may be interrupted by subordinate material and qualifiers that go on for so long that we move quite far away from the beginning of the clause and have trouble keeping it in mind, and this may be where some readers fall asleep over the book or otherwise give up on it; or the sentence may be structured in the Russian-doll pattern of one clause or phrase enclosing another enclosing another, so that unless we are alert we lose track of the first, main clause.

An example of the first type of difficulty, the insertion of subordinate material that continues at some length, is another sentence about Tante Léonie, whose existence has for years been limited to two rooms in the house and a preoccupation with her illness and the daily life of the town. (In the English, I have marked with italics and asterisks the three most striking suspensions.)

> *Elle nous aimait véritablement, elle aurait eu plaisir à*
> *nous pleurer; survenant à un moment où elle se sentait*

bien et n'était pas en sueur, la nouvelle que la maison était la proie d'un incendie où nous avions déjà tous péri et qui n'allait plus bientôt laisser subsister une seule pierre des murs, mais auquel elle aurait eu tout le temps d'échapper sans se presser, à condition de se lever tout de suite, a dû souvent hanter ses espérances comme unissant aux avantages secondaires de lui faire savourer dans un long regret toute sa tendresse pour nous et d'être la stupéfaction du village en conduisant notre deuil, courageuse et accablée, moribonde debout, celui, bien plus précieux, de la forcer au bon moment, sans temps à perdre, sans possibilité d'hésitation énervante, à aller passer l'été dans sa jolie ferme de Mirougrain, où il y avait une chute d'eau.

She truly loved us, she would have taken pleasure in mourning us; had it come at a moment when she felt well and was not in a sweat, *the news** that the house was being consumed by a fire in which all of us had perished already and which would soon leave not a single stone of the walls standing, but from which she would have ample time to escape without hurrying, so long as she got out of bed right away, **must often have lingered** among her hopes, since *it combined***, with the secondary advantages of allowing her to savor all her tenderness for us in an extended grief and to be the cause of stupefaction in the village as she led the funeral procession, courageous and stricken, dying on her feet, ***that other much more precious advantage* of *forcing her**** at the right moment, with no time to lose, no possibility of an enervating hesitation, ****to go and spend* the summer on her pretty farm, Mirougrain, where there was a waterfall.

In this example, there are three major suspensions: in the first, the subject ("the news") is separated from its predicate ("must often have lingered among her hopes"); in the second, the subject and verb ("it combined") are separated from the object ("that other much more precious advantage"); and in the third a phrase depending on that object ("of forcing her") is separated from the infinitive that completes it ("to go and spend the summer on her pretty farm").

That sentence opens, by the way, with an intriguing *paratactic* structure: "She truly loved us, she would have taken pleasure in mourning us"—two independent and equivalent clauses side by side. The mystery is the absence of connective, so that it is hard for us to know just how Proust meant to relate the two clauses: "She truly loved us, *but* she would have taken pleasure in mourning us," or "She truly loved us, *and therefore* she would have taken pleasure in mourning us"? What we have is simply the implied, cryptic "*and* she would have taken pleasure in mourning us." If a translator inserts a connective here, perhaps opting for *but*, she goes rather further into the territory of interpretation than perhaps she should, in my opinion.

The second type of difficulty is the series of interrupted clauses enclosing one another like the Russian doll. The following example is taken from one of the Verdurins' dinner parties, where the gentle old man Saniette happens to be out of favor, quite unfairly, with the hostess and some of the guests:

> *Saniette**, who****, after hurriedly giving the butler his plate, which was still full, ****had plunged** back into a meditative silence, **emerged* from it at last to tell them with a smile the story of a dinner he had attended with the Duc de la Trémouille at which it

turned out that the Duc did not know George Sand
was the pseudonym of a woman.

Saniette,*
   who,**
      after hurriedly giving the butler his plate,
         which was still full,
    **had plunged back into a meditative silence,
  *emerged from it at last

In a deft syntactical sleight of hand, the first three words
of the sentence ("Saniette, who, after") begin three different structural parts of the sentence, a pattern that Proust
produces occasionally elsewhere in the book. "Saniette" begins the main clause ("Saniette emerged from it"); "who"
begins the first subordinate clause ("who had plunged back
into a meditative silence"); and "after" begins a prepositional
phrase that will be completed immediately ("after hurriedly
giving the butler his plate"), but that will be followed by yet
another subordinate clause hanging off "plate" ("which was
still full"). Growing by "irradiation," in other words, what
could have been a simple enough hypotactic sentence—
"Saniette, who had plunged back into a meditative silence,
emerged from it at last"—is first enlarged to: "Saniette, who,
after hurriedly giving the butler his plate, had plunged back
into a meditative silence," and then enlarged further to:
"Saniette, who, after hurriedly giving the butler his plate,
which was still full, had plunged back."

Proust does not "help" us in these complex sentences by
setting off clauses with dashes or placing them inside parentheses. If he uses a dash (usually no more than one per page)
and, less often, a set of parentheses, they merely serve to
allow him to exploit his digressive tendencies still further—

they provide yet another space in which to expand the sentence. For punctuation, in fact, he usually relies on commas alone, and he usually deploys them very sparingly to achieve a sort of all-inclusive fast-forward momentum.

The rhythm and sounds and syntax of the language are large elements of a work, even when they are not the most important elements, and a translator who for the most part chooses to ignore these is omitting one aspect of the work. But since compromise is an inherent part of any work of translation—the multiple small compromises involved in so many of the millions of decisions that are made in the course of a project—one can when necessary justify sacrificing rhythm, sound, syntax in the interests of something else, like characterization, dramatic tension, narrative coherence, clarity, and so on. And it is interesting to see how, given one's engagement with the unfolding narrative of *Swann's Way*, with Proust's complex thoughts, his multifaceted characters, his detailed descriptions, and all the many other elements of the novel, which are all present in a translation even when significant rhythmical and syntactical elements are missing, the work in translation, imperfect as it must be, is still so powerful. Perhaps one measure of the richness of Proust's work, or any great work, is that even when the translation is not faithful to the particulars of the way in which a thought is presented, so much is retained that is compelling.

2003

An Alphabet (in Progress)
of Proust Translation Observations,
from *Aurore* to *Zut*

D

    dictionaries
    dont

E

    etymologies
    exact equivalents
    exclamations
    expressions

F

    faire constructions
    false friends and words whose meanings have changed
        over time
    flensed
    fugitif

G

    genre
    gingerbread
    gourmand
    Grieve, James
    grille: "gate" or "fence"?

H

    hélas

I

    idioms
    the *imparfait*
    inversion
    involuntary habits in writing English

recurring words in the original
reflexive verbs
revisions (1): some of the changes and the reasons for
    them
revisions (2): the many revisions for the British paperback,
    the American hardcover, and the American paperback

S

the Scott Moncrieff translation coinciding with mine
the Scott Moncrieff translation and its revisions: addi-
    tions, substitutions, and errors in English constructions
slang and colloquial speech
soir
solitude
sounds of words in English
sounds of words in French: one suggested by another
stages of the Proust translation
style, conversational or not
syllable counts
synonyms
syntactical structures

T

tension of the mouth
thoughts concerning the translation
title
tortillard
tranche, and the novel's closing sentences

U

usage, in English

V

vigne vierge
vocabulary, cultural
vocabulary, precise
volonté

W

"way," with its two meanings
word by word translation
word choices, individual

X

Y

y in French syntax

Z

zut

PREFACE

I began translating Proust's *Du Côté de chez Swann* in 1997
and continued to revise the translation, after its UK publication in 2002 (for which it was titled *The Way by Swann's*,
that choice being a story in itself), for two further editions
of what was by then being called *Swann's Way*—the American 2003 hardcover and 2004 paperback. In working on the
Proust translation, I tended to consider and reconsider even
the smallest questions, and some of these struggles interested
me enough to record them. I noted their progress in what
became a Proust translation diary, which also included discoveries about language and about Proust and his subjects,

and generally useful information—finding one of Proust's botanical words in the title of Monet's *Nymphéas*, which shows pink-flowered water lilies; or recording an English expression that was timeless enough to be put in the translation, like "common as blackberries"; or observing Proust's use of extended metaphors for characterizing people in the novel, à la Charles Dickens (for instance, Mme Verdurin compared to a bird).

Eventually, I began to write up some of my debates in the form of an "Alphabet of Proust Translation Problems." When I came to expand this "Alphabet," taking from the many notes I had made in the pages of the translation diary, I found myself interested in including more than just the problems, and widened the scope of the entries to include observations about such subjects as Proust's themes, writing style, and word choices, and also features of the other translations I consulted at later stages in my work, as well as comments about the French language and a description of the dictionaries I used during the translation.

This "Alphabet" is still in progress—as will be evident from the fact that some letters in the Table of Contents have no entries and some entries listed in the Table of Contents do not exist in the body of the text—they represent ideas and plans, only. There are many more possible entries that could and perhaps will be developed, of course. And some letters will be easy to supply, eventually, like the letter Q, given the intriguing possible conundrums involving *qui* and *que*.

A

S'AMUSER
Consistently difficult for me has been finding a good translation for *s'amuser*. It is common in French, but its literal

translation is not as common in English, so quite often a different equivalent needs to be found.

The word occurs in *Swann's Way* most crucially in the closing passage of the "madeleine episode," in the metaphor in which Proust compares the memories evoked by the taste of the tea-soaked madeleine cake to the unfolding of a paper flower in a glass of water. The sentence begins:

> *Et comme dans ce jeu où les Japonais s'amusent à trem-per dans un bol de porcelaine rempli d'eau de petits morceaux de papier.*

In my first version, I translated it this way:

> And as in that game in which the Japanese amuse themselves by filling a porcelain bowl with water and steeping in it little pieces of paper.

In my last version, it became:

> And as in that game enjoyed by the Japanese in which they fill a porcelain bowl with water.

An improvement, at least, in that the two *in*s are not quite so close together. But in both English versions, there is more emphasis on *enjoyment* than there is in the French version, in which *s'amuser* is more casual.

Scott Moncrieff's version:

> And just as the Japanese amuse themselves by filling a porcelain bowl with water. (leaving out Proust's *jeu*, "game")

This was revised by Kilmartin and Enright to read:

> And as in the game wherein the Japanese amuse
> themselves by filling a porcelain bowl with water.

The problem also occurs in *Madame Bovary*, as Emma,
bored at dinner with her husband, Charles, "*s'amuse à . . .*"
In my English translation:

> Charles took a long time eating; she would nibble
> a few nuts, or, leaning on her elbow, amuse herself
> drawing lines on the oilcloth with the tip of her knife.

But in a later edition, I changed this to:

> she would nibble a few walnuts, or, leaning on her elbow,
> pass the time drawing lines on the oilcloth. (*Walnuts*
> should have been *hazelnuts*, one of the easily avoided
> mistakes I made through momentary inattention.)

It may be that we, in English, used to employ *to amuse
oneself* earlier in our literary history more as the French do
still. For instance, I find the phrase used in a way that reminds me of Proust's passage as I'm reading Gilbert White's
The Natural History of Selborne, which consists of letters
written by the amateur naturalist Rev. Gilbert White to a fellow naturalist in the latter part of the eighteenth century.
This sentence is from a letter dated 1774: "In the garden of
the Black Bear Inn, in the town of Reading, is a stream or
canal, running under the stables, and out into the fields on
the other side of the road: in this water are many carps, which
lie rolling about in sight, being fed by travellers, who amuse
themselves by tossing them bread."

Another problem word of the same sort—that is, a word common in French whose direct equivalent in English is more awkward, is *passant*, meaning "passerby." In French, *passant* is easy, quick, and quite common. But in English, the closest translation, meaning the same, is an awkward word and not terribly common, sounding a little stilted, a little foreign when used.

Another word more common in French that sounds cumbersome in English is *interlocuteur*, "interlocutor." In French, it is a quick way (despite its five syllables) to say "the person one is speaking to." It serves the same purpose in English, but, because of the history of our use of it, sounds far too stiff and technical to be easily used in vivid prose fiction.

Neither *s'amuser* nor *passant* nor *interlocuteur* is a serious problem, only bothersome.

ALLITERATION

Here is a perfect example, though such a short one, of a "Proustian" sentence, in its balanced construction, its use of alliteration, and its content:

Le désir fleurit, la possession flétrit toutes choses.

I came upon this in one of my dictionaries, *Le Petit Robert*. It is quoted from Proust's 1896 nonfiction work, *Les Plaisirs et les jours*. *Fleurit* = causes to blossom; and *flétrit* = causes to wither and fade. The initial consonants *fl-* associate the two words, as does the final vowel sound, -*it* (*t* not pronounced), whereas the slightly different initial vowel sounds contrast the two words. In English, this could read: "Desire causes a blossoming of all things; possession causes them to wither or fade away."

Alliteration functions to associate two words aurally, as in this example, in a passage about the steeple of Saint-Hilaire releasing a volley of crows:

> *il lachait, laissait tomber à intervalles reguliers des volées de corbeaux*

Notice the close association between *lachait* and *laissait*. I came across my translation of this by chance, while searching for something else, and was not pleased with the way my two verbs went together, though I liked both verbs in themselves: "it loosed, dropped at regular intervals, volleys of crows." When I looked back at the French, I saw how the sound of *lachait* led quite naturally to the sound of the next verb, *laissait*. Perhaps I could have used alliteration myself to link the two English verbs more naturally (and at the same time come closer to the French *laissait tomber* and absence of comma), thus: "It loosed, let fall at regular intervals volleys of crows." As I reread this, I hear another nice link created by sound: ". . . -vals volleys." This is present in the French, also, despite two intervening words: *intervalles reguliers des volées.*

One last example of striking alliteration, still on the subject of the Saint-Hilaire church, this instance coming at the close of a paragraph, where Proust often takes particular care with his effects, it seems to me:

> *et, par un matin brumeaux d'automne, on aurait dit, s'élevant au-dessus du violet orageux des vignobles, une ruine de pourpre presque de la couleur de la vigne vierge.*

Note the four neighboring *v*'s and the similarity in sounds of the side-by-side *pourpre presque*. I did not make a special effort to reproduce this effect in English, but in my close translation there was some alliteration by chance:

and on a misty morning in autumn one might have
thought it, rising above the stormy violet of the vine-
yards, a ruin of purple nearly the color of a wild vine.

It seems to me now that *misty autumn morning* would have
been better, for sound and concision. And perhaps *close to* instead of *nearly* would have created a nice further alliteration
with *color*.

ARTICLES, DEFINITE

A translator working with sound cannot do much about the
difference between the constantly recurring French definite
articles *le*, *la*, and *les*, and the English *the*. The article will be,
inescapably, repeated throughout the book, and in itself creates a major difference in the sounds of the two languages.
The *l* sound is, of course, more liquid, more pleasant to the
ear, while the voiced *th* sound softens and muffles each noun.
And the French article, when placed before a word that begins
with a vowel, creates an alliteration—say between *l'extrémité*
and *l'abandon*—that does not exist in the words without the
articles. Even though the English article, *the*, is also placed in
front of the words—*the extremity*, *the abandonment*—there is
a separation between the article and the noun, so that we do
not hear them as both starting with *th*.

AURORE

The word *aurore* occurs in a passage where Proust is writing about the interior of the church at Combray. He is
describing a stained-glass window and refers to *des flocons
éclairés par quelque aurore*, which literally would be: "snowflakes illuminated by some aurora." In Scott Moncrieff's
version, the phrase is: "flakes illumined by a sunrise." The
Kilmartin-Enright revision of Scott Moncrieff corrects *sun-*

rise, changing it to: "snowflakes . . . illumined by the light of dawn."

I consulted *Le Petit Robert* because *aurore* seemed to me an unusual choice for "sunrise" or "dawn"—why didn't Proust use the more common *aube*? I discovered a differentiation that surprised me: the *aube* is the first light that begins to whiten the horizon; the *aurore* is the brilliant pink, rosy, or yellow-gold gleam that appears in the sky following the *aube*; then the sun itself appears. As I did so often when translating Proust, I looked up the English words, too, to make sure I knew my own language. In English, *dawn* and *daybreak*, too, mean the first appearance of light in the morning, and would be the equivalent of *aube*, whereas the English word *aurora*, in fact, means the same as the French: the redness of the sky just before the sun rises. We tend to be familiar with that word only in the term *aurora borealis*, which means "northern dawn."

The perfect equivalent of *aurore* is therefore *aurora*. But *aurora* will not be very expressive; it has not accumulated the same emotional and metaphorical associations for us as *dawn*. And so, for some time, I thought I would compromise: the perfect equivalent existed, but it would mean less than something more approximate or wordier; perhaps I would opt for "snowflakes illuminated by some rosy dawn." But in the end I was not willing to give up the perfect equivalent, and I returned to *aurora*. If a less familiar word may be less immediately evocative, it does add something else of its own to a text—its surprise, its novelty, and of course its perfect match to the French original.

AVOIR (AND *RECEVOIR* AND OTHERS)
I began to notice, as I worked on the translation, that Proust was particularly fond of the word *avoir*, "have." I began try-

ing consciously to retain it even when the sentence would have been tighter and neater if I had eliminated it—which often would have been easy to do. Did his choice of *avoir* signal a further, subtler emphasis on the theme of *possession* to which he reverted so often in other ways, and should I be careful to reproduce that?

Example: something as quotidian as *le capucin que l'opticien avait à sa devanture*, literally translated as "the monk [or friar] which the optician had in his front window"—a sort of barometer, with the monk's hood going up when the weather threatens to be inclement. I did eliminate, rightly or wrongly, the explicit possession in this phrase, and tightened it to "the little hooded monk in the optician's window." I would now, if I revised further, probably restore the *had* and remove the *little*.

Other examples of *avoir* occurring where it does not need to: *la voiture qu'elle avait*, "the carriage that she had"; and *elle avait dans les cheveux des fleurs*, "she had flowers in her hair."

Along with *avoir*, the verb *recevoir*, "to receive," is also associated with possession and is another of which Proust is particularly fond. An instance, I think, of a deliberate and unnecessary use of *recevoir* is "I received its caress" instead of "it caressed me" in the following passage, in which Proust compares the gaze of Mme de Guermantes to a ray of sunshine: *comme un rayon de soleil qui, au moment où je reçus sa caresse, me sembla conscient* ("a ray of sunshine which, at the moment I received its caress, seemed to me conscious").

He "receives" also, in memory, his mother's heart in a kiss, a few pages later, as he describes "that untroubled peace which no mistress has been able to give me since that time because one . . . can never possess their hearts as I received in a kiss my mother's heart" (*cette paix sans trouble qu'aucune maîtresse n'a pu me donner depuis puisqu'on . . . ne possède jamais leur coeur comme je recevais dans un baiser celui de ma mère).*

There are also instances of phrases like "offered my imagination" and "gave me the sensation" that further enhance the impression of the narrator as the passive receiver, the receptacle, or perhaps an active receiver, awaiting the sensations and impressions that would be given to him by the world.

B

BALANCE OF SOUNDS IN THE PROUSTIAN SENTENCE
Here is another example of the balance of elements in a Proustian sentence. It occurs at the beginning of another very long sentence: *et alors, pensant à l'admiration et à l'amitié que les gens . . . lui prodigueraient.* The balance is achieved by placing a pair of assonantal nouns (*l'admiration* and *l'amitié*) in the middle and two *p-* verbs (*pensant* and *prodigueraient*) on either side.

Another brief moment of exquisite balance: *l'éclat, mais non la clarté* in which the same consonantal sounds (*-clat, clart-*) and vowel sounds (*é, a*) occur but with the vowels reversed the second time they occur. We don't tend to hear, or pay attention to, the little words (*mais non la*) that come between the two nouns that are associated not only by meaning (Proust is contrasting the two) but also by sound.

One more, almost a tongue twister (quotation marks Proust's): *reperce et "restitue" la rue des Perchamps.* Here there is the heavy alliteration of the *r*'s but also the balance of vowel sounds in: *-per- . . . -tue; rue . . . Per-.*

BAVER
The sentence containing the problem word *baver* occurs in a passage in which the narrator, as a child, runs a serious risk of

punishment by waiting up for his mother, in his bedroom, to demand the kiss that she has not given him downstairs. He opens the window and sits at the foot of his bed. He is very still, and outside, things seem frozen in mute attention also.

> *Ce qui avait besoin de bouger, quelque feuillage de mar-ronier, bougeait. Mais son frissonnement minutieux, to-tal, exécuté jusque dans ses moindres nuances and ses dernières délicatesses, ne bavait pas sur le reste, ne se fondait pas avec lui, restait circonscrit.*

My version:

What needed to move, a few leaves of the chestnut tree, moved. But their minute quivering, complete, executed even in its slightest nuances and ultimate refinements, did not spill over onto the rest, did not merge with it, remained circumscribed.

I had gone over the entire passage many times because the sentence that preceded these two was not easy either: "the moonlight . . . duplicating and distancing each thing by extending its shadow before it, denser and more concrete than itself, had at once thinned and enlarged the landscape like a map that had been folded and was now opened out." (Note, incidentally, Proust's characteristically lavish use of pairs.) But I was stuck on *baver*, which was most familiar to me as "drool." I could not seem to find a good equivalent. I did not really understand the reason for Proust's choice.

Then I saw it. The extended metaphor here was one of drawing or sketching: the shivering of the leaf was the subject of the drawing. Proust was saying that the lines with which it was sketched did not *run* or *smudge* or *bleed* over onto the rest. I understood, now, but was still stuck. *Run* would be confusing; *smudge* would be clumsy and not quite right; the sense of *bleed* was right, but, of course, I could not use that entirely different metaphor, one that would introduce such violence and color into the quiet moonlit scene. *Baver* is very wet: "spill over" was the closest I could get, still a compromise, since it does not sustain the drawing metaphor. For comparison, Scott Moncrieff changes metaphors entirely, to a musical one, with "made no discord." The Kilmartin-Enright revision replaces that with the far more abstract "did not impinge." I thought *impinge*, abstract though it is, might have at its etymological root the Latin *pingere*, "to paint," which would make it technically not a bad choice, but no, it derives from *in* and *pangere* and originally had the more violent meaning of "thrust at forcibly."

C

CHAUD

Here is a petulant question: Why does French not distinguish between "warm" and "hot" in the word *chaud*, which can mean either? The translator must rely on context, and sometimes context is lacking.

Why does French not distinguish between "to like" and "to love" in the word *aimer*, which can mean either?

Not to speak of *soir*, which can sometimes mean afternoon and sometimes evening.

CONTEXT

The importance of context for understanding the meaning of a word (as for example *chaud*), phrase, sentence, or passage became very evident, concretely, when I played the game I enjoyed sometimes, at a certain stage in the first draft of the translation: I would translate one word at a time, without reading ahead to the end of the sentence, without reading ahead at all. Or I would see how few words I had to read at once in order to know the meaning of the first word, retroactively, as it were. Sometimes the meaning of a word or phrase would shift as the context accumulated in the course of the sentence. Either a word would be clear in and of itself, or I would anticipate its context and it would be clear because of that, or it would not be clear. The game was interesting to me because it shed light on the way we understand speech as it unfolds, how much context helps us understand or anticipate what is about to come. I wondered how many words a native French reader would have to read in order to understand each word—would he or she have to read two words ahead to understand the previous one or two?

This became trickier, and more interesting, when Proust used inversion. For instance, he would start a sentence with the prepositional phrase *De Balbec* and there would be no way of knowing, just then, at the start of the sentence, whether he meant "From Balbec" or "Of Balbec." In this case, what came later in the sentence would provide the context that would allow me to understand the opening. How do we understand as we read, then? Do we keep both "From Balbec" and "Of Balbec" in suspension in our minds until we have progressed further in the sentence?

An example of context determining meaning: Once I knew the family hadn't had dinner yet when they went up to see Aunt Léonie, I decided they were saying "good evening" to her rather than "goodnight."

CONTIGU

The word *contiguous* occurs five times in *Swann's Way*, or it may be more accurate to say that the word *contigu* occurs at least five times in *Du Côté de chez Swann*; I decided after some debate to use the closest equivalent, the cognate, in each of these occurrences in my English version. I like the word, although it is a little chilly or prickly: it contains crisp sounds—the hard *c*, *t*, and *g*—and a good rhythm—four syllables with the accent on the second. It's one I don't come across often, it is certainly not common in speech or writing, yet people have some idea what it means, especially in context. In translating Proust, I attended closely to just such details of sound, mainly because he himself did, but also because, beyond the meaning of the prose, I wished to translate, or try to find an equivalent for, its sound. It was necessary to pay attention to syllable counts, internal rhymes, good alliteration, clumsy alliteration.

Contiguous is applied, in these five occurrences, to: states of mind; houses; houses again; the details that go to form a true story; and the impressions that, together, make up one's memory of one's life—that is to say, to three abstract ideas and two concrete objects.

1.
Et de la sorte c'est du côté de Guermantes que j'ai appris à distinguer ces états qui se succèdent en moi, pendant certaines périodes, et vont jusqu'à se partager chaque journée, l'un revenant chasser l'autre, avec la ponctualité de la fièvre; contigus, mais si extérieurs l'un à l'autre, si dépourvus de moyens de communication entre eux, que je ne puis plus comprendre, plus même me représenter dans l'un, ce que j'ai désiré, ou redouté, ou accompli dans l'autre.

I translated this as follows:

And so it was from the Guermantes way that I learned
to distinguish those states of mind that follow one another in me, during certain periods, and that even go
so far as to divide up each day among them, one returning to drive away the other, with the punctuality
of a fever; contiguous, but so exterior to one another,
so lacking in means of communication among them,
that I can no longer understand, no longer even picture to myself in one, what I desired, or feared, or
accomplished in the other.

It may be that part of the attraction of using *contiguous* in
this passage, rather than the more familiar *adjacent*, derives
from the close proximity of *fever*, and thereby the association
of *contiguous* with *contagious* (which would work the same
way in French, since *contigu* is close in sound and appearance
to *contagieux*). The last phrase of the passage offers a very
good example of Proust working with parallel structure, and
with pairs, something he does quite consciously throughout
the novel. It can be arranged to show this more clearly:

contiguous,
but so exterior to one another,
so lacking in means of communication among them,
that I can no longer understand,
no longer even picture to myself in one,
what I desired,
or feared,
or accomplished in the other.

2.
*L'isolement et le vide de ces courtes rues (faites presque
toutes de petits hôtels contigus, dont tout à coup venait*

rompre la monotonie quelque sinistre échoppe, témoi-
gnage historique et reste sordide du temps où ces quartiers
étaient encore mal famés), la neige qui était restée dans
le jardin et aux arbres, le négligé de la saison, le voisinage
de la nature, donnaient quelque chose de plus mystérieux
à la chaleur, aux fleurs qu'il avait trouvés en entrant.

My translation:

The isolation and emptiness of these short streets (almost all of them made up of small contiguous private
houses, whose monotony would suddenly be interrupted by some sinister street-stall, the historic sign
and sordid remains of a time when these districts were
still disreputable), the snow that had stayed in the garden and on the trees, the slovenliness of the season, the
proximity of nature, added something mysterious to
the warmth, the flowers that he found when he went in.

Hoping by some miracle to reproduce not only the substance
but also the form of the novel, and keeping my translation
as close as possible to the original, here, too, I attempted to
begin and end each sentence and paragraph with the same
elements ("The isolation and emptiness . . . the warmth, the
flowers") in the same order as Proust's original.

3.
S'il arrivait après l'heure où Odette envoyait ses domes-
tiques se coucher, avant de sonner à la porte du petit
jardin, il allait d'abord dans la rue où donnait au
rez-de-chaussée, entre les fenêtres toutes pareilles, mais
obscures, des hôtels contigus, la fenêtre, seule éclairée, de
sa chambre.

I translated this as:

> If he arrived after the hour when Odette sent her ser-
> vants to bed, before ringing at the gate of the little
> garden he would first go into the street onto which
> looked out, on the ground floor, between the win-
> dows, all the same but dark, of the contiguous houses,
> the window, the only one illuminated, of her bedroom.

This was a tricky sentence to translate because of the succession of short phrases, all given rather equal value, into
which it is broken up toward the end; because of the inversion: "onto which looked out . . . the window . . . of her
bedroom"; and because of the placement of the qualifying
phrases "all the same but dark" and "the only one illuminated." It might have been easier to combine some of the
phrases, thus:

> he would first go into the street onto which looked
> out, on the ground floor, between the windows of
> the contiguous houses, all the same but dark, the only
> one illuminated, the window of her bedroom.

Or maybe:

> the only lit one, the window of her bedroom.

But I opted to reproduce Proust's chopped-up arrangement, thinking he had some reason for it, since he so often
does the reverse—omits commas where one would expect
them. I may not have understood why he did what he did,
but I preferred not to change what I had not yet understood.

4.

Proust is discussing, here, Odette's habit of lying to Swann.

Elle se trompait, c'était cela qui la trahissait, elle ne se rendait pas compte que ce détail vrai avait des angles qui ne pouvaient s'emboîter que dans les détails contigus du fait vrai dont elle l'avait arbitrairement détaché et qui, quels que fussent les détails inventés entre lesquels elle le placerait, révéleraient toujours par la matière excédente et les vides non remplis, que ce n'était pas d'entre ceux-là qu'il venait.

My translation:

She was wrong, it was precisely this that gave her away, she did not realize that the true detail had corners that could fit only into the contiguous details of the true fact from which she had arbitrarily detached it, corners which, whatever might be the invented details among which she placed it, would always reveal, by their excess of material and unfilled empty areas, that it was not from among these that it had come.

I translated the French *angles* as "corners," which is one of the meanings of the word, but it could also be "angles," and in a future edition I may change it to that. Proust's first English translator, Scott Moncrieff, tending as he does to add to the original, translates the end of this passage as "gaps which *she had forgotten* to fill" for the sparer original *vides non remplis*—"gaps not filled" or "unfilled empty spaces." In adding, Scott Moncrieff is also interpreting: in his version, the gaps were not filled because she had not filled them;

and she had not filled them because she had forgotten to fill them. This interpretation actually gets in the way of the simpler, cleaner image of the jigsaw-puzzle piece that does not fit. "It was not from among these that it had come" becomes "its proper place was elsewhere." This is certainly not "close" translation. Is it an adequate equivalent?

My last instance comes at the very end of the book, which is why I paid particularly close attention to this word, and probably why I went back and looked at all the other occurrences of it.

5.

> *La réalité que j'avais connue n'existait plus. Il suffisait que Mme Swann n'arrivât pas toute pareille au même moment, pour que l'Avenue fût autre. Les lieux que nous avons connus n'appartiennent pas qu'au monde de l'espace où nous les situons pour plus de facilité. Ils n'étaient qu'une mince tranche au milieu d'impressions contiguës qui formaient notre vie d'alors; le souvenir d'une certaine image n'est que le regret d'un certain instant; et les maisons, les routes, les avenues, sont fugitives, hélas, comme les années.*

I translated this as:

> The reality I had known no longer existed. That Mme Swann did not arrive exactly the same at the same moment was enough to make the avenue different. The places we have known do not belong solely to the world of space in which we situate them for our greater convenience. They were only a thin slice

among contiguous impressions which formed our life
at that time; the memory of a certain image is but regret for a certain moment; and houses, roads, avenues
are as fleeting, alas, as the years.

One thing to note here is the variety of different verb forms
Proust uses in these sentences, as though running through
them again, at the very end of *Swann's Way*, to reflect the
mix of varieties of past and present in the novel and in his
very approach to the experience of life lived in time. In sequence, they are: past perfect, imperfect, imperfect, subjunctive, subjunctive, perfect, present, present, imperfect,
imperfect, present, present.

Now, in choosing *contiguous* over *adjacent* and *adjoining*
I was guided in part by the sound of the word, in part by
opting for a cognate whenever appropriate, and in part
by searching for the most exact equivalent. And one element
of my search was always into the etymology of the word,
the deeper layers of its evolution and especially the concrete
metaphor from which it evolved. In this case what I found
for the three choices was:

adjacent: from the Latin *ad-* and *jacent* meaning "lying
near"

adjoining: from the Latin *ad-* and *jungere* meaning "to
join with"

contiguous: from the Latin *contiguus* meaning "border-
ing upon" (Related to the English *contingent*, *tangent*, and
contact.)

And here I discovered that in fact *contiguous* and *contagious* do derive from the same Latin root, *contingere*. I
further discovered, looking at the handy comparison of synonyms provided by my worn old copy of *Webster's Seventh*

New Collegiate Dictionary, that whereas *adjacent* does not necessary imply touching, and *adjoining* does imply touching but not necessarily at more than a single point, *contiguous* implies "having contact on all or most of one side," so that for a house or for the jigsaw-puzzle piece of the mendacious Odette's "true detail," this word really is the most appropriate and the most exact equivalent of Proust's. And the possible association (either conscious or unconscious, in Proust's mind) of *contiguous* and *contagious* in one of the passages above confirms another of my reasons for trying to keep as close to Proust's original as I can: not every reason for his choices has yet been discovered—or may have been obvious even to him. I want to preserve these choices as nearly as I can, for further investigation.

D

DICTIONARIES

In my translating of Proust, I used mainly a large, red two-volume *Harrap's New Standard French and English Dictionary* till it was well worn out, the spine taped and hanging in slivers, the pages separating in blocks. I kept Volume A–I on my left as I worked, on a separate little table perpendicular to my desk, and Volume J–Z on my right, on a shelf that slid out from the old white metal office desk. But, often, I preferred to use my cream-colored *Le Petit Robert* French–French. I would read the various definitions of the word in *Le Petit Robert*, then the literary quotations illustrating some of the definitions, and then decide what the best English for that meaning would be, in the given context. This was, when I think about it, a more natural way of arriving at the best English equivalent. For English–English, I relied on my battered old, humble, tan *Webster's Collegiate*, or sometimes walked over to the six-inch-thick *Webster's New International* on its stand at the end of the room, or, if necessary, got out my magnifying glass and my tiny-print two-volume *Oxford English Dictionary*.

I found, as I worked, that because I was regularly consulting and reading *Le Petit Robert*, I was also regularly reading quotations from a host of French writers I had never read before, or not deeply, such as Daudet, Loti, Duhamel, and others, and becoming gradually curious to know more of their work. I was also beginning to guess what sorts of writers they were, if I did not know already, and when they wrote. And this became another game: to see if by reading only these fragments I could form a sense of them, or come to know the body of their work, in my mind.

Every time I looked up a word in a dictionary, or almost every time, certainly once every day, I would learn some new meaning of a familiar word, or an entirely new word. For example, did I know, before, that *brochure* came from *brocher*, "to sew" (because of the way the pages are attached to each other)?

I also acquired, at a certain point, a much older dictionary, the *Grand Dictionnaire Français–Anglais et Anglais–Français*, edited by Fleming and Tibbins and published by Librairie de Firmin Didot Frères in 1885, the year Proust turned fourteen. It had the advantage, of course, that none of the English would or could date from later than Proust's childhood years, and none of the English interpretation of the French words and phrases would be modern ones. I used it only sparingly, however, because its pages were so dry and brittle. I would come to a word or phrase that made no sense given the meanings available to me in my head and in the other dictionaries and suspect there was once a slightly different meaning, now fallen into disuse. I would then consult the old dictionary.

Even lifting the dictionary was risky, and opening it was worse. In addition, some pages were dog-eared, hiding information under the flap. I knew that if I folded back the dog-ear to see what was under it, the chip of paper would break off. So I had to decide if finding out what was under it was worth further damage to the dictionary.

Here are two instances, however, in which the old dictionary was helpful: *habitudes* (which I would have translated as "habits") = acquaintance (in the plural sense, meaning the people one knows); and *superstition* (which I would have translated as "superstition") = "excess of exactitude, obsessive preoccupation, excessive preoccupation." In other words, some of these seeming exact equivalents had become, over time, "false friends."

One more example: a *demi-castor*, literally "half-beaver," is a mixed beaver hat, a hat not made entirely from beaver pelt. But the expression *c'est un demi-castor* is a derogatory one for which the old dictionary had a nice, slightly circumlocutory translation that I don't think I used, but easily could have: "He's not far from a scoundrel."

It is possible that, in the course of my decades of translating, I have read more in my French dictionaries than I have in French literature itself.

DONT

Here comes the short but densely constructed sentence about the man's voice. Swann, after going home from seeing Odette, becomes suspicious and returns to see if she is with another man. He walks around to the back of her house, into the little street onto which her bedroom window looks out. He sees a light through the closed shutters and hears voices.

Il se haussa sur la pointe des pieds. Il frappa. On n'avait pas entendu, il refrappa plus fort, la conversation s'arrêta. Une voix d'homme dont il chercha à distinguer auquel de ceux des amis d'Odette qu'il connaissait elle pouvait appartenir demanda:

"Qui est là?"

He raised himself on his tiptoes. He knocked. They had not heard, he knocked again more loudly, the conversation stopped. A man's voice which he tried to distinguish from among the voices of those of Odette's friends whom he knew asked:

"Who's there?"

This small paragraph is actually a good illustration of some of the types of sentences in *Swann's Way*. First you have two simple sentences, one extremely brief—and Proust could, mercifully, be extremely brief: "He raised himself on his tiptoes. He knocked." Then you have a nice paratactic sentence—that is, three elements of equal value and similar in form follow one another without a connective: "They had not heard, he knocked again more loudly, the conversation stopped." (As it happens, in the original the sentence is roughly symmetrical, with the shortest clause in the middle; in my translation the sentence is also roughly symmetrical, but with the longest clause in the middle.)

For comparison, in this sort of sentence, C. K. Scott Moncrieff will often supply connectives where they are lacking in the original, or separate the clauses by semicolons instead of commas, whereas I chose to leave the parataxis the way it was, reproducing Proust's choices, including punctuation, even when I did not entirely understand the reason for them.

In this case, Scott Moncrieff inserted three semicolons,

giving the sentence four parts instead of three, but retaining the somewhat staccato rhythm of the original: "They had not heard; he knocked again; louder; their conversation ceased."

Following the two short sentences and the rather clipped paratactic sentence comes a highly complex sentence of the Russian-doll type, even though it, too, is not very long. This is the sentence that interested me and that I struggled over a long time, ultimately failing, however, to do all that I wanted to (which is why it is a blessing to have to translate a sentence like: "He knocked" or "Who's there?" where you can feel successful). The sentence is:

> *Une voix d'homme dont il chercha à distinguer auquel de ceux des amis d'Odette qu'il connaissait elle pouvait appartenir demanda:*
>   *"Qui est là?"*

A man's voice which he tried to distinguish from among the voices of those of Odette's friends whom he knew asked:
    "Who's there?"

There are no punctuation marks in the sentence at all until the colon before the question. I wanted to preserve that. Also, Proust has managed to construct it in such a way that, of the five words toward the end of the sentence, before the colon, four are verbs, three of them the closing verbs of clauses he has begun earlier—he has put four of the six verbs in the sentence together close to the end, by doing one of his Russian-doll tricks in which the main clause, "A man's voice asked," encloses the second clause, "concerning which he tried to distinguish," and a third clause, "to which . . . it might belong," which in turn encloses a fourth clause, "of those of Odette's friends whom he knew." This is the sort of stylistic manoeuvre which Proust performs that is so tricky and delightful you are obliged to think Proust enjoyed writing it as much as we do reading it.

(1) *Une voix d'homme*
   (2) *dont il chercha à distinguer*
      (3) *auquel de ceux des amis d'Odette*
         (4) *qu'il connaissait*
      (3) *elle pouvait appartenir*
(1) *demanda:*

I wanted to have no punctuation at all until the colon, jam up as many verbs as possible at the end, keep the same order in which the sentence unfolded, and put a string of prepositional phrases in the middle, as Proust had it: *auquel de ceux des amis d'Odette.*

The following completely literal translation demonstrates that if you do not aim to create a pleasing sentence in English it can, grammatically, be done:

A man's voice concerning which he sought to distinguish to which of those of the friends of Odette whom he knew it might belong asked:
   "Who's there?"

This retains the string of *ofs*—"of those of the friends of Odette"—and the logjam of four verbs at the end: "he knew it might belong asked."

Another version, with a tiny change, tightened a little but sacrificing the string of *of*s, and still not pleasing, might be:

> A man's voice concerning which he sought to distinguish to which of those of Odette's friends whom he knew it might belong asked:
> "Who's there?"

But "concerning which" is no good and can't successfully take the place of the elegant monosyllable *dont*—and it is that *dont*, so useful in constructing a good sentence in French, which has, as many times before, created a problem for me.

After a lot of fiddling, by successive compromises, I reach my final version, which does some but not all of what I wanted it to do. It has no punctuation until the colon and it unfolds in the same order, but it has only two instead of four verbs at the end, sacrifices the string of *of*s, and—a worse failure—leaves out one clause, and thus one idea, entirely— "it might belong":

> A man's voice which he sought to distinguish from among those of Odette's friends whom he knew asked:
> "Who's there?"

Returning to this solution after some time, I realized that the word *those* was ambiguous, trying to refer to both "voices" and "friends," and I decided that a better choice, even though it contains a repetition not in the French, might be:

> A man's voice which he sought to distinguish from among the voices of those of Odette's friends whom he knew asked:
> "Who's there?"

It is interesting to compare Scott Moncrieff's version of the sentence:

> A man's voice—he strained his ears to distinguish whose, among such of Odette's friends as he knew, the voice could be—asked:
>   "Who's that?"

As always when I look at Scott Moncrieff's solution to a problem, I can see clearly what his intentions were, and what dictated his choices; as I worked on my translation, my respect for him kept growing, even while I almost always disagreed with his solution.

Scott Moncrieff takes care to begin and end the sentence the same way Proust did, he allows it to unfold in the same order, he retains the idea of "whose . . . the voice might be" for "to which of the friends . . . the voice might belong." However, he inserts a pair of commas and, more radically, a pair of dashes, to make it read more easily. In doing so he changes the overall hypotactic structure to a paratactic one and stops the forward flow of the sentence. He does not entirely solve the problem of reproducing the strangeness of the jammed-up verbs in French—"he knew it might belong asked"—though with his dashes he comes close: "as he knew, the voice could be—asked." Also, characteristically, he heightens the drama of the situation by inserting material of his own: "*strained his ears* to distinguish" instead of Proust's plainer "sought to distinguish."

James Grieve's version of *Swann's Way* demonstrates yet again just how many ways one sentence can be translated. Since he works from a somewhat different set of guiding principles in his translation practice, Grieve brings in more punctuation, changes the order in which the sentence unfolds and ends, and uses the conjunction *and* to form a larger paratactic structure that is not as typical of Proust:

> Then a man's voice asked, "Who's there?" and Swann, thinking of the men-friends of Odette, tried to iden- tify which of them it sounded like.

E

ETYMOLOGIES

It was while working on the Proust translation that I first began regularly to read etymologies of French words. Some of what I learned was not surprising, but other word origins were unexpected. In particular, I always enjoyed coming upon a word derived not, say, from Latin or Italian but from deep in the early history of the land itself: from the languages of the Franks or Gauls.

Very different in nature, for instance, are two words for *pride* in French. *Orgueil*, so much more primitive in sound with its guttural *g*, is derived from the Frankish *urgoli*, or *orgollja*, whereas the wispy, fleeting *fierté* comes from the Latin *feritas*, "wildness, savagery." (I have just discovered that there is actually an English word, *ferity*, meaning approximately the same thing.)

Example from the Gaulish: *frogna*, "nose," in *(se) ren-frogner*. *Frogner* used to mean "wrinkle one's nose." *Se renfrogner* means "to grimace" or "scowl."

Interesting word history info department: *bien famé* first appeared in the fifteenth century, whereas *mal famé* not until the eighteenth century, about three hundred years later.

Another interesting etymology: *calvaire*, "calvary," comes from *cauvaire*, "skull." The Latin *calvariae locus* is the translation of the Hebrew *Golgotha*, meaning "place of the skull," the name of the hill where Jesus was crucified.

EXACT EQUIVALENTS

My intention, from the beginning of the project, to produce a translation as close as possible to the original without sacrificing natural or pleasing English became only more focused as I proceeded, and I grew fascinated by how exact a translation of a word or phrase could be.

A more exact translation of *revenir* (*re* + *venir*) would be "come back" (since we can't say *re-come*). *Return* keeps the *re-* but completes the word with *turn*.

For the phrase *ma grand'tante elle-meme*, a perfectly acceptable translation would be "even my great-aunt," but closer would be "my great-aunt herself," if I could use it.

I was given license to make all the revisions I wanted to, in preparation for the American hardcover of *Swann's Way* and then again for the American paperback. It was at one of those points that I realized I could change the perfectly good and accurate "catastrophic deluge" to a much closer replica of the French, "diluvian catastrophe," which I found delightful in its slight strangeness.

There are many more instances of the difference between a perfectly accurate and a more exact translation.

EXCLAMATIONS

Exclamations were particularly difficult, whether coming from the mouth of the servant Françoise or from another character. I began collecting English possibilities from nineteenth- and early twentieth-century writers in English, such as George Eliot and Henry James.

Mon Dieu, literally "my God," which was polite in

French, could not be translated literally into English, since it would sound too rough, coming from a dignified old woman, for instance. Better would be "dear me," "heavens!," "good heavens!"

But whereas *Mon Dieu* was polite, *bon Dieu*, "good God," was not.

Dame, literally "lady," derived from the Old French *par Nostre Dame!*, was equivalent to *ma foi*, literally "my faith," and might be translated by "bless me" or "to be sure." Or: "indeed," "what else," "I should think so."

I would also collect possibly useful exclamations I heard around me on the street or indoors in a public place. For instance, in a restaurant, a woman at a table near me once said, emphatically: "I should say!" Out came the notebook and pen.

An archaic possibility was "gramercy!" expressing gratitude or astonishment. It was the equivalent of another old one, "mercy on us!"

One of the hardest exclamations to translate was *Ah!*, although sometimes it could be translated simply as "Ah!" or "Oh!" My trusty *Le Petit Robert* gave the sixteenth century for the first appearance of the word in writing and explained that this exclamation indicated a lively feeling—of pleasure, pain, admiration, impatience, etc. Other possible translations might be "Well!" or "Now then!" or "I see!" or any one of dozens of other exclamations. "Ah!" and "Oh!" appear regularly in Henry James, "Oh!" for surprise or dismay, "Ah!" for enlightenment or when enlightening another.

EXPRESSIONS

I also began to collect expressions, in case I could use them, though I'm not sure I ever did. Here are some:

"Mad as a meat axe" (Australian)

"He must have swallowed the dictionary" (of someone who uses very long words)

"Oh, to be shot at dawn!" (jesting, said by someone
in trouble)

"You're slower than the second coming of Christ!"

"To eat vinegar with a fork" (to be sharp-tongued or
snappish)

"You'll just have to climb fool's hill and sow your
gawkseed" (said by an aunt to my father, as reported by him)

"Her tongue is hung in the middle and wags at both
ends" (said by same aunt)

"Stole my thunder"

"In the twinkling of a bedpost"; or, "in the twinkling
of a bedstaff" (instantly)

"They just want to shine your buttons"

"He's swinging his cape around" (showing off)

I also tried to remain alert to expressions often repeated by
certain of Proust's characters, such as Swann and his *tout de
même* ("all the same").

F

FAIRE CONSTRUCTIONS

Among the most consistently difficult problems were the
verb constructions using *faire*, "to make" or "to cause," as
an auxiliary. So quick and simple in French, so cumbersome
to translate into English.

Example: *faisait monter*: "caused to mount or rise." In

the following example I cheated, in a sense, by using the transitive verb *walked* for moving the image both over the curtains and up to the ceiling, thus skipping *faisait monter* altogether.

> *l'image de Geneviève de Brabant, ancêtre de la famille de Guermantes, que la lanterne magique promenait sur les rideaux de ma chambre ou faisait monter au plafond*

> the image of Geneviève de Brabant, ancestor of the Guermantes family, which our magic lantern walked out over the curtains of my room or up to the ceiling

For *faisait monter*, I could perhaps have said, not "caused to rise," but "raised."

Another example of a *faire* construction: *faire naître* = (literally) to cause to be born. To avoid that awkward literal version, one could use "inspire" or "produce" or "instigate" or some other neat verb. For this phrase, in one instance, Scott Moncrieff's translation is "kindle," creating a metaphor not in the original. (See M: Mixed Metaphors.)

FALSE FRIENDS AND WORDS WHOSE MEANINGS HAVE CHANGED OVER TIME

I am thinking, in particular, of those words in English identical or close to identical to their French counterparts but whose meanings have changed over time, so that, once equivalent to the French meanings, they no longer are. (See also James, Henry.)

One of these words is *effusive*: in 1885 it had more sincerity attached to it than it does now. Now, it carries a suggestion of the hypocritical.

Sournois used to mean "somber," "melancholy"; it now means "who hides his/her real feelings, often with a malicious intent."

Jour (which we understand usually to mean "day," "light") can also mean "opening." The English *light* can also mean "window" or "opening," as in the definition of *mullion*: a slender vertical pier between lights of windows, doors, or screens.

Iris once meant "rainbow." The French *iriser* means: "to make iridescent"; "to color with the colors of the rainbow."

More false friends: *coquet; fastidieux; sophistique; intelligence.*

Fatigue in the singular means "fatigue," "weariness." But in the plural, *fatigues* means "hardships," "strains."

Volontaire does not necessarily mean "voluntary," but can mean "deliberate," "intentional," or "willed."

Maniaque does not mean "maniacal" but "finical," "finicky," "fussy."

Pathétique can be "pathetic," but also "touching," or "moving."

Perdu can mean "lost" or "wasted" (as in the general title of Proust's novel, *À la Recherche du temps perdu*) but it can also mean "isolated" or "distant," as in *pays perdu*, an out-of-the-way place.

Confidence can only mean "confidence" in the sense of a secret, something you confide, which is the less common meaning in English. *Confidence* meaning "self-assurance" is a little different in French: *confiance.*

A remark can be *inoffensif*, "inoffensive," but, in French, a dog can also be *absolument inoffensif*—"absolutely harmless, not dangerous."

And so forth. This is why I turned to my dictionaries so constantly.

FLENSED

The lovely word *flensed*, which I could not use in my translation, would have occurred in a passage that describes the
young narrator's outings to the Champs-Élysées, where he
goes faithfully day after day, when his mother lets him, in
hopes of meeting the object of his infatuation, the red-haired
Gilberte. The weather becomes important to him: if it is too
unpromising, his mother may not allow him to go out or
Gilberte herself may not appear. (A paragraph or two before
the passage in question, for instance, he has been watching
anxiously for the clouds to pass, and is overjoyed when he
sees on the stone of the balcony the shadows of the elaborate wrought-iron support of the balustrade at last alight like
birds, "pledges of calm and happiness.")

On his outings to the park he is always, though he wishes
he were not, accompanied by the servant Françoise. On this
particular day, he has little hope of seeing Gilberte on the
snow-blanketed lawns and paths, but by the end of the day
will be happily surprised. *Flensed*, if I had used it, would
have occurred early in their outing, while Marcel was still
struggling with his disappointment over Gilberte's probable
nonappearance.

> *Françoise avait trop froid pour rester immobile, nous
> allâmes jusqu'au pont de la Concorde voir la Seine
> prise, dont chacun et même les enfants s'approchaient
> sans peur comme d'une immense baleine échouée, sans
> défense, et qu'on allait dépecer.*

My version:

> Françoise was too cold to sit still; we walked to the
> pont de la Concorde to see the frozen Seine, which

everyone including the children approached without fear as though it were a beached whale, immense, defenseless and about to be cut up.

This sentence interests me because of the pair of rhymes in the French, which can be reproduced in English (as is the case more often than one would think), and a third rhyme in English that would have been so perfectly apt and yet could not be used for a couple of reasons. But there are other features of the sentence to look at, two more instances of the inevitable compromises involved in translation.

First, the rhymes: they occur near the end of the sentence. The whale to which Proust compares the Seine is described as *immense* and *échouée, sans défense*. The rhyme of *immense* and *défense* is clearly audible. It is also easy to echo in English: "immense, defenseless." Now we come to the fourth qualifier for the whale (the third is "beached," in English), which Proust has rather awkwardly tacked onto the end of the sentence, as he sometimes does, almost as though to disrupt his own lyricism: *et qu'on allait dépecer*, "and that they were going to cut up," or "and that was going to be cut up."

Dépecer, from the Old French *pèce*, "piece," means "to cut to pieces or dismember," when applied to an animal. A butcher may *dépecer* a lamb for Easter dinner. Or a lion may do the same—here is the word in a sentence of Flaubert's: *Ils tiraient à eux les morceaux de viande . . . dans la pose pacifique des lions lorsqu'ils dépècent leur proie.* "They drew the pieces of meat toward them . . . with the peaceful mien of lions dismembering their prey."

Now, when *dèpecer* is applied specifically to a whale, says my *Harrap's* French–English dictionary, our word for it would be "flense," even though, as I discover when I check it in my *Webster's*, *flense* means more exactly to cut the blubber from a whale. But this would be an apt enough equivalent and a fortuitous rhyme for *immense* and *defenseless*. It might have been one of those happy accidents the translator encounters less often than the impossible cruxes. Yet there are two problems with writing "immense, defenseless, about to be flensed." The word is not familiar enough to English readers to be comprehensible, even with the help of the context; and—perhaps in part because of the unfamiliarity of the word—the rhyme would have been excessive and intrusive, more appropriate for humorous verse than for a lyrical description of a frustrating winter afternoon. And so I abandoned *flense*, though it continued to haunt me as being an unusable perfect solution.

As for the compromises, the first is: "which everyone including the children approached without fear." A better alternative would perhaps have been "which everyone, even the children, approached without fear." *Even* would have been closer to *même* and it would have sounded better, echoing "everyone" and being a nimbler, less pedestrian word than *including*. But at the time I opted for it, I had only recently realized, by looking specifically at Proust's punctuation, how sparing he was with his commas and how often I could reproduce that light touch in English. Fresh from that discovery, I wanted to avoid using the comma pair there, so as not to slow the sentence more than Proust does. (Already, my semicolon in place of his comma in the first line had stopped the forward motion.)

The second compromise is the order of images in "beached whale, immense, defenseless." *Beached* comes first in English; *immense* comes first in French: the French gives us *immense baleine*, "immense whale," then continues with *èchouée*, "beached" or "stranded." (Though *beached* and *stranded* are both correct for the image, we in English tend to use *stranded* metaphorically so much more often than literally that it has lost some of its concreteness. I therefore opted for *beached*.) I preferred to keep the rhyming words side by side: "immense, defenseless." If I had chosen to follow the French order of images, I would have written "immense whale, beached, defenseless," which would have been perfectly good. As often, it was something of a toss-up.

G

GENRE

At the end of the section of *Swann's Way* titled "*Un Amour de Swann*" or "Swann in Love," the closing, climactic sentence is the one in which Swann marvels over his emotions:

> *Dire que j'ai gâché des années de ma vie, que j'ai voulu mourir, que j'ai eu mon plus grand amour, pour une femme qui ne me plaisait pas, qui n'était pas mon genre!*

In my translation:

> To think that I wasted years of my life, that I wanted to die, that I felt my deepest love, for a woman who did not appeal to me, who was not my type!

The word *genre* was the one, in this sentence, that several people asked me about: How are you going to translate that?

Scott Moncrieff chose "who was not in my style!"—admittedly rather unnatural, at least to our ears. The Kilmartin-Enright revision changed this to "who wasn't even my type!"—adding the intensifying "even," not in the French original. James Grieve opted for keeping the intensifier and repeating "a woman": "A woman who wasn't even my type!" and I chose, at first, "who was not my kind!" Now, of course, the word *kind* strikes me as less natural than *type*. Perhaps I was trying to be consistent, since at another point in *Du Côté de chez Swann*, Proust uses the three possible synonyms in one sentence: *genre, sorte,* and *type.*

When Swann is first introduced to Odette, we are told right away that her beauty was not the *genre* ("type," or "sort," or "kind") that he found very attractive—she was *non pas certes sans beauté, mais d'un genre de beauté qui lui était indifférent, qui ne lui inspirait aucun désir* ("certainly not without beauty, but of a kind of beauty that left him indifferent, that awoke no desire in him")—and the word *genre* is followed a few lines later by the word *type—de ces femmes . . . qui sont l'opposé du type que nos sens réclament* ("one of those women . . . who are the opposite of the type that our senses crave"), as though the words were perhaps, for Proust, interchangeable.

On the next page, again, *genre* reappears: "*il regrettait . . . que la grande beauté qu'elle avait ne fût pas du genre de celles qu'il aurait spontanément préférées* ("he was sorry . . . that the great beauty she possessed was not of the type of those he would spontaneously have preferred").

After I was questioned about this word and started thinking more closely about the three possibilities, I realized I myself tended to use *sort,* in speech and writing, far more often than *kind* or *type.* Is *sort* less specific? One so easily says "a sort of glow," "some sort of pleasure." But perhaps *kind* can be used just as casually: "I'm kind of worn out today," "It wasn't her kind of thing." Is *type* a little more technical? "What type of work does he do?" As usual, supposed synonyms are never exactly the same.

GINGERBREAD

Pain d'épices—literally "spice bread" or even more literally "bread of spices"—makes more than one appearance in *In*

Search of Lost Time. It is prized by Charles Swann as a remedy for what he calls his "ethnic" eczema and his "constipation of the Prophets," and he sends a servant to purchase it from one particular vendor, a woman in the Champs-Élysées who is for that reason "particularly nice" to Swann's daughter, Gilberte, and the smitten young narrator.

More than one French–English dictionary defines this food as "gingerbread," but it is not really the equivalent of what we in America think of as gingerbread—a soft cake, really, with perhaps only a little resistance in its slightly sticky crust, sweeter and much spongier and lighter than a *pain d'épices*. *Pain d'épices* is a dense cake made with rye flour, honey, sugar, and spices (notably anise). It could be called "spice cake" or "spice bread," but is in any case more a bread than a cake. Oddly, we have the word *bread* in our *gingerbread*, but we no longer even hear it as meaning what we think of as "bread." Did the cake itself use to be something closer to the French *pain d'épices*?

H

HÉLAS

In my investigations of the etymologies of individual words that I encountered in the course of the translation, I came to pick apart *hélas*, "alas," in order to see if I could rebuild something better (I thought) than *alas* in English. The word first appeared in written form in the twelfth century and was formed of the exclamation *hé!* and the adjective *las*, meaning *malheureux*, "unfortunate" or "unfortunate one." It was an interjection of complaint, expressing pain (affliction, sorrow) or regret. *Hélas* occurs seventeen times in *Swann's Way* and was a problem for me. I never did write "oh, unfortunate one!" in the translation. But I wondered if I should use the word *alas* at all, since it seemed to tip over into the excessively archaic. (I had also, at one point, decided not to use somewhat old-fashioned words like *hasten* for *hurry* until I was persuaded otherwise by an advocate of the beauty of such language, particularly of *hasten* itself.) Then I noticed that it appeared in emails from my friends from time to time; it obviously still had a place in contemporary language. After I discussed this with a friend well versed in the classics, she began using, in her correspondence, the Latin for *alas*—*Eheu*, a nice sort of sneeze. I did keep all seventeen occurrences of *alas* and eventually began to hear the recurring word as a sort of Greek (or Latin) chorus repeating its general comment on the events that were unfolding in the plot.

I

IDIOMS

Idioms are difficult for the translator. One example, which recurs throughout *Swann's Way* and must be translated differently in each instance, depending on the context, is *il s'agit de*. This is most directly translated as "it's a matter of" or "it's a question of" but can be (often should be) translated in many other ways, such as "what we're talking about here" or "what we're concerned with here" or "what I mean is" and so on. For instance: *quand il s'agit de* may be "when it comes to." There is a lot of room in how one translates it. By contrast, I welcome the relief of translating a word like *beurre*, which can (usually) mean only "butter."

THE *IMPARFAIT*

Any discussion of the *imparfait* verb tense in France, roughly equivalent to the imperfect in English, becomes complicated. The imperfect is the verb depicting an ongoing or prevailing condition, or a habitual action, a repeated action, as opposed to a one-time, finite action, and it was heavily used by Flaubert in *Madame Bovary*, in part to emphasize the tedium of Emma's life, as she experienced it.

Proust was particularly struck by what he saw as Flaubert's innovative use of the verb form. It was an important form for him, too, because of his interest in the role of habit in our lives.

In English, we most usually express the imperfect by the auxiliaries *would* or *used to* with the infinitive (*would go, used to go*), or *was* with the present participle (*was going*). It is also the tense used, in English, for the "background" or "context" action in which the more finite or immediate action takes place: "I *was walking* [imperfect] to the store when I *saw* [past perfect] my friend Joe"; "I *was living* [imperfect] in France when I first *put* [past perfect] endives in my salad."

In the first published edition of my translation of *Swann's Way*, at that time titled *The Way by Swann's*, I made heavy and repeated use of *would* to construct the imperfect in English—"would go," "would imagine," etc. I can't remember now if I had a clear reason, at the time, for choosing all those *would*s. The problem is that whereas the French *imparfait* verb ending *-ait* that repeats throughout the book—*allait*, *imaginait*—has an easy, open sound that bears repeating, the same cannot be said for our thudding, end-stopped *would*. Although there is now and then, in translating, a good reason for retaining a word or phrase that slightly offends the ear, in this case there was not. After a little time had passed and I could reread my first version objectively, I saw this somewhat too heavy use of *would* as clumsy—although some readers whom I questioned had not noticed it at all. I realized that I could start a sentence or passage in the imperfect—"would go," "would imagine"—to signal that what was involved here was repeated action, and then slip unobtrusively into the perfect tense—"went," "imagined"—without creating confusion. I could occasionally return to the imperfect, when necessary, for clarity. Thus, in the following passage, describing the narrator as a boy returning from a family walk, "I would be dragging my feet, I would be ready to drop with sleep" became "I was dragging my feet, I was ready to drop with sleep."

The passage occurs about one-quarter of the way through *Swann's Way*. It displays Proust's gentle humor and presents a harmonious picture of the protagonist's family life; it also contains some lovely images and conceits. At the close of the passage, Proust explicitly brings in the notion of habit itself.

As for us, since it was Sunday the next day and we would not get up until time for high mass, if there was moonlight and the air was warm, instead of having us go home directly, my father, out of a love of personal glory, would take us by way of the calvary on a long walk which my mother's incapacity for orienting herself, or knowing what road she was on, made her consider the feat of a strategic genius. Sometimes we went as far as the viaduct, whose spans of stone like great strides began at the railway station and represented to me the exile and distress that lay outside the civilized world, because each year as we came from Paris we were warned to pay careful attention, when Combray came, not to let the station go by, to be ready ahead of time because the train would leave again after two minutes and would set off across the viaduct beyond the Christian countries of which Combray marked for me the farthest limit. We would return by way of the station boulevard, which was lined by the most pleasant houses in the parish. In each garden the moonlight, like Hubert Robert, scattered its broken staircases of white marble, its fountains, its half-open gates. Its light had destroyed the Telegraph Office. All that remained of it was one column, half-shattered but still retaining the beauty of an immortal ruin. I was dragging my feet, I was ready to drop with sleep, the fragrance of the lindens that perfumed the air seemed to me a reward that one could win only at the cost of the greatest fatigue and that was not worth the trouble. From gates far apart, dogs awakened by our solitary steps sent forth alternating barks such as I still hear at times in the evening and among which the station boulevard (when the public gardens of Combray were created on its site) must have come to take refuge, for, wherever I find myself, as soon as they begin resounding and replying, I see it, with its lindens and its sidewalk lit by the moon.

Suddenly my father would stop us and ask my mother: "Where are we?" Exhausted from walking but proud of him, she would admit tenderly that she had absolutely no idea. He would shrug his shoulders and laugh. Then, as if he had taken it out of his jacket pocket along with his key, he would show us the little back gate of our own garden, which stood there before us, having come, along with the corner of the rue du Saint-Esprit, to wait for us at the end of these unfamiliar streets. My mother would say to him with admiration: "You are astonishing!" And from that moment on, I did not have to take another step, the ground walked for me through that garden where for so long now my actions had ceased to be accompanied by any deliberate attention: Habit had taken me in its arms, and it carried me all the way to my bed like a little child.

INVERSION

Another hard problem: that French can invert when English can't. In a single sentence, I would encounter an inversion that could not be reproduced in English—"illuminated obliquely the room"—and then an inversion that also worked perfectly well in English: "encrusting with little pieces of gold the lemon-wood of the commode."

In some cases, the inversion could remain when there was substantial content in the different parts of the sentence—for instance, "with little pieces of gold" and "the lemon-wood of the commode"—whereas if there had been less content, the inversion would have been awkward, as in "encrusting with gold the commode," which becomes possible with just a little more content in the object, either here: "encrusting with gold the lemon-wood of the commode," or here: "encrusting with gold the commode which stood in the corner."

Here is another example, in which the complexity of the second part makes the inversion necessary—the indirect object, a prepositional phrase, must be slipped in before the direct object: "which . . . projected on the world the mysterious light in which he saw it." Had the direct object been more complex and the indirect object simpler, no inversion would have been necessary: "which . . . projected a mysterious light on the world as he now saw it." (See also section 3 of *Contigu.*)

There is much more to say about inversion, of course. And as soon as one starts thinking about it, one notices examples of its different functions. Here are two from J.R.R. Tolkien's essay about *Beowulf.* These are inversions at sentence openings for emphasis: "So potent is it" begins one sentence. Another, soon after, reads "So excellent is this choice as the theme of the harp that maddened Grendel lurking joyless in the dark without that it matters little whether this is anachronistic or not." (Note that *without* means "outside.") Actually, that second example is a reasonable instance, also, of dispensing with commas.

INVOLUNTARY HABITS IN WRITING ENGLISH

I noticed that when I came to translate *plus loin*, I chose "farther on" when speaking of the course of the Vivonne river, and, in the same passage, "farther off" when speaking of the surface of the water. I seemed to prefer "farther on" when travel or progress was suggested, and "farther off" when what was suggested was surveying the distances from a stationary position.

Each individual translator no doubt has many involuntary writing habits, including involuntary syntactical preferences and a preferred habitual vocabulary, and these are in part what inevitably make each translation of the same text different.

J

JAMES, HENRY

The language of Henry James in *The Portrait of a Lady*, published in 1881, contains English words that in his day meant the same as their French equivalents, whereas these meanings are no longer current in English, while they have not changed in French.

Example: "tables charged with knickknacks." The French would also use the verb *charger*. We, now, would say "loaded" or "covered." Or maybe "laden."

Another: James writes "quitting her," as the French would use *quitter* and we now would say "leave."

Two more: James has "history" (French *histoire*) for "story." And "fixed them" (French *les fixait*) for "stared at them."

James is comfortable with an ample use of every variety of *which* construction, including the equivalent of the neat French *dont* that I envy so. For instance this, including an inversion, close to the beginning of *Washington Square* (1880), in a description of an admired doctor: "He was a thoroughly honest man—honest in a degree *of which* he had perhaps lacked the opportunity to give the complete measure."

Similarly, the Jamesian sentence may include the sort of balance we find in Proust, as well as the alliteration. In the following, note the two pairs of alliterated verbs and the rhythm of seven beats with a silent eighth:

"She has waited and watched and plotted and prayed; but she has never succeeded." Note also the symmetry of the vowel sounds in *waited, watched; plotted, prayed*.

At a certain point in my work on the translation of *Swann's Way*, I thought I should go through at least one James novel marking every such verb that then carried—but no longer—the same meaning, or usage, as the identical or cognate French verbs today. This was one of several ambitions I have not fulfilled. (Another being to look up and read all the writers important to Proust, such as Ruskin, Anatole France, and Leconte de Lisle.)

L

LATINATE VS. ANGLO-SAXON

I was very aware of the choice of Latinate vocabulary versus Anglo-Saxon as I worked on the translation of *Swann's Way*.

The vocabulary of French would be mainly Latinate; for the English, I could follow the French and employ that vocabulary or I could take advantage of English's parallel vocabulary of Germanic words whose nature was entirely different and so very characteristic of English. Of course I would decide on the suitable word choice in each individual case, but what I declared that I wanted, at a certain point, was balance: a wealth of formal, Latinate (abstract, conceptual) vocabulary if at other times I had hefty doses of Anglo-Saxon. Although on the whole I am more naturally fond of the punchy, emotional, vivid Anglo-Saxon vocabulary, the monosyllables of Tyndale's translations of the Bible, it was also true that the more formal, Latinate diction was often a language of grace and sometimes greater precision. I also leaned more than usual toward the Latinate in the case of this translation because of the nature of Proust's language. His own vocabulary was of necessity heavily Latinate and polysyllabic.

Here was one instance of my considering an Anglo-Saxon versus a Latinate choice of words. Describing Swann's thoughts about the moon and Odette's face, Proust writes: *il pensait à cette autre figure claire et légèrement rosée comme celle de la lune, qui, un jour, avait surgi devant sa pensée et, depuis, projetait sur le monde la lumière mystérieuse dans laquelle il le voyait.* In my translation, "he would think of that other face, bright and tinged with pink like the moon's, which, one day, had appeared in the forefront of his mind and, since then, had cast on the world the mysterious light in which he saw it." I am naturally inclined to use *cast* rather than *project*, for the single syllable and the clean, clear sound of it. And *cast* is more or less married to *shadow*, which we so readily associate with the sun or the moon or any other source of light. (A film, on the other hand, is *projected* from a *projector*.) I wondered, though, if there might be a good

reason to remain closer to the more complex, multisyllabic
original. But generally, in English, *project* is more suited to
an abstract idea: "I'm afraid I have projected my own feelings
onto him." In Proust's text, within the metaphor, the image is concrete. For Proust, there might have been no other
alternative. But I opted for *cast*. (For comparison, the revised Scott Moncrieff translation has "shed": "shed upon the
world the mysterious light in which he saw it bathed." But
I read *shed* as more than simply *cast*, rather as *cast off*—as a
snake *sheds* its skin.)

LITERAL TRANSLATION

In my first draft, typed rather fast (though with many long
pauses) into the computer file, the sentences would often
come out nearly as I would eventually keep them in the final
draft. I stayed very close to the word order, and the wording, of the French original. Sometimes I thought the closest
translation was not possible, until, in a later draft, I checked
Scott Moncrieff's version and saw that he had managed, successfully, to stay even closer, though so much of the time
he strayed as he thought best. (See S: The Scott Moncrieff
Translation, etc.)

The more literal will sometimes be strange. But is it
good-strange, or bad-strange? In other words, is it fresh and
invigorating language, or is it awkward translationese? What
context can allow for fresh and strange language, and what
cannot?

Close translation and literal translation are not the same,
though people confuse them and though they can coincide.
The close translation departs from the literal when the literal
would be more awkward than the original or uncharacteristic
of natural English style. But, having the aim of being close,
one can also, frequently, be literal.

When translating another language quite closely, one is reproducing its characteristic patterns: the way it moves, the way it thinks, and the way the author thinks, of course. To what extent was I willing to lose that by moving away from the very close?

A fairly simple example: Where Proust had *ceux qui ne sont pas du même avis*, I had two choices. I could translate it very closely, even literally, retaining the rather formal locution, thus: "those who are not of the same opinion." I could also, while still preserving the meaning, translate it less formally as "those who do not agree." I opted for the first, more formal and closer. I did this in order to match the French more closely but also to keep in the text the word *opinion—avis*. The text had its own word-hoard that I was loath to subtract from. I also liked the more flowing rhythm, and even the elegance, of the longer choice, over the blunter and shorter choice.

LITTLE WORDS

Some of the most difficult were the "little words" like *comme*, *d'ailleurs*, *enfin*, which depend so much on context, and/or serve general purposes in dialogue and narration, of expressing surprise, or function as connectives, or attenuate (soften) a statement.

Comme is used in French in certain situations in more or less the same way as our "like" is used colloquially in spoken exchanges and has been for the last twenty years or so, though not before. But the French *comme*, of course, has not at all the same casual ring to it. It has the same intention, though, of moderating a comparison or a description.

Example from *Swann's Way*: *il fait de notre vie comme une étendue émouvante*. Here, *comme* means "a sort of," "in some sense," "something akin to," etc. A fairly straightforward translation can be found in the revised Scott Moncrieff: "makes of one's life a sort of stirring arena." This was changed from Scott Moncrieff's longer and more elaborate (and perhaps more accurately conveying the meaning): "makes of our lives a vast expanse, quick with sensation." James Grieve also enlarged the clause, into "transforms our whole life into . . . an ambience of shared pervading sentiment." Both Scott Moncrieff and Grieve have omitted the idea of *comme* and gone straight to the unmoderated simile. The Kilmartin-Enright revision of Scott Moncrieff restores the *comme* with "a sort of," though "stirring arena" in itself is quite strange.

M

MIRROR
Proust said the writer is the mirror—it is not the event that matters but how it is reflected.

He also said that his desire was to "exhaust the real."

MIXED METAPHORS
In a passage about Swann, his social position, and his flirtations, there occurs a sentence about his attraction to women "beneath" him socially. Instead of finding some more "proper" dalliance, he chooses to pursue a woman from a family "whom it would have been more correct for him to make no attempt to know" (as Scott Moncrieff translates it in a pleasingly convoluted way). Proust explains that Swann chooses not to *tromper le désir qu'elle avait fait naître*, which would be literally rendered as "cheat the desire she had caused to be born," which has the difficult-to-translate *faire* construction in *fait naître*. I translated this first as "cheat the desire she had inspired." In a later edition, no doubt bothered by the

incidental (= careless) rhyme of *desire* and *inspired*, I changed this to "cheat the desire she had awoken in him"—better. For this phrase, Scott Moncrieff has "cheat the desire that she had kindled in him," which seems a fairly good solution, considering how awkward "caused to be born in him" would be, in any case. True, perhaps there is a mixed metaphor in the idea of "cheating" something that was "kindled"—can you cheat a fire or flame? But perhaps you can't, either, cheat something born, inspired, or awoken? In any case, this is changed in the Kilmartin-Enright revision, perhaps for that reason, or perhaps because Kilmartin or Enright was bothered by the word *cheat*. In any case, that revision, unfortunately, manages to introduce another, slightly different, but more glaring mixed metaphor: "stave off the desire she had kindled in him." Now we have desire compared, via *kindle*, to a flame or fire, and we have the action of "staving" it off. This really produces an impossible image.

Here are a couple more examples of Kilmartin's (or Enright's—I simply can't always check to see if Kilmartin changed something before Enright assumed the responsibility of further revision) propensity for mixed metaphors: "Disseminating . . . the horror that had gripped him." In this metaphor, horror is being compared to seed which you can cast about. Acceptable, though a little odd. But then, in that case, horror can't also be something capable of gripping.

A second example: "The shattered creature which these crushing words had made of him." The creature must be either crushed or shattered, not both. The Scott Moncrieff translation, before the revision, reads: "the utterly spiritless creature which these crushing words had made of him." The French being: *l'être sans forces qu'avaient fait de lui ces accablantes paroles. Sans forces* simply means drained, weakened, or debilitated. As happens fairly often, James Grieve entirely recasts the sentence, changing its structure; his translation of this part is: "instantaneously prostrated by this horrific speech."

MONOSYLLABLES IN PROUST'S DIALOGUE
Although so much of the narration in *Swann's Way* revels in polysyllabic locutions, there are passages of dialogue, in particular, that are strikingly monosyllabic.

Example, in two pieces of dialogue, in an exchange between Swann and Odette as he tries to ferret out the truth from among her lies, also striking for its lack of punctuation:

Swann: "*Je ne sais quoi que j'ai su ne pas être vrai.*" Not a single polysyllable. In my translation, there are more: "something or other that I knew at the time wasn't true."

Odette: "*Oui, que je n'y étais pas allée le soir où je t'ai dit que j'en sortais quand tu m'avais cherchée chez Prévost.*" Here, six two-syllable words punctuate the stream of monosyllables, at one point eight in a row; one comma. My translation is longer but still full of monosyllables, only five polysyllables, and limited to the one comma, as Odette admits to lying about her whereabouts: "Yes, that I hadn't actually been there at all that evening when I told you I had just come from there and you had been looking for me at Prévost's."

O

OMISSIONS FROM THE TRANSLATIONS
The Scott Moncrieff translation occasionally misses a phrase or so from the text, apparently overlooking it. The Kilmartin-Enright revision does not always restore phrases missing from the Scott Moncrieff translation.

For example, in a passage about the hardships of having a love affair, Proust says this about the devoted lovers: *en qui le sacrifice qu'ils font de leur repos et de leurs intérêts à une rêverie voluptueuse fait naître un charme intérieur.* The phrase missing from the translation is: *à une rêverie voluptueuse* (literally, "to a voluptuous daydream"). Scott Moncrieff's version is: "in whom the perpetual sacrifice which they are making of their comfort and of their practical interests has engendered a spiritual charm." The revised Scott Moncrieff, which has not restored the missing phrase, becomes: "in whom the perpetual sacrifice they make of their comfort and of their practical interests engenders a sort of inner charm." Here, it is worth pointing out, also, that that troublesome phrase *faire naître* ("cause to be born") is really most closely translated by "engenders." But the context does not always allow one to use that word. "Brought forth" might be another possibility, though not here. Or "brought into being." In my translation, I found yet another possibility: "in whom the sacrifice they are making of their sleep and their other interests to a dream of sensuous pleasure produces an inner charm." But now I'm doubtful about "other interests." And perhaps even "produces." And what is an "inner charm"?

Another example: *sans qu'il sache seulement s'il pourra revoir jamais celle qu'il aime déjà et dont il ignore jusqu'au nom.* In this case, Scott Moncrieff did not omit any part of the original sentence, but in the process of revision the Kilmartin-Enright version dropped one entire phrase and idea, that of *celle qu'il aime déjà*: "the one he already loves" or (because "the one" is feminine in French) "the woman he already loves." In Scott Moncrieff's version, we have: "without his knowing even whether he is ever to see her again whom he loves already, although he knows nothing of her, not even her name." (Gracefully written and close, though the last part—"knows nothing of her"—is an expansion of the original.) The revision shortens this, dropping an idea, probably inadvertently, and changing the order: "although he does not even know her name or whether he will ever see her again." My version is: "without his even knowing if he will ever see this woman again whom he loves already and of whom he knows nothing, not even her name." I have expanded the sentence a little, too, perhaps unnecessarily. Better might have been, if I can lift what I like from Scott Moncrieff and try again: "without his knowing even whether he will ever see her again whom he loves already, though he does not know even her name." The repetition of "even" is unfortunate, but at the moment I don't see how to avoid it. "See her again whom he loves already" is somewhat unfamiliar as a construction, but interesting.

At yet another point, the Kilmartin-Enright revision of the Scott Moncrieff omits a phrase. Here is, first, the French: *Ainsi un voyageur arrivé par un beau temps au bord de la Méditerranée, incertain de l'existence des pays qu'il vient de quitter, laisse éblouir sa vue, plutôt qu'il ne leur jette des regards, par les rayons qu'émet vers lui l'azur lumineux et résistant des eaux.* Scott Moncrieff's translation: "So will a traveller, who has come down, on a day of glorious weather, to the Mediterranean shore, and is doubtful whether they still exist, those lands which he has left, let his eyes be dazzled, rather than cast a backward glance, by the radiance streaming towards him from the luminous and unfading azure at his feet." This is rather pleasing, in itself, but there are a few problems here, perhaps—Scott Moncrieff has expanded the bit about the lands left behind, and he chooses to replace "the azure . . . of the waters" or "the azure . . . of the sea"—which is how the sentence ends in French—by "the azure . . . at his feet," implying rather than declaring the presence of the water. Nice, for instance, is the rhythm of the whole sentence and the conjunction of sounds in his "left, let." The Kilmartin-Enright revision changes "who has come down" to the closer, and briefer, though not as lovely, "arriving." It makes other minor changes in the direction of a closer translation, but once again omits an entire phrase: "rather than cast a backward glance." The sentence now reads: "So will a traveller, arriving in glorious weather at the Mediterranean shore, no longer certain of the existence of the lands he has left behind, let his eyes be dazzled by the radiance streaming towards him from the luminous and unfading azure of the sea."

OVAL—AND OTHER ENGLISH WORDS YOU THINK YOU KNOW

As you translate, you find yourself looking up words in your own language that you think you know but in fact do not know well enough. I consulted a dictionary for the word *oval* because Proust refers to the sun's "oval" shape. I suddenly wondered: Could a circle be one type of oval, just as a square is one type of rectangle? Maybe it was, somehow, a perfectly circular oval? But no, of course not, especially since the answer is right there in the word: *oval* comes from the word for egg. It is Proust who chose to see the sun as oval, perhaps in a certain hazy light.

Then there is the word *stagnant*. We have gradually given it a negative connotation; even when it is applied nonmetaphorically to water, we see the water as murky and afloat with decaying vegetation. But in fact it means, quite simply and more neutrally: "still," "not moving," "not flowing," "motionless." I discovered this by researching the French *mare*, whose near synonyms are *flache, flaque, lagon*: a *mare* is a small shallow sheet of water that stagnates; it is a body of still or standing water. The French definition of *stagner* ("to stagnate") is: *rester immobile sans couler, sans se renouveler* ("to remain motionless without flowing, without renewing itself").

The English word *plaid*, like the same word in French, *plaid*, derived from the Gaelic for "cover," did not originally mean the pattern that we now associate it with. It meant a piece of clothing of the Scottish highlanders, a checkered wool cover draped to serve as a cloak; it also used to mean a man's or woman's ample traveling cloak.

P

PAST PARTICIPLES AS ADJECTIVES

The difficulty, sometimes, of translating past participles functioning as adjectives.

For instance, in this sentence, the word *redevenues* (literally, "re-become," if only one could employ such a word), which can be so neatly and economically used in French as an adjective: *Les romans champêtres de George Sand qu'elle me donnait pour ma fête, étaient pleins . . . d'expressions tombées en désuétude et redevenues imagées, comme on n'en trouve plus qu'à la campagne.*

I translated this, in the end, as, "The pastoral novels of George Sand which she was giving me for my saint's day were full of expressions that had fallen into disuse and turned figurative again, the sort you no longer find anywhere but in the country."

But before opting for that, I regretfully put the impossible *re-become* to one side and listed to myself the other possibilities, all of them less concise than the French: become again; once again become or become once again; having once again become or having become once again; having reverted to, having returned to; now once again; and, finally, turned . . . again.

Then there is a past participle related to the troublesome
redevenu, "re-become," and that is *devenu,* "become," which
is freely used in French and presents the same problem for the
translator, for instance in this description: *La lumière tombait
si implacable du ciel devenu fixe que l'on aurait voulu se sous-
traire à son attention*: literally, "The light fell so implacable
from the become-fixed sky that one would have wanted to
withdraw oneself from its attention," which in more natural
English could be, "The light fell so implacably from the now
still sky that one would have wanted to elude its attention."

One more example: A description of the crows and their
flights from the steeple of Saint-Hilaire, the village church,
employs both *devenu* and *redevenu* as adjectives in succeeding sentences. The first: *comme si les vieilles pierres . . . ,
devenues tout d'un coup inhabitables.* Here, I did not treat
devenues as an adjective but rather made it part of the active
verb: "as if the old stones . . . had suddenly become unin-
habitable." The next sentence includes this characterization
of the church steeple: *de nefaste redevenue propice,* literally
"from baneful re-become benign." Here, I opened the adjectives out into a subordinate clause, translating them much
less concisely (nine words as opposed to four) as "which was
no longer baneful but once again benign." I think I needed
the "which was" so that "no longer baneful but once again
benign" would not (grammatically) qualify the crows rather
than the tower.

THE PLAIN TRANSLATION VS. THE MORE ELABORATE

VERBS

One of the differences between my translation of *Swann's
Way* and the previous ones is that almost without exception
I translated Proust's verbs by the closest English equivalent,

while the other translators (Scott Moncrieff, his two revisers, and James Grieve) might opt (though they did not always) for a more "developed" translation, most often one that incorporated information gathered by the translator from the context.

Proust's plain *répondit*, for instance, the most direct translation of which, in the context of a passage of dialogue, would be "answered," "responded," or "replied," is translated by Scott Moncrieff, at one point, by "broke in," which of course adds content that Scott Moncrieff derives from the scene in which the verb occurs—it is not in the word itself. For the same word, James Grieve elaborates in his own way, more extensively and with a different interpretation from Scott Moncrieff's, by translating it as "made the following suggestion."

In another scene, when Swann has at last found Odette, after searching for some time, he climbs into her carriage and "tells" his carriage to follow; he does not "order" it, as Scott Moncrieff chooses to translate *dit*.

In a scene between the young narrator and the family friend Swann, the boy modestly declines a favor offered by Swann in relation to a much-admired author, Bergotte, but does venture to "ask" him "some questions" about the author (*posai à Swann des questions sur Bergotte*). In Scott Moncrieff's translation this becomes "bombarded Swann with questions," quite out of keeping with the hesitant deference otherwise expressed by the young narrator. The Grieve translation respects the narrator's modesty, but expands the simple "asked Swann some questions," changing it to "took the opportunity to ask Swann a few questions." The taking of the opportunity is certainly implied in the situation, but a reader absorbs that idea from the simpler French and from a more direct translation.

For *autrefois*, meaning "in earlier times," "in the past," etc., the revised Scott Moncrieff gives us the extrapolation "as a boy."

NOUNS

Before Swann finds Odette that evening, his old servant offers his "opinion" (*avis*) that Monsieur had best give up the search and return home. Scott Moncrieff translates this as "advice."

VERB AND NOUN

Where Proust writes *pris quelque chose d'humain* ("taken on something human," as I translated it most plainly), the Kilmartin-Enright revision has retained Scott Moncrieff's choice, "endued a vesture of humanity." I knew the word *vesture*, meaning a "covering garment," though I did not encounter it often, but *endue*, meaning "to put on," "to don," was new to me. (The words of the Christmas carol—"don we now our gay apparel"—could be changed to "endue we now our gay vesture.") Once again, Proust's relatively plain and straightforward language has been rendered archaic and obscure in English—the everyday *taken on* become *endued*, the everyday *something* becomes *a vesture*—and this English is thus, once again, not a true reflection of the style of the original.

PRESENT-TENSE NARRATION

Every so often, in *Swann's Way*, Proust will leave the past tense in his narration and continue, briefly, in the present tense. Sometimes it is as though what he is describing is "now" still the same as it was "then," in the story he is telling us. (Flaubert does this, too—as though landscapes and towns that feature in *Madame Bovary* will be found to be the same now, no matter when the reader's "now" is, as they were at the time of the story he is telling.)

For instance, Proust describes the Vivonne river thus: "Soon the course of the Vivonne is obstructed with water plants." Or "But farther on, the current slows down." The Vivonne, he implies—though the "Vivonne" itself does not exist—will be found to be the same "now."

A few pages later, Proust is talking about the Guermantes family, and here comes the present tense again. Amid a past-tense narration, he remarks that there emanates (present tense) from that syllable—*antes*—an orange light. The Guermantes family, by implication, really exists, exists eternally, and what Proust perceives about their name will continue to be true "now."

Here is yet another fleeting instance of this use of the present tense, again in describing geography: and again, although the landscape of the story is fictional, the present tense implies that it is not. The scene is the walk the young narrator is taking with his father and grandfather along the boundary of Swann's estate. His elders have gone ahead while he lingers, looking through the fence. Then, in my translation, "I had to run to rejoin my father and grandfather, who were calling me, surprised that I had not followed them along the little lane they had already entered which leads up to the fields." The momentary present tense is in the word *leads*. The story is in the past, but Proust offers us the illusion that the little lane, even now, and eternally, leads up to the fields. Here is that bit in the French: *étonnés que je ne les eusse pas suivis dans le petit chemin qui monte vers les champs.* (The Kilmartin-Enright revision avoids this present tense by translating it, more or less reasonably, as "surprised that I had not followed them along the little path leading up to the open fields." (*Chemin* is another difficult word for the translator, by the way, since it can mean "path," "lane," or "road" . . .) Scott Moncrieff avoids it, too, with his "surprised that I had not followed them along the little path, climbing up hill towards the open fields, into which they had already turned." But I savor the, somehow, intimacy of the word *leads*, which seems to invite us, more than the past tense, into a familiarity with this place.

One more example, but one in which the present tense is used a little differently. Proust writes in the present tense in an extended passage close to the end of the second section of *Swann's Way*, as he is describing how the two alternative "ways" of going for a walk have marked him permanently. This use of the present tense functions in another manner: here he is bringing us with him into the present, his present, but he is an integral part of the continuing story, not something that exists in perpetuity outside the story.

PUNCTUATION, ESPECIALLY COMMAS

The following passage is taken from a point just before the end of the section of *Swann's Way* titled "Swann in Love"—a self-contained story within the novel. It concerns the feelings of Charles Swann for his mistress and (though he doesn't yet know this) future wife.

> Having in the past often thought with terror that one day he would cease to be in love with Odette, he had promised himself to be vigilant and, as soon as he felt his love was beginning to leave him, to cling to it, to keep hold of it. But now, corresponding to the weakening of his love there was a simultaneous weakening of his desire to remain in love. For one cannot change, that is to say become another person, while continuing to acquiesce to the feelings of the person

one no longer is. Now and then a name glimpsed in a newspaper, that of one of the men he thought could have been Odette's lovers, restored his jealousy to him. But it was very mild and as it proved to him that he had not yet completely emerged from the time when he had suffered so much—but when he had also known so voluptuous a range of feelings—and that the hazards of the road ahead might still permit him to catch a furtive distant glimpse of its beauties, this jealousy actually gave him a pleasant thrill just as to the sad Parisian leaving Venice to return to France, a last mosquito proves that Italy and the summer are not yet too remote.

Following the shapes and structures of Proust's sentences as closely as possible, word by word and phrase by phrase, in my translation, eventually applied, also, to matching his punctuation when I could. Many a sentence is constructed in such a way that we do not find out the subject of the main clause until the end of it, and requires close attention and readerly patience. But most of the sentences in the novel are not excessively long, and the long ones are often deployed strategically following a buildup of shorter sentences to convey the reader more deeply into the complexities of a particular thought that Proust is developing. In the passage above, for instance, the sentences, in order, extend over three lines, two lines, two lines, three lines, and six lines—shorter sentences leading up to a longer and more complex one.

The question of stopping or not stopping the flow within a Proustian sentence comes up regularly in translating him. Whereas at first I paid little attention to Proust's punctuation as such—aside from respecting the obvious larger stops, the semicolons, colons, and periods—but concentrated on other aspects of the sentence, punctuating in the way that was natural to me, to "my ear," at some point in the translation I realized that I should be more diligent in trying to respect his placement of commas as well, if I could. Some commas are indispensable for clarity of meaning, as in "to cling to it, to keep hold of it" in the passage above, but other commas are optional (as right here at this point in this sentence and from here to the end) and can be included if the writer wants to slow the sentence down or omitted if the writer wants an unbroken and perhaps rather fast pace to the sentence. (For instance, this last sentence of mine can be radically peppered with commas to read, "but other commas are optional, as right here, at this point in this sentence, and from here to the end, and can be included, if the writer wants to slow the sentence down, or omitted, if the writer wants an unbroken, and, perhaps, rather fast, pace to the sentence." Eleven commas in this latter version, none in the former.) One extreme example of omitting commas and yet maintaining grammatical correctness is this sentence by the master syntax-manipulator Samuel Beckett: "For could one not in his right mind be reasonably said to wonder if he was in his right mind and bring what is more his remains of reason to bear on this perplexity in the way he must be said to do if he is to be said at all?" A shorter example comes from John Ashbery's "If You Said You Would Come With Me": "One of the women however came to greet us in a friendly manner." There he has dispensed with the pair of commas that might be placed around "however." To return to the Proust example, the deliberate omission in the following sentence fragment—*et voulant d'autre part pour lui-même exprimer*, where we might expect commas around *d'autre part*—allows the sentence to trip right along or charge ahead with an equal weight on each word, the asides (*d'autre part*) being subsumed in the forward motion of the whole, not stopping it.

In the six-line sentence above, for instance, which begins "But it was very mild," Proust has only two commas (along with the pair of dashes) to break the forward momentum. It required no special acrobatics for me to include only two, in the same places, in mine. C. K. Scott Moncrieff, however, chose to slow the sentence by including no fewer than ten commas. Speaking of Swann's jealousy, Proust opens with *Mais elle était bien légère et comme elle lui prouvait qu'il n'était pas encore complètement sorti de* . . . (no commas), and I chose to match his punctuation with, "But it was very mild and since it proved to him that he had not yet completely emerged from . . ." Scott Moncrieff's version, punctuated in a more standard way, reads, "But it was very slight, and, inasmuch as it proved to him that he had not completely emerged from . . ." The added commas are not intrusive there. More markedly, further along in the sentence, Scott Moncrieff's version is: "this jealousy gave him, if anything, an agreeable thrill, as to the sad Parisian, when he has left Venice behind him and must return to France, a last mosquito proves that Italy and summer are still not too remote." He slows down with five commas what in Proust's original is slowed by only one: *Cette jalousie lui procurait plutôt une excitation agréable comme au morne Parisien qui quitte Venise pour retrouver la France, un dernier moustique prouve que l'Italie et l'été ne sont pas encore bien loin.* (This is a nice moment in the novel, as Proust gives a small role even to a *moustique*, or "mosquito." One of the admirable qualities of his approach to his material is that about certain subjects, in any case, he is not sentimental.)

Proust could easily have inserted a pair of commas around *plutôt* and another after *agréable.* My version, equally eccentric but not impossible, has no more commas than the Proust original: "This jealousy actually gave him a pleasant thrill just as to the sad Parisian leaving Venice to return to France, a last mosquito proves that Italy and the summer are not yet too remote." If I had not been making the deliberate effort to try it without commas, if I had been punctuating "by ear," I would probably have put a comma before "just as," which begins the simile. I would also have put a comma after "just as," because of the comma before "a last mosquito." This would feel natural and correct—but these same placements of commas might have felt natural and correct in the original, too, and Proust chose not to include them. (And often I did not believe such faithful adherence to Proust's punctuation would work until I made myself try it "at least in the first draft.") In fact, the effect of not interrupting the sentence is to give the words a more equal, even staccato measure, quite changing the effect of the sound of the prose. And, curiously, this lack of commas, I think, makes the text sound more contemporary to our time—and yet the choice was Proust's, not mine, which may say something about how much more modern he has always sounded to French ears than he has to his readers in English, during the many decades in which Scott Moncrieff's translation was the only one available.

For another comparison, it is interesting to look at James Grieve's version, since his working method is so very different from mine and from Scott Moncrieff's, perhaps indeed quite opposite, as he often disassembles and reassembles the original in his own fashion, though with special attention to meaning and narrative liveliness. Grieve inserts paragraph breaks where Proust has none; he amplifies sentences, so that, for instance, the three-word sentence "He was mistaken" becomes the eight-word "In this, as it happened, he was mistaken." He breaks up the longer sentence quoted above with a semicolon and two more commas, changes the paired dashes to parentheses, and renders the phrase quoted above thus: "They [his twinges of jealousy] caused him some not unpleasant qualms of agitation, as the irritation of a last mosquito may remind the morose Parisian, reluctantly leaving Venice for France, that the summer in Italy is not yet a thing of the past." The mosquito is introduced before the traveling Parisian, it is enhanced by "the irritation of," Proust's strong "proves" is weakened to "may remind," Italy and the summer, two separate things in Proust, are collapsed into "the summer in Italy," and, lastly, Proust's simple "not too remote"—which refers to both time and space, is both figurative and literal, as the landscape recedes with the motion of the train—is altered to refer only to time: "not yet a thing of the past." Which is different, incidentally, from "not too remote."

The many detailed decisions a translator makes in the course of translating a long book add up to an overall effect: just as Scott Moncrieff's regular amplifications make the text in places wordy and redundant where the original is not, while his euphemisms make it coy where the French is plainspoken, his many more breaks in the sentences of this long novel make it generally more hesitant, more halting, than the original, and, curiously, because of the buttonholing effect, seem to shift the reader's attention a degree or two away from the text and toward the writer.

R

RECURRING WORDS IN THE ORIGINAL

Proust is particularly fond of certain words, and they recur throughout the novel. Some of them are: *plaisir* ("pleasure"); *distinguer* ("distinguish"); and *délicieux*. I kept searching for a good equivalent for *délicieux*, since "delicious" was often not quite right. Other alternatives were "delectable," "exquisite," "divine," "marvellous."

Another favorite of his is *doux*, "sweet" or "soft" (or many other possibilities). A stormy night in February may be *doux*, as may be a house in Parma, and more than one thing connected with Odette.

Simply from observing and enumerating these recurring words, we can understand what some of Proust's themes or preoccupations were.

S

THE SCOTT MONCRIEFF TRANSLATION COINCIDING WITH MINE

The following phrases were exactly the same in my English translation (the first draft of which was done without looking at earlier translations) as in Scott Moncrieff's. I suppose I took a special interest in this and went to the trouble of noting them down because, after all, so much, of our texts in English, was far from the same and the chances, particularly in the case of the longer fragments, were against this coinciding, against these two very different people decades apart and of different cultures, life experiences, and education, and with their own preferred vocabularies and syntaxes, opting for the same phrases. Of course, these were only the examples I happened upon; there were surely more.

"abandoned in a solitary place"
"greedy for happiness"
"the air was warm"
"she complained that it was indeed very late"
"that at midnight she would send him away"
"the passion for truth"

"He knocked"

"did you see how pathetic he looked?"

"or watching Moses pour water into a trough"

"He could hear the jokes that Mme Verdurin would
  make after dinner"

"But human patience has its limits"

"physically, she was going through a bad phase"

"did not go to bed in case"

"only deepened and sweetened his sense of his own
  happiness"

"I had felt pass so painfully close to me"

THE SCOTT MONCRIEFF TRANSLATION AND ITS
REVISIONS: ADDITIONS, SUBSTITUTIONS, AND
ERRORS IN ENGLISH CONSTRUCTIONS

In taking note of the instances in which the Scott Moncrieff
translation—and usually, following suit, the revision—added
to Proust's original text, I saw that, almost always, the change
was in the direction of some sort of enhancement—either
adding an intensifying adjective or metaphor, or making an
action more violent, or in some other way raising the stakes.
Certainly, each addition changed the meaning of the original, either slightly or significantly.

ADDITIONS TO THE ORIGINAL

Some of these examples may seem minor, but they remain
misrepresentative of the original text and their cumulative
effect is not minor.

In the Scott Moncrieff translation, "get to know romantic and heroic couplets" becomes "get to know whole pages
of romantic and heroic verse."

"Incomprehensible" becomes "frankly incomprehensible."

"Old servant" becomes "old and privileged servant."

"Who liked both men" becomes "who liked both men sincerely."

"Her eyes closed" becomes "her eyes tightly closed."

"Called forth a protest" becomes "called forth an instant protest."

"Realizing for the first time" becomes "suddenly realizing for the first time."

"Trying" in the original becomes "trying desperately."

Where Proust writes *le mode selon lequel il pouvait la voir* ("the way in which he could see her"), the revision (and perhaps Scott Moncrieff's as well) adds: "more often."

The cumulative effect of such additions is to make the text risk being wordy or redundant. And sometimes the addition is more significant, as in the following:

Where Proust writes simply "we," Scott Moncrieff and the Kilmartin-Enright revision translate "we men."

Scott Moncrieff adds information not in the original. It is late in the evening; Proust writes simply that the lights of the restaurants are going off; we readers can assume the restaurants are closing. But Scott Moncrieff adds, to be explicit, "the restaurants were closing."

In perhaps the most extreme example, Scott Moncrieff seems to become carried away by the opportunity to enrich the description. Whereas the original reads, only, "these ephemeral stars which light up on gray days," Scott Moncrieff's greatly enhanced version, left intact in the Kilmartin-Enright revision, is: "these ephemeral stars, which kindle their cold fires in the murky atmosphere of winter afternoons."

MORE ADDITIONS THAT ENHANCE

In another scene, this one involving the narrator's feelings about his parents, Scott Moncrieff's "visionary longings" may be borderline acceptable for Proust's plain "dreams" (*rêves*), but the end of the sentence, *et j'étais malheureux comme si je les avais vaincus et dépravés* ("I was unhappy, as if I had defeated them and corrupted them" or "as unhappy as if"), becomes, in his translation, "as wretched as though I had ravished and corrupted the innocence of their hearts." (The plain "them" becoming "the innocence of their hearts.") I do rather like his "wretched," however, and think "as wretched as" works well. My own translation might have been improved to read: "and I was as wretched as if I had vanquished and corrupted them." James Grieve strays a little from the meaning of the French. The simile introduced by "as if" becomes an actuality: "I was saddened by the feeling that I had defeated and depraved them." His alliteration, though, works well.

MORE CHANGES THAT ENHANCE

Proust's original "possessed by another" or "belonging to another" becomes more dramatic in Scott Moncrieff's translation: "in thraldom to another." *Thrall* and *thraldom* are two of his favorite words.

The young narrator, when he imagines spurning the lovely girl Gilberte who gazes so coolly at him from inside her father's estate, pictures himself insulting her loudly and shrugging his shoulders: *Je la trouvais si belle que j'aurais voulu pouvoir revenir sur mes pas, pour lui crier en haussant les épaules: "comme je vous trouve laide . . ."* In Scott Moncrieff's translation, however, and unchanged in the revision, the boy imagines shaking his fist.

ADDITIONS OF METAPHORS

Scott Moncrieff regularly introduces metaphors not in the original. Only sometimes are these removed from the revised version. In the following, Proust is describing a failure in

a conversational gambit during a dinner party: one of the
characters has *manqué l'effet sur lequel il avait compté*, which
could be turned around but fairly closely translated as "the
effect on which he had counted had failed" (literal would
be, "he had missed [as, a target] the effect on which he had
counted"). Scott Moncrieff deploys a metaphor, translating
this as "his castle in ruins." James Grieve also reaches for a
metaphor, though a different one, referring to the "misfiring
of his little scheme." In this instance, again, Proust is plainer
and more straightforward than his translators.

Scott Moncrieff added a metaphor at the opening of this
sentence which was not in the original: "The ice once broken, every evening, when he had taken her home, he must
follow her into the house." The Kilmartin-Enright removed
it: "Now, every evening, when he had taken her home, he
had to go in with her."

At another point in the narrative, the haunting scene in
which Swann searches so long through the late evening for
Odette, Scott Moncrieff again adds a metaphor that the revision does not remove: Swann's air of indifference falls from
him "like a cast-off cloak." In the French, there is no such
simile: *Mais l'indifférence que Swann jouait facilement . . .
tomba.*

In the French original, Proust comments on people who
belong to high society and choose to abstain from pleasures
offered outside their position in the world, characterizing
their sense of *l'obligation que crée la grandeur sociale* ["the
obligation created by social grandeur"] *de rester attaché à un
certain rivage*. The most direct translation of *rester attaché
à un certain rivage* would be "to remain moored [literally,
attached] to a certain shore." In the revised Scott Moncrieff
the metaphor implicit in the original (person = boat) becomes explicit and "shore" is amplified: "to remain moored

like houseboats to a particular point on the shore of life." This has actually been reduced slightly from Scott Moncrieff's original version: "to remain moored like houseboats to a certain point on the bank of the stream of life."

At another point, Proust's "hesitant sparrows" are described, in Scott Moncrieff's translation, as "*shyly* hopping." I have a particular prejudice against anthropomorphizing birds, insects, animals, plants, in other words nonhuman animate beings, which I believe robs them to some degree of their own inherent natures by imposing human characteristics on them, so of course I particularly disapprove of Scott Moncrieff's introduction of this metaphor. One may argue that to hesitate is peculiarly human, too. I don't agree, but certainly it is not as human as to be shy. Any thinking, or conscious, creature may hesitate, including an ant or a snake. Or a sparrow. In fact, the sparrows are part of a comparison already: Proust is comparing Gilberte's friends, as they arrive one by one in the park on a winter's day, to hesitant sparrows. Grieve chooses "like timid sparrows," which is less anthropomorphic. But "hesitant" better captures the motion by which a number of sparrows, one by one, in fits and starts, may advance toward a source of food, which is, I think, what Proust had in mind.

INCORRECT ENGLISH IN SCOTT MONCRIEFF AND/OR THE REVISION

For Scott Moncrieff's "having had drilled into him as a boy," which his revisers evidently objected to since "drilled into" was stronger than the original French, the Kilmartin-Enright version substituted a better word but introduced an erroneous usage: "having had instilled into him as a boy" should have been "instilled *in* him." I became particularly exercised about the errors introduced by the Kilmartin-Enright edition, since Scott Moncrieff took great care with his writing, as did Proust, of course, and was almost always absolutely correct in his grammar and usage. In their admittedly tremendous undertaking, the project of revising the whole of the Scott Moncrieff translation, Kilmartin, and after him Enright, despite the good they did, also did some damage to Scott Moncrieff's work and thus also to Proust's.

Here is another example, more minor, from the revised Scott Moncrieff version: "And, noticing as he drove home that the moon had now changed its position relatively to his own." "Relatively" sounded wrong to me. We would now at least, I thought, say, "relative to." I was prepared to blame the Kilmartin-Enright revision. But the word also appears in Scott Moncrieff's version, though with an added comma— "had now changed its position, relatively to his own." And so I wondered if this word, so used, was correct in Scott Moncrieff's time and has come to seem incorrect only now. I consulted a good grammarian friend who in turn consulted her favorite reference works. Both references vehemently disapprove of "relative to" and completely dismiss "relatively to." Kilmartin or Enright might have changed this.

Another instance, this one of an error introduced by the revision, was correct, as follows, in Scott Moncrieff. It occurs in the scene involving Vinteuil's daughter: "It is possible that, without being in the least inclined towards 'sadism,' a girl might have shewn the same outrageous cruelty as Mlle. Vinteuil in desecrating the memory and defying the wishes of her dead father." By the time this sentence was revised, the quotation marks around "sadism" were no longer felt to be needed (Proust himself, in fact, did not use them). But in place of the perfectly straightforward phrase "the same . . . as," the Kilmartin-Enright version introduces an incorrect and awkward usage, thus: "It is possible that, without being in the least inclined towards sadism, a daughter might be guilty of equally cruel offences as those of Mlle Vinteuil against the memory and the wishes of her dead father." It is both incorrect and discordant to write "equally . . . as." The revision could easily have avoided this infelicity by writing "might be guilty of offences as cruel as those of Mlle Vinteuil." The French, for comparison, is: *Dans la réalité, en dehors des cas de sadisme, une fille aurait peut-être des manquements aussi cruels que ceux de Mlle Vinteuil envers la mémoire et les volontés de son père mort.*

The young narrator, unobserved, is watching the lovely Gilberte from a distance. If one reads the revised edition one encounters another unfortunate error: "setting aside the longing and the terror that I had of making her acquaintance." Correct may be "terror . . . of making her acquaintance" but certainly not "longing . . . of making her acquaintance"; both nouns must work correctly with "of making." First I suspected that the original, unrevised Scott Moncrieff translation would have a different, and correct, phrasing, but I was wrong again. It was the same: "setting aside the longing and the terror that I had of making her acquaintance." *Sans tenir compte du désir et de la crainte que j'avais de la connaître . . .* I was surprised. Here is another question: Is "longing" a close enough translation for *désir* and is "terror" not too extreme for *crainte* ("dread" or "fear")? I translated them more moderately as "desire" and "fear."

SLANG AND COLLOQUIAL SPEECH

Slang or colloquial speech is another problem for the translator, quite a large one sometimes. I think it needs to be timeless and placeless in English, unless it can be made to seem local to the original, and to achieve this, my solution has sometimes been to either invent it or take it from somewhere sufficiently remote from here and now—like seventeenth-century England or the Appalachian Mountains in the nine-teenth century—for it to be no longer recognizably associated with these places or times. Or I may translate it "straight"—translate the idiom literally, so that, although not necessarily familiar to a reader of English, it comes directly from France of, for instance, the late nineteenth century.

Speech, or dialogue, is one of the hardest things to trans-late effectively in any case, and especially informal dialogue and dialect speech. The speech of Françoise, in *Swann's Way*, was a challenge. It had to sound natural in English, but not odd for its time and place, in English, as it sounds natural and native in French.

SOUNDS OF WORDS IN ENGLISH

The choice of one word or phrase over another almost always involves choosing between not just two shades of meaning but also two sounds, both the sounds of consonants and vow-els and also the stresses within the word—its own rhythm.

Simple example: We might have a choice between *much more* and *far more*. The second is clearly more pleasant on the ear than the first, but in some contexts we might prefer the thick and emphatic *ch* sound in *much*.

Another pair of near synonyms, *profaning* and *desecrat-ing*, are, again, quite different in sound: three syllables versus four, the first easier both rhythmically and in the sounds of its consonants and vowels. But, again, in some contexts we might want the tooth-grinding choppiness of the second.

I realized at a certain point that I did not care as much in certain passages as in others about finding a close equiv-alent in sound or etymology. This was probably, I thought, because the style of the passage in question was more matter-of-fact or pedestrian. Maybe it was only in Proust's more lyrical passages that I looked for such close equivalents.

SOUNDS OF WORDS IN FRENCH: ONE SUGGESTED BY ANOTHER

There are many instances in *Swann's Way* in which one word in the sentence seems to have suggested another, as though the second grew organically out of the first—as probably did happen in Proust's mind.

Example: *Un moment de repos ou de repliement*, in which *repliement* is longer and more elaborate than *repos* but begins with the same sound, *rep-*.

Another example with *r*'s is *ressentait . . . ressemblait*, with the slight shift, the nuance leading on down the sentence, a short one. Here is the whole of it: *Cette souffrance qu'il ressentait ne ressemblait à rien de ce qu'il avait cru.* The *rien* following so closely after *ressemblait* eases us down from the two longer words so close in sound.

STAGES OF THE PROUST TRANSLATION

What I envisaged as the stages of translation of this project were these: first, to understand the French very precisely, down to the character and nuance of each word, consulting dictionaries as often as necessary, over and over again, even for the same word or phrase; second, in my first draft, to re-produce the French in English as closely as possible in word order and character and nuance of word in decent or even pleasing sentences; and lastly, in a second or third draft, to re-lax that high demand for closeness by a change here and there that would produce greater strength or eloquence in English.

In the first draft, I found myself more attentive to the individual words; in the second draft to larger units—the phrases, clauses, sentences; I thought that in the last draft I would concentrate on the flow of the prose in still larger sections—the effect of it. I'm not sure if I had the luxury to do that, since phrases and sentences still needed attention.

Most translators, and writers, find that each time they read something over, there is a small change that could helpfully be made.

I did translate the first draft of the book without looking at the other translations. Then I sometimes worked on a second draft of a particular sentence or paragraph or page or two before looking at the other translations and even then did not always look. I had intended to check the entire translation against at least one of the other translations, and I did check a good deal of it, but not every sentence.

My procedure in the second draft was to start by reading forward in the English, and then, if I noticed awkward English, to check against the French; to check in any case, against the original, particularly for closeness, for punctuation, especially for commas; then to check against revisions of the Scott Moncrieff translation, often also against the unrevised Scott Moncrieff, and make sure I had caught all the meaning and that I had not missed a better solution in English. I checked also, occasionally, against the James Grieve translation, not really for a possible solution in English, but sometimes for meaning.

There were two areas in which I was following my instincts where arguments could have been made for a different procedure: One was to translate the first draft without looking at previous translations. The second was to keep the translation so close, in the second draft, when small and perhaps minor adjustments might have allowed it to read more "smoothly." I thought I might make those adjustments in the last draft, but when it came to it, I usually did not. Yet consistently adjusting my text away from closeness and toward smoothness, or consistently not adjusting it, would produce two different texts. And perhaps the not-adjusted text, once one accepted it, would be fresher and more interesting.

I found that as you revise your translation, you make it very good compared to what it was, or very good compared to another translation; and then you have to forget those comparisons and just make it very good compared to some high standard of good writing. So first you're saying, "Good! It's very good!" and it is. Then you're saying, "Not so good; should be better." And it should.

We can use words without entirely understanding them. Translation requires you to understand, sometimes more and more deeply.

STYLE, CONVERSATIONAL OR NOT

Swann's Way is, in one sense, conversational in style. It is written in the first person, and many sentences begin with conjunctions: "But . . . And so . . ."

But in another way it is not written in a conversational style: many of the sentences are too long to be easily spoken in a conversation, and too confusing. They often need to be read more than once.

On the other hand, Proust himself did apparently speak in very long, complex sentences, according to his friends, full of parentheses, asides, reconsiderations, qualifications, and so on. So perhaps these long, complex sentences were close, anyway, to constituting—perhaps a heightened, exaggerated form of—a natural conversational style for the person Proust was.

SYLLABLE COUNTS

As I worked on the translation of *Swann's Way*, I began to think about how quickly pronounced and heard an individual word might be, that is, the speed with which it might enter our hearing and our understanding. A one-syllable word enters more quickly than a two-, three-, or four-syllable word. So that "just like his love" happens more quickly than "exactly like his love" or "altogether like his love." And so one chooses how much time one wants a word to take and thus how much attention we must give it and thus how much importance it assumes.

SYNONYMS

For some words in the text to be translated, there were only one or two possibilities. But for others, there was a wealth of synonyms or near-synonyms, each with its subtle difference from the others, its own associations, so that I had the luxury of several good choices.

For instance, there are so many synonyms in English for the delicious French word *frémir*: "quiver," "tremble," "shake," "quake," "shudder," "shiver."

There are so many for *se faner*: "droop," "wither," "wilt," "fade."

For *fange*, there are strong and vivid one-syllable Anglo-Saxon choices that are a pleasure to say: "mud," "mire," "muck," "filth."

For *mégère*: "vixen," "shrew," "megaera," or "bitter scold."

The French *adorable* is more frequently used than our English *adorable*, which I, for one, seldom want to use—it has an overtone of falsity, hypocrisy, or smarminess. For equivalents, we might use: "charming," "captivating," "appealing," "winning," "delightful," or "attractive."

Certain choices are clear and not difficult, are pleasant, a vacation from the difficult choices; and yet two alternatives may be quite different in sound, such as, for *bouquet*, either "bouquet" or "bunch."

But some so-called synonyms have subtle shades of difference that one must pay attention to: *presque* might be easily translated by either "nearly" or "almost." And yet the *près* in *presque* and the *near* in *nearly* make these two closer to each other than are *presque* and *almost*. And *nearly*, because we hear the *near*, feels more concrete than *almost*.

One more example: The French *torture* has many possible translations. But *torment* simply does not speak to us quite as strongly as *agony*, *anguish*, *misery*, or *distress*. Certain words are expressive, emotionally alive, while others, probably because of the long history of the contexts in which they have been used, are a bit wooden.

SYNTACTICAL STRUCTURES

One problematic syntactical structure that held me up for a large part of one day and parts of several other days occurs in a passage that comes about one-quarter of the way through *Swann's Way*. The passage describes a walk that the young narrator is taking with his family on a Saturday evening. The passage as a whole is an enjoyable one because it portrays a close, warm family life and contains pleasing images and conceits, such as the following:

> *De grilles fort éloignées les unes des autres, des chiens réveillés par nos pas solitaires faisaient alterner des aboiements comme il m'arrive encore quelquefois d'en entendre le soir, et entre lesquels dut venir (quand sur son emplacement on créa le jardin public de Combray) se réfugier le boulevard de la gare, car, où que je me trouve, dès qu'ils commencent à retentir et à se répondre, je l'aperçois, avec ses tilleuls et son trottoir éclairé par la lune.*

I translated this:

> From gates far apart, dogs awakened by our solitary
> steps sent forth alternating barks such as I still hear
> at times in the evening and among which the station
> boulevard (when the public gardens of Combray were
> created on its site) must have come to take refuge,
> for, wherever I find myself, as soon as they begin re-
> sounding and replying, I see it, with its lindens and its
> sidewalk lit by the moon.

I will compare my solutions with those of Scott Moncrieff
and of James Grieve. Scott Moncrieff's version:

> From gates far apart the watchdogs, awakened by our
> steps in the silence, would set up an antiphonal bark-
> ing, as I still hear them bark, at times, in the evenings,
> and it is in their custody (when the public gardens of
> Combray were constructed on its site) that the Boule-
> vard de la Gare must have taken refuge, for wherever I
> may be, as soon as they begin their alternate challenge
> and acceptance, I can see it again with all its lime-
> trees, and its pavements glistening beneath the moon.

Grieve's version:

> From garden-gates, set far apart from one another,
> dogs which had been wakened by our untoward
> footsteps in the silence began their antiphonal bark-
> ing, the like of which I still hear some evenings, and
> which must have become the last refuge of that av-
> enue leading from the station when it was abolished

and converted into Combray's public park, because, wherever I happen to be when those alternating barks start to sound and answer each other, I always glimpse that old street with its lime-trees and its moonlit pavement.

The main problem, as so often in Proust, is how to keep the complex syntax of the original, with its dependent clauses, and still write a sentence that sounds natural and expressive in English. This was a challenge. I will here present my thoughts somewhat in the note style of the diary.

1. The first part of the problem is the barking of the dogs. The literal translation is: "dogs awoken by our solitary steps caused to alternate barkings such as I," etc. Most natural and vivid in English would be something like "barked one after another" or "barked back and forth," but if you want to retain the structure of the sentence, two clauses—"such as I still hear," etc., and "among which the station boulevard," etc.—both need to hang off *barks* or *barkings*, and so you have to keep the order somehow, you have to keep *barkings* or *barks* as a noun following the verb.

Scott Moncrieff has: "set up an antiphonal barking." *Antiphonal* is tempting, but it carries with it an ecclesiastical association not present in the Proust: the plainer idea of *alternating* is what Proust intended. For dogs to "set up" an antiphonal barking sounds a little too organized, although Proust's "cause to alternate" is equally undoglike. Scott Moncrieff's choice of the singular *barking* means that he can't refer back to it later in the sentence with *they* but, in order to give that *they* a referent, must insert material: "as I

still hear them bark, at times, in the evenings." My solution—
"sent forth alternating barks"—doesn't sound much better,
especially when read out of context (context can be very pro-
tective), but was the only way I could see to end with the
plural needed to become the referent for *they* later in the
sentence.

Grieve's solution is to adopt Scott Moncrieff's
antiphonal—"began their antiphonal barking"—which is
all right, though there is the same problem of the singular
barking, which means that later in the sentence he must repeat material: "when those alternating barks start to sound
and answer each other." Proust tends to construct a sentence
very tightly and avoid that sort of repetition.

Note that Scott Moncrieff has *watchdogs* instead of *dogs*,
which changes the French but does add a nice alliteration
with *awakened*. Note also that he has changed "our solitary
steps" to "our steps in the silence." Grieve has expanded the
phrase: "our untoward footsteps in the silence." Both are
interpreting the original rather than translating it more directly: Proust implies but does not mention *silence*.

2. The next syntactical problem is the conceit of the boulevard taking refuge among the barkings of the dogs so that
although it has physically disappeared it lives on in the narrator's memory. Proust, typically, delays revealing the subject of the clause by inverting the word order and inserting
a parenthesis between the verbs: *et entre lesquels dut venir
(quand sur son emplacement on créa le jardin public de Combray) se réfugier le boulevard de la gare*—we don't reach the
subject until the very end of the clause. Part of my motive for
wishing to follow Proust's word order so closely has been to

offer information in the same order he did, to let the images
and ideas unfold and reveal themselves in the same sequence.
Literally, this would be translated: "and among which must
have come (when on its site they created the public garden
of Combray) to take refuge the station boulevard." Whenever possible, I retained Proust's delaying tactics, but English
can't invert word order as freely as French. I wanted to put
"the station boulevard" on the far side of the parenthesis
but couldn't think of a way to do it that didn't sound hopelessly awkward or didn't lose the idea of "take refuge among
them" or didn't sacrifice the structure of the sentence, as
Scott Moncrieff does in the following, quite elegantly, however: "and it is in their custody (when the public gardens of
Combray were constructed on its site) that the Boulevard de
la Gare must have taken refuge." Grieve changes the function of the word *refuge* and does not try to duplicate Proust's
order.

Now some lesser problems:

3. I wanted to echo the alliteration in *retentir et se répondre*,
which also has a pleasing rhythm. There were, conveniently,
several possible *r* choices for both words: *resound*, *reverberate*, *resonate* for *retentir*; and *respond*, *reply* for *se répondre*.
I thought the best choices, for meaning and rhythm, were
"resounding and replying." Scott Moncrieff loses the alliteration with his "alternate challenge and acceptance," also
reduplicates the *antiphonal* idea with his "alternate," and
adds, with "challenge and acceptance," an idea not in the
original and in fact not quite fitting, I think—if dogs barking back and forth can be thought to be challenging one
another, they are simply trading challenges endlessly, in my
experience, not accepting. Grieve stays close to the French

but loses the alliteration with his "sound and answer each other."

4. I wanted to end the paragraph with the word *moon* as Proust does with *lune*—Proust takes great care with his choice of end-words to long sentences and paragraphs. Hence my choice of "lit by the moon," and Scott Moncrieff's "pavement glistening beneath the moon." Scott Moncrieff likes to be faithful to Proust's word order, often using great ingenuity to achieve this, though he is not opposed to adding ideas and images that do not appear in the original, as here: there is no "glistening" in the French, only *éclairé*, meaning "lit" or "illuminated." His *glisten* adds the idea of sparkle or luster. As for Grieve, he retains the simplicity of *lit* but sacrifices Proust's word order: "with its lime-trees and its moonlit pavement." The alliteration of the *l*'s is not as audible and the rhythm of "moonlit pavement" is not as pleasing.

5. In Proust's original, that last phrase contains another instance of alliteration: *avec ses tilleuls et son trottoir* (the parallelism enhanced by the fact that each *t*-word also contains two syllables and is preceded by *ses*). I could not find a word for *lime-tree* or *linden* that alliterated with *pavement* or *sidewalk*, but the head-rhyme of *linden* and *lit* is at least audible.

It takes much longer to write out the debates that go on over these translation problems than it does to think them through to oneself, but then, one's thoughts are more repetitive than this writing: often I can't accept the fact that there isn't a way to solve all the parts of a problem successfully, so I go over them again and again.

Another observation, rereading this essay a few years later:
At first I think that if I were to return to this sentence now, I
would probably attempt to follow Proust more closely in the very
opening words: De grilles fort éloignées les unes des autres.
I'm not sure now why I did not. Proust must have had a reason
*for specifying so explicitly that the gates were "very" (*fort*) far*
*apart "from one another" (*les unes des autres*). Somehow, the*
image became fixed in my mind's eye of a series of large houses
lining the boulevard with not so much space between them. But
I'm guessing that Proust wanted the image of the barking to
be set within a larger landscape, the sounds to be echoing and
reechoing from greater distances. So now, I think, I might open
the sentence with: "From gates very far apart from one an-
other." But then, on second thought, I think the rather pretty
les unes des autres *is there merely to make it clear that the*
*gates are "distant" (*éloignées*) from* one another, *not from*
the family walking. Since the word apart *takes care of that, the*
phrase "from one another" is not needed. As for fort—*which*
is a more emphatic and interesting way of saying "very" here,
since très éloignées *would be difficult to say and unpleasant on*
the ear—I might include that somehow: "From gates very far
apart." Or perhaps "far" is far enough. (This is typical of the
thinking and further rethinking that go on in translating—
even years after the book, with its solutions and lingering prob-
lems, has been published.)

T

TENSION OF THE MOUTH
In some of Proust's lists, especially, I noticed a progressive
relaxation or tightening of the mouth in the pronouncing of

words as they succeeded one another. As with other stylistic practices of Proust's, this was not necessarily deliberate, or even surely not deliberate, but instinctive. Yet it was often quite marked, and it would have been nice (usually not possible) to reproduce that progressive relaxation or tightening.

Small example: The difference in tension between *violette* and *blanche*. The three quick syllables and stressed short *e* in *violette* being relatively tense, the single syllable and long, open *a* in *blanche* relatively relaxed.

More extended example: In Proust's unusually long list of adjectives describing the two spires of Saint-André-des-Champs visible across the wheat fields, which closes a paragraph, the tension progresses from more relaxed to tighter as the vowels progress from *e*'s and *i*'s to *o*'s, *o*-sounds, a nasalized *an*, and a *u*: *effilés, écailleux, imbriqués d'alvéoles, guilloches, jaunissants et grumeleux.* In English translation, with no such progression of tension, though with the three first stressed vowels echoing one another, this list could be, depending on the translator, "tapering, scaly, plated, honeycombed, yellowed, and roughened" (Scott Moncrieff's version); or, losing one of the first three identical stressed vowel sounds, "tapering, scaly, chequered, honeycombed, yellowing and friable" (the Kilmartin-Enright revision); or "tapering, scaly, imbricated, checkered, yellowing, and granulose" (my version). James Grieve abandons the list form altogether in favor of this arrangement of pairs: "spiky and serrated . . . yellowed and coarse-grained . . . intricately patterned with cusps and crinkles."(Incidentally, earlier in the same sentence, where I opt for "chiseled" to describe the spires, Scott Moncrieff chooses "crocketed," which I find delightful since I have never encountered it before.)

THOUGHTS CONCERNING THE TRANSLATION
One perception about the translation, quite early on in the work: That the things in my life were arranging themselves around it. The positions of objects in my study had changed to accommodate it. Family relations were calmer, in order to provide less distraction. My health habits were improving to promote greater alertness and intelligence; and even the basement was tidier, the mountains of cardboard boxes removed, for fear of a fire that would consume the work.

Another perception, at the same point: That by the time I was finished with the translation, I would be thoroughly trained and prepared to translate a book by Proust. In fact, I would be thoroughly trained and prepared to translate *this* book.

TRANCHE, AND THE NOVEL'S CLOSING SENTENCES
The word *tranche* occurs in another important passage, at the very end of *Swann's Way*, in the very last sentence, in fact, and it presents an awkward problem just when, as a translator, one would like to be eloquent without compromising. (And *tranche* is not the only problem posed by the sentence.)

Tranche means, most commonly, "slice." But here, "slice" reads a little strangely. Proust is creating an identification between place and time:

Les lieux que nous avons connus n'appartiennent pas qu'au monde de l'espace où nous les situons pour plus de facilité. "The places we have known do not belong solely to the world of space in which we situate them for our greater convenience" (in my translation). Then he goes on to state that these places, the places we have known, were only a thin slice . . . *Ils n'étaient qu'une mince tranche au milieu d'impressions contiguës qui formaient notre vie d'alors;* "They were only a thin slice among contiguous impressions that formed our life at that time."

We associate *slice* so firmly with foods—slice of cake, slice of cheese—that it is a little hard to apply it to anything else, especially something abstract, except for our assonantal phrase *slice of life*, which is really exactly the way Proust is using it but for us seems to be inalienable from that expression.

Tranche (which can also mean "edge," but not in this sort of context) signifies a part separated arbitrarily (in time) from an extended continuum. It is a slender portion, or a thin sliver. Now, in the years since the various versions of my translation were published, I have quite regularly heard people use the English word *tranch* quite comfortably—or perhaps it has been rising in popularity for some reason. (For instance, in a review I read not long ago, of two books about birds, the reviewer, though he liked one of the books itself, was dismissive of the publishers' motivations, accusing them of pandering to market trends by "slapping two more tranches of nature writing between hardcovers, wrapping them in tasteful jackets, and marketing them as lyrical.") I've thought about whether I could have used the word— the perfect equivalent, as is the case for other unusable word choices. But I do think it is not quite so familiar that it would not draw the reader up short, make for a moment's pause, at just the point in the novel when that would be most unfortunate.

Having decided on *slice*, I thought to change "They were only a thin slice" to "None was more than a thin slice," but did not do it, since it would have introduced a complication not in the French and because Proust himself is willing to make an equivalence between a plural pronoun and a singular noun: *Ils n'étaient qu'une mince tranche.*

The rest of the sentence, the final two parts of the three parts separated by semicolons, which has the air of a confident conclusion, is, in French: *le souvenir d'une certaine image n'est que le regret d'un certain instant; et les maisons, les routes, les avenues, sont fugitives, hélas, comme les années.*

Here, another problem is the word *regret*. *Regret* can convey the sense of "missing" something as well as "regret," and it probably does here—we miss what has receded into the past, while we don't always regret it. But I tell myself, anyway, that in this case the English *regret* can convey that longing.

Fugitives was yet another problem, for me. Should it be "fugitive" or "fleeting"? Although *fugitive* in English is the same word as in French, with somewhat the same meaning, it carries for me an association of "evasive," whereas *fleeting*, more neutrally, characterizes, to my ear, something that vanishes, flies away, escapes our grasp more innocently, and so I preferred *fleeting*. However, I was not sure whether to translate *fugitives, hélas, comme les années* as "fleeting, alas, like the years," or, more explicitly, as "fleeting, alas, as the years." Before that, within the comparison, there was the question of whether or not to include or omit the definite articles that are in the French list: should *les maisons, les routes, les avenues* be "the houses, the roads, the avenues" or "houses, roads, avenues"?

My first version, then, in the UK hardcover edition, was: "The places we have known do not belong solely to the world of space in which we situate them for our greater convenience. They were only a thin slice among contiguous impressions that formed our life at that time; the memory of a certain image is only regret for a certain moment; and houses, roads, avenues are as fleeting, alas, as the years."

I decided to change, for the sake of the rhythm and sounds, "the memory of a certain image is only regret" to "is but regret." I changed the first "that" to "which" because it came so close to the second "that," even though it was also uncomfortably close to the preceding "in which." I could perhaps have avoided the "that . . . that" problem by a different change: "impressions that formed our life then," but "then" seemed to me too vague.

The last edition (U.S., paperback) of my translation has my final changes (I did not change the first sentence): "The places we have known do not belong solely to the world of space in which we situate them for our greater convenience. They were only a thin slice among contiguous impressions which formed our life at that time; the memory of a certain image is but regret for a certain moment; and houses, roads, avenues are as fleeting, alas, as the years."

C. K. Scott Moncrieff introduces a metaphor ("map") and a mistake (changing negative to positive in the first sentence): "The places we have known belong now only to the little world of space on which we map them for our own convenience." He also introduces a diminutive—"little" world. In his next sentence, Scott Moncrieff is understandably bothered, as I was, by the mix of plural and singular (even though Proust was not) in "They are only a thin slice," and so he renders it "None of them was ever more than a thin slice." The sentence continues, "held between the contiguous impressions that composed our life at that time." Here, he has introduced a definite article in "*the* contiguous impressions" and chosen "composed" for "formed." His sentence ends: "remembrance of a particular form is but regret for a particular moment; and houses, roads, avenues are as fugitive, alas, as the years."

The Kilmartin-Enright revision retains the introduced "map" metaphor, corrects the negative/positive mistake, and removes the diminutive from "world." It adheres more closely to the French, with "memory" and "image" replacing Scott Moncrieff's "remembrance" and "form":

> The places we have known do not belong only to the world of space on which we map them for our own convenience. They were only a thin slice, held between the contiguous impressions that composed our life at that time; the memory of a particular image is but regret for a particular moment; and houses, roads, avenues are as fugitive, alas, as the years.

Now, rereading this yet again, I see the rather clumsy repetition of "only . . . only" which the revisers might have avoided. Their care with that sort of inadvertent repetition was never as great, throughout the novel, as Scott Moncrieff's, who steered clear of it in this case with his choice of "only . . . ever more than . . . but."

U

USAGE, IN ENGLISH

This was the sort of question I typically spent some time worrying over: Do you *ease* a scruple? Or do you *calm* a scruple? A scruple, etymologically, is a small, sharp stone. I often think of that etymology when I have an actual small, sharp stone in my shoe.

Another: Does pity *cease*, *die*, *die away*, *end*, or *vanish*?

V

VOCABULARY, CULTURAL

As I worked on the Proust translation, I continued to learn new English words, or had my new knowledge (gained from the translation) confirmed by my incidental outside reading.

For instance, reading Rumer Godden's beautifully written *The River* for the second time (I had read it first as a teenager), I learned that a "liberty bodice"—new to me from Proust—was something a girl would wear in adolescence; it was a sign that she was growing up. The girl in question was an English child coming of age in India; the book was published in 1946 and the setting is Bengal.

VOCABULARY, PRECISE

James Joyce always stood, for me, as the best example of a writer who seemed to have available to him a vast vocabulary of exact terms. From the opening pages of *Ulysses*, I write down these particular words—nouns, verbs, adverbs, and phrases: *stairhead, gunrest, corpuscles, equine, untonsured, grained, smartly, warily, jowl, dactyls, jejune, hyperborean, wax, rosewood, wetted ash, jagged granite,* and *stroking palps.* A writer who might equal Joyce in this respect would be Nabokov, with his immense interest in words and vast vocabulary. I'm sure *Speak, Memory*, which I read, studied, and returned to over the years, is full of examples. And wasn't it Nabokov who read the entire (English) dictionary front to back when he was young?

In any case, among the many facets of sensitivity to language that the practice of translation teaches, using precise vocabulary is one.

For instance, I have read about "castle keeps" over and over in my life, especially in guide books or in histories of medieval life, and probably have always had a sense of what they were but never precisely identified a "keep" as the strongest and most secure part of a medieval castle.

W

WORD CHOICES, INDIVIDUAL

The following illustrates the sort of debate that goes into a single word choice.

Sometimes, when I came upon a certain word in a passage of Proust's novel, I sensed that that word mattered more than some others, that it was more deliberately chosen. This may be because it was less common or because of its length or complexity of sound. And so, usually, I would take proportionately more care in finding an equivalent.

An example of this was Proust's word *contraindre*, a direct cognate translation of which would be "constrain." In French, sound and meaning coincide, because the word includes, like the English, the word *strain*, and suggests coerciveness because of the collisions of its consonants and the tightness of mouth necessary to pronounce it.

I thought of other possible *c*-choices, such as *compel* or *coerce*. The choice of the Scott Moncrieff revision was "force," that of James Grieve, "contriving," a nice enough word but without the meaning of "constraint." I wanted to use *constrain* itself, but I thought it might be too unfamiliar to have any emotional impact. We use *constraint* all the time, but not so often *constrain*. I thought *coerce* might be too forceful. *Compel* did not have the "strain" of *contraindre*, but might be the best equivalent.

At this point I thought there was the metaphor of "driving someone forward" in *compel* and wanted to check the etymologies of both *compel* and *constrain*. Yes: *compel* came from the Latin *pellere*, "to drive"; *constrain* from the Latin *constringere*, to "constrict," from the Latin *stringere*, "to draw tight"; and *coerce* from the Latin *arcere*, "to shut up or enclose."

When I checked my choices by looking at the useful little comparison in my *Webster's Collegiate* dictionary, under *force* I saw that its choice of possible alternatives was the same that sprang into my mental thesaurus—*compel, coerce, constrain*, and *oblige*. So that whereas I usually felt the choice was fairly infinite—because I worked with what came to my mind and often thought I had not exhausted all the possibilities—this time I felt there were only five options.

Still, I consulted the Microsoft Word thesaurus and found some odd ones: *concuss* and *shotgun*, as well as one other actual possibility, *require*. But I decided, as had happened many times before, to go with my first impulse, *constrain*, and see if it could work.

A simpler debate: I email a friend who has been reading parts of the translation as I go along, asking him what he thinks about the (English) word *cutaneous*, which we don't often use, I'm quite sure, though we use *subcutaneous*. He emails back to offer the alternative *cutanean*, previously unknown to me. I go to the *OED* (the *Oxford English Dictionary*, the ultimate one) and find, also, *cutaneal*. I wonder, really, if we (in English) need all three.

Z

ZUT

The following passage from *Du Côté de chez Swann* describes a moment of ecstasy on the part of the narrator when he is still a boy. He is taking a walk by himself in the autumn after the death of his aunt Léonie.

Le vent qui soufflait tirait horizontalement les herbes folles qui avaient poussé dans la paroi du mur, et les plumes de duvet de la poule, qui, les unes et les autres, se laissaient filer au gré de son souffle jusqu'à l'extrémité de leur longueur, avec l'abandon de choses inertes et légères. Le toit de tuile faisait dans la mare, que le soleil rendait de nouveau réfléchissante, une marbrure rose, à laquelle je n'avais encore jamais fait attention. Et voyant sur l'eau et à la face du mur un pâle sourire répondre au sourire du ciel, je m'écriai dans tout mon enthousiasme en brandissant mon parapluie refermé: "Zut, zut, zut, zut." Mais en même temps je sentis que mon devoir eût été de ne pas m'en tenir à ces mots opaques et de tâcher de voir plus clair dans mon ravissement.

In my English translation:

The wind that was blowing tugged at the wild grass growing in the side of the wall and the downy plumage of the hen, the one and the other streaming out at full length horizontally before its breath, with the abandon of things that are weightless and inert. In the pond, reflective again under the sun, the tile roof made a pink marbling to which I had never before given any attention. And seeing on the water and on the face of the wall a pale smile answering the smile of the sky, I cried out to myself in my enthusiasm, brandishing my furled umbrella: "Damn, damn, damn, damn." But at the same time I felt I was in duty bound not to stop at these opaque words, but to try to see more clearly into my rapture.

Given my intention to stay as close as possible to Proust's original, there were a couple of challenges in this passage. At a certain point in my work on the novel, I had observed and appreciated how sparing Proust was with his punctuation. Where I had instinctively used commas in my translation, I saw, after a time, that he had dispensed with them. I went back over my version to see whether I could dispense with them, too. I often could. For instance, Proust could have used many more commas to punctuate the passage above, particularly the sentence beginning *Et voyant sur l'eau et à la face du mur un pâle sourire répondre au sourire du ciel*, which I translated, equally comma-less, as "And seeing on the water and on the face of the wall a pale smile answering the smile of the sky."

The other challenge was more difficult: the word *zut*, which is an utterance expressing any one of a variety of emotions including anger, annoyance, surprise, amazement. I turned to the dictionaries for possible choices of meaning, looking more particularly into the etymology of the word, as I often did when stumped.

Zut is apparently a euphemistic form of *merde* ("shit"); and it is said to be onomatopoeic, although I'm not sure what sound it is imitating. I needed to find an equivalent that expressed an adolescent boy's enthusiasm or wonder—and, compounding the problem, that could be said four times in a row.

No solution seemed quite satisfactory. The dictionary that I used the most, *Harrap's*, offered these possibilities: *damn, hang it all, dash (it)*—expressing anger or disappointment (which is not what Proust's narrator is expressing). Another dictionary, the French–English Larousse, offered *dash it* or *darn it*.

It was translated by Scott Moncrieff as "Damn, damn, damn, damn." This is a little stronger than *zut* but is capable of

expressing both anger and amazement. The word was changed
by the first reviser of the Scott Moncrieff translation, Terence
Kilmartin—unfortunately, I think—to: "Gosh, gosh, gosh,
gosh." The word is milder, but can sound a little foolish and
is difficult to speak four times in a row. The choice of the only
other translator, James Grieve, was: "Oh, dash it all! Dash it
all! Dash it all!" Again, unfortunate, I think—the expression is
more local to certain segments of British society in certain periods of history than *damn* and therefore sounds odd coming
from a young Frenchman. (And it reminds some Americans,
at least, of a certain poem about St. Nicholas.) So, after much
earnest searching, I found, in the end, that the first solution
that presented itself was the one I stayed with—something
that happened often enough in this translation: Scott Moncrieff's "damn" answered the requirement of an exclamation
that could express both anger and awe; it could be repeated; it
was more universal in time and place than "Dash it all!" And
so, even though it was stronger than *zut*, it was my choice, too.

One afterthought, reading the passage in the original and
in translation now, is that I could have gotten away with being more literal in that last sentence: *Mais en même temps je
sentis que mon devoir eût été de ne pas m'en tenir à ces mots
opaques et de tâcher de voir plus clair dans mon ravissement.* Instead of the translation as it reads now, "But at the same time
I felt I was in duty bound not to stop at these opaque words,
but to try to see more clearly into my rapture," I might have
changed it to: "But at the same time I felt my duty should
have been not to stop at these opaque words and to try to see
more clearly into my rapture." Then again, maybe not. (If I
were to write a memoir about being a translator, I might title
it: *Then Again, Maybe Not.* Or, then again, maybe not . . .)

LEARNING
A FOREIGN LANGUAGE:
DUTCH

Als ik 's morgens door de verlaten
natuur fiets, merk ik dat ook de
taal me verlaten heeft. Ik heb
geen woorden tot mijn beschikking,
ik heb ze niet nodig. Later, als ik
alleen op mijn kamer zit, zijn de
woorden terug, maar ik gebruik ze
niet om te praten, want ik ben
alleen. Ik gebruik ze pas als ik
ze ga schrijven en lezen. Soms
worden ze vertaald en kom ik in
een vreemde dierentuin. Een ezel
wordt een zebra, een muis wordt
een vleermuis, een pad wordt een
paddestoel, een vink wordt een sla-
vink, een olieman een olifant, een
olifant een nijlpaard. Ik ben in een
wereld gekomen die ik herken, maar
die niet de mijne is. Ik ben rijk ge-
worden, maar mijn buurman merkt
het niet.

Before My Morning Coffee: Translating the Very Short Stories of A. L. Snijders

It was in May 2011 that I visited Amsterdam for the first time and came away with the idea that I would like to translate something from Dutch literature into English. The idea was born of the notion of reciprocity: a Dutch publisher was bringing out a book of my stories, translated into Dutch. Could I not, in return, translate at least one small piece of fiction from Dutch into English?

In fact, the idea may have suggested itself even before that trip. I remember now that a couple of years before, I was teaching a writing class that happened to have a very international student enrollment. Two of the students were fluent in Dutch. I had the previous year been published in the Dutch magazine *Raster*, in an issue devoted to the very short story. I was trying to decipher some of the other stories in the issue. One of them, by Hedda Martens, was a retelling of the story of Rumpelstiltskin, which I thought I should be able to understand, but I was not having much success. Did I ask a student for help, or did I only mention that I might call on her someday? In any case, I never did go on. But it seemed possible—after all, the words were recognizably close to English and German, which I already knew.

After I came back from Amsterdam, I wrote to several people I had met, asking them if they would recommend a writer of very short stories that I might like to translate. I was looking for stories of just a page or two, since each page would take so much effort. I had already resolved that I would do no more book-length translations—lately, each one had taken several years of my life. Two correspondents wanted to draw up a comprehensive list for me, but since school vacations were just beginning, they said they would write again in the fall. A third, however, emailed me promptly and that was Vincent, who had hosted my partner and me while we were there in Amsterdam, walking us back and forth along the Herengracht canal between the house in which my publisher had its headquarters and the hotel where we were staying, which occupied nearly a dozen interconnected townhouses fronting on the same canal and backing on another one, where the flower market was.

Vincent recommended A. L. Snijders, who had been writing very short stories for many years with more than fifteen hundred (and counting) to his credit. He had in fact invented his own term for what he wrote—*zkv*'s, short for *zeer korte verhalen*, or "very short stories." He had recently been awarded one of the Netherlands' most prestigious literary prizes. Vincent sent a story by Snijders called "Years" with his email. It was about Snijders's mother falling out of a window when she was one year old and surviving with no ill effects, her fall having been broken by an awning. I understood only a little of the story, but enough to know that I liked Snijders's straightforward approach to storytelling, was grateful for his short and fairly simple sentences, as well as his mainly concrete nouns, and found his modesty and thought-fulness appealing.

I checked with one of my other correspondents for her opinion, and she said, "Snijders's work is full of regional/cultural/political/literary references, it is sometimes more like what we call a column (a short piece in a newspaper with an opinion), so it must be selected very carefully. I like it very much and Ditte [does] too."

False friend: The *haan* in the poultry yard, in a story by Snijders, is not a hen, but a rooster or cock. The hens, along with some roosters and some chicks, regularly enter Snijders's stories, because they are a part of his everyday life, and that is what he writes about.

veters: When I first encountered it, in a story by a different Dutchman, Henk van Faassen (a newly rediscovered friend of my partner's—his landlord in Amsterdam fifty years ago), I had no idea what it was, except that it had something to do with shoes. I should have pronounced it: it is pronounced more or less the same as our English *fetters*—which is in fact one of its cognates. Then I would have associated it with tying or binding, and the answer would have been obvious: shoelaces, of course.

An added incentive for finding some very short Dutch stories to translate was the desire to respond to submission requests from literary magazines not always with a story of my own but perhaps with a translation instead—preferably from a language I didn't know well because it was new territory and a greater challenge. A translation from French, for me, has a set of challenges altogether different from those of a language I am still learning at a beginner's level.

Dutch appealed to me—on the page, anyway. I learn better when the learning is voluntary and enjoyable (which would be a nice guiding principle for teaching children). Dutch is not too hard to learn if you know some German, which I can read if it's simple enough. Also, English has the great advantage—for learning other languages as well as for one's own writing—of its enormous doubled Latinate/ Anglo-Saxon vocabulary, for example: subterranean/underground; terrestrial/ earthly; submarine/undersea; celestial/ heavenly. The Latinate vocabulary gives an English speaker a degree of access to the vocabulary of the Romance languages (as for instance the French *souterrain*: "subterranean"; *terrestre*: "terrestrial"; etc.), while the Anglo-Saxon vocabulary provides some access to the vocabulary of the Germanic languages (as in the German *Erde*: "earth"; *unterseeisch*: "underseas"; etc.). For learning Dutch, having some French also helps now and then in construing an imported word, such as the hedgehoggy *pruik* (derived from the French *perruque*, "wig") or the onomatopoeic *put* (derived from the French *puits*, meaning "well," and perhaps imitating the sound of a drop of water). There are also similarities between some Dutch vocabulary and some already-familiar words in Scots and the dialects of Northern England.

It is useful to work at first with fairly simple, straightforward texts in the new language, of course. Some people have recommended comic books. I have not found them, so far, the best way because of their choppy style and slangy vocabulary. I tried once, taking along a Mickey Mouse tale of the American Far West, translated into Norwegian, on a train trip through the mountainous Norwegian landscape, but made little progress in it. Children's books may be easier.

I think now that although German always seemed closer and more familiar to me, since it was the first foreign language I learned, it may in fact be harder for me to learn than Dutch—at least, I seem to improve more quickly in Dutch than I do in German. Dutch seems simpler: for example, it has only two words for *the*—*de* and *het*—whereas German has three in the nominative singular case alone (*die*, *der*, and *das*), never mind the genitive, dative, accusative, and then the plural forms of all those. (German does offer the slight advantage, for those lost in a baffling sentence, of capitalizing its nouns.)

> *ondoorbrengbaar scherm*: Here is quite a mouthful, but I think I can figure it out, since I recognize all the parts of it. The first thing is to break the long word into its shorter component parts: *on-door-breng-baar*. This produces "un-through-bring-able." Since the word is paired with (modifies) "shield" (*scherm*), I can guess that it means "impenetrable." My association with *scherm* is the German *Schirm*, which is most familiar in *Regenschirm*, screen or protection against the rain. Our *umbrella* has a very different provenance and climatic association: it derives from the Mediterranean (Italian) *ombrello*, "little shade"— the protection, there, is from the sun, not the rain. *Parasol* is really the same idea: *para* + *sol*: "protection against the sun." The French for *umbrella*, now that I'm thinking about this, is *parapluie*, returning to the idea of protection against the rain, and, with *pluie*, we're also back to the sound of the drops of water.

I read "Years," the first story Vincent had sent, over and over again. I chose to read it first without a dictionary, since

I found I was more deeply inside it that way, figuring out what the words meant from the context. It was also more enjoyable, like doing a word puzzle without looking up the answers. In that story, there was at least one sentence that I could understand completely without help: *We kennen elkaar niet, twee vreemden.* Using the context and cognates—probably a neat enough formula for attempting to understand a language without prior knowledge of it—I deciphered it to mean: "We do not know each other, two strangers." *We* is the same word in English; *kennen* is a cognate of the Northern English dialect word *ken*, meaning "know," as in a song I have heard from my childhood on: "D'ye ken John Peel with his coat so gay?" about a Cumbrian hunting-farmer of the early nineteenth century. (The song tended to romanticize hunting; in the 1970s, antihunting activists vandalized Peel's grave.) I'm not sure how I figured out *elkaar*, unless I was guessing from the rest of the sentence. *Twee* is a cognate of *two*, and *vreemden* a cognate of the German *fremd*, "strange, foreign."

Within a few days, I had made a rough version of the first story Vincent had sent. I was working on it, still without a dictionary, like any other word puzzle, "getting" a little more of it each time I went through it. I find that simply reading a sentence carefully a second time can yield significantly more understanding. I'm not sure exactly what happens in the brain between the first and the second readings.

Vincent helpfully said he had plenty of time to look at my rough translation, because, where he was, it was *komkommertijd*—the meaning of which he challenged me to figure out: "Good luck on that one," he said. I made some thoughtful guesses, but did not arrive at the correct answer. I knew that *tijd* meant "time" (as our cognate *tide* also did back in the sixteenth century). I imagined, of course, that *kom* and *kommer* had something to do with *come*: perhaps, in the Netherlands, it was "come-comer-time"; anyone might come by and take up some of his time, his time was available for whatever might come along. No, in fact it meant "cucumber-time," late in the summer when the cucumbers are ripening and when people are less busy, or away.

An expression: *kurkdroog—kurk-droog*, literally, "cork-dry." But we would say "dry as a bone." Why do we prefer bone to represent dryness while they prefer cork? Cork trees are not native to England or the United States, but it isn't that—they're not native to the Netherlands, either. Using cork stoppers in bottles goes far back in all three cultures.

Some of their Germanic words translate directly, not into our Germanic equivalents (such as *kurkdroog* into "cork-dry") but, more deviously, into the component parts of our Latinate equivalents. For instance, I encountered *onderwerp*, did not understand it, tried separating it into its parts, *onder* + *werp*, both of which I understood—"under" and "throw," and then, since it was a noun, moved it around to make some peculiar thing called a "throw-under." But this made no sense. When at last I looked up the word, I found that it meant "subject"—which is derived from the Latin *subjectus*, *sub* + *jectus*, "thrown under."

Another wrong guess: *fles*, which in fact means "bottle." I was at first guessing "flesh," related to the German *Fleisch*, "meat," but the cognate in this case was *flask*. We also have *flagon*, which seems further away but is actually derived from the same source.

Why so many *fl*-words in English for things associated
with liquid (or . . . flowing fluid)?

When I turned to a dictionary for help, the one I used,
at first, was very small (a little over 2" × 4"), yellow, faux-
leather-covered, a Hugo pocket version for travelers that my
mother may have bought on a trip to Amsterdam in 1964.
The cover is torn a little at top and bottom, though the book
is sturdy and won't fall apart. Some pages are stained and
a few are missing, evidently ripped out. Since these print-
covered pages wouldn't be useful for writing a hasty note,
I can only imagine they were removed to be used as book-
marks, but that seems a little odd. If there is another explanation, I'll probably never know what it is.

I still use this dictionary if I am reading a Dutch book
on a bus or a train, even though something electronic
would be quicker. Maybe I like the little interval of time between putting down the Dutch text and leafing through the
dictionary—which then sometimes doesn't have the word,
after all, either, because it is such a limited travel dictionary
or because of those missing pages. In that interval, I may look
out the window for a moment or at the visible parts of the
other passengers; we are advised, after all, to lift our eyes to
the horizon periodically when doing close work. When I'm
at the computer, though, I use about three different online
dictionaries, each of which has its own strengths and weak-
nesses. If all of these fail me, I do a general internet search for
the word or phrase and find it in one of a variety of contexts
(though sometimes, of course, the only reference is to the
piece of writing by Snijders himself), and thereby gain some
feeling for Dutch life and culture, reviewing the hours and
stock of a garden center in Rotterdam or the specifications of

different brands of tile stoves or the almost incomprehensible scraps of teenage blog-conversations.

vijf: If I'm forgetful or careless, I read it as "wife"— I am reading too fast and the word is taking a quicker, reflexive pathway to my English translation; I should be reading a little more slowly and thinking, before I jump to the translation. After all, I have known for some time that *wife* is *vrouw*, like the German *Frau*, and since *v* is pronounced like *f*, pronounced almost exactly the same—also, I actually know the word *vijf*, which means "five" and is pronounced almost the same: "fife."

I come to a new word, not seen before: *oeroud*. First reaction: No idea! (That is often the first reaction.) Then I return to it with more patience. The beginning of it—*oer*—reminds me of some of our *ae*-words, such as *aerate*, which also look strange to me; and because the word contains *roud*, I can't help thinking of "round." But I seem to remember that *oer* means "over," although some of these words, along with their meanings, do tend to drift in and out of my memory, and now I recognize *oud*. The context is a description of some stony terrain by the Black Sea, and this word is an adjective qualifying the trees there—*oeroud* trees. The second part of the word, *oud*, means "old"—close to the Northern English dialect *owd*, as in *Owd Bob*, the classic English novel about sheepherders and sheepdogs set in Cumbria. *Oud* is also part of the Dutch word *ouders*, meaning parents, or "elders." "Over-old"—I can guess that it means "very ancient," but I will wait and see if any more understanding comes, or I will simply capitulate and look it up.

When I do look it up, I see that it does mean "ancient," but that I was wrong about *oer*, which does not mean "over" (the Dutch for *over* is in fact *over*) but is related to the German (by now, in fact, our own word, too) *Ur*, meaning "primordial" or "primeval." The trees are primevally old.

Besides reading them at public events and on radio and television, and collecting them in books every few years (and winning awards for them), Snijders also sends his stories out to an email list. I have learned that he writes a story every day, in about half an hour, with few or no corrections. I'm sure he does not publish all of them. Those that he feels are good, presumably, he sends out to the list. It is a rare week or fortnight when he doesn't send one.

So, in the morning, I may open my emails to find a new story from Snijders. I may attempt a translation of it even before getting my first cup of coffee. This is partly a result of inertia: I am still tired or half asleep, and I don't want to move from my chair. If I do have my cup of coffee by me, I'm likely to sit even longer.

I begin by trying to read the story. I read the first line. More than once, it has contained the word *bosrand*, "edge of the woods"—something Snijders sees from his kitchen window and a place I like to be, or imagine. Or it has contained something about the author's problematic chickens, or his dogs. One begins with a woman (*vrouw*) in the distance (*distance* is *verte*, which, confusing me for a moment, is identical to the French for *green*, but whose root is *ver*, sharing a past with the English *far*). Still half dreaming, I am transported to the Dutch countryside, among the chickens and buzzards, foxes, shepherds, swans, and the occasional cyclist or hiker coming along the *pad* (cognate of *path*) in front of the author's house, or *huis*—actually pronounced more or less like the English and like the German *Haus*.

If I run into too many words I don't understand, or if I'm not interested in the subject (which is rare), I don't go on. But if I can read and understand most of it—if I can begin with *Ik zit aan tafel onder de lamp met mijn wollen muts op mijn hoofd* (here, I have trouble with *muts*, which looks nothing like "cap," and *hoofd*, which does not suggest to me that, like its German cognate, *Haupt*, it means "head") and figure out most of what follows, and if I like it (usually the case), then I may feel that translation-urge taking hold.

In my peaceful tabula rasa state of mind, I copy the text from the email and paste it into a new file, then type in the title and the author. I may fool myself for a moment into believing that I am just setting up the translation, that I won't return to it until later, or tomorrow. But the rest of the day is already assigned to other tasks, and if I'm going to do this at all, I must do it now, before the day begins, unofficially, on the sly—which is one way I like to work anyway. And so I start on it immediately, typing the title in English above the Dutch title, and then the author's name again under the English title, and then the first sentence: "When the roosters crow in the distance I want to go off on a journey," or "Above the path in the woods behind my house where I walk every day I see a buzzard flying among the great beeches," or "It began with . . ."—and refer back to the Dutch: *Het begon met bomen, het eindigt met stenen*. At that moment, translation, which I've found, over the decades, to be so infinitely complicated, seems very simple. It seems to be exactly what it is so often misunderstood to be by those who have no experience with it: all you need to do is read the text and then write it in English.

> *Vele schouders maken het werk lichter*. Not hard to decipher via cognates, including one from German: literally, "many [cognate is G. *viele*] shoulders make the work lighter." Compare the English version of the same expression: "Many hands make light work." Hands versus shoulders—is this because the Dutch used to carry fish, vegetables, seaweed, and perhaps other things in baskets slung from yokes that lay across their shoulders? The German version of the expression is more rhythmical, and rhymes, and has a slightly different perspective: *Viele Hände machen bald ein Ende*: "Many hands make soon an end."

Because I am tempted by these email offerings, which keep coming, I almost always start on a new Snijders story before I have finished the others. In this way, I accumulate many partial translations spread out on my computer desktop, in different stages of completion. I keep them visible so that they will not get lost in the email inbox or in the large folder (containing still more) labeled "Snijders in progress." Eventually, one by one, I finish respectable drafts, send them to usually a Dutch reader for review, incorporate his suggestions, and submit them to literary magazines here in the United States.

> *vrijgezel—vrij-gezel*: I'm amused to see that the word for bachelor includes the word *vrij* (cognate, G. *frei*), meaning "free." *Gezel* = mate, partner. *Gezelschap*, cognate of German *Gesellschaft*, means "society." I think of the Bach-Gesellschaft—the nineteenth-

century Bach Society that published Bach's complete works, the editing of some volumes faulty, some very good.

In one Snijders story, the *sleepboot* is not a "sleep boat" or "sleep-boot" but a "tugboat"; the Dutch *slepen* is a cognate of the Yiddish *schlep*, which also means to "drag," "carry," or "haul" (but with the added implication, of course, that this hauling may be unnecessary or at least tiresome and reluctantly done). So we could say "schlep-boat." And *sleeppad* has nothing to do with a pad for sleeping on, but is rather a path for schlepping—a towpath.

Although a fair number of the stories contain material that needs no footnoting—for instance, the animal life and people out in the country where Snijders lives, the neighboring farmer, the foxes, the chickens, a shepherd, a bird-watcher—it is true that quite a few of the stories, as one of my correspondents had warned, are full of references. At first I thought this would be a problem in translating his work, the Scylla and Charybdis between which I would not be able to steer: either the story, in translation, would be scattered with unfamiliar, unexplained proper names, or it would be burdened by notes that would add a whiff of the academic that might hurt the vitality of the stories, change them from fresh, newborn creations of the imagination to aged objects of study.

But then I saw the references in a more positive light. I would not want to leave them unexplained, since they were so rich in meaning for both Snijders and his Dutch readers. In researching them in order to write notes, I would learn more and more about Dutch history, geography, and literature, as would, in turn, the reader of the translation. Snijders

often refers to, and quotes, other writers, and these are, after all, most often not obscure figures, but the Netherlands'
most important or interesting early writers, such as Nescio or
Gerard van het Reve, or contemporaries such as Gerrit Krol,
Joubert Pignon, or Nicolaas Matsier. For serious readers in
our culture not to know at least the names of these writers
seemed a lack that needed to be made good. And why should
we not also know something about the Netherlands' popular
TV show hosts (Jan Wolkers, for two years, gardening program), right-wing politicians (Geert Wilders), Amsterdam
cafés (Vertigo, named after the Hitchcock film), Dutch dialects (Low Saxon), or Middle Dutch epics (*Reynaert the Fox*)?

I like being transported to another place and another
culture, especially early in the morning when I am so recep-
tive. As I translate, my own country, and maybe even my own
life, don't seem quite real to me, and there is a refreshing freedom in that. Also, I like the sound of the Dutch words in my
head—as I imagine them. (In actuality, I am surely pronouncing them quite wrong.) I even enjoy the novelty of being able
to read the stories at all. The surprise hasn't worn off.

Some words are, to my ears, comical, such as *sla*,
meaning "salad"—it sounds cool and casual. I am reminded of *slaw* in *coleslaw* though I'm not sure they
have a common source.

When I look it up, I learn that *sla* is a shortening
of the French *salade*. And that our *coleslaw* is in fact
an importation of the Dutch *koolsla*, "cabbage salad."

Sometimes Dutch-English cognates have letters reversed: *borst* = breast; *pers* = press (the media), *vers* =
fresh (*v* pronounced as *f*). And maybe also, though
I'm not sure, *vors* = frost.

No, when I check, I see I am wrong about the last one: it turns out that although the Dutch *vors* did indeed reverse letters as it evolved, it derives from *frosk*, and is an archaic word for "frog."

Some words contain cognates to older forms of our words. There is the Dutch *dorst*, for instance. It is a cognate of our *durst*, past tense of *dare*: in chronological order, I suppose we would have said, and written: he durst not say anything; he dared not say anything; he didn't dare say anything. The Dutch for that is: *hij dorst niets te zeggen* ("he durst say nothing"; literally, "he durst nothing to say").

I haven't yet lost interest in learning Dutch. I improve little by little, I don't force myself to do more than I want to, or more often than I want to. Part of my continuing interest comes from my appreciation of the stories of A. L. Snijders, which only increases as I come to know more and more of them.

I admire his variety of subject matter, his quiet sense of humor, his sensitivity to nuances of thinking, his flexibility in form, his linguistic curiosity, the unexpectedness of his conclusions. He is personal but with a keen interest, too, in the world beyond himself. He gives us fragments and facets of his life (one commentator has called his form "autobiographical fable")—from his boyhood, youth, career teaching in a police academy, adventures on the road—so that over time we form a sense of the whole. He depicts his daily life and the world close to his home: his family, his neighbors, the passersby who stop in at his house, and above all the creatures of the animal world with whom he lives shoulder to shoulder and whom he portrays with respect for their different ways of seeing and thinking and their inherent mystery. But his subject matter also ranges farther afield, to the geographically more distant world, other places in Holland and in foreign countries, places he still frequents or remembers from his past or associates with friends or correspondents. More subjects: the larger realms of his many interests—music, philosophy, sailing, politics, food, motorcycles, and especially other writers, whom he often honors by quoting a work of theirs in part or in full. In all his depictions, there is a gentle humanity, coupled sometimes with a hint of irony. There is color; characters come alive.

In "Forty Centimeters," for instance, a story about his chickens that begins quite simply but ends with several questions, he quotes from an essay by Gerrit Krol that discusses whether the pecking behavior is learned or innate: "'Innate, says one half of science, because it pecks while still in the egg. Even in the egg, says the other half, you can learn something.'" Krol continues: "'Scientifically speaking . . . both views are correct,'" and Snijders himself concludes: "Because I have no talent for science, I am always very happy with these last four words: *Both views are correct.*"

Another reason my interest in learning Dutch remains fresh is that I approach it in several ways.

—I read emails (some of them relaying tweets) in Dutch from several different correspondents. Since the context is familiar, the emails are easier to understand.

—I read books in Dutch, either with or without a dictionary.

One favorite category for language-learning is the detective novel, and for Dutch I have been reading, specifically, the classic Swedish mysteries by Maj Sjöwall and Per Wahlöö that first appeared in the 1960s and '70s. They were innovative then in that they created fully human characters for their police detectives, something we now take for granted, and incorporated political and ethical issues into the stories. I found them at Amsterdam's Schiphol airport gift shop in Dutch translation, in neat little six-euro editions.

The virtue of the detective novel is that a lot of the material in it is repeated, as the police investigators go over the evidence again and again. Repetition, of course, helps the language-learner to remember the vocabulary. But also, it is easier to learn a word when it is associated with an event, a turn in the plot, a surprising feature in one of the characters. (It is harder to remember vocabulary when it is presented as a list of unrelated words.)

Other fiction: Ariëlla Kornmehl's first novel, *Huize Goldwasser* (The Goldwasser Family—earlier, I read, in English, her good novel *The Butterfly Month*; I came to these novels through a friend's long-ongoing and fascinating research into her European family, the Kornmehls, of Austro-Hungarian origin); short stories by Sanneke van Hassel, the correspondent who said "I like it very much and Ditte [does] too"; the occasional children's tale by an old friend, Henk van Faassen; a page now and then in a Dutch classic, perhaps Gerard van het Reve's 1947 family drama, *De avonden* (*The Evenings*); or *Van oude menschen, de dingen, die voorbij gaan* (*Old People and the Things That Pass*), by Louis Couperus (published in 1906, a more complex family saga not at all easy to understand).

—I read steadily on in a grammar book: at present, it is the slim paperback I bought secondhand in Portland, Oregon, at Powell's bookstore, in the company of my fourth cousin once removed, Ruth. It is a good one, and its author, Henry R. Stern, who writes clearly and explains complicated and/or important points lucidly, recommends that you read

it through once and then start over and read it through
again. It is just a little over a hundred pages long. My plan
is to finish this one—perhaps the slimmest, most "essential"
grammar—and then acquire a slightly fatter and more detailed one and begin all over again with that one. Reading
a grammar becomes pleasurable when it answers questions
and solves mysteries. Children are given grammar instruction
the wrong way around, before they are curious to know the
answers.

—I translate Snijders's very short stories. I sometimes
translate a story by another writer, or a passage from a novel.

—I am beginning to listen to spoken Dutch. It is difficult to understand, and I have had almost no exposure. I
know there is no hurry about this: reading and translating
can come first, then understanding spoken Dutch, and last,
attempting to speak.

The owner of the bookstore in the nearest fair-sized
town, out in the country here where I live, is Dutch. I cannot
even understand her when she says the equivalent of "Hello,
how are you?"—though I know that's what she must be saying. I have only rarely understood a sentence in Dutch. I was
pleased, on my last trip to Amsterdam, to understand one
of our group, in a restaurant, when she asked where the toi-
let was.

I've recently found out that some videos in Dutch on
YouTube are supplied with optional subtitles (in Dutch). If
I use the subtitles and keep stopping the video to read and
understand what I'm hearing, I'm confident that I will get
better at understanding—though I think the subtitles themselves are sometimes full of mistakes and I also feel, dimly,
that it is wrong to keep relying on written text. I must try
to cut out the middle term and learn to hear and understand

the sounds right away without first visualizing them as written words.

—I am making more of an effort to practice speaking Dutch. Now and then, I stop in at the bookstore and read aloud some Dutch to the owner, while customers come and go, looking at us curiously and assuming confidently that the language is German. I am improving, very slowly and with mistakes and much hesitation. The next step will be to attempt simple conversation. I could practice first by myself in the car. I could also buy a CD for the car, especially for late-night drives home from the train station, when I prefer to hear a human voice speaking.

These are some of the many ways in which to pursue the project. (I can think of more: exploring some of the many websites that include discussion forums about Dutch idioms; or watching Dutch movies and television shows—I remember the pleasure I had some years ago watching *The Mary Tyler Moore Show* dubbed into Spanish.) Even the slight acquaintance I have, so far, with this complex language and culture is useful and satisfying to me. Day by day, week by week, as long as I return to it not too infrequently, it can only become deeper, richer, and more refined.

> *spoken*: Since *spoken* is also an English word, it is hard not to read this as the same word. But it is the plural of "spooks," or "ghosts."

> *zeehond*: Divided into its two parts, it is *zee* + *hond*, or "sea + dog" (cognate: *hound*). I'm guessing that it is "seal." (Confirmed, when I look it up.) Which reminds me of the story a Scottish friend of mine told me, about how, on the coast of Scotland, a certain

dog would come running down to the beach every afternoon at the same time and plunge into the surf. Offshore, waiting for him, was always the same group of seals, who gathered there at the same hour. The dog and the seals (the *hond* and the *zeehonden*) would play together in the water for a while, maybe half an hour, and then the dog would return to the beach and the seals would swim away.

2015

TRANSLATING
MICHEL LEIRIS

Paris, le 5/01/90

Chère Lydia Davis,

    Merci de votre gentil mot. Je suis, bien
sûr, à votre disposition pour vous fournir,
dans la mesure du possible, les renseignements
dont vous avez besoin.
    Bien cordialement à vous,

Over the Years: Notes on Translating Michel Leiris's *The Rules of the Game*

Over a span of nearly thirty years, starting in the late 1980s, I translated four books by the ethnographer, early surrealist, art critic, and poet Michel Leiris (1901–1990). There was, first, his collection of occasional pieces, *Brisées: Broken Branches* (North Point Press, 1989; first published in French in 1966), composed of short writings about a wide variety of subjects including language, works of literature, ethnography, the visual arts, music, film, the body, and family memoir. I then went on to translate, at wide intervals, three of the four volumes of his monumental "autobiographical essay," *The Rules of the Game*, a thirty-five-year project of self-exploration through writing, which he began in his midthirties and finished—provisionally—in his early seventies. The publication of this memoir in English has had a difficult career, but now, at last, three of the four volumes are out in a handsome edition from a single publisher. The first volume, *Scratches*, was originally published in English by Paragon House in 1991; the second, *Scraps*, by Johns Hopkins in 1997. Then, although an early draft of the third,

Fibrils, existed back in 1998, I did not complete it until some eighteen years later and it did not appear until 2017, along with reprints of the first two volumes, from Yale University Press.

While I was working on each of these three volumes, or just after I had completed it, I wrote something fairly brief about it, and I refer to these notes here. As I reread them, I see, curiously, that my attitude toward Leiris's complex writing style changed over these years, most likely for two reasons, perhaps three. One might have been that I became accustomed to it, that it came to seem natural, to a degree; a second, that possibly his style itself changed over time; and a third, that by the time I had completed the last volume, I had had, in the meantime, the experience of translating Proust's different, but not unrelated, and also challenging, stylistic complexities.

Leiris's project was, in a sense, to write himself into existence, enacting more concretely than usual a notion advanced by Michel Foucault, in an interview, that "really, someone who is a writer is not simply creating his work in his books, in what he publishes . . . his principal work is in the end himself writing his books." Leiris was a complex and contradictory person, at once a student of himself and of the greater world, demanding of our attention and modest about his own qualities, frankly admitting his failings, offering apology and self-recrimination, and yet presuming that these failings are worthy of close attention: he is modest, yet insistent; intensely private yet sharing this privacy in the most public way; revealing what is inside him to the outside world; allowing the self to be invaded by the other and the other to be encroached upon in turn by the self. He displays the agony of extreme self-consciousness yet proves also that creating a work of art that involves the frank appraisal of one's failings does not lessen the pain of those failings. His long work is full of stories, but our interest is sustained, not so much by their peripeteias as by the developments in his thinking and his discoveries about language.

If Leiris's project was to take himself as subject, with a sort of ethnographic objectivity, and write himself into being, to arrive at a sense of himself and how best to conduct his life, through the yearslong, intensive labor of exploring himself through writing, his style reflects this. His syntax mirrors his amplification and inclusiveness in its constant elaboration, qualification, provision for ruthless honesty and explicit doubt, but also his internal contradiction. Further, as the ethnographer and Leiris scholar James Clifford pointed out, in the Leiris issue of the literary magazine *Sulfur*, which he edited in 1986:

> One senses a certain hostility and fascination for syntax. The well-formed utterance, always a drastic selection of linguistic possibilities, is made to seem awkward, to stagger under excessive demands of meaning, allusion or qualification. Leiris's most complex constructions show a baroque process of thought, association, and analysis occurring *in writing*. He is suspicious of summary, peremptory expressions, preferring elaborate, careful, self-limiting performances. But there is also a subversion in this precision.

I have just reread the first, very long, sentence of *Scratches*, the first volume of Leiris's *The Rules of the Game*, published in French as *Biffures* in 1948; in it, already, we have a good, if extreme, example of how the Leirisian sentence may stagger.

But before I quote it, I will quote the short paragraph that comes a few pages later, since, here, he gives some context to the first sentence by summing up in more conventional terms the "action" that has unfolded and the revelation concerning language that he has expressed at greater length and in more detail in the preceding paragraphs:

> The lead or papier-mâché soldier had just fallen onto the floor of the dining room or living room. I had cried out "*. . . reusement!*" I had been corrected. For a moment I was dazed, seized by a sort of vertigo. Because this word, which I had said incorrectly and had just discovered was not really what I had thought it was before then, enabled me to sense obscurely—through the sort of deviation or displacement it impressed on my mind—how articulated language, the arachnean tissue of my relations with others, went beyond me, thrusting its mysterious antennae in all directions.

Although the latter concluding sentence is complex, it isn't nearly as extended as the paragraph-long sentence that, on its own, constitutes the opening of the book and narrates in more elaborate form what has happened to the boy in his little world of precious playthings: he has dropped the toy, the toy was nearly broken, and after this incident, there has been a conversation with an unnamed grown-up that reveals to him something powerful about language, the function of which, up to then, he did not fully understand. What makes the sentence especially awkward, syntactically, is the inversion that puts the main clause and climax of the sentence at its very end, the sentence having opened with a dependent prepositional phrase from which the whole rest of the long paragraph will follow:

Onto the pitiless floor (of the living room or the dining room? onto a fitted carpet with faded floral patterns or a rug with some other design on which I inscribed palaces, landscapes, continents, a true kaleidoscope delightful to me in my childishness, for I designed fairyland constructions on it as if it were a canvas for some thousand and one nights that hadn't yet been revealed to me by the pages of any book in those days? or a bare floor, waxed wood with darker lineaments, cleanly cut by the rigid, black grooves from which I sometimes liked to pull up tufts of dust with a pin when I was lucky enough to find one that had fallen from the dressmaker's hands during the day?) onto the irreproachable, soulless, floor of the room (velvety or ligneous, dressed up in its Sunday best or stripped bare, favoring excursions of the imagination or more mechanical games), in the living or dining room, in shadow or light (depending on whether it was the part of the house where the furniture was usually protected by dust sheets and its modest riches were often screened from the sun by the bars of the shutters), in the special precinct accessible only to the grownups—a tranquil cave for the somnolent piano—or in the more common place that contained the large, many-leaved table around which all or part of the family would gather for the ritual of daily meals, the soldier had fallen.

This deliberate overload on Leiris's part inevitably tempts the translator—given sudden freedom to commit excess—to go too far in the direction of a similar deliberate awkwardness, as I expressed it (somewhat floridly, or superabundantly, perhaps suffering from stylistic contagion) in the early 1990s while I was working on volume 2, *Scraps* (first published in French as *Fourbis* in 1955):

> The French language is already, to begin with, a more formal language than the English language. Now, when a writer already writing in the formal language of French writes in a way that goes beyond this formality to a further, excessive, exaggerated formality, as Leiris does, the translator would like, ideally, to produce a version that is written in an English that is also excessively, exaggeratedly formal, and because Leiris's French is not only formal but also verbose, awkward, difficult (overloaded, precious, obscure, and containing such infelicities as mixed metaphors), as he himself admits with the honesty that is such an essential part of his project of self-examination, her English will ideally, in sum, be formal, verbose, awkward, and difficult to the same degree as the French away from what might be considered a more stylistically comfortable norm in each language—though her English should, ideally, never be quite as formal as his French since the languages are to different degrees formal to begin with. But the question of degree is what is difficult. She is immediately tempted, by the permission to write formally, verbosely, and awkwardly, to do what she must always have wanted to do, and that is to produce a translation so extremely close to the French original that it departs only far enough, not to be happy and comfortable English, but to be grammatically correct and coherent. There is great joy in this, both because it is something like an acrobatic trick or the solution to a clear mathematical problem, and because it is what she has always, in her transla-

tions, had to fight against doing. But the joy in the act blinds her only so long to the results—stiff and joyless reading. And so, with a sense of betrayal, now, though betrayal of what, she is not sure, she goes back into the translation and as gently as possible moves pieces and parts of it away from the literal, close parallel to the French and farther toward a more natural or at least happier English, though even this English may in the end be a sort of inter-language, a limbo language: it is hard for her to tell because she has, by now, lost a good deal of familiar perspective, moving about more than ever before, as she herself is, in the limbo between languages which George Steiner suggests is the proper home of translations, a place she sees floating above the Atlantic and always heading toward the coast of Flanders or Normandy.

Many years later, working on the third volume of *The Rules of the Game*, I did not seem to find Leiris's prose so very awkward anymore, or perhaps it was, in fact, less awkward as it had evolved over the years (as *Fibrilles*, it was first published in French in 1966). It was not easy, it was elaborately constructed, but by now I simply relished that complexity and the trick of putting it into equally complexly elaborated English. The first part of the book is occupied by a discussion of China and the Great Leap Forward. The first few sentences are not complexly structured, but quite brief and relatively clear:

November 1955.
    I am back from another trip whose theater, this time, was the Far East, behind what the bourgeoisifying newspapers of our countries still call the "iron curtain."

Of all the trips I have taken, this is certainly the one
that has made me the happiest.

Soon, however, still on the first page, we encounter one
of those single, extended, intricately constructed sentences,
this one twelve lines long. It contains two pauses marked by
semicolons and two asides within parentheses, and its repli-
cation must be carefully handled so as not to lose the main
structure. Here, Leiris is already having second thoughts
about his enthusiasm for the new China, to which, during
his visit, he was almost prepared to move, to begin a "new
life," had the decision been up to him alone:

Well, now that those five weeks have passed, and a few
more have elapsed since my return, I am still convinced
that in just a few years China will be the foremost—
instead of merely the oldest—of all the great nations;
but I notice that after thinking I was almost on the
threshold of a new life (and not having refrained, by
any means, from telling my hosts this in the form of
toasts, each of which I would have wished to be, without its seeming to be anything much, a perfect work
of art, in the manner of a Chinese poem) I find myself
once again perceptibly at the point where I was earlier;
and that, my trip becoming more questionable as it
recedes in time and increases the already considerable
separation it derived from mere distance, a brief period
(during which I have breathed the air of Paris while
my lungs were still quite impregnated with that of Pe-
king) has sufficed for its charm to be broken.

Notice the qualifications embedded in the sentence:
China is the foremost, not "merely the oldest." Notice the

delicacy of the double negatives: "not having refrained." Notice, again, the immediate qualification of a statement: "without its seeming to be anything much." Notice also the vividness of his bringing in the physical, the body, by referring to his lungs and the air of the two cities—whose names begin alliteratively, I'm sure to Leiris's enjoyment, with the letter *P*. This extended sentence is nicely balanced by the one that follows, short and distinct: "How could something that had appeared to me rock-solid be capable of disintegrating so quickly?" As I said in my introduction to the book,

Leiris is rarely brief, rarely plain, in *Fibrils*, since every thought seems to produce a possible counter-thought that should be included. One problem for the translator is, of course, that Leiris's amplifications and qualifications—directly expressive of his own nature, the explorations entailed by his ruthless honesty, in his self-examination—enter into the structure of the sentence itself. Extended pyramidal constructions are therefore common; the work is an accumulation of syntactical architectures, sometimes very long and complex. For the translator, then, one constant exercise of wits involves syntactic acrobatics: most specifically, or most often, to be sure a given phrase or clause ends with the key word off which the next clause must hang.

His extreme precision, as he tracks his thoughts and his reactions to events, can produce a heavy weight of material within one sentence, paragraph or sequence of pages, and an impression almost of excess. The long, complex sentences can be unwieldy, with their burden of allusions and qualifications, contradictions and second thoughts. I have reproduced them as closely as

I could—with a certain pleasure in the challenge, it must be said—avoiding any simplification and retaining Leiris's formality in structure and word choice. I have rarely changed the order in which information was presented—only *in extremis*, when I could not otherwise make the sentence hang together—because that order reflects the order in which Leiris's thought unfolds. I have also respected his punctuation as far as the difference between the languages permits, especially since he took such care with it. The reader may want to read some sentences more than once in order to gather up all their meaning.

The statements about word order and punctuation echo some I have by now made about translating Proust, and indeed, I later felt that the translating I had already done on Leiris's *The Rules of the Game* had been good preparation for reproducing the intricate style of Proust's *Swann's Way*.

If the first problem in translating Leiris was his elaborate syntax, the second was that certain of his words had to be retained in French, and not only because he himself so stipulated, remarking that unlike a novel, an autobiography had its historic truth. His consistent, and crucial, wordplay centered upon the French words with which he had grown up. That wordplay was an essential part of Leiris's relationship to language. His punning and associative pairing were never arbitrary. So the French originals had to be included in the translation, as I said, first, in 1991:

Leiris's life was not an American or English life, of course, and the language of that life was not English. Certain words, phrases, labels, titles, or remarks which fell upon his ears—oft-repeated family tags like *la mai-*

son d'en face ("the house across the street"), or punning clusters that gave rise to subliminal childhood
identifications or the vocabulary of a private language,
such as *Mors, alphabet Morse, morse,* and *mors* (respectively a make of car, the Morse code, the French for
"walrus," and the Latin for "death")—are, for him,
not only sounds of sentimental importance but also
so many knots where the threads of his remembrances
and associations, ideas and moods, come together either tidily or untidily from every direction of his past
and present. This new, English text—not the "same"
text as the one Michel Leiris wrote—must therefore
be tied back to that original with these same knots,
so that the two texts may be part of the same weave.

I was completing a draft of this third volume, *Fibrils,* in
the fall of 1997, at the same time that I was beginning the
translation of Proust's *Swann's Way*—for circumstantial reasons, the two projects collided. The organizers of the Penguin
group translation of *In Search of Lost Time* had asked each of
us for a hundred-page sample (in the end, they accepted fifty
pages), to be turned in by the end of the year—in order to
appraise how differently we would be rendering our versions.
I had agreed to participate in the translation project despite
knowing that for a while the two projects would proceed in
tandem and despite some qualms as to how this would affect
my style in each. I evidently did not have the faith, then, that
I have now, that the style of the original would safely determine and differentiate the style of the translation, as long as
I stayed reasonably close.

Juggling the two projects, that fall, I tried various
schemes, giving, for instance, one day of the week to Proust
and one day to Leiris; or four pages a day to Leiris for three

days; I calculated that I needed to translate twelve pages a week in order to finish the Leiris. One page took me about an hour. I was trying to maintain certain page counts in both projects. I took notes, too, on what was evolving with regard to my approaches to translating both; certainly one aim was always to remain close. For a short period I had the idea that I should translate, on any given day, at different speeds; that it was healthy to translate sometimes very fast, sometimes at a moderate rate, and sometimes very slowly. Working fast, I would charge ahead, attempting to get ever quicker and to improve through speed alone, leaving certain problems unsolved, looking up only words I did not know at all; then, working more slowly, I would go forward at a more familiar pace, looking up every word I was not entirely sure of and making more or less final decisions, reading back over sentences or paragraphs and noting down interesting words; finally, sometimes, working very slowly indeed, I would allow myself to dwell on a single word for a long time, searching out its history, finding the way it was used in quotations from different authors, I would be in effect caressing the word. There was always the safety of the second draft, in which the passages on which I had worked very fast could be carefully corrected.

As I worked on the two books side by side, I came to feel that Leiris was marginally, at least, more interested in the expression, as such, of an idea; while Proust was more interested in the idea as such, though expressed with a similar care for nuance. There seemed to me to be more stress, in Leiris, on the single word, and more self-consciousness generally, of course, since he was writing a form of autobiography, rather than fiction, and this self-consciousness extended straight into the writing, becoming a stylistic self-consciousness.

I had highly optimistic plans: I would finish *Fibrils* before the end of the year, go on, in the following year, to translate the fourth and last volume of Leiris (*Frêle Bruit* [Frail Sound], published in French in 1976), while at the same time continuing to work on Proust, and then, once the fourth volume of the Leiris was finished, devote myself to completing the Proust. All this would be done within a little over two years. I should have known how completely unrealistic this was; but it is not uncommon for translators, biographers, novelists, lexicographers (most markedly, for instance, the editor of the *Oxford English Dictionary* James Murray, who in his early forties, working in a shed in his backyard, with some of his many children eventually assisting him, expected to compile the entire dictionary within about ten years; instead, he died an old man just after completing the letter *T*), and others embarking on long projects to believe they can dispatch the work far more speedily and efficiently than they really will, including Leiris himself, who, underestimating the scope of his project, thought *The Rules of the Game* would not extend beyond two volumes. But this optimism is surely a good thing, since otherwise many large projects would not even be attempted.

After I completed the Proust sample and sent it in, I concentrated on finishing *Fibrils*. I was doing this first draft of *Fibrils* with, in fact, the sort of ecstatic literalness that I had years before envisioned in my remarks introducing the second volume. How different the Leiris felt to me from the Proust, as I had been working on them side by side: the prospect of translating Proust had intimidated me at first, since I was going to be covering ground previously covered by no fewer than four translators, against whom I thought I would be measured. I was haunted by the suspicion that an earlier solution was better, since I was not yet looking at earlier versions, and hounded by the often impossible demand on myself to do better than the others, sentence after sentence. This initial feeling of constraint, fortunately, wore off quite soon. In the Leiris project, on the other hand, I felt wonderfully free, rightly or wrongly. No one else had ever ventured into that territory before, nor ever would again, I was sure, and his style was eccentric and excessive enough so that mine could be equally so.

The experience was heady because, for the first time in my translating life, I felt like a conduit through which the original French was effortlessly passing to become, instantly, an English equivalent, even a close English equivalent, in some way identical to the French, as though I had achieved some version of Borges's Menardian ideal—it was the same text, but now read as English rather than French, or, if it was not the Menardian ideal, at least one could read the English and see, replicated, the original French (I chose to think).

For me, this was, if it worked, the ideal mode, or ideal practice, of translation: I simply typed while reading the French, and what came out on my page was the same text, but in English. There was no need to stop and consult dictionaries or debate with myself about wording. I assume, I hope—I can't remember—that I read through this draft before sending it to my publisher. But the reader to whom the publisher then sent the translation tactfully suggested that I might want to go over the draft one more time to correct certain errors as well as a number of awkward moments.

Not long after, I sat down with the draft of *Fibrils*, hoping to correct it fairly speedily without becoming deeply embroiled in the original again for any extended length of time, since by then I was fully occupied with Proust and other, smaller writing projects. But when I began to compare my draft with the original and to go through the reader's list of detailed comments, I saw that this would not be a quick fix:

I was embarrassed by some of what I found. And so I had to put it aside for the time being, and that "time being," as other projects intruded, stretched out into years and years. When at last I returned to the work, it was for a different publisher and did indeed become the slow and painstaking, though ultimately satisfying, task of several months.

Still, even though it had been an illusion, my earlier sensation of complete effortlessness during the long-ago first draft, the experience of being merely an intelligent conduit, remained, and remains, a delightful memory, that of having achieved the acme of fluent translation practice, a form of translation practice that will continue to beckon forever, unattainable in reality, in some far-off translation heaven.

2020

AN EXCURSION
INTO GASCON

VIII.

LOU DIABLE AU CEMENTÈRI.

Bèt temps a (1), dens lou cementèri dous Carmes de Leytouro, y auéuo un nougué, e cro estat coumhengut dab lous mounges que lou campanè, que s'aperauo Barraquet, prousticré dous esquillotz. Mès arribauo souen que quant lou Barraquet s'en anauo enta lous amassa, d'autes s'éron leuatz mès maytin qu'et, e qu'y troubauo pas mês arre.

Un cop lou campanè se leuèc bien auant lou jour, e partiscouc pou cementèri dab un sac enta s'en ana hé sa recolto. Arribat sur la porto entenouc un brut, coumo de quaucoumet que cruchission. Asta lèu lou Barraquet partis a hutos, e s'en ba au coumbent dous Carmes trouba lou pèrô Benoit.

— Pèro Benoit, lous Diables soun au cementèri, e que cruchisson lous ossis dous mortz.

— Ah! lous gusards! Coumo te lous angueri acampa sens la gouto que m'es tournado dempus ajè.

— Pèro, se bouletz, bous pourteréy a perrequet.

— As rasoun, Barraquet. Bèy a la gleyso e porto me moun suber-plis, moun bounet carrat e l'aspersoun.

Quant lou Barraquet estèc tournat, ajudèc lou pèro Benoît a se besti, se lou carguèc sur l'esquio, e partiscouc pou cementèri. Lous qui hàseuon lou brut èron quoate ou cinq boulurs que minjauon es-quillotz, en attende un de sous camarados qu'aueuon mandat pana lou tessoun don moulié de Repassac (2).

— Entenetz, pèro Benoît, coumo lous Diables cruchissoun lous ossis dous mortz?

— N'aùjes pòu, Barraquet, e nou me lèches pas cayge. Dab ma pregàrio lous ban acampa coumo eau. Fuyez, esprits immondes. Vade retro, Satanas. Ah insidiis Diaboli, libera nos Domine.

1 Ecrit sous la dictée de M. l'abbé Bladé.

2) Repassac est un moulin à eau situé sur la rivière du Gers, à peu de distance de Lectoure.

Translating a Gascon Folktale: The Language of Armagnac

"Devils in the Cemetery," from which the excerpt in the following pages was taken, was a tale included in a book of stories and proverbs collected in the region of Armagnac. They were told, and transcribed, in the patois of the city of Auch, which is a local form of the language of Gascon, which is in turn a dialect language of Occitan.

Occitan is not an old form of French. It is a separate but related language, ancient and indigenous to the south and southwest of France and down over the border—that is, the Pyrenees mountains—into Spain. Occitan is still spoken today, with four main dialects, Provençal, Northern Provençal, Limousin, and Gascon, which is mostly spoken in Gascony and Béarn in southwestern France and in the Aran Valley of Catalonia (Spain). Some experts are of the opinion that there is no single language of Occitan, but rather separate languages of the Occitan region, one of them being Gascon. This folktale, in any case, is written in a particular variety of the dialect of Gascony, and that is the patois of Auch.

The word *patois* has no real equivalent in English, but it

can be defined, when the term is employed within France, as a very local type of speech in a given region, the particular way a provincial person talks in a very small part of a rural area of France. I should add, though, what I came to understand recently—that the term *patois* is just a shade derogatory, and tends to be used by people who do not think much of the language they're talking about. I do not mean to use it in a derogatory sense.

As for Auch, it is a city in the very center of Armagnac. And Armagnac, in turn, is the territory to which the name Armagnac was extended under the old monarchy and which corresponds more or less to the entire *département* of Gers. The inhabitants of Gers are known as Gersois, a very hard word to pronounce (the *G* is soft, the first *s* is pronounced like our *z*, the second *s* is silent, and the *oi* is pronounced "wah": thus, "Jhairzwah"). The *département* Gers is named after the Gers River, which is 111 miles long, rising in the Pyrenees and running not only generally downhill, like all flowing water, but at the same time north, through three *départements* altogether, before joining the Garonne River.

Gascon is not easy to read, even if you know French, to which it is related, and even if you know Spanish, which helps with some of the verb forms, those that are more like Spanish forms than French (e.g., *anar* (Gascon) = *andar* (Spanish) = to walk). It takes a lot of hard work to figure out what you are reading. One word I could not figure out at all. After searching online and in the few Occitan reference books and grammars I have at home, and just plain racking my brain, I asked, via email, the office of the Éditions Lacour-Ollé, the publisher of the book in Nîmes (France), feeling sure that everyone in the office would be familiar with several varieties of Occitan. But no—they told me they would have to wait until Friday, when the head of the firm (and descendant of the original publisher, who founded the press in 1817) would be in the office, so that they could ask him. A few days later, they sent the answer: *coumo cau*, equivalent to the French *comme ça*, simply means "like that."

This language is a linguistic code that you have to crack. Once you figure out that the French *le* is the Gascon *lou*, then you can guess that the Gascon *dous* might be the French *des*. Or you realize that quite often a French *v* will be equivalent to a Gascon *b*, so that the French *voulez* ("you want"), and *vent* ("wind"), and *rivière* ("river") become the Gascon *bouletz*, *bent*, and the rather Spanish-sounding *ribèro*. Also, you see that the Latin-derived *s* that was eventually dropped from a French word like *être* (the accent indicating where the missing *s* was) is still there in the Gascon *este*. Keeping in mind the *v* = *b* pattern and the not-missing *s* gives you a way to recognize that the Gascon *boste* might be equivalent to French *vôtre*, meaning "your." Lastly, one more example: a French *f* will become a Gascon *h*. For instance, the Gascon *hagot* is equivalent to the French *fagot* ("stick of wood"); *hè au hour* in Gascon is *faire au four* ("make in the oven," or "bake") in French. I have learned that this change is due to the influence of the Basque language, which lacks the /f/ phoneme. And how did Basque come into this?

The ancient Aquitanian language spoken in Gascony until the early Middle Ages turns out to have been an ancestral form of Basque. Basque has been described using the festive (and new to me) word *circumpyrenean*, meaning "around the Pyrenees," because the Basque language originally spread both south and north of the Pyrenees mountains as far as the Garonne River and maybe even as far east as the Mediterranean. (A similar *f* = *h* influence was exerted on continental Spanish, such that the Latin *facere* evolved into the Spanish *hacer* ["to make or do"].)

Adding to the difficulty of reading these stories, although they seem to me quite lively and charming when I can figure out what is going on in them—some having to do with ghosts and graveyards, for instance, or pigs and priests—is the fact that they were not written by a single individual, but were recited orally by native "informants," and copied down by a folklorist, Jean-François Bladé, as they were being told.

And this transcription was not done recently, but in the 1860s. The book I have, published in 1992, was reprinted in facsimile from an edition of 1867. The type is faint in some places, and pieces of some letters are missing: the present publisher apologizes gently and reasonably, saying, "The reader will please excuse, on the one hand, the slight lack of readability, and, on the other, the imperfections due to the damage inflicted by the passing decades; considering the memory of the authors and the quality of the work, it seemed suitable to reproduce it with its original characteristics."

Here is a sample, the opening of the original tale and my translation of it (*note*: the town of Lectoure is about forty-five minutes due north of the city of Auch):

LOU DIABLE AU CEMENTÈRI

Bèt temps a, dens lou cementèri dous Carmes de Leytouro, y auèuo un nouguè, e èro estat coumbengut dab lous mounges que lou campanè, que s'aperauo Barraquet, proufitere dous esquillotz. Mes arribauo souven que qunt lou Barraquet s'en avauo enta lous amassa, d'autes s'èron leuatz mès maytin qu'et, e qu'y troubauo pas mès arre.

Un cop lou campanè se leuèc bien auant lou jour, e partiscouc pou cementèri dab un sac enta s'en ana hè sa recolta. Arribat sur la porto entenouc un brut, coumo de quaucoumet que cruchisson. Asta lèu lou Barraquet partis a hutos, e s'en ba au coumbent dous Carmes trouba lou pèro Benoit.

—Pèro Benoit, lous Diables soun au cementèri, e que cruchisson lous ossis dous mortz.

—Ah! lous gusards! Coumo te lous angueri acampa sens la gouto que m'es tournado dempus ajé.

—Pèro, se bouletz, bous pourteréy a perrequet.

—As rasoun, Barraquet. Bèy a la gleyso e porto me moun suberplis, moun bounet carrat e l'aspersoun.

DEVILS IN THE CEMETERY

A nut tree once grew in the cemetery of the Carmelites of Lectoure, and the monks had agreed among themselves that the bell ringer, whose name was Barraquet, should enjoy the nuts. But it often happened that when Barraquet came to harvest them, others had risen earlier in the morning than he, and there were none left.

One day, the bell ringer rose well before daybreak and left for the graveyard with a bag to go gather his harvest. When he reached the gate, however, he heard a noise. It sounded as though someone were crunching something. Barraquet took to his heels and ran as fast as he could to the convent of the Carmelites to find Father Benoit.

"Father Benoit, there are devils in the cemetery, and they are crunching the bones of the dead."

"Oh, those good-for-nothings! How I would go and drive them away for you, if it weren't for my gout, which returned yesterday to afflict me."

"If you like, Father, I will carry you on my back."

"Good idea, Barraquet. Go to the church and bring me my surplice, my biretta, and the aspergillum."

(There follow several farcical misapprehensions about just who is in the cemetery and what their intentions are, and, after little more than a page, the tale ends as the hero flees, terrified, to his home, leaving the priest to the mercy of the devils, who are not actually devils.)

LEARNING
A FOREIGN LANGUAGE:
TWO KINDS OF
NORWEGIAN

DAG SOLSTAD

DET UOPPLØSELIGE EPISKE ELEMENT I TELEMARK I PERIODEN 1591–1896

ROMAN | FORLAGET OKTOBER

Learning Bokmål by Reading
Dag Solstad's Telemark Novel

In late spring last year, I began reading Dag Solstad's "Telemark novel," as this family saga is called, for short, even in Norway, since the full title is formidably long. It is a book described by some dissatisfied critics, in its native land, as "tedious" and "unreadable." This thick tome calls itself a novel, but, say the critics, how can it be a novel? It has been compared by some of them, in both size and dramatic interest, to a telephone directory, though it also received much admiring praise. And indeed it is something like a catalog, a catalog of ancestors, though it is far more than that.

It is a long book—426 pages, not counting the appendix. It is entirely factual, and its plot consists for the most part of detailed accounts of the births, marriages, deaths, and property transactions of Solstad's ancestors in Telemark from 1591 to 1896, with little incident, almost no real drama, much authorial speculation, and the occasional memorable character, such as the pipe-smoking widow Torhild, the spendthrift Margit, Halvor Johannesson who marries a woman forty years his senior, and the power-hungry Halvor Steinulvson Borgja (b. 1625). When, after a while, I took a look at some pages far along in the book, sure that the action would become more various as we approached our own times, I saw only more of the same.

I have finished it now. I don't often read very long books. In fact, I don't often finish even a much shorter book, even in English. I usually put it aside, however good it may be, after, sometimes, eighty or a hundred pages, or less, having in some sense not only absorbed its nature but saturated myself with it. But I have read this one right through to the end. What made me go on? Certainly a kind of suspense, but hardly one that involved the "plot" of the novel, if it can be called that—it was a complex, or multifaceted, kind of suspense involving not only the stories within the book, but also the suspense of the author's investigation, curiosity about how the book would evolve, and, probably most of all, the suspense of learning a language I did not know before.

That was what made this reading project even more unlikely, when I began it: the fact that the book is written in Norwegian, and I did not know Norwegian, beyond a few words, like the strange *ikke* for "not" and *og* for "and," the grandmotherly *gammel* for "old," the not-quite-right *til* for "to" (as well as "until"), and the fact that—what seemed even stranger, and was not true of any other language I knew—in Norwegian the definite article, *the*, is often tacked onto the end of a word, appearing only as a suffix.

I was reading the book for the most basic of reasons: it did not exist in English, and would, I thought, perhaps never be translated into English, so if I wanted to read it—and I did, and right away—I would simply have to start in and do my best to understand it. Soon after beginning, I decided to continue for as long as I could, making my way word by word, regardless of how much I understood, through the whole of the book. I would also do it "cold," without looking anything up in a dictionary and without seeking help (*hjelp*) by turning to a native Norwegian.

FIRST NORWEGIAN LESSONS

The seeds for this adventure in learning Norwegian were planted more than a year ago, when I was visiting Oslo for a literary festival. By now I know that if I am in a foreign place, I will always be intrigued by the language and, though I may vow not to, will begin trying to figure it out from reading billboards, bilingual menus, signs in restrooms, train stations, hotel rooms. So this time, in advance, I asked the organizer if he could arrange a few Norwegian lessons for me. He found me a teacher, close at hand—my own Norwegian translator, Johanne.

Each day for three days, as long as I stayed in the city, we had an hour-long lesson in the hotel lounge, on a comfortable sofa. Johanne decided on the method, and it suited me very well. She produced from her bag an old-fashioned children's picture book with family scenes in bright colors. Speaking only Norwegian, she pointed to the pictures and described what was happening: Mother was standing in the garden, the children were playing with the dog, Father was picking apples from a tree. Johanne, though far younger than I am, has a nice, motherly manner—she is in fact the mother of a five-year-old—and I felt a little like a child as I watched and listened, tried to understand, and occasionally spoke.

I did pick up a few words. Take the middle letters out of *mother* and you have the Norwegian word for her, *mor*. Do the same to *father* and you have *far*. As for *child*, the Norwegian *barn* is close to the Scottish *bairn*. And then, logically, but pleasingly, the odd-looking *mormor* (nothing to do with *murmur* or *marmoreal*) is "mother's mother," or "maternal grandmother," while *farfar* is "paternal grandfather," and *barnebarn* is "grandchild."

THE FIRST WORD LISTS

After our language lessons were over, I went on studying a little on my own. Johanne had given me a children's picture book called *Mo i mørket*, by Sara Li Stensrud, about a little girl, Mo, who wonders if she still exists, and is the same person, *i mørket*, when the lights are off. We had looked at the first page together, and with some rereading and stopping to think, I could understand some of it. It took me a while, though, to see that *mørket* had nothing to do with *market*, for example, but meant "the dark," Mo in the Dark—that *-et* was the pesky tacked-on *the*. An English cognate would be *murky*. (Cognate = born together, and means that the words come from the same original word or root.) I began to make lists, on small pieces of paper, of the words I was learning from this book.

I did not make my way through all of it before the time came to leave on a side trip to Bergen. The next stage in my learning of the language began in the train station at Bergen as I prepared to return to Oslo. Someone had suggested that another good way to start a foreign language was to read comic books. So before I boarded the train heading back over the mountains, I browsed the shop in the station and found the adventures of *Mikke Mus i grenseland* (in frontier country). (The front cover incited kids to buy it with the words *Ny!* ["New!"] and *Kul!* ["Cool!"].) So my next vocabulary lists were from the comic book and included words like: *mystery rangers, gang of robbers, right!, jail* (*fengsel*), *we're freezing!, supernatural, gold, black magic* (*svartekunster*), *we're alive!, Just as I thought!* (*Som jeg trodde!*), and *Out with it now!* (*Ut med det nå!*).

Reading the comic book was interesting, but not easy. I misunderstood things. I did not at first see the relationship between *spøkelse* ("ghosts") and our *spook*. I had to readjust my expectations to exclamatory comic-book-style dialogue: "Quick—after him!" (*Fort—etter ham!*). And to the one-word responses: "Wrong!" (*Feil!*).

The train trip was seven hours long, and during that time I managed to read very slowly through only one story. "Read" meant put my eye on a word, hear it in my head, try to figure out what it was, reread it, try again, go on to the next word. Of course, a great deal of the time I was also staring out the window at the mountain peaks, clouds, lakes, snow, snow tunnels, roads, hiking trails, cycling families, railway stations, and lonesome huts.

The small population of Norway is thinly spread over the land, so there is a lot of unpopulated scenery. The vastness of the mountains and fjords makes the people seem very small dark figures against the expanses of land and water, both the people of now, at least from a train window, and also those in photographs from earlier times. In Bergen, I had found the photos of the nineteenth-century photographer Knud Knudsen in a museum gift shop. His black-and-white images of the dramatic and wild landscape, and the families in that landscape, and also the city streets, exist as individual cards in shops, and also in great numbers online, but, strangely, were not at that time collected into any obtainable book.

ACQUIRING THE SOLSTAD NOVEL

When I returned to the United States, I did not go on with my Norwegian studies—I had lost some of the immediate motivation. But some months later, Johanne came on a visit, and in the course of a conversation, I described to her the difficulties I was having with a project of my own involving several generations of my ancestors, one that promised to be long, complex, and confusing. She recommended a new book she admired by the writer who is considered by many to be Norway's preeminent contemporary novelist, Dag Solstad (pronounced "Soolstad" or "Soolstah"), then in his early seventies. I had already dipped into the two paperbacks of his that I had in English translation. Johanne told me this new one was highly unusual, and quite controversial: How could it be called a novel? She said that although I would not be able to read it, I might find it interesting "just to browse." I could at least look through it and get an idea of what he was doing.

So in late May last year, I wrote to the Norwegian publisher hoping to buy the book directly from them. They offered to send me a copy, commenting that in their opinion Solstad was truly one of the greatest authors in not only Norway but the whole of Scandinavia. I was anticipating a colorful mix of contents: photographs, drawings, charts, family trees, maps. I looked forward to leafing through it, studying the decorative loops of the old handwriting and the somber nineteenth-century portraits, picking up helpful ideas for an approach to at least organizing my own problematic family saga.

It arrived in June. It was a fat hardback with a strikingly austere and handsome white dust jacket. The letters are black and red; the words of the title are all in capitals and are run together with no spaces between the words, as in classical Greek and Latin inscriptions, so that *Det uoppløselige episke*

element i Telemark i perioden 1591–1896 becomes: DETU-
OPPLØSELIGEEPISKEELEMENTITELEMARKIPERI-
ODEN1591–1896, except that it is laid out on the jacket
like this, forming a column of strange non-words:

DAGSOLSTAD
DETUOPPLØS
ELIGEEPISKE
ELEMENTITE
LEMARKIPER
IODEN1591–1896

Nothing interferes with this block of text on the white
space, because the only other words present, ROMAN
("novel") and the name of the publisher, FORLAGET
OKTOBER, are in minuscule point size, thus:

ROMAN | FORLAGET OKTOBER

directly under the last part of the title, so much smaller
that from a distance you don't see them at all, thus (more
or less):

IODEN1591–1896
ROMAN | FORLAGET OKTOBER

The design seemed to me brilliant, so striking that I asked
about it. I was told that the designer responsible for it was
one of the most distinguished book designers in Norway,
Egil Haraldsen. Credited along with him, in the book, is El-
len Lindeberg.

I don't yet understand the whole of the title. It is something like "The un-*oppløselige* epic element in Telemark in the period 1591–1896." I might have been able to figure out the unknown word when I encountered a form of it again, for only the second time, near the end of the book, but I could not, and now I can't find it again.

This design is not only handsome in itself, but of course appropriate for the form this novel takes: the run-together words reflect the choice Solstad has made, to present his text in almost unbroken blocks, with no chapters and few paragraph breaks. (The running-together of the words also, oddly, contradicts the directive with which the book opens, which asks us to read the book one word at a time.) Later, the cover design also came to seem symbolic, in two ways, of my confrontation with the unfamiliar language: the letters formed an almost impenetrable wall, and the words were almost all strange to me.

I opened the book and I was surprised. Yes, the endpapers front and back were maps of the towns, rivers, and mountains of Telemark, and an appendix gave the genealogy of each line of Solstad's family that he discusses in the book. But there were no charts, no photographs, no drawings. The book consisted, page after page, for 426 pages, of solid blocks of text, margin to margin, with rarely any sort of break. I wondered what to do with it.

I had been all set to examine it carefully, live with it a while, pick up some useful ideas. I also wanted to read it, now that I had it. I was frustrated: this was a book I wanted to read, and it did not exist in English. I wondered if I could simply start reading, one word after another, and find out if I would begin to understand. I had done something like this before, with two other languages, though in both cases I had had much more of a head start than I did this time. Having acquired the rudiments of Spanish on my own, as a teenager, decades later I read *Las aventuras de Tom Sawyer*, which turned out to be a good choice, since I knew the story so well. Years and years after that, by now interested in Dutch, I read several detective novels in that language. As the police figured out the crime, the details of it were repeated over and over, which helped me to understand. I was carried along by both the unfolding story and my changing grasp of the language.

I RESOLVE TO READ IT

If I wanted to know at first hand what Solstad was doing in this book, the only way to find out was to try to read it. I was intrigued by what Johanne had told me about it. So, seeing no alternative, I opened the Dag Solstad Telemark novel to the first page and started in on the opening sentence: *Les langsomt, ord for ord.* I was encouraged by the fact that I understood the first two words, and not because Johanne had taught them to me, but because I guessed them from their German cognates, *lesen* ("read") and *langsam* ("slow"): "Read slowly." That was good advice, and I would have to follow it in any case.

It took me a few more minutes and several rereadings to realize that *ord* had nothing to do with *order* or the German *Ort*, "place," but meant "word": "Read slowly, word for word." I went on: *hvis man vil forstå hva jeg sier.* This was more difficult, but I understood some of it: "Read slowly, word for word, *hvis* one will [or wants to] understand [G. *verstehen*] *hva jeg sier.*" I thought *jeg* could mean "I" (Fr. *je*). By now I know that the whole sentence contains a surprisingly apt directive: "Read slowly, word for word, if you want to understand what I am saying." Having got this far, I then made up my mind that I would simply keep reading. Even if at first I understood almost nothing, I thought, I would in time understand more and more, and perhaps actually learn to read Norwegian.

WHY I FOUND THE BOOK SO ENTRANCING

It is hard to explain why the book became so entrancing. On the face of it, I would not have said that to read, laboriously, word by word, in a language I did not know, understanding only a little, a book with very little plot and a multitude of three-named Norwegians of centuries past would be such an inviting prospect that I was eager to wake up in the morning and go read—read for several hours, often, reluctant to put the book down and turn to other things.

One part of the pleasure, I know, was that through this reading I journeyed so far away, both geographically and in time. I journeyed into a landscape thinly populated even now, necessarily more so in centuries past, and characterized by dramatic scenery that stretched away into the distance or loomed over the people who lived there.

In the photographs of Knud Knudsen, in the rural scenes, the people, dwarfed by the landscape, gather by the shores of a lake or river or fjord, preparing to embark for a wedding celebration across the water, or they trail along a winding dirt road on foot alongside a cart and ox or horse. These photographs would sometimes come to mind as I read Solstad's novel, though of course we enter the nineteenth century only after we're well along in the book.

It was therefore partly the attraction of the foreign that drew me, foreign in place and time. There were multiple layers of a figurative mist in front of me as I read (with some breaks in the mist, more and more as I went along): the mist of my incomprehension, the mist of the past stretching back, the mist I imagined over the landscape of Norway, even wilder then than now, and the mist of the telling: the intervention of the narrator between us and the people or the documents. Reading it in a language unfamiliar to me removed it even further in time and space. And perhaps I absorbed this landscape and these characters more deeply because I dwelled on each sentence so long, long enough to figure some of it out, and then also returned to it, dwelling on it again.

The past was mysterious in part just because so much of it was missing, so much was unknown. The novel goes far back in time, and there is very little information about each character. There was a real, though quiet, suspense in wondering what would happen next to these people of Telemark so many years ago: who married whom; which children survived to grow up; whether they lived on a *stor* farm or a more modest one; if widowed, whether they remarried; what the children thought of their new stepmother, the extravagant Margit, with her chests of linens; what was inside the lunch bag packed by the lonely widow and opened by the itinerant carpenter in a clearing in the woods; and why old Erik Sakeson hanged himself.

There are dramatic stories in the book, and they are a welcome burst of color when they come along. They come without warning, told in the same even tone as what came before and what will come after. They are usually brief. A man gets into a fight at a wedding feast, after drinking too much *øl* (which I mistook, in an earlier passage—where it appeared in a list of household food and drink—for "oil"), and kills another guest, then goes into hiding for two years before being found, brought to trial, sentenced, and beheaded.

The fact that these events actually took place heightens

the interest, for me. Because the plot turns were not invented by the author, but were determined by chance, character, genes, environment, they are often abrupt and surprising: not only the births and deaths, but also the wildly mismatched marriages, the thefts and murders, the evictions of poor widows, the accumulation of wealth, the descent into destitution.

Solstad does not just give us the answers, he takes us along with him in the process of finding out. He speculates in detail about one possibility, we find it plausible, and we believe he is right. Then he shows us, as though working it out for himself, why that possibility is unlikely. And then why another possibility is more likely, or must in fact be the case. And some of his speculations are frustrated and we are left, with Solstad, simply not knowing. So this is another kind of suspense: Solstad's historical investigation.

Certainly Dag Solstad is very present in the book, regularly commenting, sometimes exclaiming (*Hva??*—"What??"), as though spontaneously. On the very first page, he explains that originally he had intended to write a completely different kind of novel (*Jeg skulle opprinnelig ha skrevet en helt annen roman*) but that he found this family material so compelling, when it was collected and sent to him by a younger relative, the *sønn* of his *kusine Birgit*, that he changed his plan.

Occasionally he bursts out with an opinion, sometimes quite emotional. So, the author's own emotional involvement in the book is another part of its power, for a struggling reader.

But of course for me one of the most exciting aspects of the experience, adding to the suspense, was the adventure of gradually learning the language, beginning the book without knowing it and gradually acquiring it as I went along, seeing more and more mysterious words become familiar. In the beginning, as I made my way into this partly incomprehensible Telemark of the 1600s and 1700s, I felt, pleasantly, all the further away from home in both time and culture for not knowing half of what I was reading. Then the mists began clearing, and each page offered another reward: not only the unfolding story, but also a linguistic revelation—again and again came the little burst of understanding, like a little light coming on, as a word that looked so mysterious—*miljø*—abruptly revealed itself: "milieu."

This confrontation with the densely printed text in the unknown language turned out to be oddly exhilarating. It was like diving, or jumping, into the deep, cold, and mysterious waters of a mountain lake. Or, to change the metaphor—I'm searching for a way to express just what this project was like—it was like confronting a rock face, or a mountain that I had to climb. The fact of doing it by myself, independently, without help, was part of what made it exhilarating. No one was going to lift me up that mountain. I would have to find the handholds and footholds by myself.

As I went along, I understood more and more—one bit of understanding helped me to another; the more words I understood in a sentence, or the more clearly I understood its construction, the easier it was for me to guess or figure out the rest. The mists were clearing a little; or the mountain was leveling off a bit, or offering more small passes; or the forest that had been almost impenetrable was opening some small paths and clearings.

And so, in fact, the experience of reading the book kept changing for me as my understanding improved; it was never quite the same experience one day as it had been the day before.

The activity also became something of an addiction. I became very dedicated to my daily immersions in the tales of Solstad's ancestors in distant Telemark. Every part of the reading was a pleasure: the clean, large, white page, the sharp pencil for making notes, the comfortable armchair, the bright light, the complete erasure when I erased a misspelling or an awkwardly written letter, and most of all, of course, the progress word by word through the narrative, with an occasional touch of frustration, but far more often with satisfaction.

MY METHOD OF READING AND LEARNING: NO DICTIONARY

I read without a dictionary, understood some of each sentence, did not understand quite a bit of it, and was willing to read on ahead without understanding everything I had read.

There were several reasons why I did not want to use a dictionary. First, it was more comfortable not to be constantly picking up a dictionary, or sitting in front of a computer. Since, at first, there would be a quantity of words on any given page that I would not know, I would have been looking up many, many words, and this would have been a cumbersome chore. I wanted to sit with this heavy book in a comfortable chair, with nothing more, besides the book, than a sharp pencil and piece of paper.

Second, though, and more important, the work of trying to figure out what the words meant was stimulating and completely absorbing. I realized, after a while, that using my brain for something as difficult as this made thinking a very physical act, much more so than the easier, almost unconscious use we make of our brains most of the time.

Third, I remembered the words far better when I figured them out on my own. I even remembered words that I couldn't figure out, so that when I met them again later in the book, I recognized them (without knowing what they meant). I saw that finding the unknown word in another context might give me the answer.

I remembered the words better, too, because I encountered them in an interesting context. I learned *respekt* (though that word was obviously an easy one) on page 303, in December, in the context of *respekt* for the *døde* ("dead"), particularly for the *døde fedrene* ("dead forefathers"), *respekt* that ought to make one hesitate before disturbing an old burial mound (*gravhaug*). But that did not stop one of the foremost theologians (*teologer*) of the time, a bishop (*biskop*) keen on archeology (*arkeologi*). The story is longer than this, but the short version is: He obtained permission from the owner of the property to hire some workers to excavate the *gravhaug*. The work was still going on when he had to return home (*måtte reise hjem*). But the workers had noticed something (I did not understand exactly what) that made them believe there was a money chest deep in the hole. The owner of the land ordered them to cover over what they had dug. But later, after some underhand activity that, again, I could not understand, a chance passerby (if that is what *tilfeldig mann* means) discovered a chest full of silver coins (*sølv-penger*) below the bathhouse (*bad-stue*). He told no one, but took them to an old woman (*gammel kone*) to be washed. There is more.

But I will skip to a related story, about what the landowner himself found in another mound on the same property: a large sword, a heavy iron key, a silver plate with engraved circles and spirals, and a heavy gold cross (*gullkors*). The owner of the property, not realizing the cross was gold, sold it to a certain sergeant (*sersjant*) who was well aware of its value and became suddenly wealthy (*plutselig rik*) (cognates G. *plötzlich*, "suddenly"; Eng. *rich*).

But now, I must add—since it reveals something about his narrative technique—that Solstad denies this last part of the story, and tells us the sergeant's sudden wealth was only *folks fantasi*.

Words occur in Solstad's book that occurred earlier in the only previous reading I had had in Norwegian: in *Mo i mørket*, people look down from the windows (*vinduene*) and see Mo in the street below with her orange ball—there goes Mo, they say. In the Solstad novel, the wealthy and pitiless Halvor Borgja, who is known to drive his workers like slaves (*som slaver*) hangs his red hat in the *vindu* of his room so that a hired man, toiling in the field, who stops work for a moment to catch his breath, will look up at the windows of the main house and believe that the boss is there watching from under the brim of his hat, and will bend down to work again. And so, as a language does when one learns it this way, *vindu* is beginning to gather associations for me.

Similarly, a character in the *Mikke Mus* comic uses the word *trodde*, "believed," in his exclamation: "Just as I thought!" (*Som jeg trodde!*) At one point in his narrative, Solstad, as he speculates about his grandmother's childhood, also uses the word: he mistakenly *trodde* something about her foster parents that turned out not to be true. So for me, now the word *trodde* is gathering associations that it wouldn't have if I had learned it off a list of vocabulary to be memorized.

Another reason I did not want to use a dictionary or ask anyone for the answer was that, almost right away, this experiment interested me qua experiment, and I wanted to keep it quite pure. I was trying to learn a language the way we learn our own native language from babyhood on up. Words are repeated in certain contexts, some contexts the same and some different, and eventually, over time, with much repetition, we learn what the words mean.

BLIND IMMERSION

This experience with Norwegian was not my first experience of learning a language more or less from zero and with very little help, mainly through immersion. There was, to begin with, my original acquisition of my native language, English, as baby and child—with quite a lot of active coaching, I'm sure, from two parents interested in language and from an older sister and an older brother. Then there was my experience at the age of seven in the first grade of the Ursulinenkloster Schule (Ursuline Cloister School) in Graz. It was my first experience of a foreign language, if I don't count the snatches of French I had been so surprised to hear in Paris, where my family and I stopped for a few days on our way to Austria, and where I went out to play every day in the Tuileries Garden with my hoop and stick.

I had been given no prior preparation or coaching in German, and the first-grade teacher spoke only a little halting English. But she was a kind woman, anxious to help me along, and my classmates were friendly. Every day I sat in the schoolroom, dressed like the other girls in long woollen stockings, sturdy buckled shoes, a dress and a smock, my hair cut short, and listened and watched, and stared down at the attractive pages of the grammar book, with its pretty illustrations, the words printed very large in the beginning of the book and progressively smaller as the book went on. After about a month, when the teacher called on me to read aloud, I was able to, and during the rest of that year I continued to learn more and more rudiments of German, not only how to read it and speak it, but also how to form the letters of my script in the German way, with loops in the upper parts of the *o*'s and *a*'s and *d*'s and *g*'s. By the time my family left to return to the United States, I had a well-ingrained and "natural" understanding of the basic syntax of German and a good pronunciation, and could talk fluently within a child's limited range of vocabulary and syntax. Back in the United States, I missed the German language.

In the present case, true, I had had those three lessons with Johanne, and some preliminary vocabulary gained from two other texts, and I also brought to the language my previous experiences of other languages, so this experiment was far less "pure" than the experience in the Graz classroom, which was in turn less pure than my original acquisition of English.

MARKS ON THE PAGE

On the first page of the novel, which was page 5, I learned these words: *read, slowly, word, for, will, I, material, a, must, also, begin, with, not, shall, written, whole, other, from, my, cousin, was, gathered, son, and, me, use, over, time, work, equally, it, we, after, ago, understand, then, in, copy, four, years, eight, months, so, strong, basis, as, long, that, mother's father, goes, back, us, are, many, no, idea.* I know this because I wrote them in pencil in the white spaces at the top of the page and on the blank facing page.

Some of the words I wrote down on that first page have question marks after them, though none of them was in fact wrong. But I saw that because so many words were going to be new to me as I read on, I could not continue writing them in the margins, because there would not be room for them all. So I started keeping lists on separate pieces of paper.

LONGER WORD LISTS

The reward of figuring out a word was to write it down in a running list and see how my vocabulary grew and grew. Some words were followed by a question mark. Some words recurred on the list more than once, even many times, still with a question mark. Some I had wrong.

The reason to keep a list was in part acquisitive: I *had* this word now, I had acquired it. Then I had another. I was collecting them.

But there were other reasons: The act of writing out the Norwegian word made me pay close attention to what it was, how it was spelled. Writing out the English helped me to remember it. Having the word there on paper allowed me to review it, and to search for the same word on another page, since words that were difficult for me I wrote down more than once.

After a while, becoming impatient with myself that I could not remember certain basic and important words, I would write them in capitals, or put asterisks next to them.

On June 15, I noted, on the back of a vocabulary list, that I was not writing down some new words because I would always recognize them, such as *reagerte*, "reacted." Other words easy to recognize were *motivet*, "the motive"; *resultatet*, "the result"; *insolvente*, "insolvent"; *pekuniær*, "pecuniary"; *introduserer*, "introduces"; *instinktivt*, "instinctively." Later, I did write down obvious or easy words, too, because, as part of my experiment, I wanted to see how many new words I was learning in all.

From *instinktivt* and other easy words, such as *sarkastisk*, "sarcastic," I learned that Norwegian did not seem to use a *c*. Where we in English had a hard *c*, their equivalent word had a *k*.

Learning that their *k* might be our *c* gave me another clue to deciphering a word that looked strange. Easier words early in the book were *kusine*, "cousin," and *kom*, "come." Later in the book, *kalkylene*, "calculations." But a stranger-looking *k*-word was *auksjon*. When I substituted our *c* for their *k* and tried to say it, I saw what it was: "auction." Figuring out this word gave me another possible spelling hint: *sj* might always be pronounced "sh." I had first suspected this reading the *Mikke Mus* comic, when, among the vivid words for sounds that sprawled in fat letters across the frames, I encountered *splæsj* ("splash") and *krasj* ("crash"), along with others: *splooosj*, *svooosj*, *flasj* (cameras popping), *svisj* (pursued and pursuers racing past), and the sound of a sneeze—*atsjoo*—from a character concealed among some burlap sacks of soap powder. Knowing how to pronounce *sj* might help me with other odd-looking words.

There are certainly words that look strange as written in Norwegian but that are not difficult once you give them a moment of attention, or try saying them out loud. For example, *miljø* ("milieu")—which also tells you how to pronounce the *j* and that odd (to me) letter *ø*, whose name I don't yet know.

CREATING A GRAMMAR FOR MYSELF

Fairly early on, I realized it would be helpful to devote one page of the word list to the main verbs and their principal parts as I learned them: *do*, *make*, *have*, *see*, *say*, *know*, etc.

Some were quite confusing, and I still have to look at that page sometimes. For instance, *see* is *se* (pronounced "seh," I think), past tense *så* (pronounced "so"), while *say* is *si* (pronounced "see"), past tense *sa* (pronounced "sah"). See, *se*, saw, *så*; say, *si*, said, *sa. Give* and *go* are also confusing.

On the same page, I grouped all the *hv*-words together in an irregular box that became more and more crowded as I found more of them: *hvor, hva, hvis, hvordan, hvem, hver, hverandre, hvortil, hvilke, hvorav, hvorfor*, etc. These words that begin with *hv* are, many of them, equivalent to our English words that begin with *wh: where, what, whom, which*, etc. The English and Norwegian words were closer in the past: in Old English, our *wh*-words were *hw*-words: *what* was *hwaet*, etc. Our present-day *wherefore* was in Old English *hwarfore* and meant, as the Norwegian *hvorfor* means, "why." "Wherefore [why] art thou Romeo?" (when you could belong to some other family with whom my family is not feuding).

I also made a list of *d*-words: *de, dem, den, der*, etc. They mostly corresponded to our *th*-words: *the, them, that, there*, etc.

I learned from its function in a sentence that when a word that looked to me like an adjective had a *t* added to the end of it, as in the case of *instinktivt*, it became an adverb. Other examples would be *generelt*, "generally," and *formelt*, "formally." I made a note of that. And when I began noting how adverbs were formed, I realized that I was not only accumulating vocabulary in this new language, but also creating my own grammar.

Another piece of grammar I learned was that *-es* added onto the root of a word seemed to indicate the passive voice. *Vites* = is known.

Once I realized I was creating my own grammar of the language, I saw the similarity between what I was doing and what an anthropological linguist does (and what some Christian missionaries used to do, and may still do) when attempting to record the language of a people whose language has not previously been studied: living with the people, they learn the language through day-to-day immersion, devising symbols for the sounds and deriving syntactical rules.

Figuring out the grammar for yourself is an adventure. When you stumble on the answer to a question that has been plaguing you, a problem that you haven't been able to solve, it is a satisfaction, and a relief. (Perhaps you find it out by "cheating," either by reading a book of Norwegian poetry with facing translations, or by allowing yourself to ask just one question of a Norwegian friend: What does *hos* mean??) It is far more satisfying to have one's own urgent question answered by learning a point of grammar than to have to memorize that point of grammar before you actively want to know it, as in conventional language instruction.

MARKS ON THE PAGE (CONT.)

After I started keeping lists on separate pieces of paper, at first I did not underline the words on the page. Maybe, out of respect for the handsome book, I wanted to keep it relatively clean of marks. That lasted only for a short time, because my system of marking changed through the course of reading the book. After that first page, the only marks, for a while, were little straight lines dividing the different parts of a difficult word to help me figure it out. And sometimes I underlined the name of a character or wrote it at the top of the page.

On June 19, at about page 80, I noted that in half an hour I wrote down fourteen words. Some of those words were repeats. When I had trouble remembering a word, and was learning it over again, I would write it down again. Sometimes the same word occurred only many pages after I had first read it, so that I had more or less forgotten it. Writing it down again also helped me remember it.

This is one of the reasons that reading without a dictionary, and writing down the words I learn, is more effective for me as a way to learn to read a language I don't know. The effort to think what a word means, often rereading the sentence once or twice and taking time to think about it, coming to the answer myself, and then taking more time to write it down, all help me remember the new word better than if I looked it up and found the answer right away. More generally, in this case as in others, I liked doing this exercise myself rather than having the work done for me (by the dictionary).

I also liked using the pencil. I liked sharpening it to a fine point, and I liked being able to erase a mark cleanly and rewrite correctly on the page with the sharp point. I sharpened the pencil often with a little rose-colored plastic "portable" sharpener. Later I used, instead, a heavier sharpener that resembled a glass inkwell.

Sometimes, then, my penciling was a notation of how long it had taken me to read (which at that time still meant: decipher) a passage. Often, it seemed, one page took half an hour. I did become so absorbed in reading this book that one, two, or even three hours would go by before I could drag myself away from it. I would read it with my first cup of coffee—it became a motivation for getting up in the morning. Then I would read it while I ate my breakfast, which I would eat very slowly. At last I would have to get on with the rest of my day. But for quite a few weeks, in the beginning, I also read it again in bed before going to sleep, until I decided that it was too stimulating to my brain and did not help me get a calm and deep night's sleep. So there were some days on which I read as much as ten pages, others on which I had time only for two, three, or four.

MY METHOD OF FIGURING OUT THE WORDS: BREAKING THE WORD INTO ITS COMPONENT PARTS

In contrast to the elided words of the book's title on the cover, one of my strategies in trying to understand a word was to break it into its component parts, which were, in fact, its root, prefixes, and suffixes. Often, especially in the beginning, I marked only the suffix, when it was the tacked-on article: *fjord|en*, "the fjord"; *kong|en*, "the king"; *provins|en*, "the province"; *barn|et*, "the child"; *munk|ene i klostr|ene*, "the monks in the cloisters."

Although I knew long ago, before I began this, that in Norwegian and other Scandinavian languages the definite article (*the*) is usually (not in certain cases) tacked onto the end of the noun, it is still one of the hardest things for me to grasp "instinctively" or automatically. As I read along, I had to keep reminding myself, and saying "the" aloud in my head where it didn't seem to appear with the word.

I learned early on that *u* at the beginning of an adjective would probably mean "un-" or some other negating prefix, an example being: *u-tro-lige*, "un-believ-able." Once I learned what *u* meant, I could separate it with that line: *u|lykka*, "mis-fortune" (cognate, Eng. *luck*); *u|tallige barn og barnebarn*, "countless [un-countable] children and grand-children" (cognate, Eng. *tally*).

Here is a good example of learning the word by separating it into its root and prefixes and suffixes: *uavhengighet* =

u-av-heng-ig-het = un-from-hang-ing-ness = independence (page 325). In fact, come to think of it, you can separate the English word, *independence*, into almost exactly the same elements. But because it's derived from the Latin, we don't see the root *hang* quite as clearly: in-de-pend-ence = un-from-hang-ness. Another example: *mektig* means "powerful." *Allmektighet* = *all-mekt-ig-het* = "all-might-i-ness," or, the Latinate version, "omni-pot-ence."

MISTAKING THE COMPONENT PARTS

Breaking the word into its component parts was usually helpful, although occasionally I would break it the wrong way, into parts that didn't mean anything. For instance, I looked at the phrase *opparbeidet seg* (page 290), about the activities of one Jørund; first I saw *op-par-beid*—even though I should have known that since *opp* is a word ("up") it should remain intact; *par* and *beid* meant nothing to me. Then I looked again and saw it divided the right way: *opp* and *arbeidet*. The German cognate (*Arbeit*) gave me the clue that this word had something to do with work, even though I did not fully understand it (up-worked himself?; worked his way up in the world?; improved his position?).

Another word that I more recently separated the wrong way was a word in a poem by Olav H. Hauge, after I started attempting a few other texts in Norwegian: *snøkvelden*, which I separated into *snøk* and *velden*. *Velden*, I thought vaguely, could be "world" or "field," but what was a *snøk*? Then the correct division came to me: *snø* and *kvelden*—"snow" and "(the) evening," an evening of snow, a snowy evening. (The word *kveld* figures also in Solstad's novel, in a story about a resurrected Swede.)

Another misunderstanding, late in the book, in a passage about crossing a lake, was *sjøormen*, which I separated into *sjø-or-men*. I knew that *sjø* was "lake," and because of the water, I carelessly, reflexively (for the brain will sometimes be lazy and reflexive unless one directs it firmly) interpreted *or-men* to be "oar-men"—that is, men employed to row people across the lake. Not at all, of course. The correct division was *orm-en*, the noun was *orm* with its suffix *the*. Since *orm* is "worm," or "snake," the *sjø-orm-en* was probably some kind of water creature, no doubt mythical.

THE BOOK'S ELUSIVE TITLE

Then there is that word in the title of the book that I still don't know: *uoppløselige*. I break it into its parts: *u-opp-løse-lige*, "un-*oppløselige*," "un-up-*løse*-able." I keep returning to it, but I haven't yet been able to figure it out. I have a feeling its root has something to do with solving, but that may just be because I am so occupied with trying to solve the problem of this word.

MARKS ON THE PAGE (CONT.)

Soon, I began to make a mark on the page when I saw that Solstad was doing something interesting in the writing of the book. I would often mark it with an asterisk in the margin. On page 83, for instance, I marked a spot where a paragraph break would very naturally have gone, but where Solstad had chosen not to make one. The break might have occurred after this sentence:

"But [now let's get] back to the will left by Aslak Veinung-son Fossheim."

At page 92, I started making more marks on the clean pages. First, I began putting a long diagonal line in the side margin where I was beginning the day's reading, with the date below it. That particular day happened to be June 20. On that day, I also noted in the margin, "description of house," since I was interested in what a house would have been like in those long-ago days of Solstad's earliest documented ancestors. Of course, I could read only part of the description:

"The main house was an old *stue* [farmhouse? house?] with a *tilbygd* ["to-built": built-on?] *bu* [building, structure?] with a loft over it, and a *spon*-roof. There is reason to believe that this *tilbygget* [built-on addition?] was added when Kittil Jonson from Baugerud in Hitterdal came and moved to the farm and the farm had two families. Then one family, Ingerid Tweitan and her husband Ole Samundson, lived in the old farmhouse, while Anne Eivindsdatter and her husband and later her large flock of children lived in the added-on section w/ loft." (Here I am also translating Solstad's abbreviation of *with*: *med* becomes "*m.*" Part of the charm of the book is his occasional casualness.)

At about this point, although I was not yet writing new words in the margins of the book, I began underlining the new words I was acquiring.

A BREAK FROM NORWEGIAN

On June 24, I had to suspend my reading. I was going off on a trip that would take me into July, with another, complicated trip on the horizon for August and into September. I was then going to be teaching a short course, for which I had to prepare; and I had other work to catch up on. I did not resume my reading until mid-October—after a break of four months. I had stopped at page 120. I wondered if I would have the same interest and dedication when I took the book up again. (Strangely enough, I did. Too often, my enthusiasms tend to get left behind with the passage of time.)

BERLITZ: BENDING THE RULE A LITTLE

During the month of teaching, in the fall, however, I did try adding something to the project, I was going to be spending more time in the car, so I acquired a Berlitz language-learning booklet plus CD, designed, of course, for the casual tourist in Norway, not necessarily the reader of Solstad. I did not intend to study the booklet, not at first anyway. I had bought the CD because I wanted more exposure to the sound of the spoken language.

Since, however silently I read, I always hear in my head whatever I am reading, I had been hearing my own version of the Norwegian words for some time now. After weeks of mispronouncing the words one by one as they passed before my eyes, I was frustrated and impatient with not really knowing how they were meant to sound. I therefore did not particularly mind if the sentences on the Berlitz CD all had to do with such things as airplane flights, hotel reservations, and ordering a drink, as long as I could learn to pronounce the words. And so, for the month of October, driving back from the class late in the evening, I would listen to the CD in the car. It was rather a relief, after three hours in the classroom discussing plot, character development, and (English) sentence structure, to say over and over again in the dark, as correctly as possible: "*Kan du anbefale en bra restaurant?*"— "Can you recommend a good restaurant?"

It is true that, as I was in this way bending my rule a little, I did learn a few words that had mystified me in Solstad's novel.

BACK TO THE NOVEL: MY METHOD OF FIGURING OUT THE WORDS: COGNATES

After separating a word into its parts, if it's a long one, I can usually figure out the prefixes and suffixes easily enough: *un-*, or *up-*, or *out-*, or *to-*; *-ly*, or *-able*, or *-ness*, etc. I search my mind for what may be the possible cognates of its root— the essential, core part of the word (e.g., *pend* in *independence*). A cognate may give me the answer to what the word means, or at least a hint.

Here is an example of a short word and its cognate: if a *bekk* runs through a farm, a handy source of water, and if one remembers the Northern English word *beck*, then one can assume this is a little stream.

Here is an example of a large sentence fragment that can be understood entirely via cognates: one of Solstad's regular "connecting" statements, in his narrative, is: *Vi skal komme tilbake til* = "We shall come to-back to." (All English cognates.)

Sometimes I was able to find the cognate by removing that strange (to me) *j* that seemed to creep into certain words: remove the *j* from *kjøp* and I would have nearly the Dutch *koop*, meaning "buy." Remove the *j* from *gjerne* and I would be closer to the German *gern*, "gladly."

MISTAKING THE COGNATES

The word *flyttet* occurs again and again in the Telemark novel, right from the beginning of the book. A character often *flyttet* away from the place he lived, often *flyttet* from one farm to another. The word resembles the English words *fleet*, *flit*, *flight*. So I thought *flyttet* had to mean "flew," or "fled"—the character was running away in fear of something like an enemy, or from debt. But no. I knew after a while this couldn't be right, because Solstad's characters were so constantly doing this. It simply meant "moved," as in "moved house" or "moved away."

I thought the Norwegian *ferd* was related to the G. *Pferd*, "horse," but it is not: the Norwegian for *horse* is *hest*.

When I first encountered it, I thought *giftet seg* (literally "married oneself," got married)—a phrase that occurs over and over in this book, since it is so much about one person marrying another—must have something to do with poison, because of the G. *Gift*. But after a while, I realized that it wasn't possible, of course, for his characters to keep poisoning themselves and then having children. So I understood what it had to mean. Complicating things, though, as I later learned, the Norwegian *gift* by itself also does, like the German, mean "poison." Solstad's great-grandmother, clever Aaste, although she is, as a child, so good at her catechism, grows up to have a tongue that is rather *giftig*.

I was easily misled by some Norwegian words having to do with time. The word *time* itself, *tid*, I understood fairly soon, though its cognate in English is *tide*, so the relationship is not direct. But then, to confuse things, their word for *hour* is *tim*, cognate with our *time*. And their word for *while*, as in *a while*, is *stund*, cognate with German *Stund*, "hour." So *to timer* is not "two-timer" or "two times," but "two hours." And what about our *hour*? The only word resembling it that I could think of, on my own, was *houri*, Persian for a beautiful young woman.

Then, two days after I had been stopped by *hour* and the irrelevant *houri*, I learned the Norwegian *ur*, meaning "watch" (as in *wristwatch*), which I had not known before, and of course that reminded me of a word I should have remembered, the German *Uhr*, also meaning "watch." These are the cognates of *hour* that I was looking for.

Solstad imagines the fearsome and powerful Borgja, in his afterlife, watching his descendants from where he sits up in the heavens, in the *skyer*. *Sky*, with the indefinite plural suffix *-er*, must be "skies," or "sky," of course. Of course! But no, it is "clouds."

MARKS ON THE PAGE (CONT.)

Around page 140, soon after resuming my reading, I began writing in the top or bottom or side margins, occasionally, words I was having trouble with that were repeated regularly, like *enda*, "still," as in *enda tidligere*, "still earlier." This way, I could compare instances. For most of the book—324 pages—I had trouble with *I tillegg til*. Then at last (why after so long?) I understood it: "in addition to."

On October 25, on page 161, I changed the approach yet again: I abandoned my system of writing new words on those folded sheets of typing paper, which had been a bit of a bother, after all, and went back to what I had done the first day: I wrote my newly acquired words directly on the page. I could have done this long before, because, by now, I was learning fewer new words on each page—I knew a lot of the basic vocabulary, and a lot of it repeated. Writing the words directly on the page was not only easier, but much better for reviewing the new words in context and comparing them to earlier instances. There might be as few as six new words on a page, or even just one, or, sometimes, as many as fifteen. Recording just one new word on a page could be good or bad. It could mean I understood almost everything on the page, or it could mean any combination at all of knowing the words already and not being able to figure out any of the ones I did not know.

I loved the way the book looked, its handsome production, not only the front cover design, but the inside, the solidity of it, the quality of the paper, the blocks of text on the pages. Each time I turned a page, what I saw were two clean pages—large in format, with good heavy paper, clear, large, dark type. Then I would begin reading, and by the time I left a page, it was covered with thin, faint pencil marks—words and lines, the occasional box and the rare circle, not always neatly done. I was reading the page in an active way. I wrote as I read. The fresh, unread page was beautiful, the page once I had read it was less so.

MY METHOD OF FIGURING OUT THE WORDS: CONTEXTS

I learned the words from cognates and also from their context. Cognates allowed me to guess (sometimes wrongly, but usually correctly) what the word might mean. The context would confirm this, or further limit the word, narrow the possibilities of what it could be.

I realized at a certain point that this, too, followed a model from science. When I was not certain of a word, I made a guess, based on cognates, context, etc. That was my hypothesis. Finding the word again, in another context, was a test of my hypothesis. It might confirm that I was right, or disprove my hypothesis, in which case I would have to form a new hypothesis, or it might do neither, simply leave me in doubt. Eventually, another context (and maybe a little more thinking it through) would allow me to form a hypothesis that could finally be proven to be correct.

Here are two examples of how a context teaches a word, the first one easy and immediate:

1) I learned the word for *tower* as soon as I read it, from the association with Babel. Since I knew already that an *s* on the end of a noun, with no apostrophe, most often indicated the possessive, *Babels tarn* had to be "Babel's tower," or "tower of Babel."

2) In one passage, Solstad lists animals a couple of times—I know these are animals because he is talking about what things are on two different farms and I recognize *hest* ("horse"), and (I think) *sauer* ("sheep"). In one of the lists he includes *gris*, which I don't recognize—it doesn't resemble any likely word I can think of—and then he remarks that the new owners of that farm will have a *gris* for Christmas (*jul*, pronounced more or less like the English "Yule"). I assume that the animal they will want to slaughter for Christmas is a pig, or hog, so *gris* must be "pig," or "hog." But I realize now that it could also be a goose. In this case, I'm not sure, but the possibilities are at least limited by the context: either hog or goose. (Not *lam*, in any case, also on one of the lists, which would probably be for Easter.)

3) Just one more example, which combines both cognate and context: *spelemann* is probably "play-man," if I choose to trust the German cognate *spiel*, meaning "play," and therefore could be *gambler*, *actor*, or *musician*. But the context here decides it: this *spelemann* is in demand at weddings—so

he isn't likely to be an actor or a gambler, and must be a musician.

4) I'll add a fourth example, because it shows how the scientific experimental model works, how one context leads me to a first, tentative hypothesis that is then disproven by the next context.

It is a continuation of the story of the bishop and his desecration of the ancient burial mound. The family is now plagued by misfortune and the people believe it is because of this desecration. They say: Those who dwell underground, the *underjordiske*—the *døde*, or "dead"—do not like to be *vanæret*. I thought—and I knew it was a little odd—that *vanæret* might have something to do with "exposed to the air" because of the root *ær* and its resemblance to our *aerate*. I let that hypothesis stand and went on reading the story. A few pages later came another word with *ær* in it, characterizing a certain lineage as *ærverdige*—"*ær*-worthy." Well, then, *ær* could not have anything to do with "air," after all. Thinking more about it, and considering the context, the lineage and its worthiness, my memory was jogged enough for the German *Ehr*, "honor," to come back to me. *Ær* most probably meant honor. Farther down the page, Solstad confirms this new hypothesis quite explicitly, by saying the same thing two ways: *De underjordiske . . . skal æres, og ikke vanæres.* "The underground-dwellers [i.e., the dead] . . . shall be honored, and not dishonored."

Sometimes a mysterious word appears in a context in which it is the only missing part in the drama of the sentence—and the story. For instance, well on in the book, one character always wanders the roads carrying a *ljå*. Solstad tells the reader this more than once. Each time he repeats it, I don't know what a *ljå* is. I imagine, and imagine, this character walking down the roads with something, but can't guess what. How much did it change the experience of reading those passages not to know what he was carrying?

Much later, I find the missing piece of the image in a poem I am reading that has a facing translation in English. I am cheating a little, or, rather, changing the rules. The change in the rules is that if a helpful book comes my way *by chance* (in this case, the book of poems was a gift from a Norwegian friend), I am allowed to look at it and be helped by it. The book was by the very well-known (in Norway) and much-quoted twentieth-century poet Olav H. Hauge, who lived all his life in the same place, tending an orchard on his small farm. A *ljå* is a scythe. This surprises me, since to me the word *scythe* looks almost Norwegian; the word for it should be almost the same, I think somewhat indignantly. But now, because of my earlier struggle, and because of the vividly described character who is carrying it, I probably won't forget what a *ljå* is.

MY METHOD: REREADING

I also discovered how important rereading was. It was a rule from the very beginning that I couldn't simply skip over a sentence and go on, but had to work on it until I either understood or saw that I could not. So, unless I did understand it right away, which happened more often as I continued to read the book, I would have to reread the sentence. The first reading of a word or sentence might reveal nothing at all, and leave me mystified. But with just the small increase in familiarity that came from reading it a second time, the words would begin to suggest themselves. I wondered what happened in the brain, between the first and the second reading.

MARKS ON THE PAGE (CONT.)

Eventually I added a little box around the date of the day's reading, so that I could quickly find the days as I leafed through the pages.

I would occasionally write the word's meaning directly above the word—and I continued to do this to the end of the book—especially when the word was one that could mean several things. One of the tricky ones was *som*, which could mean "who" or "which" but also "as." This was not meant to be a note that I would return to later, but was an active way of reading, an aid to comprehending as I went along.

I sometimes underlined a phrase of two or more words, so that I would read it as such. Later I began collecting phrases, such as *mer enn nok*, "more than enough," writing them on a blank page in the back of the book.

In the top and bottom margins, sometimes, I added names of ancestors being talked about, if they were important or if theirs was an interesting continuing story. Sometimes also the topic of a story (e.g., "extravagant Margit" or "Erik Sakeson kills himself" or "murder at a wedding feast" or "Ole Hovdejord and his two artificial hands"). In the side margin, sometimes, along with the name of an ancestor, I added birth dates, and children, if I wanted to keep track. But I'm not sure why I wanted to keep track—maybe this was my reaction to feeling overwhelmed by the enormous cast of characters.

One of the interesting stories: Ole Hovdejord, alone and unarmed, comes unexpectedly face-to-face with a bitter enemy, one Kaptein Nägler, and loses his right hand to the sword of the captain's bodyguard. Ole runs to the nearest smithy (*smid*), which lies in the valley next to Hitterdal church, and sticks his bleeding stump into the glowing embers to stanch the blood. Long afterward, he has two artificial hands made for himself, one of silver (*sølv*), for Sundays and holy days, and one of iron (*jern*), for everyday use.

We will never know anything more about Ole Hovdejord, because that is the way it is with the stories that come from public records, from a limited collection of primary documents, and that are not supplemented, or not much, by the writer's imagination.

WHAT I DID NOT DO ENOUGH OF

I simply did not review my word lists enough, or copy them often enough into my "master" word list—the alphabetical Norwegian Word List that I at some point began compiling in a computer file. Regular reviewing—rereading and reviewing—would have helped my comprehension. I was too impatient.

Also, I could have compiled a list of problem words and where they could be found, so that I could regularly compare contexts and figure them out.

For instance, I see that on page 293 I have figured out that *ledd* means "generation," but not even ten pages later, on page 302, I seem to have forgotten all about that, and think that *ledd* means "layer." Of course, on some days, I must have been tired, or for some other reason not thinking clearly.

I should have copied new words into my Norwegian Word List at the end of every day's session of reading, so that I did not have to learn them all over again.

SOME OF THE WORDS, PHRASES, AND
EXPRESSIONS I ENCOUNTERED

The strange little word *og*, meaning "and," is not unlike the Dutch *ook* and the German *auch*, both of which mean "also." But how did it come to mean "and," whereas the Germans have *und*, so much closer to our word?

What about the dropped *w* in their *ord*, "word"—or is it that we added the *w*? There is another case of it: *orm* for "snake," like our *worm* but without the *w*. I look up both word histories: back in the proto-Germanic, where both have their source, the *w* was present.

Some words I became quite fond of, without knowing why: *tvil*, for "doubt." The sound, the modesty? Did it remind me of the material (in English), twill?

Another pair I liked, so short, so economical, so cheerful: *hit*, *dit*, meaning "hither," "thither." This pair made me think again about the *h-*, *th-*, *wh-*sets in English, something I always like to think about: the most common set is *here*, *there*, *where*—words we use all the time. A matching set is *hence*, *thence*, *whence*—of this set, we use *hence* quite often, but less often the other two; and all three have a slightly precious sound to them now. And the last (or is there another?) would be: *hither*, *thither*, *whither*—these we never, or very rarely, use, except in *hitherto* (even more precious). Oh, there is a fourth, or part of a fourth: *therefore*, *wherefore*. *That* and *what* are probably part of another set, the third member of which is not *hat*. Now that I go on thinking about them, I remember some combined forms: *thereupon*, *whereupon*; *thereof*, *whereof* (the Norwegian equivalent of which is *hvorav*); *heretofore*; *thereafter*, *hereafter*, *herein*, *therein*, *wherein*.

The Norwegian for *throw* is *kaste*, which of course is cognate with our *cast*. And our *cast* was once more commonly used than it is now. *Cast* has declined in use, certainly in the casual use meaning "throw." Although *kaste* and *cast* share a very early source, *throw* would appear, I think, to be a very old word, too. I look up the answers: *cast* comes from Old Norse *kasta*, "to throw"; *throw* comes from Old English *thrawan*, "to twist," or "turn." That's a surprise. Early on, then, the idea of *throw* had, it seems, an element of twisting in it; to throw was to cast with a twist.

Sometimes a Norwegian expression that is the same as one in English will yield a few new words: for instance, on page 115, I was reading a passage describing the extreme poverty of one Johannes, who, despite this, managed to marry "up"—a priest's daughter. In the passage, I was pleased to come upon the expression *blakk som en kirkerotte*. I knew *kirke* (Sc. *kirk*), so it wasn't hard to guess "poor as a church-mouse," or maybe *rotte* is "rat," and their expression is slightly different. On page 134, reading the story of Torhild, the hardworking widow who is so fond of her pipeful of tobacco, I encounter the same expression as ours: she *røyker som en skorstein*—"smokes like a chimney."

Abbreviations: these can be a challenge. Again, context helps. If Solstad is about to give some examples of something, and precedes his remarks by *f.eks.*, I can guess that *eks.* is short for *eksempel*. I tend to pronounce it, in my head, with a certain pleasure, "fecks." Others, harder, are *dvs.* = *det vil si* = that will say = in other words; and *bl.a.* = *blant annen* = among others. And there were two that I think he might have made up. Two men he was discussing had the same names. Tired of writing out "the older" and "the younger," he abbreviated them *d.e.* and *d.y.*

Sometimes—on page 356, for instance—he describes what he means by a word and therefore defines it for me. I was in doubt about the word *venner*, though I had some guesses. These *venner* acted as godparents to the child of a young couple. Then he went on to describe who they might have been: "not relatives, either on Anlaug's or on Anders's side, but *venner*, people they could *stole* on ["count on"?], without being in the same family, we must assume. . . . People they had met, often married couples in the same generation, through the fact that they were, like them, *leilendinger* ["occupiers of rented property"?] and *husmenn* ["farm managers"?]." *Venner* = friends.

In other cases, he will say the same thing in two ways, and therefore allow me to learn a new word. A clear and simple example of this is his introduction of the word *oldemor* on page 130: *min mormor Birgithe Andersdatters mor, min oldemor*—"my grandmother Birgithe Andersdatter's mother, my great-grandmother." Farther along in the same sentence, since this *oldemor* marries him, I learn the word *oldefar*. Later in the book, in the same way, I learn the perky-sounding term for yet one further generation back: *tippoldemor* for "great-great-grandmother."

Another example is the word *eneste*, or "only one," which is clearly "taught" in the following sentence, the second part of which in effect repeats or enlarges upon the first: "Halvor Johannesson did not marry again; his marriage as a young man, aged twenty, to a widow who was more than forty years older than he, remained his *eneste*."

SPEAKING OF HALVOR JOHANNESSON: A DIGRESSION ABOUT THE NAMES IN THE BOOK

The ancestors, or characters, in Solstad's book are always at some point identified by their full names, and they always have three—unless, exceptionally, they have four, some people having two "first" names. There is the given name—Halvor, for example—the choice of which is ruled by several principles that I won't go into, except to say, about these principles, that Solstad was sometimes able to use them to make useful deductions about relationships and lineage from studying a first name; and that there existed a curious custom, which was that the first son born to a widow who remarried would generally be named after her previous husband.

As for the middle name, it was always "son of" or "daughter of" plus the father's name. This, of course, conveniently allows a genealogist to make a good guess as to who the male parent was.

The last name was the name of the place where the person was born or where he or she now lived. So, interestingly, although the first and middle names did not usually change during the person's lifetime, the last name might change, if the person moved, and might even change more than once, if the person moved several times. This, too, gives the genealogist clues as to where the person was living at the time of a baptism or marriage, or, in some cases, with which place a person chose to identify him- or herself.

Thus, these three-part names identified individuals quite thoroughly, in three different ways.

Last names became fixed in at least one family line, Solstad says, in the second half of the nineteenth century. Why then? Why not before, and why not after? What also changed, at about that time, was that middle names might be given for no other reason than that the parents liked them, as happens here in our country, now.

DIFFICULTIES

Certain phrases I stumbled over every time, because they were counterintuitive: one was *en eller annen*. I figured out that it meant "one or another," but the fact that *en* meant "one" or "a" and *eller* was a longer word meant that I kept thinking, first, that it meant "an *eller*," *eller* meaning some kind of a thing. Or I thought *eller* was an adjective modifying *annen*, "an *eller* sort of *annen*," Right up to the end of the book, I stumbled over that, even though I knew it.

In June, I thought *skiftet* meant "funeral." But in November, I decided it meant something like "will," though by the end of the book I still wasn't sure what it meant, because there were contexts in which both "funeral" and "will" made sense, but others in which those words did not. Maybe it had more than one meaning. *Skiftet ut*, for instance, was a fate about to be suffered by a couple of horses in one story, who were included in the farm bought by the hardworking Peder, or Per, Håkonsson Moen and were apparently too old to continue pulling the plow and the carriage—they would probably be "traded out"—in other words, gotten rid of.

Later still, I decided that one meaning of *skifte* had to be "change."

I tended to keep mixing up pairs of words that looked somewhat alike, such as, at first, *også* and *altså*, later *enda* and *ennå*, *våre* and *værre*, *enke* and *ekte*, *vist* and *visst*, *skjedde* and *skjebne*, *jul* ("Christmas") and *juli* ("July"), *nettopp* and *neppe*, *må*, *mål*, *måle*, *mat*, *måte*, *måten*, *måtte*. To a Norwegian, these words are miles apart in meaning, perhaps; it's laughable to mix them up. But I mixed them up because, after all, the first thing you encounter, looking at a page of unfamiliar language, is not the meaning but the appearance of the words, the way they look.

Trying to learn, or to be sure of, the word *mat*, which I think means "meal," as I read my way into the beginning of another book of Solstad's, an earlier novel called *Armand V.: fotnoter til en uutgravd roman* (*Armand V.: Footnotes to an Unexcavated Novel*), I compare the *mat* in a student cafeteria to the *mat* in the Telemark novel's story of the wandering (and fugitive) Swede—the *kvelds-mat(en)* during which he dies very suddenly—to make sure I'm not mixing this word up with another of those *m*-words. (There is also, in another story, *mat* and *drikke* flowing freely at a wedding feast in the year 1684 that ends in a fatal stabbing.) (Of course, our English cognate would be *meat*.)

The story of the fugitive comes late in the novel: a Swedish miner who is on the run because of a murder he has committed is in the home of strangers, eating his evening meal (*kveld-maten*), when he drops dead. They lay him out in the *koven* (I'm not sure what that is—maybe an alcove?). The next day, his wife finds her way to the house, asks if they have seen a wandering Swede, hears the news, and shrieks.

At the sound of her cry, her husband comes back to life and appears in the doorway.

As you struggle to learn something difficult, you are constantly aware of the limits of your brain's strength, agility, alertness, etc. You look at a word—*ser*, for instance—and you know you know it, but you can't recall it. Where is its meaning, in your brain, and where are you, in your brain, as you try to find that meaning? It comes to you after a while, or you come to it, somewhere in there. In fact, it means "see."

Sometimes I "get" the word, I know what it means, but a perceptible few seconds go by before the equivalent English word comes to me (in the latest case, it was *confirm*). I experience this as quite physical, when it happens: the understanding is there, somewhere nearby in my brain, I am in touch with it, but it is still unarticulated, still formless or inchoate; then a connection is made, and the English word appears.

It took me quite a long time to realize that *andre* meant more than just "other" or "another" (G. *andere*), as in *ene etter den andre*, "one after another." It could not mean "other" in the sentence "she was his other wife"—since the early Norwegians were not polygamous. Eventually, I understood that it could also mean "second." Another example:

Hun var 47 år. Hun ventet på sin andre ektemann. På mannen.

Translation: "She was forty-seven years old. She was waiting for her second husband. For a husband."

This occurred in a nice little story about a widow and a carpenter. A widow hires an itinerant carpenter, Ole Olson, to build something for her on her farm. He is there for several days, does good work, and she evidently takes a liking to him. When the job is done and the time comes for him to leave, she packs him a substantial lunch to take with him. He goes on his way. When, after an hour or so, he grows hungry and stops in a clearing in the woods to see what she has packed for him, he finds, gleaming behind the sausages and other food, the key to the *stabbur* (which I first thought meant "cupboard," then "storeroom"). He understands the message, turns around and rides back, and she is standing there waiting for him. They marry, etc. This was in the year 1678.

But, says Solstad, the real sensation (*sensasjonen*) happens two years later, when the hitherto childless forty-nine-year-old gives birth for the first time. Almost a virgin birth, he nearly said—says the narrator of the novel, or Solstad—but kept it to himself (he says). (Another interesting narrative trick.)

I am sometimes slowed down by the French words in my head, like *vide*, "empty," when I try to understand *utvidt*, *ut-vidt*. It is not "emptied out," but "extended" (out + widened).

It is hard for me not to read *det* as always meaning "that"— and often enough it does mean "that." Many of Solstad's sentences begin with *Det er*. *Er* means (conveniently) both "is" and "are." So I would like, always, to read *det er* as "that is," or "it is." But *det* also means "there," and often enough Solstad is saying "there are." As in English, one word can have several meanings, and one phrase can have several meanings. But whereas I take this for granted in English and am completely used to it, it surprises and frustrates me when I am trying to learn a new language.

For means "for," which is easy enough. But it also—when it wants to—means "too." *Få* means "have," but it can also mean "few."

Something I learn about the word *penger*: In the Telemark novel, since so many of the historical records concern financial transactions, I encounter the word *penger* (*peng* + the suffix *-er*, the indefinite plural) over and over, and I always understand it as "coins" rather than what it also is: "money." That is, in the contexts in which it appears—sales of property, wills, etc.—I read it as something concrete, whereas the more usual translation would be something I see as more abstract—"money."

I do not know this until I am watching a Norwegian movie with subtitles. A character says *penger* and the subtitle reads "money." (Here, by watching this movie and reading the subtitles, I am again bending or modifying just a little my "no-help" rules.)

In all this reading and studying, I am also watching how the brain works—or, sometimes, doesn't work. My brain opted for the concrete, coins, over the abstract, money.

WHAT THE WORDS I LEARNED TOLD ME ABOUT ENGLISH

The revelations were not only about Norwegian, but also about the roots it shares with English. From reading this book, and from learning some Norwegian, my English words became at once newly strange, and richer.

When I learned *svar*, I glimpsed the source of the ghostly presence, the unpronounced *w*, in our *an-swer*. I knew *neighbor* was related to *nigh*, "near"; when I learned that the Norwegian *bor* meant "dwell," I could see *neigh-bor* for what it is: one who (for better or worse) lives nearby.

I learn the Norwegian word for *bells*: *klokker*. I say to myself: that looks so much like the English *clock*! And the German for *bells* is rather similar—*Glocken*. Did our English *clock* once upon a time mean "bell"? And could that have been because we told the time from listening to the church bells? And what about the nautical way of identifying the time: eight bells, etc.? I haven't yet put it all together.

I learned, or relearned, *klokker* in the story of Erik Sakeson's suicide, since the church bells (*kirkeklokker*) rang loudly at his funeral, and were heard by a woman imprisoned on the other side of a mountain, and the sound of the church bells gave her hope, though I am not sure why (since some words were missing for me) or why she was imprisoned.

MEASURING MY PROGRESS IN COMPREHENSION

PAGE 78 I noted on June 15 that as I read on in the book, I would turn back to the first page now and then, to see if I understood more. By about page 78, I could read and understand almost the whole of that page, missing only a few words.

PAGE 226 By page 226, I could sometimes read two pages in half an hour.

PAGE 346 By page 346 (eighty pages from the end), I could read many sentences "fluently" without stumbling. True enough (*riktig nok*), there were almost always a few words I could not figure out. But more and more rarely did I find myself caught for a moment in a small thicket of impenetrable language.

PAGE 426 On January 12, 2015, I finished the book.

But in late January, unable to break my habit, I began another novel by Solstad, the one called *Armand V.*, consisting of footnotes to a nonexistent novel. I had not planned to read it, but one morning I simply opened it out of curiosity and read the first page. Then I went on.

MARKS ON THE PAGE (CONT.):
CHARACTERISTICS OF SOLSTAD'S WRITING

In addition to marking names of characters (from the beginning), dates of events (irregularly starting halfway through the book), words I learned (starting on page 161), material that interested me (now and then, from the beginning), along with, beginning on page 92, the date of that day's reading, I also noted the following:

on page 129, a particular sentence rhythm of Solstad's;

on page 132, how he tells a story;

on page 142, an exclamation of his;

on page 145, a comment about what we know about the characters' lives versus what they knew;

on page 151, a shift in his narrative mode as he explains something in a different way;

and, on succeeding pages, to the end of the book: his changes of pace; variation of short, very short, long, and very long sentences; use of refrains; inclusion of the reader with the word *our*; occasional English words; specificity; speculations; invitation down false trails; rare information about the larger historical context; frustration that he can't write something here if he does not know for certain that it is true; a single account of visiting an ancestral site for his research; a decision not to investigate something, a thing which, he decided, like so much else, "shall remain lying untold in darkness."

One recurring feature of his style was his use of repetition—of facts, epithets, opening phrases purely for the rhythm of the sentence ("Fortunate were those . . . Fortunate were those . . ."). For me, this repetition became a truly lyrical sort of drill, of the words and phrases I was learning, but I was also more and more aware, as I struggled less with the language, of its rhetorical beauty.

THINKING AS I WAS READING

I realized, now and then, that because my attention was mostly on learning the language, I was not reading the book with the wider, and deeper, and more thoughtful attention with which I would have read it in English: I was not absorbing it effortlessly while at the same time thinking about it, as I would have been doing in English. Because my brain was so busy trying to understand it, in the most basic way, I did not tend to remember much, from page to page.

I was not trying to keep track of the family lines, or the relationships. I was not trying to remember the characters, especially since, usually, we would be moving on and leaving them behind quite soon. Although I was very interested in it, and planned to think about it later, I was only occasionally

thinking about the form of Solstad's novel, what he was doing, why he was doing it, what effect it had.

But, increasingly, I did stop to think about it, and now
that I've read it, I can think more.

SOME WAYS IN WHICH HIS BOOK IS DIFFERENT
FROM A CONVENTIONAL NOVEL

From the beginning, I was curious about whether this book
would change as it went on, and also whether it would eventually feel to me like a novel. But what interested me most,
at first, were the ways in which it was not like a conventional
novel.

For one thing, it was not the author, but fate, that determined the plotlines. Solstad then decided in what order to
organize and narrate them, and how to present them. Solstad
refused to fictionalize, tempted though he sometimes was
(page 392: "I burn to tell about that"). The principal material in the book seems to have been the information collected
by his cousin's son. Solstad set himself the challenge of writing a "novel" that was entirely nonfiction.

So, then, all the premises shift, concerning what is dramatically or narratively interesting or important: because so
much is unknown to Solstad himself, or to anyone, since the
plot turns may happen quite unexpectedly, with no fore-
warning, we learn to have no expectations. And these sudden turns of event cannot be seen as artistically arbitrary or
gratuitous, because we know they did happen.

Solstad is able to conjure up a character's life working only
with the traces left behind: if a child was five when his mother
remarried, and seven when his mother then died, Solstad
can imagine that these were difficult years for the child. He

can state this plainly, and the child comes to life dramatically. Reading this book confirmed for me that it is possible to create dramatic interest using just the few "dry" facts at hand, combined with the author's distinct voice and strong style.

I find it very affecting to be given a fragment of a story and know it is true. At the same time as the meanings of the words I am reading become clear, or remain obscure, the characters in the book appear suddenly and disappear just as suddenly. But while they are here, they are fully present, and all the more striking because the rest of their lives "shall remain lying untold hidden in darkness," as Solstad says.

There was something eerie about the events of the book, because they seemed to have been fated to happen just as they did happen—but fated only in retrospect. For instance, there is the case of the German ancestor who enters on page 367. We meet him as he is crossing a lake on his way to church on the Sunday following Trinity Sunday. But no sooner do we welcome him into the story, prepare to remember him, to see him developed, to witness the ups and downs of his life, than, in the next sentence, he falls overboard (the words are hard to mistake: *faller over bord*), drowns, and disappears forever—from his own life, from future historical records, and, quite soon, from this story.

Because this German, Lauritz Türninger, drowned, and because the officials recorded this, we know his name and what he was doing on that particular day. And when he died, he left behind a son, so that—not at the moment he drowned, but in time, after his children had children, and after those children in turn produced further generations— he came to be an ancestor of Solstad's.

Or, because a boundary was revised in 1887, and because this boundary change was recorded, and certain families were living in the vicinity of the change, and their names were recorded, we know what we otherwise would not have known—where the little foster child Bergit, eleven years old, was living in the year 1887, this child who was not yet, in that year, but would grow up to become, Solstad's grandmother.

A RECURRING THEME: THESE ARE HIS ANCESTORS; AND THE CHANCE EVENTS THAT RESULT IN A PERSON BECOMING HIS ANCESTOR

I sometimes forget, for a while, that these are his ancestors. Then he reminds me not only of that, but of the strangeness of how haphazard it all is: for instance, at the top of page 142, how a financial calculation on the part of one man—a father choosing a suitable husband for each of his daughters—causes another man (and thus, with him, a whole widely branching line of previous generations) to become part of Solstad's own lineage.

THE PLOT OF SOLSTAD'S OWN INVESTIGATIONS: HOW HE DISCOVERS WHAT HE KNOWS

There are the story lines of the various characters he tells us about; but there is also another story line that appears and disappears, the story of his own investigations, what he is able to find out and what he is not able to find out, what he guesses or assumes or doubts.

What I learn from this is something I had already suspected: how interesting the tale of the investigation itself can be. It solves another problem I had been facing in my own project, the project that was the impetus for reading Solstad's book in the first place: that the investigation that I would carry out, with all the small dramas of its mysteries and solutions, hints and discoveries, would be more engrossing than any neat presentation of the results, as formulated in the eventual book. Now I see that the investigation itself should also be written into the book.

ANOTHER STORY LINE, ONE THAT DOESN'T APPEAR VERY OFTEN: HOW THIS BOOK WAS SHAPED

Another story line consists of Solstad's thoughts and plans about how to shape the novel itself, what to include when and where. It arises every so often, though rarely, and when it does, it brings me as a reader actively into partnership with him, as I witness him deliberate on how he will shape this novel I am reading.

THE STRAIGHT FACTUAL ENLIVENED NOT ONLY BY EXCLAMATIONS AND OBSERVATIONS, BUT ALSO BY BRIEF DRAMATIC STORIES

Solstad offers detailed facts about births, deaths, marriages, and property transactions for many pages at a time, unenlivened by any drama, but I tolerate it, partly because of the ongoing excitement of learning the language, but also because I sense the animating spark of Solstad's strong emotion and personality, and because I am moved by the very style of the writing, which I can perceive even from the beginning, when I do not understand many words.

Can I, too, be exact and factual, detailed and meticulous, about fairly dry data throughout certain passages of the book I have in mind, and will a reader tolerate that? (Can I, in fact, come to think of it, be a little too detailed at certain points in this present essay, about words that were exciting for me to learn, but are perhaps not exciting for a reader to hear about, and can I perhaps go on for too long, and yet rescue myself with certain other passages?)

Because so much of the text is in this sense "dry," the moments in which there is imagery or a sustained dramatic narrative enter the novel with heightened vividness. There is, for instance, the story of "Pipe-Torhild," who at the age of twenty-seven was left a widow with a two-year-old son, and who was remembered in later years for two things—her industry and the fact that she smoked a pipe. She managed two farms on her own, and, according to the stories people told, she would wake up in the morning on one farm and milk the *dyra* ("animals") there before walking the long distance to the other, where she went out into the fields and scythed the day's portion of grain before walking back to the first farm and doing the evening chores. This was in 1680.

Or the story of "the great (or fearsome)" Halvor Borgja hanging his red hat in the window to deceive his workers, and the decline in the fortunes of his family in later years, down upon which Solstad wishes Borgja could have gazed, from up among the *skyer*.

THE END OF SOLSTAD'S BOOK—AND THE REACHING BACK OVER THE GENERATIONS

Close to the end of the book, on page 401, Solstad recounts the one memory his mother had of her grandfather. And this single vivid memory on the part of Solstad's mother, of her grandfather—the only memory she has of him—is enough to bring him to life, for Solstad and thus, in turn, for me as reader. Of his great-grandfather, he says, he has this one "wholly concrete picture," the oldest he has of any of his ancestors.

"My mother sees her old grandfather go *målbevisst* away to a barrel with *sild* that stands *gjemt* under a roof of *skrot* in the *fjoset*, or some such. She sees the old man lift the barrel, with a strength-*anstrengelse*, and drink from it. She sees him set it down and turn his face directly toward her, the little nine-year-old granddaughter. She sees that the *silde*-fat is running down his face. Just that. That is what she remembers. And that is the picture of the ancestors. Of my great-grandfather, and all his ancestors."

THE END OF THE BOOK—AND THE IMPORTANCE OF DETAIL

The memory that Solstad's mother had of her grandfather is the sort of ordinary memory we all have in great numbers in our minds—of small incidents and encounters, odd and fragmentary. It doesn't matter that the moment was undramatic, even completely inconsequential. In fact, that may make it all the more effective, because the memory is taken from ordinary, everyday life and thus makes that everyday life seem very present, very close. What matters is that it is concrete, and detailed, and thus vivid—that one moment seems to prove that Solstad's great-grandfather existed, in flesh and blood.

THE END OF THE BOOK—FLESH AND BLOOD

Solstad, after starting with the remote ancestors in 1591, at the end of the book comes all the way down to his grandmother (married in 1896), with whom he spends time when he is a child. He sees her in person, and listens to her talk, and watches her. It is satisfying to us, the readers, after having witnessed so many of his ancestors from afar, active in very small portions of their lives, to be in the presence of a living forebear of his. The little girl who emerged from the mists of the past through her birth date and the facts of the place where she lived, just as so many other ancestors of Solstad's emerged, for a moment, only to slip back into obscurity, now stays in the present, remains visible, sits by the window and watches the highway.

IS THE BOOK A NOVEL?

In my effort simply to read it and find out what is in it, for a long time I put aside the larger question of whether I would consider this book a novel. Or rather, I did return to it now and then, but did not concentrate very hard on it. Actually, I did sometimes concentrate hard on it, but I could not arrive at a definition of a novel that would include this one, until I did arrive at such a definition, but was left a little unsatisfied by it.

It is already an unusual book. For a novel, it is even more unusual.

The fact that Dag Solstad chose to call this a novel has been much discussed in Norway. About half the critics admired the book and its unique project, and the book was nominated for several important prizes. The other half were provoked or bored, and could not see how this could be called a novel—along came that comparison to a telephone directory. It also added fuel to the larger debate in Norway about what a novel is or can be.

The debate must already have been well underway since the publication of Karl Ove Knausgaard's long autobiographical novel. That novel is not as purely factual as Solstad's, or I should say as dryly factual, or as well documented. But it does claim not to have invented anything; all of its contents, if one makes allowances for undependable memory, are taken from Knausgaard's own life. If we think a novel needs to include stories, that one certainly does, and it is also one larger continuous story—as, really, the Solstad Telemark novel is, too.

Apparently Solstad and his editor did not talk about the question of genre. Nor, apparently, did those in the publishing house discuss it among themselves. They simply saw the book as truly original and groundbreaking, and were prepared for the fact that it might not be a book to everyone's taste. It has its many devoted fans. One Norwegian friend said she was completely obsessed by it last winter—she read it all and was sad to finish it. Readers in Norway feel that the book is written in Solstad's characteristic style, even if the material is unusual. My Norwegian friend feels that the way Solstad sequences the facts and the way he handles them, along with his interjections and the rhythms of his prose, make it very much a characteristic novel of his.

I mentioned the novel to an editor here (American), and he said he had heard Solstad read from it last fall and there was something mesmerizing about the language. About the question of whether it is a novel, he said that the project itself seemed like an interesting challenge, how to narrate factually and yet get "the lift of fiction." After he said this, I thought about the word *lift*, since it seemed he was pointing out something that fiction might give and that nonfiction might not give. I would interpret *lift* to mean a sort of transcendence: we are lifted out of our lives, imaginatively, into another realm, perhaps a realm full of surprises, either factual surprises, or stylistic ones, or emotional ones. Perhaps Solstad's treatment of his material, in a "novelistic" sort of way, and with his own characteristic stylistic turns, and his injection of his own passion, give it, in the end, the "lift" of fiction.

I've been told that Solstad does not see himself as a historian, but as a novelist. And this leads, as several paths lead, to what I feel, for now anyway, is one definition that could include this book as a novel. It is perhaps too basic, or too simplistic. It is that if an author feels, and declares, that his or her book is a novel, then that is enough to define it as a novel—of some sort. To qualify that a little: If an author truly sees and intends his or her book as a novel, then it is some variety of novel, and it is up to the reader, or critic, to figure out in what way it can be seen as a novel. I believe this, for the time being anyway.

OTHER THOUGHTS AS I READ

Was my Solstad-Norwegian language project a misguided one? Should I not have been doing it? Did I not have other things I had planned to do? What things will I now never do because I did this? But, on the other hand: Which projects are a "waste of time," anyway? The projects one had not planned to do? But does such a thing as a waste of one's time even exist? Or, in a larger sense, in the end, is not everything in one's life equal—whether washing a floor, figuring out a page of Norwegian, or writing something one had promised to write, or talking to a neighbor for an hour on a winter afternoon about the risks involved in continuing to take certain medications?

The homeliest thought: I see, as I pursue this project, how, doing a little each day, if it is done regularly, adds up to a lot. (There are many mottoes to this effect.)

I am still trying to figure out whether a beginner in a language understands a surprising amount, considering she knew so little a year ago, or whether she understands vastly little. Or maybe, contradictorily, the answer must be: both. In other words, I'm surprised that with an accumulation of a quantity of fairly basic vocabulary, including those so-important, so-revealing prefixes and suffixes, I can read and understand so much of not only the Telemark novel, by now, but also the other Solstad novel I am reading, *Armand V.* But on the other hand, I'm aware of how much I am missing, on every level, and must necessarily miss, without years of study and a wide range of reading, and, preferably, some time living in Norway and conversing with Norwegians.

Now that I've read the book, if I were to try to have a conversation in Norwegian, my vocabulary and idioms, and my syntax, too, would be almost entirely limited to what I know from this one book. Aside from whatever few scraps have remained in my head from last year's *Mikke Mus* and *Mo i mørket*, and more recently the poetry of Olav Hauge, I wouldn't know anything beyond this material and this way of speaking about it, or this way of speaking, period. Conversing with a Norwegian, I could say that my son had the strength of a bear—*har krefter som en bjørn*—as Solstad says of the hardworking Peder Moen, *hammermester* and farmer, or that my husband had plowed a field with his grandfather behind two horses (which he did, as a child). But I could not talk about the internet, or airplane travel, high-rise buildings, streetcars, or many other things.

It also occurred to me, as I bent over my thin pencil scratches on the handsome pages of the book, that we read selfishly—and we read in whatever way we choose. The author has no say in how we approach the book and what we do with it. He controls his creation while he creates it, but then, when it is published, he must abandon control of it. In this case, for example, Solstad might object to my reading it without understanding all of it. He might also object to my marking every page with my own discoveries and ideas. He might object to my being just as interested in learning the language as I am in the book itself and how he has conceived and written it. He might object to my telling some of the most dramatic stories here in this essay, out of context. And more.

A somewhat desolate thought, though a familiar one and inflected by resignation: Because most publishers these days are usually reluctant to publish a book that may not sell in great numbers, the most innovative and adventurous—and therefore the most "difficult" to read and to sell—contemporary literature, including Solstad's Telemark novel, may never appear in English. So the fiction writers of the world who read only English, or only English as their second language, but no other foreign language, such as Norwegian (or Icelandic, or Faroese), will be denied the vital stimulation of reading the most avant-garde work of many, many other cultures. And there are only so many languages we can try to learn in order to read the books that will not be translated into our own language.

I'm thinking about words all the time as I continue this project (continue, because I'm reading another novel by Solstad). Words on their own. Words in sentences. The histories and changing meanings of words. I occasionally return to some very basic, mathematical thoughts: There are only so many letters in our Roman alphabet. It is then by the power of the math—the infinite (or not strictly infinite, but huge) number of combinations of letters—that we have so many words. But then, further expanding the number of possibilities, truly to infinity, one word (one combination of letters) can have multiple meanings. Further multiplying the number of meanings, even within one given dictionary definition of a word, is the effect of its context, both immediate and larger, which can endow it with, again, an infinite number of subtly differing shades of meaning. Further enriching the single word, within and beyond its contexts, is one's own personal associations with it, either from one's reading or from one's life experiences.

I copied out these two words, recently, which I did not know and still have not looked up, from an American novel of the twentieth century: *temulent* and *succedaneum*. Even in one's own native language, there are a great many words, meanings, and shades of meaning that one simply doesn't know and may never encounter.

2015

Reading a Gunnhild Øyehaug Story
in Nynorsk

After writing about my "translation" of the children's classic *Bob, Son of Battle* (aka *Owd Bob: The Grey Dog of Kenmuir*) into easier English, I heard from an emeritus professor and scholar of Danish history who retained a fond schoolboy memory—a bright spot in a generally bleak school experience—of listening, rapt, every Sunday evening as the book was read aloud to him and his schoolmates by their otherwise cruel and capricious headmaster.

In the course of our ensuing correspondence, I mentioned to him that I had been attempting to learn Norwegian. I thought that as a Dane he might be interested. I had for the moment forgotten the rivalrous history shared by the countries. He advised me against continuing, warning that the project would be especially daunting because Norway has in fact two languages, the older Bokmål, most widely used, and the nineteenth-century Nynorsk, devised in an attempt to re-create a form of the language as it might have been without four hundred years of, in fact, Danish influence. Fifteen percent of the population do use Nynorsk, I discovered, and it is said to lend itself particularly well to poetic expression.

Notwithstanding my correspondent's advice, I went on with my self-imposed and perhaps misguided project—to make my way word by word, regardless of how much I understood, through the whole of Dag Solstad's "Telemark novel," abiding by the resolution with which I had begun the project: to decipher what I could using only the clues contained within the narrative, the words and phrases themselves and their functions within the sentences. I was gaining proficiency with each page.

When the time came for me to set off on a brief trip to speak at a college on the West Coast, I did not want to stop reading Norwegian. By then I had become very attached to my daily immersion in the tales, some quite dramatic, all curiously entrancing, of Solstad's ancestors in distant Telemark. But the handsome hardcover was too heavy to take along. I had been waiting hopefully for the arrival of a packet of more of Solstad's novels, sent by a friend in Norway, but it did not come in time. I would have preferred to continue with the same author—I did not know if I was ready for a whole new vocabulary and a different style of writing. However, I looked to see what else I had.

Among several in my "Norwegian" pile was a slim paperback collection of stories called *Knutar* (*Knots*) by a young Bergen writer, Gunnhild Øyehaug, whom I remembered as one of the quieter ones in a group of writers assembled for a harborside fish dinner in the old Hanseatic city last autumn. The trouble with trying to pick out a book to read in a language you don't really know is that although you can decipher some opening sentences, you can't cast your eye casually down the pages and get a sense of the whole book.

I could see right away, though, from certain differences in the language, that the book was written, not in the Bokmål I had become somewhat used to, but in Nynorsk. Many of the words were the same (*han* for "he"), and many more were quite close (*ikkje* instead of *ikke* for "not"), though others were strange (not *hun* for "she," but *ho*). Yet I believed I would be able to understand it. There was plenty of overlap in basic vocabulary, and, fortunately, repetition is a stylistic feature of Øyehaug's writing, as it is of Solstad's—very helpful to the beginning language student.

But the content of the stories turned out to be a little racier than Dag Solstad's. In his novel, for instance, a man gets into a fight at a wedding feast after drinking too much and kills another guest, is eventually brought to trial, sentenced, and beheaded. Solstad does not refer to letters or diaries, and may not have consulted any, but rather seems to have worked from church records (*kirkeboka*) and legal documents, and he chooses not to imagine his way into the bedrooms of his characters unless the "long arm of the law" (*lovens lange arm*) has already entered.

On the first leg of the flight west, I took out book and pencil and settled in to my reading, doing my best to ignore the rather agreeably busy life around me—my tattooed seatmate, absorbed in her iPad; nearby laptops displaying mostly food programs; the tiny "emotional support" dog snuffling under my seat; the flight attendant backing away down the aisle calling out "Water? Water? Water? Water? Water?" One of the first stories I read also seemed to include a killing, maybe even a double murder. Since I was missing some of the words, perhaps the crime happened only in the mind of the hero, Frans. But along the way, to my surprise—since the meanings came to me so slowly—I found myself accompanying him into the *bade*, where he gets into the *dusje* (cognate Fr. *douche*) and *onanerer* (at first I thought this meant that his mind was wandering) while imagining an encounter in the basement laundry room with the seventeen-year-old *jenta* from the *etasje under* (Fr. *étage* + Eng. *under*). (Which, we learn later, causes his perceptive girlfriend to become *sjalu* [Fr. *jaloux*].)

I changed planes in Las Vegas, walking past the banks of flashing slot machines, though spotting only perhaps one or two of the desperate gamblers I had imagined seeing. I belted myself in for the short connecting flight, and went on reading, this time a story that was more my sort of thing: Grandmother stands by the kitchen window (*kjøkkenvind-auget*) on her ninetieth birthday and stares up at the mountain (*fjellet*) that looms over her *små hus*, deciding finally not to open the door to her seven children (*sju barn*) and her many more grandchildren (*barnebarn*), who are descending upon her to celebrate.

That evening, in the hotel room, after making a different sort of linguistic mistake—having misunderstood the label on the slim tube of *crema de afeitar* picked up on an earlier trip, I found myself brushing my teeth with shaving cream—I lay in bed continuing to read Øyehaug's book, which I was by now enjoying and admiring: every story a formal surprise, smart and droll. Outside, beyond the pocket-size balcony, were tall palm trees; down below in the courtyard, the voices of a few guests enjoying a hot tub, though the November air seemed chilly to me; within the room, the other odd sounds of a strange hotel, always somewhat the same, always a little different—the steady hum of a ventilator fan, the ping of the minifridge cycling on or off, the intermittent, ragged coughing from the other side of the wall.

I thought ahead to the translation seminar the next day. I would probably mention to the eager students—as I always imagine them—how one language opens the door to another, Spanish to Portuguese, Dutch to Afrikaans, Norwegian to Swedish, Danish, Icelandic, and even Faroese. I would probably not mention the shaving cream, the soapy taste of which still lingered in my mouth.

2015

ON TRANSLATION
AND
MADAME BOVARY

Buzzing, Humming, or Droning: Notes on Translation and *Madame Bovary*

BOUFFÉES D'AFFADISSEMENT

Not long ago, I was chatting with an older friend who is a retired engineer and also something of a writer, but not of fiction. When he heard that I had just finished a translation of *Madame Bovary*, he said something like, "But *Madame Bovary* has already been translated. Why does there need to be another translation?" or "But *Madame Bovary* has been available in English for a long time, hasn't it? Why would you want to translate it again?" Often, the idea that there can be a wide range of translations of one text doesn't occur to people—or that a translation could be bad, very bad, and unfaithful to the original. Instead, a translation is a translation—you write the book again in English, on the basis of the French, a fairly standard procedure, and there it is, it's been done and doesn't have to be done again.

A new book that is causing excitement internationally will be quickly translated into many languages, like the Jonathan Littell book that won the Prix Goncourt two years ago, sensational in part because the story was told in the voice of a former Nazi SS officer who participated in the atrocities of the Holocaust. It was soon translated into English by a good translator, Charlotte Mandell, and if it isn't destined to endure much beyond the next few decades, it will probably never be translated into English again.

But in the case of a book that appeared more than 150 years ago, like *Madame Bovary*, and one that is an important landmark in the history of the novel, there is ample time, and some demand, for a number of different English versions. For one thing, the first editions of the original text may have been faulty, and over the years one or more corrected editions have been published, so that the earliest English translations no longer match the most accurate original. For another, the earliest translators (as was the case with the Willa and Edwin Muir rendering of Kafka) may have felt they needed to inflict subtle or not so subtle alterations on the style and even the content of the original so as to make it more acceptable to the Anglophone audience; and with the passing of time, we come to deem this a betrayal and ask for a more faithful version. And lastly, earlier versions may simply not be as good in other respects as they could be—let another translator have a try.

Each version will be quite distinct from all of the others. How many ways, for instance, has even a single phrase (*bouffées d'affadissement*) from *Madame Bovary* been translated:

> gusts of revulsion
> a kind of rancid staleness
> stale gusts of dreariness
> waves of nausea
> fumes of nausea
> flavorless, sickening gusts
> stagnant dreariness
> whiffs of sickliness
> waves of nauseous disgust

DANTE ON TRANSLATION

"Nothing which is harmonized by the bond of the Muses can be changed from its own to another language without having all its sweetness destroyed."

EVERY GENERATION NEEDS A NEW TRANSLATION

Wise people like to say: Every generation needs a new translation. It sounds good, but I don't believe it is necessarily so: if a translation is as fine as it can be, it may match the original in timelessness, too—it may deserve to endure. In fact, it may endure even if it is not all it should be in style and faithfulness. Although the C. K. Scott Moncrieff translation of Proust's *In Search of Lost Time* (aka *Remembrance of Things Past*) was written in an Edwardian English more dated, and more ornate, than Proust's own prose, and departed consistently from the French original, it had such conviction, on its own terms, and was so well written, if you liked a certain florid style, that it prevailed without competition for eighty years. (There was also, of course, the problem of finding a single individual to translate a four-thousand-page book—an individual who wouldn't die before finishing it, as Scott Moncrieff had. Translating Proust's novel into Norwegian brought fame, for her near-thirty-year labor, to Anne-Lisa Amadou, but English has yet to find a single individual willing to take this on again.)

But even though a superlative translation can achieve timelessness, that doesn't mean other translators shouldn't attempt other versions. The more the better, in the end.

ANOTHER PESSIMIST: AUDEN ON TRANSLATION

"When, as in pure lyric, a poet 'sings' rather than 'speaks,' he is rarely, if ever, translatable."

A SWARM OF FLIES

For a while I thought there were fourteen previous translations of *Madame Bovary*. Then I discovered more and thought there were eighteen. Then another was published a few months before I finished mine. Now I've heard that yet another will be coming out soon, so there will be at least twenty, maybe more that I don't know about.

It happened several times while I was doing the translation that I would open a newly discovered previous translation of *Madame Bovary* and my heart would sink. I would say to myself: Well, this is quite good! The work I'm doing may be pointless, after all! Then I would look more closely, and compare it to the original, and it would begin to seem less good. I would get to know it really well, and then it would seem quite inadequate.

For example, the following seems good enough, until I look at the original: "Ahead of them, a swarm of flies drifted along, humming in the warm air." But they were flitting (*voltigeait*), not drifting—a very different motion—and they were buzzing (*bourdonnant*), as flies do, not humming. ("Warm air" is not a problem.)

Another example concerning insects occurs on the last page of the novel in a different translation: "Cantharides beetles droned busily round the flowering lilies." Again, this seems fine until you check the French: *des cantharides bour-donnaient autour des lis en fleur.* Then you have to ask, why the gratuitous and rather clichéd addition of "busily," which personifies the beetles—especially when Flaubert was at such pains to eliminate metaphor wherever possible? And Flaubert is again using the verb *bourdonnaient*, for the noise made by the beetles. Is "drone" the best choice? Maybe; in this case, we need to pay more attention to the insect and less to the dictionaries, in order to decide on the best verb.

If a translation doesn't have obvious writing problems, it may seem quite all right at first glance, or even all the way through, if we don't look at the original. We readers, after all, quickly adapt to the style of a translator, stop noticing it, and get caught up in the author's story and vision of the world. And a great book is powerful enough to shine through a less than adequate translation. Unless we compare it to the original, we won't know what we're missing.

HALFWAY THERE

A badly written translation, we could imagine, has been abandoned in a state of transition. What is written is not natural English, it does not sound right, yet it now exists, and its very existence seems to justify it. It is certainly a translation of sorts, because it is no longer French—it is English. But it is not English as any gifted native English writer would write it.

It could be considered an earlier stage of a finished good translation. It needs some rewriting, some different vocabulary choices. But often it is left at that stage, and published.

ANOTHER INSECT

Nabokov, in his lecture on *Madame Bovary*, discusses one of the early descriptions in the book, of the interior of the room in which Charles, on a visit, finds Emma sewing on a summer day. He quotes from the Eleanor Marx Aveling translation, making his own alterations:

"Through the chinks of the wood the sun sent across the stone floor long fine rays that broke at the angles of the furniture and played upon the ceiling. On the table flies were walking up the glasses that had been used, and buzzing as they drowned themselves in the dregs of the cider." (The second sentence in the original: *Des mouches, sur la table, montaient le long des verres qui avaient servi, et bourdonnaient en se noyant au fond, dans le cidre resté.*) (And there is that verb, again, this time for the flies as they drown: *bourdonnaient.* And a third choice for translating it: "buzzing.")

Nabokov goes on to comment:

"Note the long fine sun rays through the chinks in the closed shutters, and the flies walking up the glasses (not 'crawling' as translators have it: flies do not crawl, they walk, they rub their hands)."

I was impressed, when I read this nearly thirty years ago—I was teaching a translation workshop and used passages from *Madame Bovary* to compare translations—by the care and objective, scientific precision of Nabokov the stylist and lepidopterist. I now paid more attention to flies. Certainly they seemed to walk. But what did it mean, to crawl, anyway? I looked up *crawl*—more than once—in my favorite old *Webster's Collegiate*. In crawling, the body must also be in contact with the surface, not just the feet.

Of necessity, we get to know our own language even better when we are translating. When we are writing our own work, our choices are less deliberate, more involuntary, at least in the first draft. It is our natural vocabulary that springs to mind. As we translate, it is not our own choice that confronts us, but the choice of another writer, and we must search more consciously for the right words with which to convey it. It is then that we summon all the so-called synonyms in our own language, in the hope of finding just the right one. For of course they are not exact equivalents, they are all a little different, with different origins and different registers.

When we write our own work, we can be spontaneously, thoughtlessly confusing, confusing by chance or accident. But when we translate, if we are confusing, we are deliberately confusing—which is all right only when we translate closely and faithfully a confusing original.

And when we translate, as opposed to when we read passively, we can't simply skip over the things in the original text that we don't understand.

COLLABORATING WITH THE DEAD

Madame Bovary is the first book I've translated that has already been translated many times into English. Since I looked again and again at about eleven of the other translations—a twelfth as I made changes for the paperback edition—I came to know them well.

It did occur to me from time to time, as I studied them—as I felt, in effect, surrounded by them as a group—that a group effort might be interesting. This translator is better informed than I am about French history (or rather, I later realized, looking more carefully, she found someone good to do her endnotes); that one is especially clever at dialogue; another seems to have a naturally rich vocabulary;

and yet another is a decent writer and might give a useful critique of the style of my version: together we might produce a wonderful translation. Of course, the earliest of us lived in the 1880s, and most of the others, too, have died by now.

INDEPENDENTLY WEALTHY

If a translator is poorly paid, she must work quickly in order to earn anything like a living. If she is well paid, she can work more slowly. The independently wealthy can work as slowly as they like on a translation.

On one book, one of Maurice Blanchot's interesting and difficult novels, I worked at a snail's pace, even though I was not independently wealthy, and later calculated that in translating that book I had earned about a dollar an hour—a good wage at various times in the nineteenth century.

FOR THE RECORD

I thought I had first read *Madame Bovary* in my teens or early twenties, but I wasn't sure. The answer to the question came via a strange coincidence that occurred at about the same time my translation of the novel appeared. I received an email from a woman who identified herself as the person who, with her husband, had bought the first house I owned. I was in my early thirties when the house changed hands. She told me that when she, in turn, came to sell the house, after living there twenty years (so that I was by then in my early fifties), she discovered an old journal of mine, and, she confessed, she had waited another ten years before contacting me (by now I'm in my early sixties). Would I like it back? Of course I would! (To me, the answer is obvious, but I have discovered that some people, strangely, are not interested in their past, and some are horrified by the very thought of reading an old letter of theirs.) When I read it, I found a list of the books I had read over the previous months, during which time I had turned twenty-three. There, in the list, was *Madame Bovary*. But, very disappointingly, although I had comments for some of the other books I said nothing about this one:

September 27, 1970.

For the record, as we like to say: I graduated in June, to my great surprise, in general; since then, the four months have slipped by with nothing substantial to show for them.

My position now, at the end of September, is this: a great uncertainty about future and jobs, and a rather pervasive depression about it.

To mention some reading so as not to let it slip away out of memory: two books by Céline, which are Journey to the End of the Night and Death on the Installment Plan. Gulliver's Travels, which I intend to re-read at some point. The Brothers Karamazov, Madame Bovary, Oliver Twist, Dead Souls—and I only wish Gogol had written a great deal more. Some of Hebdomeros and I want to finish that, certainly, one of the most beautifully-written in the purest of prose styles.

A LOVE STORY

Although I say nothing in my journal about *Madame Bovary*, I know I was left with an impression of it that was more negative than positive. I had probably read it expecting something quite unlike what I found. I had probably come to it expecting . . . another *Jane Eyre*? I did not like the heroine, the story was a grim one. And where was the style for which Flaubert was so famous? Now, knowing better, I can enjoy all of Flaubert's little gibes. I can catch his irony, the way he pokes fun at what he considered the stupidity of the bourgeoisie, the priesthood, the self-styled enlightened rationalist. But that was evidently not what I was hoping for when I read it the first time. This love story was not at all a love story—or a very peculiar one, maybe the story of the gentle, oblivious Charles's abiding love for Emma.

HENRY JAMES ON *MADAME BOVARY*

"Anything drearier, more sordid, more vulgar and desolate than the greater part of the subject matter of the romance it would be impossible to conceive."

FLAUBERT'S STYLE

I know that I wondered, as I read *Madame Bovary* for the first time (in English) all those years ago, and after I was done reading it, what was so distinctive about the style for which Flaubert was famous. But although even in high school I was aware of translators and translations, it never occurred to me that the reason I did not like the novel might have been not only its mostly unsympathetic characters and its unmitigatedly gloomy story line, but also the style of the translation.

There is great trust in translations, on the part of many people who don't know any better and even many who do.

Now that I'm aware of how many previous translations of *Madame Bovary* there are, and of the fact that none of them reproduces Flaubert's style, I know that whichever one I may have read at that time (and it was probably Francis Steegmuller's), I was not reading the novel in the style in which Flaubert wrote it.

HENRY JAMES ON *MADAME BOVARY*

"It is a work . . . in relation to which sincere opinion may easily have the air of paradox."

My sincere opinion: I find that if I do not love *Madame Bovary* as a whole—certainly not as I love Flaubert's last, unfinished novel, *Bouvard and Pécuchet*—I do relish many parts of it, individual lines and whole passages, a good proportion of what is in the whole novel. In other words, I relish many parts of the book without relishing the whole.

In translating it, I embrace it actively, and I particularly relish the English results of certain passages, though others remain frustrating.

HENRY JAMES ON *MADAME BOVARY*

"To many people *Madame Bovary* will always be a hard book to read and an impossible one to enjoy."

BUT ALSO

"M. Flaubert can write nothing that does not repay attention."

SOME FACTORS DETERMINING THE QUALITY
OF A TRANSLATION

The quality and nature of a translation (let's say from the French) depend on at least three things: the translator's knowledge of French language, history, and culture; his or her conception of the task of the translator; and his or her ability to write well in English. These three variables have subsets that can recombine infinitely, which is why one work can have such widely differing translations. Publishers selecting a translator seem to proceed on the assumption that the most important qualification is the first. "Let's ask Professor X, head of the French Department at Y!" Often they completely ignore the second factor—how will Professor X approach the task of translating?—and certainly the third— what is Professor X's writing style like? (I am judging perhaps unfairly and from limited experience within the walls of a publisher's editorial meeting room; and it is true that a translation sample is usually asked for; but I don't believe I'm wrong about priorities, generally, here.) All three factors are vital, or at least important, but in many instances, if one has to rank them, the third—how well the translator writes expressive English—may be the most important qualification, followed closely or equaled by the second—how he or she approaches the task of translating, especially how narrowly or how liberally; it is the first that must be given last place, since minor lapses in knowledge of the language, history, and culture are, in an expertly written, generally faithful version, fairly easily corrected, especially with the help of a meticulous editor and/or copy editor, whereas a misconception of the task of the translator and, worse, an inability to write well, will doom the entire book through its every sentence.

MARX AVELING—AND PAUL DE MAN

Eleanor Marx Aveling, daughter of Karl Marx, produced the first translation of *Madame Bovary* in 1886. What is known as the Paul de Man revision of the Marx Aveling translation (Norton, 1965, 2005) retains some of her old-fashioned or inappropriate vocabulary, such as "heretofore," and "conjure" (for "beg" or "plead"). It adds explanations or identifications to the text (what Flaubert called "the Chaumière," because everyone knew it becomes "the Chaumière dance hall")—undoubtedly helpful to the reader, but a betrayal of the original—and the writing style regularly falters, the revision often making matters worse, as in this passage from the end of the book, concerning poor grieving Charles just before he dies:

> and Charles was suffocating like a youth beneath the vague love influences that filled his aching heart. (Marx Aveling)

> and Charles was panting like an adolescent under the vague desires of love that filled his aching heart. (de Man revision of Marx Aveling)

Quite apart from the comic absurdity of "panting like an adolescent," especially unfortunate coming just at a point in the story when we should be filled with sympathy for Charles, the revision drops the word "suffocating," an important one that recurs several times in the novel at moments of intense emotion.

For a while, the de Man–Marx Aveling seemed to me the very worst among the eleven. It isn't—maybe it's the second worst. But then, such a thing is hard to judge, because in certain specific passages, it *is* the worst. The de Man–Marx Aveling version exists for a couple of wrong reasons, and people buy it for another wrong reason. Wrong reason number one: Norton chose to use the Marx Aveling translation because it was in the public domain and wouldn't cost anything (I'm assuming this, or I was told—I can't remember which). Wrong reason number two (I'm certainly guessing here): They asked Paul de Man to revise and edit it not because he was conscientious and an excellent writer in English but because he had prestige, a reputation, and scholarly intelligence. He then apparently handed most or all of the work over to his wife, and did not acknowledge her. (This I was told by a reliable source.) Wrong reason number three: People buy the book not because it is an excellent translation of this important novel, but because the volume includes informative essays and other useful critical apparatuses—it is handy for a teacher, for instance. So, readers have a collection of useful material to read *about* the novel, but are reading this, one of the most important novels in the history of the novel, in a less than excellent translation.

FLAUBERT'S LETTERS

I read them to know him better and to hear him grumble, usually, about *Madame Bovary* and the experience of writing it:

> My head is spinning with annoyance, discouragement, fatigue! I've spent four hours without being able to write *one* sentence. I haven't written one line

today, or rather I've scrawled a hundred! What atro-
cious work! What a bore! Oh, Art! Art!

Most of his letters were to his lover, the poet Louise
Colet. He would write them usually at one or two in the
morning, after he was finished working for the day. It was
really too bad for all of us Flaubert enthusiasts and scholars,
both amateur and professional, when he and Louise Colet
broke up two-thirds of the way through his writing of the
novel.

I also read his letters to see what his style was like when
it was spontaneously produced and probably uncorrected. (I
doubt that he went to the trouble, at that hour of the night,
to make a fair copy of a corrected letter.)

THE OTHER TRANSLATIONS

I did not study the other translations while working on the
first draft of my translation, because I had to establish my own
approach, my own style, and my own understanding of what
I was reading before I could risk exposure to the rhythms
and eccentricities of the others striking my ear and possibly
creeping into my prose. (As in translating Proust's *Swann's
Way* and most of the previous books I had translated, I also
did not read ahead more than a paragraph or at most a page,
so that the material would be new to me, a surprise.) Then,
in the second draft, as I revised what I had written, I looked
again and again at the previous translations—sometimes at all
of them, in the case of a particularly sticky problem, but usually at five or six that were proving useful in different ways.
Over time, I began inevitably to imagine the translators.

JOAN CHARLES

The Joan Charles translation (I'm looking at an abridged Garden City Book Club edition from 1949) follows the original very closely—she wouldn't dream of adding or omitting material with the writerly flair of, for instance, Francis Steegmuller (American, 1957) or Gerard Hopkins (English, 1948), authors of what were for a long time the two "classic" and most popular translations of *Madame Bovary*—one for each side of the Atlantic. Nor does she rearrange the sentences much.

JOAN CHARLES, AGAIN

For a while I liked Joan Charles—I saw her as prim, correct, neat, sober, honest, frank, clear-eyed. I thought of her as a sort of ally in what I was trying to do. I thought she was unjustly ignored and passed over by the later translators, who didn't mention her. Then I became somewhat disillusioned, as she made the occasional mistake and tended to lapse into a rather wooden style. Eventually I came to see her as tight-laced and humorless.

BY JOVE

It was not she, but several of the other translators, who put such a discordant exclamation into the mouth of Rodolphe, Emma's first lover and a wealthy young landowner, who is made to say (remember, this is France in the 1830s) "By Jove!" (Even worse, one of the most recent translators has him say, on another occasion, "No way!"—immediately bringing him into the twenty-first century. And at yet another point, in this translation, he says: "Good Grief.")

Should each of the major Translation Sins have a number? Shall we call this Number Six? (I haven't yet decided what the first five are.) It is the sin of magically, but heedlessly, transferring the action, character, and dialogue into a different time and culture—in this case from the 1830s Pays de Caux in Normandy to England in, say, the early 1900s, or whenever "by Jove" was most dashing and fashionable.

TRANSLATION SIN NUMBER SEVEN

Since several translators committed this sin at that particular spot, it may also be evidence of Sin Number Seven on their part: relying too trustingly on a previous translation. This is a tricky sin, of which I have been guilty myself. Certain translation situations are fairly desperate: What in the world is the author saying? Any amount of cogitating and searching—in reference books, online, in correspondence with smart native speakers—yields nothing. And here at hand is a group of reasonably intelligent minds, of whom one, two, three, four, and five have come to the same conclusion—or, more likely, opted to follow the example of number one. It is very tempting to do the same. I can also imagine the Translation Jury ruling that if six translators opt for it, it is not an unreasonable choice; I have the illusion, anyway, of safety in numbers. I yield to temptation and follow suit, but with a feeling of uneasiness that doesn't go away. Usually I return to the problem and make an independent choice after all.

CONSTANCE GARNETT

The solution adopted by Constance Garnett, the prolific translator of Russian, to the word, phrase, or passage in the original that utterly confounded her: Leave it out.

FINE EDITIONS CLUB: THE WORLD'S GREATEST BOOKS

The translation of *Madame Bovary* by Eleanor Marx Aveling that I have is the Fine Editions Club edition, published in 1948. In the "Member News" flyer that came with the book (small format, four small pages), no mention is made of the translator, though the illustrator, Laszlo Matulay, and the author of the introduction, Carl Van Doren, are both identified here. The brief description of the novel on the first page of the flyer is as follows:

"Emma Bovary, wife of a country doctor, is beautiful, bored, romantic . . . unable to face reality. Here is her story, told with consummate skill in the inimitable French manner."

It is the last part of the quote that intrigues me. What is the "inimitable French manner"?

And that also brings us back, of course, to the differences among the translators of *Madame Bovary*. If there is an inimitable French manner, there is not one single manner of translating it. Eleanor Marx Aveling's close (if sometimes inaccurate or old-fashioned) approach is quite different from Francis Steegmuller's elastic one: consider Marx Aveling's "whilst she wrote" (for the very simple *en écrivant*, "while writing") compared to Steegmuller's "as her pen flew over the paper"; or Marx Aveling's "his feet were bare" (exact for *ses pieds étaient nus*) compared to Steegmuller's "his feet were innocent of stockings." The latter style hardly conveys what the Fine Editions Club flyer describes as Flaubert's "spare, unadorned prose." The flyer adds some perfectly sensible and unarguable statements about the novel and then concludes that it "well merits publication in the Fine Editions Club's rich leather binding."

Marx Aveling's was the translation that Nabokov used in teaching the novel at Cornell. For a while, I was convinced that Nabokov's opinions about this translation, and his own suggested alternatives for certain words and phrases, must be correct—brilliant writer in English with profound understanding of French and this novel. And so I looked carefully at what he said in his lecture on the novel, collected in his *Lectures on Literature*.

Then I discovered that Nabokov's teaching copy of the translation was in fact not far away, housed in the Berg Collection of the New York Public Library at Forty-Second Street, and that I could go in and study it. So I took a notebook and went in, sat in front of the book with the usual fascination one feels in the presence of a historical artifact (I did not have to wear white gloves, but the book was placed on a felt-covered book stand and the room was presided over by a watchful attendant), and began writing down in my notebook his changes and comments to certain passages. On my next trip into the city, I did better, carrying along my own copy of the Marx Aveling translation so that I could reproduce, in it, Nabokov's penciled marginal notes just as they appeared, in effect creating a replica of his book. I did this perhaps two or three times. But the work of copying went very slowly, and I was also beginning to lose some of my confidence in the soundness of every opinion of Nabokov's. I would come across instances of marginal notes that I did not agree with— either his understanding of the English choice did not seem quite right to me or his alternative seemed too far away from the original. (For instance, Marx Aveling's "Once, during a thaw, the bark of the trees in the yard was oozing" is one correct solution for *Une fois, par un temps de dégel, l'écorce des arbres suintait dans la cour*. Nabokov's replacement of "oozing" by "glossy with dampness" is perhaps nicer, but it inserts too much of a Nabokovian flourish, I think—a problem that would come under the heading of "approach to translation" in the list of criteria for a good translator.) I abandoned my project, much though I would have loved to own a replica of Nabokov's teaching copy of *Madame Bovary*.

I took a few more moments, however, to copy down some of the English words Nabokov had evidently found difficult: he had written them out with diacritical marks indicating how they were to be pronounced, should he have to speak them to the students: *prívet, clématis, bígoted, pólypany, múltiple, cátechism, sólace, péctoral, Botocúdos, málleable, nastúrtium*.

MORE ON FLAUBERT'S STYLE

"A good sentence in prose," says Flaubert, "should be like a good line in poetry, unchangeable, as rhythmic, as sonorous." To achieve a translation that matches this high standard is difficult, perhaps impossible. Of course, a translation even of a less exacting stylist requires millions of tiny, detailed decisions; many reconsiderations; the testing of one word or phrase against another multiple times. In the case of *Madame Bovary*, there are unusually many previous translations, and it is intriguing to observe how differently previous translators have made these decisions.

Curiously, in the case of a writer as famously fixated on his style as Flaubert was, many of the translations do not try to reproduce that style, but simply to tell this engrossing story in their own preferred manner. And so the reader in search of *Madame Bovary* has a wide choice: Gerard Hopkins's 1948 version, with added material in almost every sentence; Francis Steegmuller's nicely written, engaging version, smoother than Flaubert's, with regular restructuring of the sentences and judicious omissions and additions (1957); the stolidly literal, sometimes inaccurate version by the very first, Marx Aveling (1886), which caused Nabokov much indignation in his marginal notations but to which he resorted in teaching the novel; that version as revised (not always happily) by de Man (or by his unacknowledged wife), who chose to omit the italics, for example. There is *Madame Bovary* with fewer of those pesky semicolons, with serial *and*s supplied, with additional metaphors. There is a version in which Charles is made to sob on the last page, another in which he is made to say "Poor thing!" (not in the original) when his first wife dies. There is even Flaubert complete with the involuntary repetitions that he so disliked.

Perhaps Flaubert was mistaken when he believed that the success of the book would depend entirely on its style—since various of his translators over the years have composed versions that readers find deeply affecting but that do not reproduce the style. Yet Flaubert would not listen, but was infuriated, when Zola remarked that there was more to the book, after all, than its style.

NOT ALWAYS PAINSTAKING

It should be noted that painstaking as Flaubert was about certain features of the prose, he was quite casual when it came to others, particularly pronoun references and capitalization. Ambiguous pronoun references are sometimes quite confusing, but for the most part I chose to retain the ambiguity in my translation. As for his inconsistency in capitalization (as in the frequent variations of "Square" and "square"), I also chose to retain it. This inconsistency was apparently not the result of an editorial oversight, since the original French text went through numerous editions by different hands in which it remained, surviving even into the most definite 1971 Gothot-Mersch edition. Evidently, either Flaubert did not care, as Proust believed he simply did not care about certain pronoun references, or, perhaps more likely, he capitalized instinctively, unthinkingly, guided by some less conscious but still deliberate purpose. In any case, since it is part of the experience of the French reader of the original, I let it stand.

THE COMMA SPLICE

Flaubert also regularly wrote sentences containing what is called the comma splice, in which clauses are strung together in a series separated only by a comma and without a conjunction. The clearest example of this is one of the shortest sentences, near the end of the novel: "Night was falling, rooks were flying overhead." One effect of this construction is to give each clause equal weight and value. Another effect, sometimes, is to speed the action forward, speed our thoughts as readers forward through time or material, so that even the full stop at the end of the sentence seems a momentary pause. There is a suggestion of the notational, of the quick noting of facts or details, so that this construction sometimes counterbalances lyrical or dramatic material by the subtlest hint of a certain matter-of-factness on the narrator's part. I considered it important to retain this feature of his style, too, rather than soften it or smooth it out with conjunctions.

EQUIVALENCY

"Smooth" and "flowing" are not inevitably compliments when applied to a translation.

If a passage in the original is graceless or peculiar, then the translation must be graceless or peculiar in that spot, too.

But one could say the only justification for making a certain passage better than the original is a sort of mathematical one: in other passages, the translation may unavoidably be worse than the original, therefore the improvement makes up the balance. You could say you want to achieve a sort of overall equivalence, when all the parts are added up.

THE IDEA OF EQUIVALENCY IN TRANSLATION, REITERATED

The translated text should roughly *add up* to the original; it does not need to attempt equivalency at each point.

The translation is like a problem in math—using different numbers, the answer must be the same, different numbers must add up to the same answer. If you can't reproduce a pun here, maybe you can create one over here. If your description in this passage is less lyrical than the original, maybe in another passage it can be more so.

WITTGENSTEIN'S NOTION

That translation is like a kind of mathematics: a solution can be arrived at, but there is no rule for how to arrive at solutions.

THE IDEA OF EQUIVALENCY IN TRANSLATION, AS EXPRESSED BY CICERO, CONCERNING HIS TRANSLATION OF DEMOSTHENES

"I have not felt myself obliged to pay out each and every word to the reader. Instead, I have paid out an equivalent in value."

THE IDEA OF COMPENSATION, ACCORDING TO JOYCE

In his opinion, the French compensated for their relatively barren language by inventing great style—by employing balance and precision to superlative effect. He said: "They have a rather poor instrument, but they play wonderfully well."

THE FORMALITY OF THE FRENCH LANGUAGE

A fellow translator of mine in the seven-translator Penguin edition of the entire *In Search of Lost Time* was praised by a reviewer for one sentence in particular:

"I could tell [the weather] from the first street noises, whether they reached me muffled and distorted by dampness or twanging like arrows in the empty, resonant space of a wide-open morning, icy and pure."

The reviewer picked out one phrase in particular, her "twanging like arrows," as a good solution for the French original's more formal and neutral *vibrant comme des flèches*—he called it "a brilliant touch that taps an indigenous resource of English while honoring the French." I was startled by but also rather admiring of the flair of that "twanging." In my thoughts, I kept returning to the sentence and her solution. I was experiencing something of a struggle, because I knew that the use of "twanging" represented one approach to translation—to draw on the full Anglo-Saxon riches of English even if that gave a bit of an Anglo-Saxon flavor to the prose—but that I, despite loving that vocabulary, would almost certainly have opted for the more literal, and less colorful, "vibrating like arrows." No flair in that, alas.

There is something about the formality of the French that I find compelling—or perhaps what I find compelling is that even if French is more formal because of having more limited resources (as Joyce would assert), or by tradition, or because of the strictures of the Académie française, its formality is part of its distinctive character, and I would be very hesitant to change that—even if an equivalent formality in English is not really equivalent, but actually *more* formal because we are, in our literary traditions, cumulatively less formal.

BECKETT TRANSLATES PAUL ÉLUARD

One line:

Le passage de la Bérésina par une femme rousse à grandes mamelles.

Literal: "The crossing of the Beresina by a red-haired woman with large breasts."

Beckett: "The Beresina forded by a sandy jug-dugged woman."

Elsewhere in the same poem, for *habitants*, Beckett in his translation chooses "denizens" rather than the more literal and colorless "inhabitants"; for *immobile*, "rapt" instead of the less colorful "motionless," "immobile," or "still."

A NOTE TO MYSELF, SOME THIRTY YEARS AGO, WHEN I THOUGHT THAT ONE'S APPROACH TO TRANSLATION COULD BE VERY SIMPLE

"Very simple: know the text thoroughly: sense and style, tone, mood, etc.; and write the English text so that its style, tone, sense, mood match the original."

Part of the sentence was crossed out. I had said: "write the English text *very beautifully and* so that its style . . ." Crossed out, not because I did not think it should be beautifully written *if the original was*—but that the original might *not* be beautifully written, and therefore *to write beautifully* could not be part of any *general* rule of translation.

APROPOS OF "BEAUTIFULLY WRITTEN" WHEN THE ORIGINAL IS NOT

My discomfort with the opening passage of my translation of Pierre Jean Jouve's *Hélène*, back in 1993:

There is something mysterious and inexhaustible in the relationship among these regions. There is a quality about it that never comes to an end. There are several tiered regions, enclosed in the hundred blue valleys of the hollowed mountains.

I knew it read awkwardly in English, and I knew that the French (in my opinion) also read awkwardly, and I knew that I could easily be accused of having produced a poor translation, or of writing poorly. On the following page, the prose relaxes and becomes more rhythmical:

I was going to leave this paradise that same day. I was going to leave the valley of the Bondasca with its fresh and dreamy forms, my soul full of the poetry of my sixteenth year, for other countries more ordinary, less dangerous.

Sometimes a carefully written translator's note lets the reader know that the translator is perfectly aware of how less than graceful a passage sounds. In the case of *Madame Bovary*, I was in fact asked by the editors of one edition to point out in my introduction that certain of the more awkward moments of the translation were deliberate and mirrored the original, as for instance the lack of parallel structure in this description of the young Charles, early in the book: "He was a boy of even temperament, who played at recess, worked in study hall, listening in class, sleeping well in the dormitory, eating well in the dining hall."

PRESERVING THE SEMICOLONS

This desire, on the part of a translator or an editor, to smooth out prose or poetry that appears rough or too eccentric can be compared to the first publications of Emily Dickinson's poetry, and the changes made to her punctuation toward the creation of something perceived to be more normal, better, less barbaric—specifically, her dashes replaced by commas, semicolons, and periods.

Flaubert's punctuation, too, has been altered for the most part by previous translators—I mean altered beyond what is necessitated by the differing requirements of French and English syntax. As important to him as Dickinson's dash must be the semicolon. The semicolon often halts the sentence in midstride, rather than brings it to a conclusion, as a period does. Several semicolons within one sentence bring it to a halt several times. The effect is often to make it more deliberate, heavier.

I can take an example of this from two versions of my own translation, the first in the hardcover edition, where I, too, "normalized" the punctuation unnecessarily; and the second, my correction for the paperback edition. I still do not understand why I didn't follow Flaubert's punctuation in the first edition, since there was no reason not to and since I had it very much in the forefront of my mind to follow him as closely as I could wherever possible, even to his punctuation.

I discovered what I had done only as I was preparing to visit a translation seminar. I was planning to show the class Gerard Hopkins's version of this passage and contrast its wordiness to the original and explain my own choices in translating it. The passage comes from the scene toward the end of the novel in which Emma visits her former lover Rodolphe hoping for a loan. They haven't seen each other since he disappeared on the eve of what was to have been their elopement. Here is the original French:

> *Elle se laissa prendre à ses paroles, plus encore à sa voix et par le spectacle de sa personne; si bien qu'elle fit semblant de croire, ou crut-elle peut-être, au prétexte de leur rupture; c'était un secret d'où dépendaient l'honneur et même la vie d'une troisième personne.*

The single sentence has three sections separated by semicolons, and within those sections a sparing use of commas— three in all. And here is Gerard Hopkins's version with its different construction, the single sentence broken into three separate sentences, and the additions of material, including a fourth whole sentence adding content not at all in the original. I have italicized his additions.

> She let herself be beguiled by his words, *and,* still more, by *the sound of* his voice and the sight of his person. So *powerfully did these things affect her* that she pretended to believe, perhaps *even* did *actually* believe, in the pretexts *he put forward* for having broken with her. *He couldn't, he said, go into details.* A secret was involved on which depended the honour, *nay, perhaps* even the life, of a third person.

The passage in his translation is seventy-six words long, compared to the original's forty-seven words. The difference is most clearly seen in this unnecessary expansion: from "perhaps did believe" to "perhaps *even* did *actually* believe."

But, as I prepared for this seminar, copying out the French original and my own version, I was surprised and disappointed to discover that although mine hewed more closely to the line of the original, it did not follow the punctuation of the French when it could have, quite neatly. Here is my first version (fifty-seven words):

> She allowed herself to be persuaded by his words, even more by his voice and by the sight of his person, so much so that she pretended to believe, or perhaps did believe, the excuse he gave for their break: it was a secret on which the honor and even the life of a third person depended.

Fortunately, there was time to make changes in the punctuation for the paperback.

> She allowed herself to be persuaded by his words, even more by his voice and by the sight of his person; so much so that she pretended to believe, or perhaps did believe, the excuse he gave for their break; it was a secret on which the honor and even the life of a third person depended.

ANOTHER EXAMPLE OF HOPKINS'S TENDENCY TO INFLATE

For "reflecting," he has "in an agony of indecision."

M. FLAUBERT CAN WRITE NOTHING THAT DOES NOT REPAY ATTENTION

One becomes aware of the motifs within the novel: belts (the belt of Emma's life that constricts her—one of the metaphors

Flaubert allowed into the novel—and the apothecary Homais's newfangled magical Pulvermacher belt at the end); things built in layers (Charles's cap in the beginning, the wedding cake, Emma's nesting coffins at the end, etc.); water and bodies of water (the recurring image of a carriage rocking as though carried by waves, Emma near the end of the novel standing in a plowed field as soft as water, Emma's lie to Léon that she was once involved with a sea captain, Emma's coffin compared to a boat rocking in the waves, etc.); the theme of writing (Père Rouault's letters, Homais's articles, the officials' speeches, Rodolphe's farewell letter, Emma's love letters, Homais's note to the doctors, Charles's instructions for the coffining); many others.

ANOTHER RATHER EARNEST NOTE TO MYSELF, MANY YEARS AGO

"Extremely important obligation of translator a) to be faithful to meaning, b) to spirit, and c) to present a *good* work in English."

(Faulty parallel structure, there.)

I must have been trying a little desperately, once again, to isolate the most important principles of translation, even though of course they were obvious to me and already inherent in the way I approached any translation.

However, over the years, I seem to have shifted the emphasis in my thinking—not in my practice, which has remained quite consistent—away from concern with the *spirit* of the original work to fascination with reproducing the *style* of the original. Not because I regard the spirit as less important than I used to, but because, in my experience, the spirit comes through intact if the style, meaning, and types of word choices of the original are respected, and because what is hardest to reproduce, what requires the most conscious effort and ingenuity, is the style.

YET ANOTHER ATTEMPT AT A DEFINITIVE
STATEMENT, YEARS AGO

"There can be no 'total' translation because languages and cultures differ: every translation is an approximation."

Yes, I can't disagree. But some languages are closer to each other, as some cultures are closer.

OTHER LANGUAGES:
THE PLEASURES OF GERMAN

The concreteness of their word for (our Latinate) *multiplication*: *Einmaleins* (= "one-times-one").

The economy or condensation of their *Wildbachbrücke* (= wild-brook-bridge = a bridge over a mountain stream).

One of my favorites is a word I remember from a Peter Handke novel but cannot now find within it, search as I may. I find it elsewhere, though, in an article about a 5,300-year-old corpse preserved by a glacier and discovered in the Alps by a *Bersteigerehepaar* (= mountain-climbing-married-couple).

This is internet-automatically translated more concisely as "climber couple"; as for the corpse, it is described as "freeze-dried."

OTHER LANGUAGES:
THE PLEASURES OF SPANISH

ahogarse en poca agua = to drown in little water = to
   worry unnecessarily
dar a luz = give to light = give birth
entre dos luces = between two lights = at twilight; or
   half-drunk, confused

ANOTHER OLD NOTE TO MYSELF

"Know the context of your work as fully as possible."

I agree with this. In the case of *Madame Bovary*, as in
the case of many translations I've done, I intended to read
widely so as to become thoroughly familiar with the context
in which it was written: nineteenth-century France in all its
aspects, cultural, political, literary, etc. I did do some reading, but not nearly as much as I had intended. My note goes
on to say:

"This can be carried to infinity."

BACKGROUND READING

Always: I have ambitions to do more background reading
than I do, in the end.

Always: I acquire more books than I actually read. The
ideal of thoroughness pleases me—I will know *everything*
there is to know about Flaubert—but there are other demands on my time, the hours of reading don't get done, or
not all that might be desirable.

Often: I do some laborious background work for the

translation that proves not to be very useful. In the case of the Flaubert, I decided I should read, or reread, some English novels written in the mid-nineteenth century, to remind myself, in particular, how the dialogue might sound. I did reread Edith Wharton's *The Age of Innocence*, though it was written a little later than *Madame Bovary*. I reread George Eliot's *Middlemarch*, copying out in a notebook typical expressions of the various characters: for example, Mr. Brooke often repeats "you know" and "that will not do" and "that kind of thing" and, standing alone, "A great mistake." Mrs. Cadwallader often begins a sentence with "Why" or "Come, come," "Oh" or "Bless you," and was fond of the word "Capital!" I thought I could attribute some of these words or phrases to characters in the Flaubert novel—though not "Capital!" which sounds to me so British. In the end I did not. I still think it is a good idea, but it never became necessary.

APROPOS OF CONTEXT, THE CONTEXT OF FLAUBERT'S WORLD

Flaubert describes the covered market in the town of Yonville-l'Abbaye, where Emma and Charles live for most of the novel, in the following way when he first introduces us to the town:

"The market, that is, a tile roof supported by about twenty posts, takes up about half of the large Yonville square."

The word he uses for "posts" is *poteaux*, so my translation was quite exact just there. He mentions the market-place three more times in the novel, however, and each time he now refers to the *poteaux* as *piliers*, or "pillars." I thought this was too massive a word for an element of a market structure, and I chose not to follow him but to retain "posts."

Then, on a trip to France, following the GPS instructions to go north by way of a small town called La Bastide-sur-l'Hers, we turned left through the main square and I saw a covered market whose tile roof rested on what were undeniably massive pillars.

Fortunately, there was still time for one more change to the paperback edition.

LIGHT IN THE MARKETPLACE

On Emma's first night in Yonville, as she is walking home with her husband and others, a brief description of the scene:

> *Le bourg était endormi. Les piliers des halles allongeaient de grandes ombres. La terre était toute grise, comme par une nuit d'été.*

> The town was asleep. The pillars in the marketplace cast long shadows. The earth was gray, as on a summer night.

That was my version. The little passage becomes distinctly more lyrical in Francis Steegmuller's slightly amplified version:

> The town was asleep. The pillars of the market cast long shadows, and the pallor of the road in the moonlight gave the effect of a summer night.

Gray earth is certainly less romantic than a pale road in moonlight: here, Steegmuller has "improved" the original, which I find wrong. But I do like his "pillars of the market" better than my "pillars in the marketplace" and would readily make the change for a future edition.

At these times, rejecting or adopting another translator's solution, the act of translation becomes briefly a collaboration.

EARLIER DRAFTS OF *MADAME BOVARY*

Flaubert worked from successive plans of *Madame Bovary*, following them, then revising them. He also wrote numerous drafts of every passage, often rewriting and perfecting it only to cut it out, then, altogether. At one point he estimated that he had 120 finished pages but to achieve them had written 500. (He revised by cutting, whereas Proust revised by expanding.) In rewriting he would watch for poor assonances, and bad repetitions of sounds and of words, especially *qui* and *que*, which he occasionally underlined and apologized for even in his personal letters. Zola remarked that "often a single letter exasperated him."

He did not burn these early drafts but left them for us to pore over—approximately 4,500 pages in all, which now reside in the Municipal Library in Rouen. They are available to us in clearly legible form, even online (at www.bovary .fr), because they have been transcribed with amazing meticulousness by volunteers under the direction of Yvan Leclerc, at the Centre Flaubert de l'Université de Rouen, who have reproduced every rejected scene, every false start, every cross-out. The drafts are an invaluable resource for scholars and, of course, for translators.

Flaubert's intensive cutting meant that occasionally the omission of a sentence or phrase rendered a passage ambiguous, or puzzling, or simply left room for an assumption that might turn out to be mistaken. What was in the little bottles held by the ladies in their gloved hands at the La Vaubyessard ball? Why did Charles, when a student, use to stamp his foot on the wall of his room while he ate lunch? Why was the church hung with straw mats?

Thanks to the volunteers, it is possible to look at all of Flaubert's earlier drafts, and when a passage is puzzling, it is sometimes helpful to see what Flaubert wrote in an earlier draft, especially since, as he generally cut out material when revising, the earlier draft is likely to be longer and more explanatory. (It was sometimes in cutting that he made the passage puzzling, by assuming too much knowledge on the part of the reader.)

DISCOVERIES, FROM FLAUBERT'S EARLIER DRAFTS

Some things I discovered:

The miniature of Emma that Rodolphe had, in his box of keepsakes, was oval, not rectangular, and therefore the "corners" that got "knocked" were not the corners of the miniature but the corners of the box.

The "gold-stoppered bottles" held by the ladies at the ball in their gloved hands contained vinegar, not perfume, vinegar to revive them if they, in their tight corsets in the overheated room, became faint.

In the list of things endowed by Emma with the affectionate possessive *our* in the hotel room where she meets her lover Léon—our room, our carpet, our chairs—we can be confident that Flaubert in fact did not write "*my* slippers" by mistake, as is often assumed, for the reason that he deliberately repeats it from one draft to the next, to the next.

The piece of green velvet that Charles specified for covering Emma after her death was to be laid directly over her body in the innermost coffin, not over the outermost coffin.

The straw mats in the Yonville church were hung on the wall to protect the congregation from the cold; they were not nailed to the seats of the pews.

Of course I could not be more specific in the translation than Flaubert was in his final text; I could not put vinegar in the gold-stoppered flasks, for instance, nice as that would have been; but I also knew enough not to write something that would have changed what Flaubert intended—by putting perfume into the flasks, for instance, as some of the translators did.

A MORE EXTENDED EXAMPLE OF INFORMATION FROM THE EARLIER DRAFTS

A more extended example of how Flaubert rethought one moment of a scene may demonstrate the fascination of watching him at work. This example shows Charles's interactions with others at Emma's graveside. From a careful reading of the final, printed version of the French, we may suspect that Charles did not in fact take in his hand the aspergillum (brush or other instrument for sprinkling holy water) that was held out to him by Homais, even if it is tempting to overleap the plain text and assume that he did. And if we test our suspicion that he did not, by looking at earlier drafts, we may be impressed by the care with which Flaubert reimagined the transaction, from draft to draft: in the earliest, Lheureux (not Homais) passes the aspergillum to Charles, who drops it; in the next draft, Lheureux offers it to Charles, but he refuses it; in the third, Homais holds it out to him, but Charles "does not want it." In the final draft, Flaubert cuts out any reaction at all to the aspergillum on Charles's part: Homais simply holds it out to him, and Charles does not explicitly refuse it or explicitly take it, instead falling to his knees and throwing the loose earth into the grave by the handfuls. If we simply trust the words of the original and translate them as "held out to him" rather than "passed to him," we will get it right.

CHANGES TO SUCCEEDING EDITIONS

Also consistent: I see more corrections or changes to be made after the translation is in print. I made about fifteen hundred changes to *Swann's Way* from the British edition to the American, and then another couple of hundred from the American hardcover to the American paperback. I was not correcting mistakes, but simply making further revisions in the writing. If you imagine that on any given page of the 433-page book it might be easy to see three small changes that could be made in the writing, it is not so many.

A translation, one worth taking trouble over, is always a work in progress: It can always be improved. The translator can always learn more that will make it better, or can always think of a better way to write a sentence.

For instance, I have just learned more than I knew before about the history of women's fingernails, and now I'm planning another endnote for a future edition of the translation. As the wearing of gloves declined, in the nineteenth century, women paid more attention to their fingernails, a filbert-shaped nail being highly desirable, for instance. On Charles's first meeting with Emma, he particularly admires her fingernails, and Flaubert takes some care to describe them—in fact, they are the first things he describes about Emma in any detail, though the nut in question is not the same:

"Charles was surprised by the whiteness of her fingernails. They were glossy, delicate at the tips, more carefully cleaned than Dieppe ivories, and filed into almond shapes."

ENDNOTES

I included, at the back of the translation, a host of endnotes. They were provided "blind"—that is, without marks on the pages of the text referring to them—so that there would be no visual intrusion on the page between the reader and the experience of the novel. It should be possible, I believed, to enjoy the book as French readers enjoyed it in the original, uninterrupted, but if more background information was wanted, it was available. I felt, too, that footnotes on the page or superscript numbers referring to endnotes would turn the book from a living novel into the subject of an academic study—they would change the nature of the book and the experience of reading it.

These endnotes attempted to be as detailed and extensive as is reasonably possible. They went beyond explaining mysterious references that would be difficult to research, such as "Pulvermacher hydroelectric belts" and Homais's remedies, and clarifying historical references, as to King Henri IV, "the Bearnais." Erring on the side of inclusiveness, they defined such domestic items as fabrics and types of carriages, medical practices such as bloodletting, and distinctive social signals such as the yellow gloves worn by dandies. Most of these latter sorts of notes were meant to identify the multitude of possessions deeply embedded in the bourgeois customs and culture of the time in which the novel was set, things whose meaning would have been self-evident to its readers at the time of its publication. Flaubert, after all, deliberated at length about what should be included and what should be left out of this assiduously pruned novel, so we must assume he had strong reasons to specify fabrics such as cambric, barege, and twill, or carriages such as the landau, berlin, and tilbury, and perhaps even took pleasure in naming them; it is reasonable that we should make some attempt to understand what they are. Similarly, pastimes such as whist and *trente et un* or common sights in the street, such as the stone *bornes*— sometimes guard stones, sometimes milestones or boundary markers—should at least be not entirely mysterious to the twenty-first-century reader.

THE PROBLEM OF DIALOGUE AND IDIOMATIC LANGUAGE

Always: I enjoy translating descriptions and do not, at this point, enjoy translating dialogue. Dialogue is a problem: How do I persuade this innkeeper to speak English in a way that will convincingly create the illusion of a Frenchwoman speaking French in the nineteenth century, without making her sound archaic or stilted or too well educated, etc.?

While I was translating Proust, I thought of the solution to the problem of translating slang or idiomatic speech but then never employed it. The tricky thing is that slang and idiomatic speech are so local to their time and culture. If you translate into American or British slang—one French character saying of another, as in some example I read long ago, "He'll never set the Thames on fire," or, in a previous translation of *Madame Bovary*, Rodolphe exclaiming "By Jove!" or "No way!"—it will usually sound impossibly out of place. But some idioms can probably, depending only on their associations, work as well for nineteenth-century France as twentieth-century America, for example: "singing from the same hymn book" (religious); "sold for buttons" (domestic/mercantile); "take the wind out of my sails" (nautical); "keeping their powder dry" (military); "not a bad apple" (domestic/agricultural).

You can also translate an expression literally, which I like to do but which some people object to: in *Madame Bovary*, I have the innkeeper remark, "Don't worry, we've got hay in our boots!" This is an expression meaning that she is well prepared against adversity. I like the unfamiliarity of it, while, at the same time, I believe the meaning is clear from the context. Another instance of a straight translation of a French idiom is Homais's brusque dismissal of the blind man toward the end of the novel: "As if I didn't have other dogs to whip!" (Previous translators had: "other fish to fry"; "enough on my hands"; "enough on my plate"; "nothing else to see to"; "other things on my mind"; "all I need"; "enough things to be seeing to"; "enough to deal with"; "more important fish to fry.")

The third alternative I thought of—what I decided could be the solution but then never used—was to invent a convincing slang or idiomatic expression such as, to be used ironically, "happy as a slug on a bed of salt" or, unironically, "happy as a slug on a lettuce leaf." It would sound as though it might belong to the culture of the time and place, and its meaning would be clear enough. Another example of an invented idiom came recently from a friend. She remarked, concerning a quarrel and whether to let it escalate or not: "It might be better to take the kettle off the fire."

EXAMPLES OF SOME KOREAN SAYINGS

The following, taken from *Land*, by the Korean Pak Kyung-ni, a very long novel translated by Agnita Tennant and recently published by Brill, might work just as well in a contemporary American text or a nineteenth-century French one:

> "Less than the blood in a bird's leg."
> "Sometimes the sun shines in a rat hole."
> "If it's your fate to die, you'll drown in a saucer of water."

DEBATABLE STATEMENT

Here is a note to myself that I probably disagree with, though I'm still thinking about it:

"We translate constantly—whenever we read a text written in a different time or from a different culture. The farther away in time or culture, the greater the gap, the more difficult the act of translation—"

I now believe we don't bring it into our own time and culture by working transformations on it, but rather go to it and, through it, enter its own time and culture.

ANOTHER NOTE TO MYSELF

"Each [new] translation causes the work to be reborn—and extends its life."

I agree with the first part, but not with the second: it is very hard to know if the life of the original has been extended through a new translation, especially if the new translation is not as good as previous versions. But certainly the work is reborn in another guise, with each new translation.

The paradox, however, is this: that each new guise may be quite different from previous versions while the work itself remains more or less the same, surviving every translation, if it is a powerful work.

REPAYS ATTENTION: NAMING, IN THE NOVEL

One thing that is unavoidably lost in any translation of *Madame Bovary*: the fact that the name of Emma Bovary's young maid means "happiness," unless the reader sees the resemblance between *Félicité* and *felicity*. This naming is, of course, another ironic gesture on Flaubert's part.

REPAYS ATTENTION: RECURRING WORDS

Words that recur throughout the novel, in various forms: *escape*, *abandon*, *disappear*.

Also, *continue*—emphasizing the theme of sameness, monotony, which is so deadly to Emma and so important to the novel:

> After the weariness of this disappointment, her heart remained empty, and then the succession of identical days began again.
>
> So now they were going to continue one after another like this, always the same, innumerable, bringing nothing!

At Emma's funeral, the soil "continues" to trickle down into her grave. After the funeral, Charles begins to forget Emma even as he "continually" thinks of her.

PROBLEM WORDS IN THE REVISION

The word *continue* also occurs in the description of the hostelry called the Croix Rouge at the edge of Rouen, where Charles and Emma stay once on a visit to the city: inns of this kind, says Flaubert, were *continuellement pleins de monde, de vacarme et de mangeaille*.

And the first problem of the day, on one particular day, as I was putting in revisions for the paperback, was the inadequacy, I felt, of my translation here: "full of people, noise, and food"—generic and colorless equivalents of words that in the French are more vivid: *monde* is a more colloquial word than *gens* for "people"; *vacarme* is a din or racket or commotion, not just a noise; and *mangeaille* (a derogatory *-aille* ending on the word for "eat") is a slangy word for food that is abundant and *médiocre* (another favorite word, and concept, of Flaubert's)—so the plain *food* lacks all the force of the original.

None of the twelve translations I checked was very satisfactory. Some made an attempt—"people, and racket and fodder," or "people, hubbub, and food," or "people, bustle and victuals"—but the latter, for instance, does not fall very well on the ear, with its three *l*'s, and employs the old-fashioned *victuals* that may have been effective fifty and more years ago but that many readers of English now will simply not even understand. Also, *bustle* is a noun describing motion rather than noise. In this case, exceptionally, the de Man–Marx Aveling, which departs from the structure of the original, may be the most natural in English for conveying what Flaubert had in mind: "crowded, noisy, and full of food"—though still generic. "Full of food," while a little strange, does suggest that the food is not very good.

APROPOS OF *MANGEAILLE*

Another unfortunate discordance, as pointed out by a reviewer of the Penguin Proust translation of 2002, discussing one of the later volumes, also involves the word *mangeaille*, though here not used in a derogatory sense: *cette raffinée mangeaille* was translated as "this superb nosh."

It is not only a question of whether the word, phrase, idiom, proverb can be transposed into the culture of the original text without bringing along inappropriate references (e.g., a rat and its hole can be transposed to almost any time or place, but the Thames cannot, nor can a "nosh"), but also a question of what our associations are with the phrase.

I was brooding about this on a train recently and overheard a garrulous woman across the aisle—who was disturbing the other passengers by doing a lot of her office work loudly via cell phone—use the expression "dead in the water." She said: "Then you're dead in the water until we get you access."

I wondered if one could use the expression in a translation of a nineteenth-century novel, since people then and there, too, were sometimes dead in the water—but I think our associations with the expression simply inescapably place it in our contemporary culture.

The same would be true of the phrase "not an option." It might appear neutral and straightforward, yet if we use it without subject or verb, or even with subject and verb— "That is not an option"—it will sound too contemporary and of our culture.

ANOTHER EXAMPLE OF CULTURAL AND
TEMPORAL DISCORDANCE

Otherwise praiseful, a reviewer objected to the insertion, into the translation of a poem by the seventeenth-century Francisco de Quevedo, of a "Hershey's kiss." (The entire line in translation is: "If [you're] a Hershey's kiss, you need some foil"; the original is *Si [eres] un pan de azucar, en Motril te encajo.*

MOMENTS OF HUMOR IN *MADAME BOVARY*,
AMONG MANY POSSIBLE EXAMPLES

When we think of *Madame Bovary*, as when we think of *Swann's Way*, their humor is not what comes to mind first, and yet both novels are well leavened by amusing passages or moments. Here are some examples in Flaubert's novel.

Part II opens with a description of the region in which the town of Yonville-l'Abbaye lies. As we embark on reading it, we expect this description, from our long training in reading novels, to be positive or at least neutral. But, after discussing such things as the origin of the name of the town, the river, the appearance of the valley, the "ferruginous springs," there comes this remark, typical of sour Flaubert:

"It is here that they make the worst Neufchâtel cheeses in the whole district."

In Emma's restlessness, in her boredom, this rather random and short-lived impulse:

"She decided to learn Italian."

Homais's command to Charles after Emma's death. What makes it funny to me is all in the way it is written, the repetition (redundancy):

"And [Charles] wept.

"'Weep,' said the chemist."

As Homais gropes awkwardly for some way to divert the grieving Charles, at the end of the book, as they are keeping vigil in Emma's bedroom, he picks up a carafe in order to water the geraniums that Emma used to care for. What amused (and impressed me for its sleight of hand) was the bit of free indirect discourse in the last three words, which cause us immediately to enter the complex mind of Homais with a statement so unambiguous, so unsurprising:

"Then, to distract him, Homais thought it appropriate to talk a little horticulture; plants needed humidity."

Earlier in the story, there is Homais's offer to run for some vinegar to revive Emma when she has fainted, after the departure of the perfidious Rodolphe:

—*Je cours, dit l'apothicaire, chercher dans mon laboratoire, un peu de vinaigre aromatique.*

It is difficult to translate *Je cours* so that it captures the humor of the original. The pomposity suggested by the placement of those two words (literally, "I run" or "I'm running" or "I'll run") followed by the deliberate rhetorical pause ("said the apothecary"), in turn followed by his mention of his laboratory and the particular substance, aromatic vinegar, that he plans to fetch, is funny. But how to capture that?

I gave up any hope that it would be as funny in English:

"'I'll just run to my laboratory,' said the apothecary, 'for some aromatic vinegar.'"

Only one of the other translators chose to break up his remark, yet I think the slight pause is important to suggest Homais calculating (as he always does) the effect of his speech.

The solution of W. Blaydes is very close to mine, and possibly better:

"'I will run over to my laboratory,' said the apothecary, 'for a little aromatic vinegar.'"

BLAYDES'S TRANSLATION

I did not acquire the Blaydes translation (1902) until I was halfway through my revisions for the paperback, and I did not look at all of it. It is a very close translation, and often quite well written, though not always. My translation would still benefit from a careful comparison, as long as I did not think I could adopt words like *sward* (meaning an expanse of short grass).

This translation was mentioned to me by an older friend of mine. It was one volume of a handsomely bound set of French classical romances that had been given to him when he was a boy by his father, who was otherwise rather a renegade and often absentee parent. (That restless soul had *actually* run away to join a circus when he was young.) The book had made a deep impression on my friend.

DIFFICULT TO TRANSLATE

They are not "false friends," because in some contexts they can be translated into the same word in English, but in this novel, these words, which recur quite often, cannot always be translated directly and are not easy to translate:

vague
médiocre

MARIANNE MOORE ON TRANSLATION

"The natural order of words, subject, predicate, object; the active voice where possible; a ban on dead words, rhymes synonymous with gusto."

REPETITION, GOOD AND BAD

I would often repeat a word if it was repeated in French and if it would sound reasonably good repeated in English. For example:

Cette lettre, cachetée d'un petit cachet de cire bleue.

"This letter, sealed with a little seal of blue wax."

Flaubert was very sensitive to poor, involuntary repetition so his repetitions, in particular, were likely to be deliberate, most of the time.

ANOTHER OLD NOTE EITHER FOR MYSELF OR TO BE CONVEYED TO MY STUDENTS

"Watch sentence endings. Reproduce strong endings, weak endings."

"Watch paragraph endings, stanza endings, and the ending of the whole text."

(I would now add, of course: watch beginnings.)

THE CLASSICIST D. S. CARNE-ROSS
ON TRANSLATION

"True translation is much more a commentary on the original than a substitute for it. Like criticism, to which it is closely allied, its role is interpretative. . . . Where it is seen as a substitute for the original, the stress is likely to fall on literal accuracy."

I have always had trouble seeing translation as interpretation, in most of what I have done. Most people do see it as interpretation—what am I not understanding? I agree that some statements may need interpreting in order to be translated. But if I translate "the grass is wet," what kind of interpretation am I doing?

TO THE EXTENT POSSIBLE

I suppose I am looking to create a substitute for the original: I am looking to create something so close that a student of Flaubert can see exactly, or as exactly as possible, what Flaubert was doing in the original.

In the case of a classic like *Madame Bovary* or *Swann's Way*, what I am translating is not only a living piece of literature, a work of the imagination that should be fully alive for a reader in English, but also an artifact, something much studied and examined in detail. I therefore want it to follow the original closely enough so that it can be studied as the original is studied, or to the extent possible.

GUY DE MAUPASSANT'S DESCRIPTION
OF FLAUBERT AT WORK
(NOT ON *MADAME BOVARY*)

"And then he would begin to write, slowly, stopping and starting all the time, crossing out some words and adding others, filling up the margins, writing words across the page, covering twenty sheets of paper with black ink to produce a single page of finished text, groaning with the mental effort like a man laboriously sawing wood."

MY CRITERIA FOR GOOD TRANSLATING,
YEARS AGO

Some of my criteria for a good approach to translating were the same years ago, and some were different:

"Three essentials: thorough knowledge of original; skill in writing; courage to make your own piece.
"Then: enjoyment of the original; enjoyment of the act of translating; enjoyment of writing.
"Then: patience; readiness to work a problem."

2011

ONE FRENCH CITY

The City of Arles

INTRODUCTION

What follows is part of an ongoing piece of writing that I could best describe as being the elaborated notes of what I have been discovering in my explorations of the history of the French city of Arles—a history that goes back nearly three thousand years, so there is a lot to read. This essay began as notes taken during a visit to Arles in November 2018, when I gradually came to notice how, within the small area of the old city, over the centuries of occupation by different cultures, so many of the structures remained intact and were reused, adapted, enlarged, rebuilt, etc., or if they were dismantled, the materials of which they were built were reused for another construction—this repetitive progression very well embodying the principle taught in basic science, that no matter is either created or destroyed. The nuns of Santa Clara, for instance, after rehabilitating the buildings of an earlier monastic order just outside the city walls for their own use, were forced one hundred years later by the city to vacate them, at which point the stone and sand of those buildings were used to reinforce the city ramparts.

Arles is in the South of France, in Provence, on the lower part of the Rhône River, the marshy Rhône delta, on a limestone hill twenty-five meters above sea level. It was settled, successively, by Ligurians, Greeks from Phocaea, Celts, and in 46 B.C. by the Romans as a retirement colony for Caesar's Sixth Legion. Curious outsiders have been visiting the city for hundreds of years, many of them first drawn by the most outstanding attractions: the Roman monuments and the carved portal of the St. Trophime Church. For instance, important visitors, back in the 1300s, would be taken down to see the obelisk from the Roman circus, which had been discovered buried in a vegetable garden. Much more recently, tourists also included in their visit the places made famous by Van Gogh when he lived there, though his stay was only a little longer than one year.

What I have been writing about Arles takes the form of short, titled sections.

THE IMPRESSION OF AN EARLIER TRAVELER

Joseph Bard, in 1834, described it this way: "It is an old city, of an incredible opulence in debris, lost in the swamps."

THE HILLSIDE

The city is built on a gentle slope, an outcropping of limestone, with the amphitheater close to the top. There are perspectives up, and down, and, from the top, out over the countryside. And even as you walk down into the flatter areas, you have a sense, always, of where you are—the slope of the hill behind you, the broad river always to your right, beyond the houses. You are heading away from the Roman arena and the Roman theater, down toward the middle of the old city; in the center, as you rest for a moment in the

very heart of it on the Place de la République, you share a
bench with an older woman, who has greeted you before sitting down and who, after looking for a while calmly around
at the city hall and the St. Trophime Cathedral and the clus-
ter of people laughing and jostling by the fountain and by
the Roman obelisk, which was rescued from the vegetable
patch and three hundred years later brought up the hill to
this square, takes a nail file out of the depths of her purse and
discreetly works on her nails. Here, in this very peaceful sunlit square, you are in the historical center of power of Arles,
ecclesiastical and civic; the archbishops' palace is also in front
of you, with, out of your view, its courtyard where the lion of
Arles was once kept. Then, when at last you leave the bench,
taking care to say goodbye to the older woman, who nods
and smiles, you go on down into La Roquette, into what
once was a neighborhood of farmers, sailors, fishermen, and
dockworkers, and, finally, to the end of the city, and maybe
even beyond it to the old Roman circus, built outside the
town by the Romans and still outside the old town, where
the obelisk once stood.

THE MARSHES

In earlier times, the Abbey of Montmajour, on a hill about
five miles away from Arles, appeared to be an island, rising up
out of the marshes (*marécages*) that surrounded it.

THE MOSQUITOES OF ARLES

John Murray's *Handbook for Travellers in France*, the standard nineteenth-century guide, warns that Arles is unhealthy

"at certain seasons" because of the marshes and pools in the vicinity. Even today, there are hosts of mosquitoes in Arles clear into the month of November, and no screens on the windows, so that if you expect to have a good night's sleep, you must swat as many of the little insects as possible against the walls and ceiling of your hotel room, where they tend to rest, and not open the window until your lights are out.

THE FIVE MAIN AREAS OF ARLES

There are five main neighborhoods within the preserved old part of Arles: the Cavalerie, in the north; the Hauture, which is the highest part, on the hilltop, in the northeast; the Cité, in the center, where the city hall and the St. Trophime Church are; the Méjan, in the middle, along the riverside, historically the main commercial area; and the old neighborhood formerly of fishermen and farmers to the west of the center, La Roquette. La Roquette used to be called the Vieux-Bourg, the "old town," and in the twelfth century was still walled off from the rest of the city. The Cavalerie used to be called the Bourg-Neuf, the "new town." The Cité was the center of power, both church and civic. The Méjan, the middle, was a district of merchants and included the Jewish quarter.

THE CHANGING FUNCTIONS OF BUILDINGS

In the Hauture district at the top of the city, the former parish of La Madeleine was once important enough to engulf another whole parish. Now, the small church building, its steeple gone, set back from the road, resembles a modest old stable. It is privately owned, used as a garage and workshop.

NOTABLE FIGURES OF ARLES: ST. CAESARIUS

St. Caesarius (ca. A.D. 470–543) lived at a time of intersection of late antiquity and the early Middle Ages. Roman law was still in force, as well as institutions such as slavery.

The Camargue and its marshes still began, then, "at the gates of Arles." St. Caesarius describes them, in his sermons, as harboring useless plants and disgusting creatures.

In his day, the common language was still Latin, and it was in Latin that he spoke to his congregation. Not all the population was Christian: there were also adherents of the Arian heresy and even pagans who still worshipped Jupiter.

St. Caesarius condemned a provision of Roman law, still practiced at the time, that allowed a young man to keep, before his marriage, concubines whom he would then abandon after several years in order to take a legitimate wife. "They do this with the support of civil law," said St. Caesarius, "but certainly not with the support of heaven."

THE ROMAN AMPHITHEATER AND ITS
TRANSFORMATIONS

The Roman arena of Arles, built in the first century B.C., was in use for about four hundred years, for gladiatorial combat of various kinds, including gladiators versus wild boars, tigers, and other wild animals, and, when filled with water, for staged naval battles. We know from the remaining Roman stone seats that the width of a seat for a spectator in Roman times, of whatever social class, was just under sixteen inches. Sailors operated the movable roofs that were extended over the arena to shade the spectators or protect them from rain.

By the eighth century, the arena had been converted into a fortification, with four stone towers, three of which are still standing.

Also in the Middle Ages, the outsides of the arches were filled in, and houses were built inside the arena and up against its outer walls, so that in time, over many years, a fortified village was created within the arena, complete with streets, a public square, and two chapels, one containing the remains of St. Genesius, patron saint of notaries. The village continued in existence until the 1800s, described in the Murray guidebook, in harsh terms, as being "filled within and choked up without by an accumulation of mean hovels, occupied by the poorest and worst part of the population of the town to the number of 2000." Then, in an upsurge of interest in the city's Roman heritage, the decision was made to raze the houses and clear out the village. This began in 1823 and was mostly accomplished by 1844; when Stendhal visited the city in 1837, there were still a few of what he calls "poor dwellings" inside the walls. Despite these remaining houses, the first event to take place in the arena after the clearing was a race of the bulls in 1830, held in celebration of the conquest of Algiers.

THE TORTUOUS STREETS OF ARLES:
HENRY JAMES

Henry James, visiting in about 1883, in writing about Arles, complains about the streets—he calls them "tortuous and featureless," just as John Murray in his *Handbook*, some thirty years earlier, had described them as forming "a labyrinth of dirty narrow streets, more intricate than any other perhaps in France." James complains about the material with which they are surfaced, which he calls "villainous little sharp stones." He is referring to the stones brought to the city from the valley of La Crau, that place called by one guidebook a "weird wasteland," to pave the streets.

James goes on to say, more emphatically, that "the rugosities of its dirty lanes affect the feet like knife-blades." Those stones are, it is true, sharp and small. But they no longer pave the streets of Arles, except for one short street near the top, and the streets of the old center of Arles, though still narrow and tortuous, and, many of them, once you are away from the cafés and restaurants, dark at night, despite the regularly placed old-style lamps standing on lampposts or affixed to house walls, and empty of people at night, are kept very clean except for the very occasional corner or patch of wall, where a mysterious heap of personal trash may be piled up. Every morning, early, a small white cleaning truck comes along with its revolving brushes, pausing by a diminutive metal trash-bag holder for the crew to remove and replace the suspended trash bag. Supplementing this vehicle

are individual men in yellow vests with brooms, working by
themselves here and there during the day or in the dark just
before dawn.

THE OVERLAPPING OF CULTURES

The Christian sarcophagi, in the fourth century, show figures
of importance wearing Roman togas.

St. Caesarius, in the early sixth century, wished to found
a convent. One who aided him, in his fundraising, was The-
odoric, King of the Ostrogoths.

In A.D. 539, the Frankish king, Childebert I, arranged
for combats of gladiators in the Roman arena.

The earliest form of the parish church of Notre Dame
de la Major, on the highest eminence of the city, was built
on the remains of a Roman temple to the so-called Good
Goddess, perhaps an aspect of Cybele.

THE PLACE DE LA RÉPUBLIQUE AND
THE PLAN DE LA COUR

The Place de la République, the center of the city, was also
known, earlier, as the Place du Marché, when the market was
held there, or the Place Royale, and then the Place de l'Hôtel
de Ville because that was where the Hôtel de Ville stood. It
still stands there. Leaving the spacious, light-flooded square,
which has been compared to an Italian piazza, you can walk
straight through the atrium of the Hôtel de Ville as a shortcut to the streets on the other side, and many do. You enter
from the Place de la République, pass under the complex and
celebrated ceiling of intersecting shallow vaults, ignoring,

for the moment, the little corner room off to your left from which you could, if you wanted, gain access to the damp, gloomy underground cryptoporticus, and ignoring, for the moment, up the flight of stairs to your right, on the first landing, the reproduction of the statue of Venus that was found in the Roman theater and that Arles reluctantly gave to King Louis XIV, so that it was taken away to Versailles, and walk straight out the other side, through what used to be the main entrance, onto the Plan de la Cour, which, though narrow and short, and small now, compared to the Place de la République, used to be the more important square, when the Place de la République was considerably smaller than it is now.

Inside the entry hall of the Hôtel de Ville, as you stare up at the intersecting vaults of the ceiling, you see the people taking the shortcut first silhouetted against the bright sunlight bathing the Place de la République, then passing you, then disappearing at your back out into the bright sunlight of the Plan de la Cour. You have also watched, from a different angle, outside, a boy on a scooter take this shortcut. He, with his mother, who is pushing a baby carriage containing an infant sibling, has left the daycare center that lies on the far side of the courtyard of the archbishops' palace, has come out of the courtyard, which also opens onto the Place de la République. He looks up to ask his mother's permission, his mother grants it, and with vigorous thrusts of his little right leg he propels himself toward the doorway of the Hôtel de Ville while his mother hurries up the street parallel, alongside the Hôtel de Ville, so that she will be there on the other side when he comes out. He is swallowed up inside the Hôtel de Ville as she disappears along the street and around the corner to meet him in the Plan de la Cour.

THE WINDS OF ARLES

The mistral, the famous wind, is usually the prevailing wind in Arles, but it is not, and was not the only named wind. There are pictures called wind roses, directional wheels showing all the winds of Provence, with their names. There were not just four named winds, or even eight, or even sixteen or twenty-four, but, on one wind rose I consulted, thirty-two named winds, each blowing from a different direction. And in a document drawn up by the Clarisses, the nuns of the order of Santa Clara, as they prepared to sell their house in the rue Vallat, describing in detail how the neighboring properties abutted their property, they in fact referred to certain directions using the names of the winds. One was, in Provençal, *auro drecha*, a direction not north by northwest, but north *of* north by northwest, in other words almost due north. Another direction they called *marin*, by which they meant southeast. More common names they used for directions were *levant* and *couchant* or *ponent*—in other words, in the direction of the rising or the setting sun.

THE ROMAN FORUM AND THE CRYPTOPORTICUS

In a newly established city or military camp, the Romans customarily laid out a main north–south road called a *cardo* and an intersecting main east–west road called a *decumanus*; in Arles, what was in Roman times the cardo is now the rue de l'Hôtel de Ville, the street that runs past the Hôtel de Ville; the decumanus is the rue de la Calade, which descends the hill from the remains of the ancient Roman theater to intersect with the rue de l'Hôtel de Ville close to the city hall itself. The Roman forum was customarily built at or close to the intersection of these two roads, and that is the case in Arles, too, although the Roman forum itself is mostly gone. What remains are a few traces aboveground and the very extensive cryptoporticus underground, which once supported the arcades of columns aboveground and which is almost fully visible, with its double arches, though rather dark and in certain seasons wet and muddy underfoot, and on the whole forbidding for its gloom and emptiness and the continuous drips from its ceiling.

It was along the old Roman north–south cardo, now the rue de l'Hôtel de Ville, that the young mother with her baby carriage hurried, almost running, to meet her small son who was passing swiftly on his scooter through the shadowy atrium of the Hôtel de Ville out the other side into the sun-bathed old Plan de la Cour, once the grand square before the main entrance.

INDIVIDUAL CITIZENS OF ARLES WE ENCOUNTER IN THE HISTORIES

The homeowner in the rue Balze who, in 1654, tried to prevent the construction of a chapel by the Jesuits across the street from him, complaining that it would block his light and sunshine: This was Gaspard Reynaud.

The man whose house was bought in 1884 and torn down to clear a site for the Amédée Pichot fountain that greets visitors to Arles if they enter the city from the direction of the railway station, walking up the rue de la Cavalerie: This was a wigmaker named Sautecoeur.

The man whose hand was eaten in 1407 by the lion of Arles, as reported by Bertran Boysset in his chronicle: This was Johan Envezat, who survived the incident and lived on thenceforth with two arms but only one hand.

The man and woman who sold their property in 1368 to the Jewish community for a cemetery inside the city wall close to the Porte du Marché Neuf: These were Renouard de Ville, an apothecary, and his wife, Jacquette Guigue.

The fisherman whose house by the Rhône was bought and torn down to clear a site for the defensive tower called the Tour de l'Ecorchoir, erected in 1372: He was Estève Léon. The tower, for this reason, was sometimes known as the Torre del Leonet.

The man whose wife owned a malformed white hen that had three legs and feet on one side and one on the other, as reported by Bertran Boysset in his chronicle in 1397: This was Juanet de Poquieras, probably of the Vieux-Bourg neighborhood.

The man who, with his wife, was hired in 1442 to act as guardian of the Jewish cemetery at Bourg-la-Crau after marauding wild animals became a problem there: This was Berengarius Barrani.

The butcher who, in 1453, was paid twenty florins for providing the meat for the lion of Arles kept in the palace courtyard of the archbishops, the courtyard through which, many centuries later, the young mother, baby carriage, and boy on scooter passed on their way from the daycare center: His name, in Latin form, was Hugonicus Davidis.

THE RUE DES CARMES

There is a short street near the Place de la République called the rue des Carmes. It has a dogleg bend in it, and just at the bend is the doorway of a bookshop specializing in small-press poetry books. You learn that when you walk down this street, south from the rue de la République, which is at your back, you are walking down the center of what used to be the nave of a large church, the church of the Carmelites.

Between that bookshop and the rue de la République, where the street originates, on the east side, there are several buildings owned by a chef whose restaurant is located in one of them. He has another restaurant, through an archway and across a courtyard. On the far side of the courtyard, to the right, you see a line of smaller arches now filled in, and one half of an arch. Later you realize that this is part of the cloister of the old church. It was falling into ruin and was sold to a neighbor.

It was after the Revolution that the church was taken down. The crypts, which had served as burial places, were either simply abandoned or filled in with rubble. For a time, because of the now disused crypts below, where the dead had lain, the newly created public street, running down the line of the center of the nave, was called the rue des Morts, or "street of the dead." On a day of fair weather, a cool, sunny day, the windows and doors of the houses and shops now lining the street will be left open. Then you can look into them and see stone vestiges of the old church—bits of the chapels' vaulted ceilings, columns, or capitals.

THE JEWISH CEMETERIES: THE SECOND, AT PORTE DU MARCHÉ-NEUF

Not far from the site of the church and cloister of the Carmelites, you go in search of a shoe-repair place that might be able to sew up your watchband. There is one just south of the intersection of the rue de la Rotonde and the rue du President Wilson. The shop is a very small place. Just two people inside, standing at the counter, fill the space entirely, and a woman approaching the shop outside, coming along the sidewalk, turns away quickly when she sees that it is full. You later learn that when you crossed the intersection, on your way to the shoe-repair shop, you were walking directly over the ground of what used to be a cemetery of the Jewish community in Arles, their second cemetery.

This cemetery lay just inside the medieval ramparts, in an area that then had the strange name of "Old Lettuce." To create the cemetery, in 1368, the Jewish community bought a piece of land from an apothecary and his wife for fourteen florins.

The Jews of Arles had not only their own school, baths, cemetery or cemeteries, and charitable institutions, but also their own gallows, first across the river outside the village of Trinquetaille, then on the road that led to the village of Raphèle.

ARCHITECTURAL TERMS YOU LEARN WHEN IN ARLES: DRIPSTONE

A *dripstone* is a molding over a door or window that deflects rain and decoratively enhances the opening, typically in medieval architecture.

A dripstone may also be called a "hoodmold." A hoodmold may terminate in a "head-stop"—a small sculpted head.

REUSE IN LES ALYSCAMPS

Near the Roman necropolis of Les Alyscamps, which lay outside the city on the Aurelian Way, in 1852, on the neighboring farms, cattle drank out of stone troughs which were in fact empty sarcophagi. The lids of the coffins were used as little bridges over the ditches.

At the far end of Les Alyscamps is an early church, St. Honorat. Parts of St. Honorat were built using pieces of stone from the sarcophagi.

Three early Christian sarcophagi were brought into the St. Trophime Church. One, dating back to the fourth century, was set into the northern gutter-bearing wall and serves as an altar for baptisms.

Starting in 1848, railway yards and locomotive sheds were built in the middle of the Roman necropolis, wiping out one of the handsomest burial grounds of antiquity. Also occupying the grounds of the necropolis were, later, factories, a canal, and a housing estate. Of the nineteen chapels once standing in the cemetery, only two are left. One of them serves as the ticket booth from which admission to the cemetery is sold.

In the 1860s, the young Frédéric Mistral and his friends were wandering there one night after drinking at a tavern, when they heard a sepulchral voice issuing from the depths of one of the coffins. It was a homeless person using the sarcophagus as a place to sleep.

NOTABLE FIGURES OF ARLES: THE LION

The lion of Arles was a symbol of the city depicted on various coats of arms and other decorative elements. The oldest seal of the community depicts the lion on its reverse. There was also an actual lion in the history of Arles, or rather, a succession of lions, kept by the city in the courtyard of the palace of the archbishops, and there enclosed within an iron fence.

One lion was given to the city by the Count of Provence, and at that time he paid for its upkeep. Later, the city assumed the expense of its upkeep, and there exists, extant, dated 1453, a receipt from the butcher who furnished the lion's meat, called, in the Latin of the document, *nutrimenti leonis.*

The lion was made to engage in fights, one with a bull in the courtyard of the archbishops' palace, and one with a ram, also inside the lion's enclosure. The lion once tore off the arm of an incautious locksmith, who died of his wounds, and once ate the hand of another man, who survived.

By the mid-sixteenth century, the city had decided the lion cost too much to maintain and eliminated it, we don't know how.

FOURCHES PATIBULAIRES

Bertran Boysset, the fourteenth-century surveyor and chronicler of Arles, describes a hanging, in 1394, across the river on a hill in Trinquetaille, now a part of Arles but then a separate fortified village. When he refers to the "forks of elm wood" used for the hanging, it is not immediately clear what he means. Later you understand: two forked poles or tree limbs would be fixed in the ground, and a transverse pole of wood laid between them, and from this the condemned person would be suspended.

Boysset writes: "The forks of elm wood had been planted on an elevation of earth or a height. . . . On this elevation of earth or height no one had ever before seen forks or a hanged person. The man remained on the forks for a year; then he was taken down and buried, at night, in the cemetery of St. Pierre de Trinquetaille with the permission of the Archbishop of Arles. The forks remained planted in that spot until they fell of their own accord because their bases had rotted."

BOYSSET'S ORCHARD AT THE PORTE DE LA ROQUETTE

In the days when Bertran Boysset was writing his chronicle, this gate in the medieval rampart was called the Porte de Sainte-Claire, or, as he wrote it in Provençal, *lo portal de Santa Clara*. He records that on December 3, 1384, he planted, inside the wall, on the east side of the gate, a white poplar.

Ten years later, on December 18, 1394, he planted in the same place, which was an orchard belonging to him, a walnut tree.

TWO NOTES CONCERNING THE LANGUAGE
OF ARLES

In the sixth century, the most commonly used language in
Arles was still Latin, though the city was for periods under
Visigothic and Ostrogothic control, so that some Gothic may
have been spoken as well. It was in Latin that St. Caesarius, for
example, delivered his sermons, adopting a less formal style in
order to communicate effectively with his congregation. In
the streets, conversational Latin would, over the following
centuries, evolve into something like present-day Provençal.

Alphonse Daudet, in the 1860s, listening to his friend
Frédéric Mistral read aloud to him some of his verses, remarks that the "beautiful Provençal language" is "more than
three-quarters Latin."

VAN GOGH AND THE HÔTEL-DIEU

When Van Gogh temporarily lost his reason on the night of
December 23, 1888, cutting off the lobe of one ear, which
he took to a prostitute of his acquaintance, who fainted at the

sight of it, he was transported to the Hôtel-Dieu, also known as the Hôtel-Dieu Saint-Esprit. This was a set of buildings, including a two-story arcade, forming a rectangle around a courtyard planted with trees and flower beds and including a fountain and a well. It was founded in the sixteenth century to bring together under one roof all of the city's thirty-two charitable institutions. It accommodated not only the sick but also abandoned infants, impoverished children, and orphans. The buildings continued to function as a hospital until 1974. In 1986, the complex was turned into a cultural center and it now houses a multimedia library, the municipal archives, a literary translators' college, and a part of the University of Arles. It also contains, on the ground floor of one wing, two gift and souvenir shops and a crêperie.

It was a petition on the part of his neighbors that caused Van Gogh to be incarcerated a second time in the same place. They were disturbed by his peculiar appearance and behavior.

THE SIGNING OF ACTS IN ARLES

Acts and other legal documents, created over the centuries and deposited in archives, included not only signatures and dates, but also mentions of the places in which they were signed. This is sometimes our only source of the information that such a place existed.

Church documents were often signed in a room occupied by a church official that had many functions but included that of bedroom (*camera*, in Latin).

They could also be signed by a church official in a hallway or gallery (*corritorio*).

The act granting the Jewish community a new cemetery—

not their second cemetery, which now lies several feet beneath the intersection of rue de la Rotonde and the rue du President Wilson, with its busy foot traffic, but their third cemetery, in Plan-du-Bourg, outside the city walls—was signed in the home of the Jewish scholar Izak Nathan.

THE PEOPLE OF LA CAVALERIE AND THEIR PETITION OF 1864: THE PLANTINGS OF THE PLACE LAMARTINE

One of several requests to the city by the petitioners of La Cavalerie in 1864 was that the plantings of the Place Lamartine, then known as the Place de la Cavalerie—the same (trapezoidal) square on which Van Gogh's "yellow house" would later look out, in 1888—be improved, and this request was granted, resulting, eventually, in a growth of lush thickets and mature shade trees. These plantings were to provide Van Gogh, twenty-four years later, with a subject for painting that was right across the street from his house. The traffic circle that exists there still has several mature shade trees on it, and some grass, but none of the thickets and winding paths that Van Gogh painted. Another part of the former gardens, on your right-hand side as you walk up to the old city from the railroad station, is now for the most part paved over in concrete and, at least part of the year, obstructed by the shuttered booths of an out-of-season funfair.

A SINGLE SHEEP AND A DOORWAY

Because we have photographic evidence, in a postcard photo of a flock of sheep filling the rue du Quatre Septembre, in Arles, many decades ago, and because we can recognize, in the photo, a certain doorway that still exists, we can walk up to this doorway, in the now empty street, look at its threshold, and know that on that spot, many decades ago, a single sheep, out of a flock of several hundred, paused to turn her head and look back at the rest of the flock coming up behind her.

REUSE: THE TOUR DE L'ECORCHOIR

At the far end of the old city, the downhill end, the south-westernmost end, the Tour de l'Ecorchoir, known first as the Torre del Leonet, "Leonet's tower," after the fisherman whose house was demolished to make way for it, was built in 1372 as a defensive tower on the site of the fisherman's home, to defend the city of Arles at its southwest corner from attacks coming from the river, on whose banks it stood. It was later renamed Torre Nova, "new tower," at a time when it was undergoing reconstruction and repair.

The Tour de l'Ecorchoir was for a time also known as the Torre Santa Clara, after a nearby city gate by the same name. The city gate, the Portail Santa Clara, was, in turn, named after a nearby convent that was occupied in the thirteenth century by the Clarisses—the nuns of the order of

Santa Clara who were eventually to be required to leave their convent.

After it ceased to be used for the defense of the city, the tower became a slaughterhouse and was renamed the Tour de la Boucherie, "tower of the butchery," or the Tour de l'Ecorchoir—an *écorchoir* being a place where the carcasses were flayed. After it was no longer needed as a slaughterhouse, it was used to store furniture.

By 2018, but presumably long before, it was in partial ruins and overgrown with vegetation. One could walk up to its darkened window hole on the ground floor, look in, and see signs of occupation by campers or the homeless—sleeping bags, collapsed tents, and various personal possessions strewn among the rubble in the dim light on the tower floor.

REUSE: TWO OLD BUILDINGS OUTSIDE TOWN

Two structures on what used to be the northern slope of the Mouleyrès hill, outside town to the northeast, were known as "La Morgue" and "La Poudrière"—"the morgue" and "the powder-house"—and still existed in 1992. They were at that time being used for storage by the Municipal Service for the Distribution of Garbage Bags.

HYPOTHESIS ABOUT POMPEII AND ARLES

We read a study of the remains of the ancient Roman city of Pompeii and wonder if, by closely examining what is known about Pompeii, we can tell something about the types of structures and the layout of the shops, homes, workshops, and streets, including the widths of the streets, of Roman

Arles, which was about 134 years old at the time Pompeii was buried under volcanic ash. The side streets in Pompeii that ran off the broad main Via dell'Abbondanza varied in width, but most were three to five meters wide. These widths easily correspond to the widths of the smaller streets of the old center of Arles.

THE ROMAN ROADS: BURIED

In the city of Narbonne, another important Roman colonial city of Provence, a section of Roman road has been uncovered and is on display in the main square, before the city hall. It is conceivable that throughout the old part of Narbonne, and also throughout the old part of Arles, the Roman roads remain, three or four meters below the surface of the present-day pavements.

THE VANISHED PARISH CHURCH

Where the cafés, houses, and shops now line the east side of the Place du Forum, including the famous café now painted yellow that Van Gogh depicted in his *Café Terrace at Night*, there once stood a parish church, St. Lucien, and its cemetery. We walk downhill through a narrow street in the evening, with the intention of entering the Place du Forum and passing through it on our way to dinner. The street we walk down, downhill, to reach the Place du Forum, having been mostly straight all the way down, when it is nearly there strangely bends to the right and then to the left again just before it reaches the *place*. What it is doing is skirting the spot where the old cemetery was. The same road, as it was a few hundred years ago, swung wide of the cemetery, and so does the road as it is now, though the cemetery is no longer there. "Historiographic tradition" has it that the foundations of this church date back to the sixth century. Parts of it, specifically the lower, southern side of the nave, are preserved in neighboring houses. And if you go into the Hôtel de Ville, which is nearby, and down the metal staircase into the gloomy, damp Roman cryptoporticus, and walk through it to its northern gallery, you will be able to see, underground, the apse of this church and the base of the altar of the lower chapel.

BRIEF NOTES

Little girls of the sixth century might wear gold earrings and bracelets, and might chatter among themselves in church.

Within the famous and much visited St. Trophime cloisters, with their finely carved and not uniform pillars, the central space, now a rectangle of mossy gravel and crisscrossing paths, was once the canons' cemetery.

In the fifteenth century, some of the Jews of Arles, in their wills, would include legacies of olive oil for lighting lamps in the synagogue.

The Gallo-Romans were great consumers of bread and gruel (*bouillie de gruau*).

French writers writing about France and French history sometimes refer to the country as "our hexagon."

In the vestibule of the chapel of the Blue Penitents, one could still see, in the eighteenth century, a door that was once that of the synagogue. But the destruction done to the Chapel of the Penitents in the late nineteenth century during the construction of the waterworks wiped out the last vestiges of the synagogue.

From Murray's *A Handbook for Travellers in France, Part II* (1884 edition): "The country about Arles is solitary, and suspicious-looking tramps are often seen prowling about. A good thick stick, therefore, is an appropriate companion for a pedestrian."

Murray's *Handbook* notes that the Camargue, in its climate, soil, and even fauna, resembles Africa and the borders of the Nile more than it does France.

The Plan de la Cour, in the eighteenth century, was once laid with fine polychrome paving. Carts, carriages, and wagons were not allowed into the courtyard, only people on foot.

Most of the buildings of the old part of Arles are from the seventeenth and eighteenth centuries.

In official documents of the Middle Ages, at least some of them, nobles were always identified as nobles, at each mention of their name, and Jews always identified as Jews.

At the time of the Revolution, there was a well called the Puits de la Trinité in the rue de la République, in front of the Hôtel Laval-Castellane, a private house that is now a museum, the Museon Arlatan. It was the last public well in Arles, and was gone by the late 1800s.

The stone moldings under the windows of some houses are renderings of the drapery hung out on special occasions, for royal visits, for instance. Arles at least twice hosted kings of France—Louis XIII in 1622 and Louis XIV in 1660—after the visit of the sickly young Charles IX in 1564.

In the seventeenth century, the Angelus used to ring daily from about forty churches. We heard the bells just once, soon after our arrival.

Shipping along the river was mainly of stones, wheat, salt, and fish.

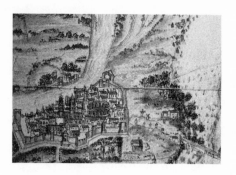

Acknowledgments

"Twenty-One Pleasures of Translating (and a Silver Lining)" is an expanded and revised version of an essay first called "Eleven Pleasures of Translating," published in *The New York Review of Books* on December 8, 2016. My gratitude to the editor, Robert Silver. That article was based on a talk given at the French-American Foundation's Translation Prize ceremony on June 7, 2016, and later expanded for a keynote address given on October 6 that year at the American Literary Translators Association's fortieth-anniversary gathering.

It was subsequently published as "Seventeen Pleasures of Translation" in *In Other Words'* "Women in Translation" issue (Summer 2018), Norwich Writers' Centre. Thanks to the editor, Samantha Schnee.

"Reading Proust for the First Time: A Blog Post" was commissioned and posted by the Cultural Services of the French Embassy in the United States, 2013, during their "2013: A Year with Proust" festival. My thanks to the organizers.

"Introduction to *Swann's Way*" appeared first, in a slightly altered form, as the introduction to my translation of *Swann's Way*, by Marcel Proust (Viking Penguin, 2002).

"The Child as Writer: The 'Steeples' Passage in *Swann's Way*" was first published as "The Steeples Appeared So Distant" in *The Proust Project*, ed. André Aciman (Farrar, Straus and Giroux, 2004).

"Proust in His Bedroom: An Afterword to Proust's *Letters to His Neighbor*" is a slightly revised version of the afterword published in *Letters to His Neighbor*, by Marcel Proust (New Directions, 2017). My thanks to the editor, Barbara Epler.

Some of the material for that afterword was, in turn, taken from an article entitled "Proust's Bedroom," originally published in *Nest: A Quarterly of Interiors* 14 (Fall 2001), New York. My thanks to the editor, Joseph Holtzman.

"Reading *Las aventuras de Tom Sawyer*" was first published in *The American Scholar* 73, no. 3 (Summer 2004), the Phi Beta Kappa Society, Washington. Thanks to the editors.

"An Experiment in Modernizing Laurence Sterne's *A Sentimental Journey*" was first published in *NOON* 1, no. 1 (2000), as "From Laurence Sterne's *A Sentimental Journey through France and Italy*: A Translated Excerpt." My thanks to the editor, Diane Williams.

"Translating *Bob, Son of Battle: The Last Gray Dog of Kenmuir*" was first published in a much shorter version as the afterword to the New York Review Book Children's Classic edition of the translation, *Alfred Ollivant's Bob, Son of Battle: The Last Gray Dog of Kenmuir* (New York Review Books, 2014). My thanks to the editor, Edwin Frank. A version including additional material appeared as a Free-lance column in *The Times Literary Supplement*, January 31, 2014, under the title "On Translating *Bob, Son of Battle*." My thanks to the editor, James Campbell. The essay in close to its present form was subsequently published online in *The Believer*, issue 133, under the title "Notes on Translating a Children's Book," December 1, 2020. Thanks to the editors.

"From Memoir to Long Poem: Sidney Brooks's *Our Village*" discusses, and quotes from, an in-progress poem, a section of which appeared in a New Directions poetry pamphlet under the general title *Two American Scenes* (along with a work by Eliot Weinberger) in 2013. My thanks to the editor, Barbara Epler. Two further parts of the long poem appeared in online and print editions of *Little Star* magazine (respectively *Little Star Weekly* 4 in 2013 and *Little Star* 5 in 2014). My thanks to the editor, Ann Kjellberg. The essay itself has not been previously published.

"Loaf or Hot-Water Bottle: Closely Translating Proust (Proust Talk I)" began as a talk delivered in several venues. It was then first published in *The Yale Review* 92, no. 2, in April 2004. Thanks to the editors.

"Hammer and Hoofbeats: Rhythms and Syntactical Patterns in Proust's *Swann's Way* (Proust Talk II)" began as a talk delivered in several venues. It was then published in French translation under the title "Les Marteaux et les claquements des sabots: Rhythmes et motifs syntaxiques dans *Du Côté de chez Swann*" in *Marcel Proust Aujourd'hui*, October 10, 2017, translation and publication arranged by Emily Eells and Naomi Toth, whose work I gratefully acknowledge. It was not previously published in English.

"An Alphabet (in Progress) of Proust Translation Observations, from *Aurore* to *Zut*" includes entries previously published as follows: C: *contigu* first appeared in *Parakeet* 1 (2004), Syracuse—my thanks to the editor, Deb Olin Unferth. Z: *zut* was first published in *New Ohio Review* 13 (Spring 2013)—thanks to the editors. A, B, C, D, F, and S were published as "A Proust Alphabet" in *Proust, Blanchot and the Woman in Red*, no. 5, in the *Cahiers* series published by Sylph Editions / AUP: Paris, 2007—my thanks to the editor, Dan Gunn.

"Before My Morning Coffee: Translating the Very Short Stories of A. L. Snijders" appeared in an earlier, much shorter version as a Freelance column in *The Times Literary Supplement*, February 28, 2014, under the title "On Translating from the Dutch." My thanks to the editor, James Campbell. A version was also subsequently published in *Two Lines* 22 (Spring 2015), under the title "Learning

Dutch." My thanks to the editor, C. J. Evans. A further, expanded version of the essay appears this year as the introduction to my translation of a selection of A. L. Snijders's stories entitled *Night Train* (New Directions, 2021). My thanks to the editor, Barbara Epler.

"Over the Years: Notes on Translating Michel Leiris's *The Rules of the* Game" was taken in part from my introduction to *Fibrils: The Rules of the Game*, volume 3, by Michel Leiris (Yale University Press, 2017). My thanks to the editor, John Donatich.

"Translating a Gascon Folktale: The Language of Armagnac" was first published in a slightly different version, along with my translation of the entire folk tale, in *NOON* 19 (2019). My thanks to the editor, Diane Williams.

"Learning Bokmål by Reading Dag Solstad's Telemark Novel" was first published in the *Freeman's* inaugural "Arrivals" issue (Fall 2015), as "On Learning Norwegian." My thanks to the editor, John Freeman.

"Reading a Gunnhild Øyehaug Story in Nynorsk" was originally published as a Freelance column in *The Times Literary Supplement*, February 13, 2015, under the title "On Reading Nynorsk." My thanks to the editor, James Campbell.

"Buzzing, Humming, or Droning: Notes on Translation and *Madame Bovary*" first appeared in *The Paris Review*, no. 198 (Fall 2011), as "Some Notes on Translation and on *Madame Bovary*." My thanks to the editor, Lorin Stein.

"The City of Arles" was first presented, in a slightly different form, as Columbia University's Trilling Lecture on March 13, 2019. My thanks to the organizers.

Illustration Credits

page vii: Cover of F. Ritchie, *Fabulae Faciles* (Longmans, Green and Co., 1937). New edition. Originally published 1903.

page 28: Cover of Marcel Proust, *Du côté de chez Swann* (Paris: Gallimard, 1965). Reprinted by permission.

page 62: Facsimile of letter 10 from Marcel Proust, *Letters to His Neighbors*, translated by Lydia Davis. Translation copyright © 2017 by Lydia Davis. Proust letters and critical apparatus copyright © 2013 by Éditions Gallimard. Reprinted by permission of New Directions Publishing Corp. and Fourth Estate / HarperCollins Publishers, Ltd.

page 86: Cover of Mark Twain, *Aventuras de Tom Sawyer*, translated by Sara Gómez (Mexico: Editorial Diana, S. A., 1974). Reprinted by permission.

page 121: Title page of Alfred Ollivant, *Bob, Son of Battle* (New York: Grosset & Dunlap, 1898).

page 122: Illustration by Marguerite Kirmse, opposite title page of Alfred Ollivant, *Bob, Son of Battle* (New York: Grosset & Dunlap, 1898).

page 186: Facsimile of opening page of handwritten *Our Village*, by Sidney Brooks, from *Our Village* (Harwich, Mass.: Harwich Historical Society, Harwich, n.d.). Reprinted by permission.

page 368: Frontispiece facsimile of A. L. Snijders's handwritten preface to A. L. Snijders, *Grasses and Trees*, translated by Lydia Davis (Amsterdam: AFdH, 2016). Reprinted by permission.

page 390: Postcard from Michel Leiris to Lydia Davis. From the collection of Lydia Davis.

page 408: Page 34 (with Lydia Davis's handwritten notes) from Jean-François Bladé, *Contes et Proverbes Populaires Recueillis en Armagnac*, 1867 edition. Reprinted in facsimile by Lacour Editeur, Nimes: 1992. www.editions-lacour.com. Reprinted by permission.

page 416: Cover of Dag Solstad, *Det Uopploselige episke element i telemark i perioden 1591–1896* (Forlaget Oktober, 2013). Reprinted by permission of Forlaget Oktober c/o Oslo Literary Agency.

page 538: Jean-Baptiste Guibert, engraving of Arles arena (eighteenth century).

page 543: Photograph of the former parish church La Madeleine, city of Arles, collection of Lydia Davis.

page 554: Photograph of stone archway depicting lion, city of Arles, collection of Lydia Davis.

page 556: Drawing of surveyors, by Bertran Boysset, from his *Treatise of Surveying* (late fourteenth to early fifteenth century). Collection of the Municipal Archives of Arles. Reprinted by permission. As found on page 28 of Dominique Carré, ed., *Arles*, translated by Penwarden and Tittensor (Paris: Editions du patrimoine, 2001).

page 558: Photograph of city wall, city of Arles, collection of Lydia Davis.

page 562: Photograph of St. Trophime cloisters, city of Arles, collection of Alan Cote.

page 564: Seventeenth-century drawing of the city of Arles. As found on page 21 of Dominique Carré, ed., *Arles,* translated by Penwarden and Tittensor (Paris: Editions du patrimoine, 2001).

Permissions Acknowledgments